2020
青岛统计年鉴
QINGDAO STATISTICAL YEARBOOK

（总　第41期　VOL.41）

青岛市统计局
国家统计局青岛调查队　编
QINGDAO MUNICIPAL STATISTICS BUREAU
NBS SURVEY OFFICE IN QINGDAO

中国统计出版社
China Statistics Press

图书在版编目（CIP）数据

青岛统计年鉴 . 2020 = Qingdao Statistical Yearbook 2020 : 汉英对照 / 青岛市统计局，国家统计局青岛调查队编 . -- 北京 : 中国统计出版社，2020.8
ISBN 978-7-5037-9219-9

Ⅰ . ①青… Ⅱ . ①青… ②国… Ⅲ . ①统计资料－青岛－2020－年鉴－汉、英 Ⅳ . ① C832.523-54

中国版本图书馆 CIP 数据核字 (2020) 第 139387 号

青岛统计年鉴 -2020

作　　者 / 青岛市统计局　国家统计局青岛调查队
责任编辑 / 钟　钰
装帧设计 / 青岛双福文化传播有限公司
出版发行 / 中国统计出版社有限公司
地　　址 / 北京市丰台区西三环南路甲 6 号
邮政编码 / 100073
电　　话 / 邮购（010）63376909　书店（010）68783171
网　　址 / http://www.zgtjcbs.com
印　　刷 / 青岛任缘印刷包装有限公司
经　　销 / 新华书店
开　　本 / 890mm × 1240mm　1/16
字　　数 / 1210 千字
印　　张 / 28.25
版　　别 / 2020 年 8 月第 1 版
版　　次 / 2020 年 8 月第 1 次印刷
定　　价 / 280.00 元　Price: 280.00 (RMB)

如有印装差错，由本社发行部调换。

全市生产总值构成（%）

Composition Of Gross Domestic Product (%)

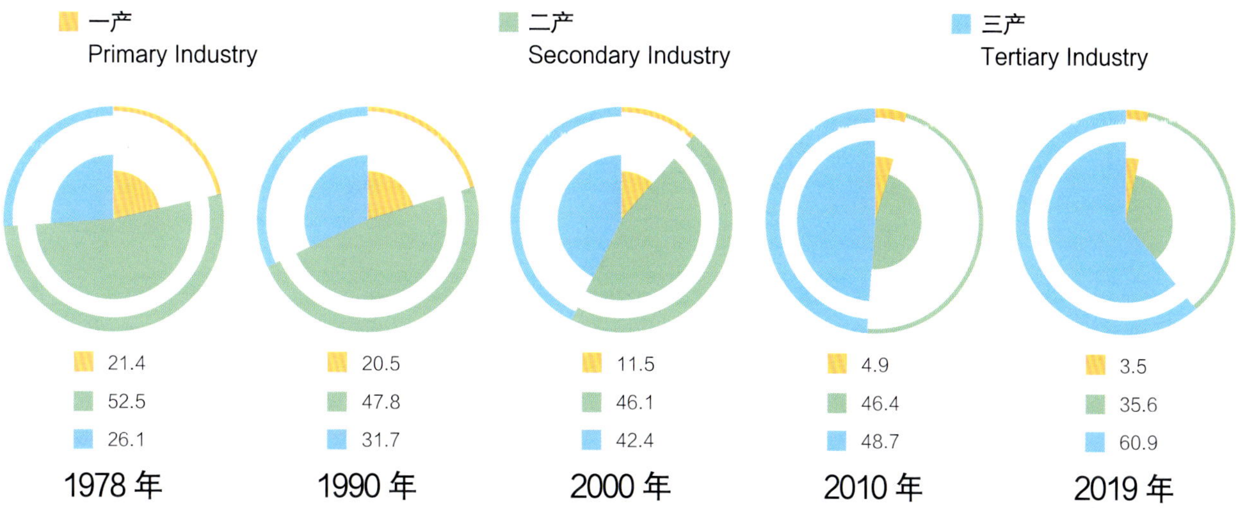

全市生产总值（亿元）

Gross Domestic Product (100 million yuan)

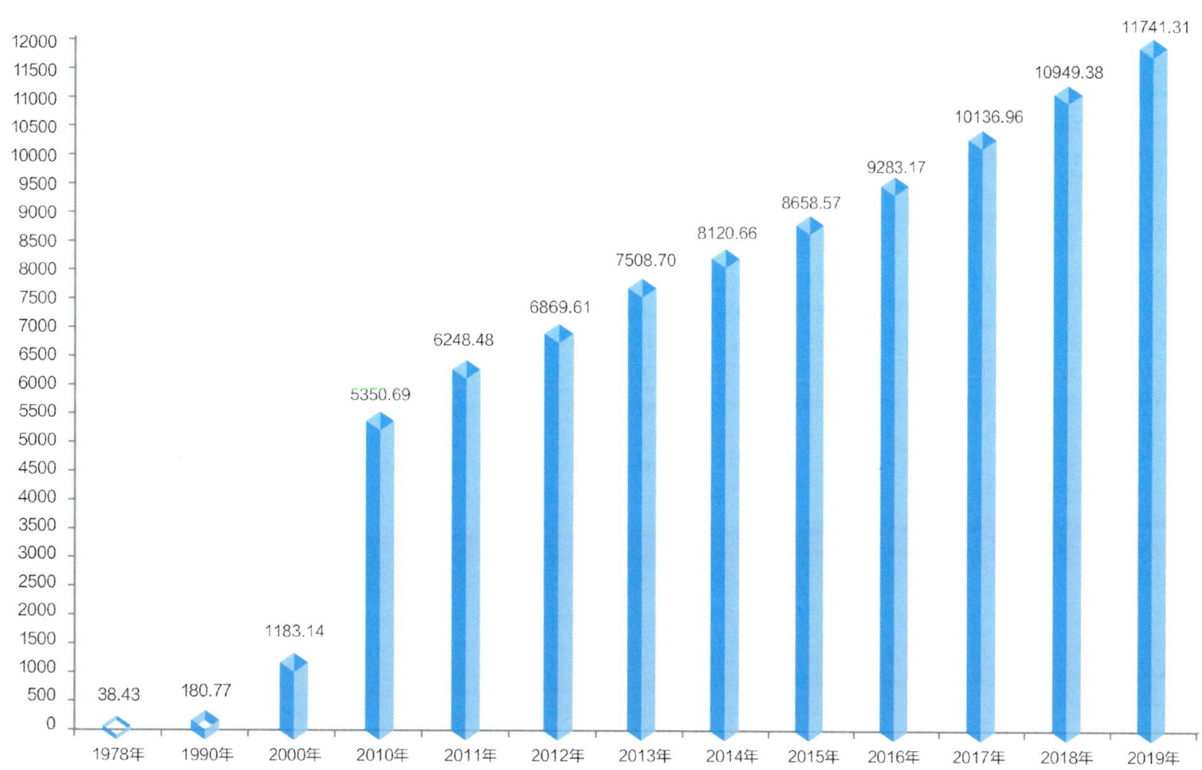

农林牧渔业总产值（亿元）

Gross Output Value Of Agriculture (100 million yuan)

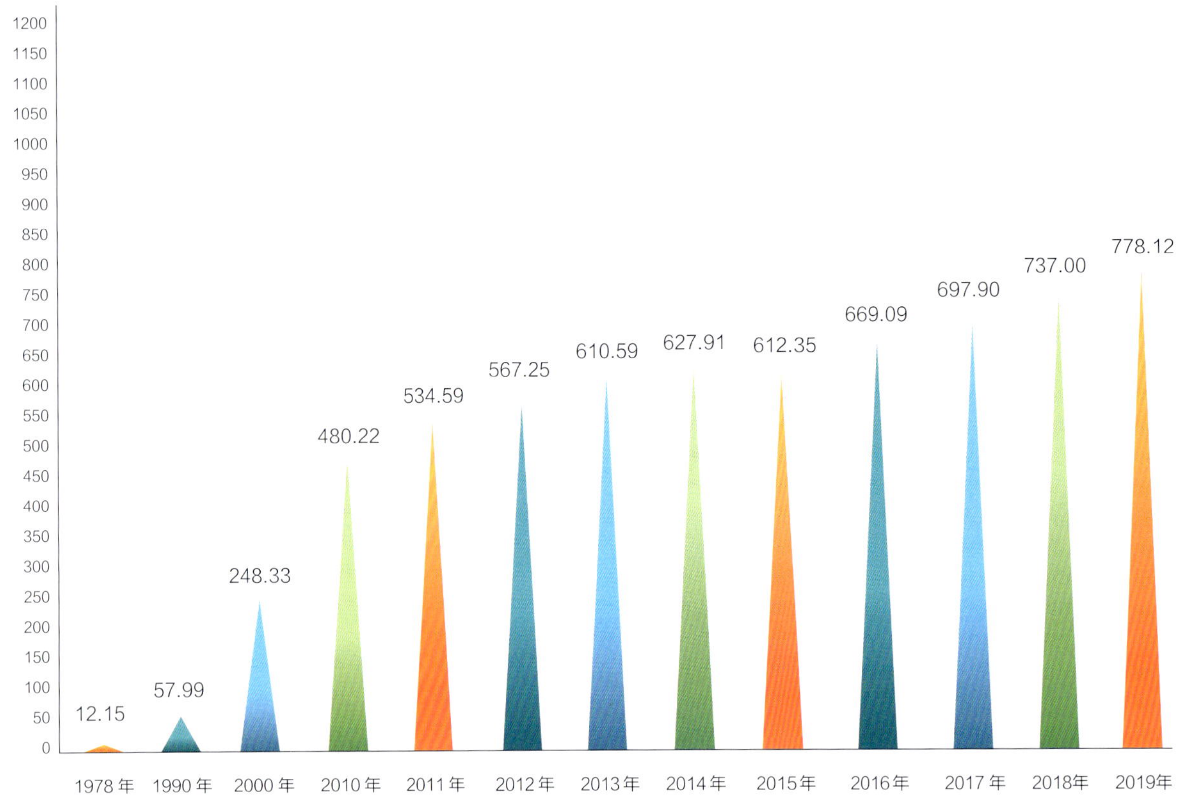

主要农产品产量（万吨）

Output Of Farm Products (10 000 tons)

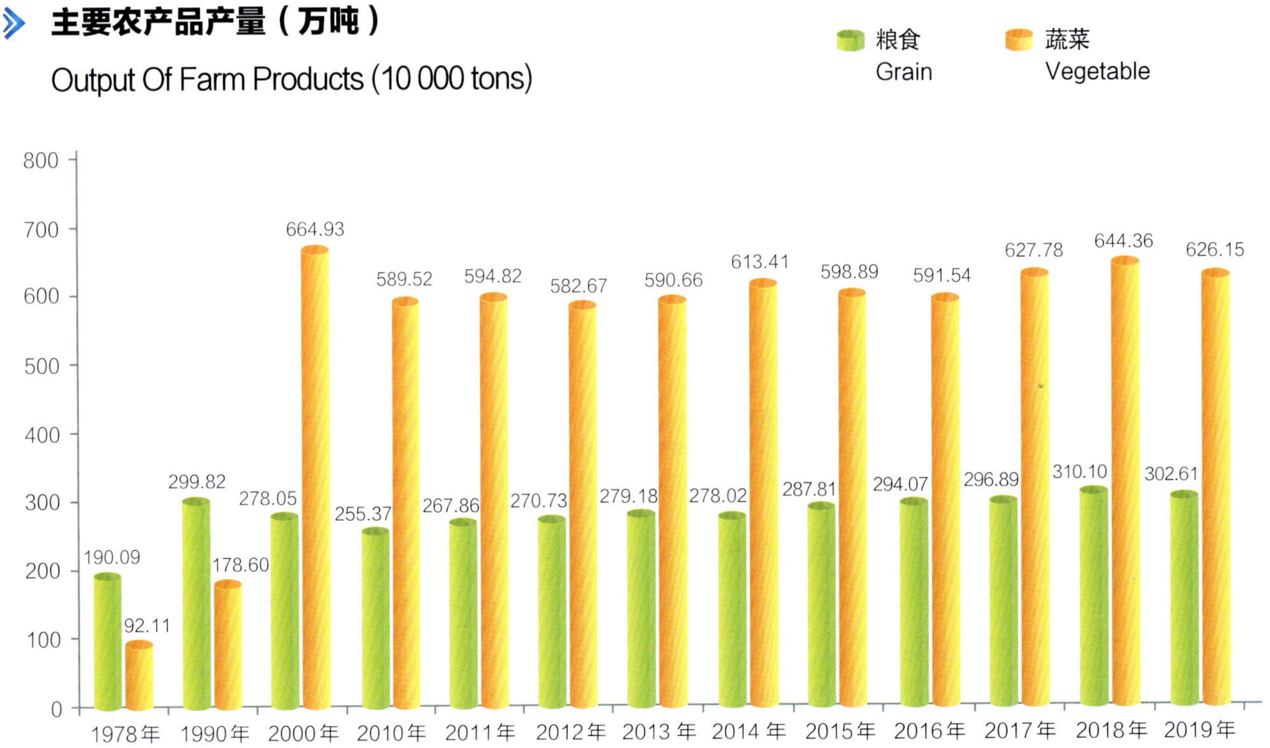

工业总产值（亿元）

Gross Industrial Output Value (100 million yuan)

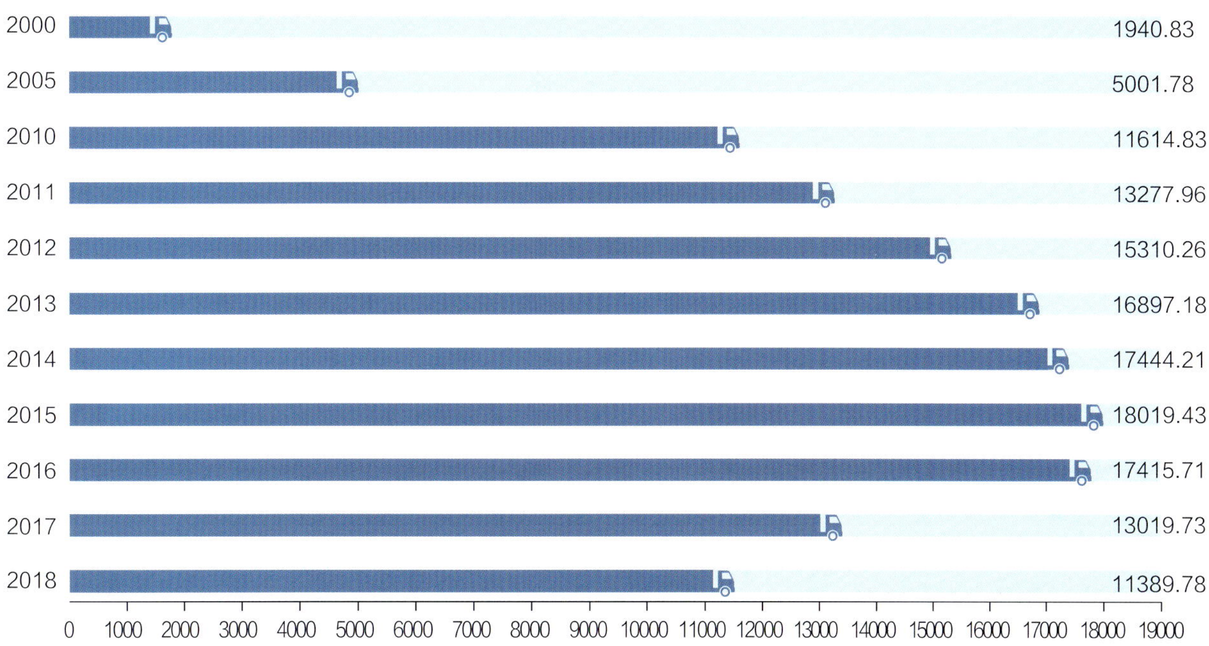

规模以上工业实现利润总额（亿元）

The Total Profits Made By The Industries Above The Designated Size (100 million yuan)

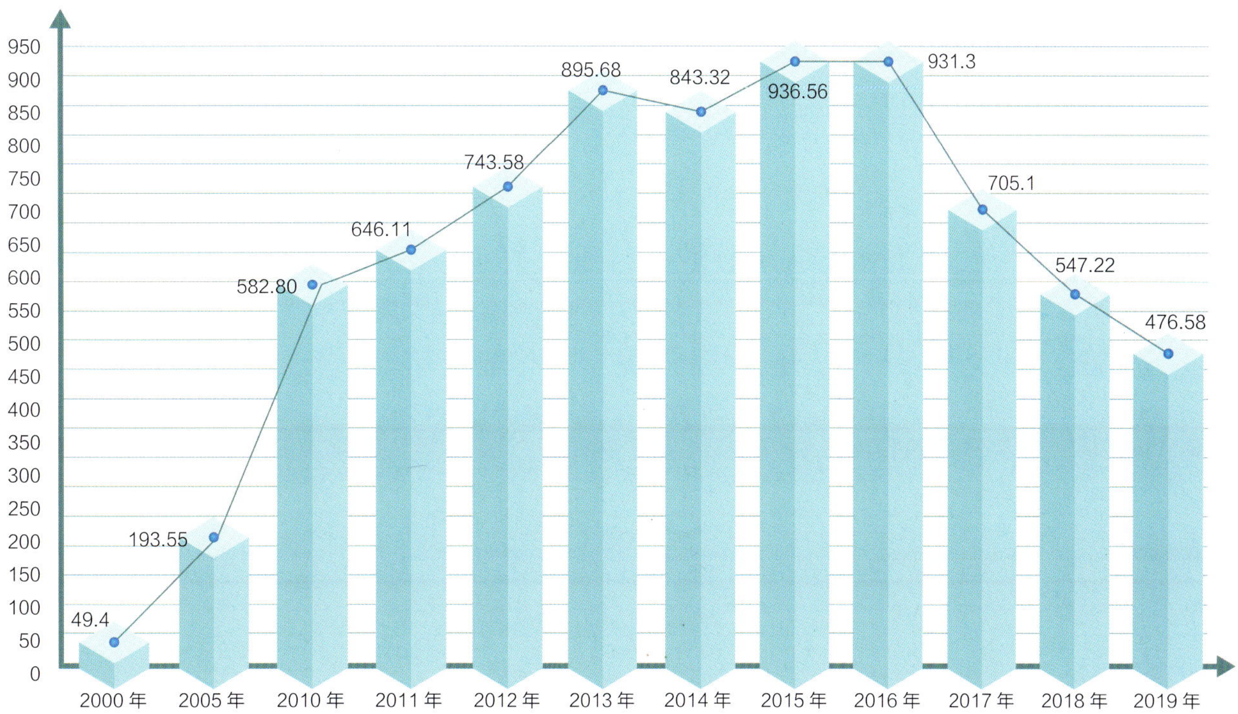

房地产开发投资（亿元）

Investment In Real Estate Development (100 million yuan)

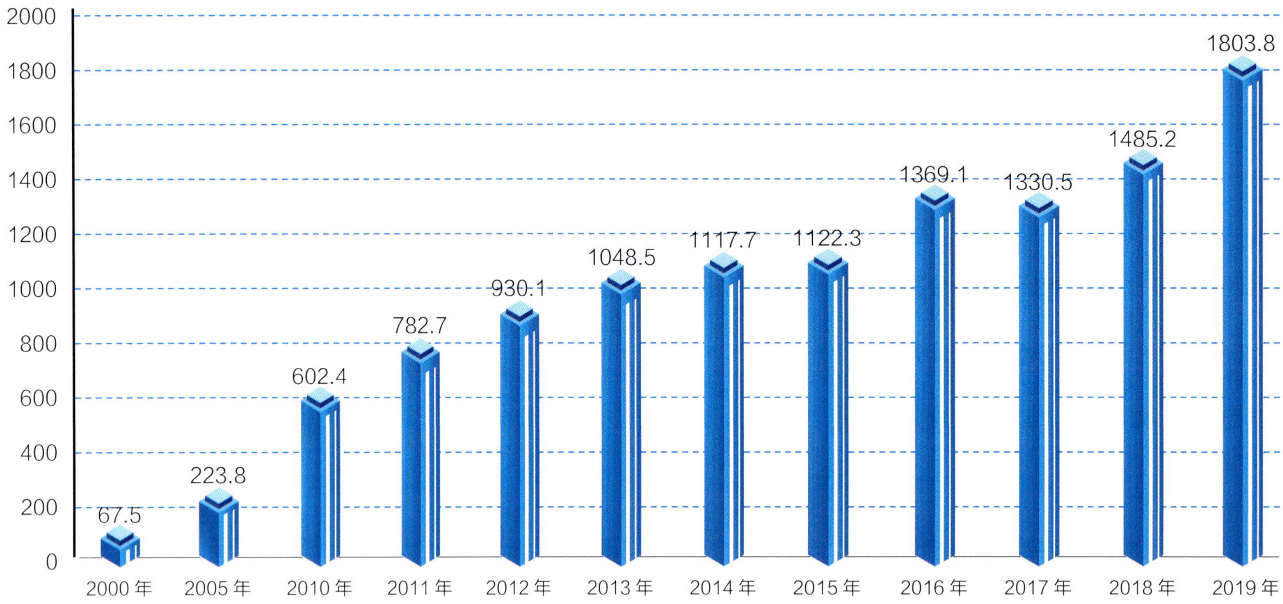

房屋销售面积（万平方米）

Floor Space Of Commercial Buildings Sold (10 000 sq.m)

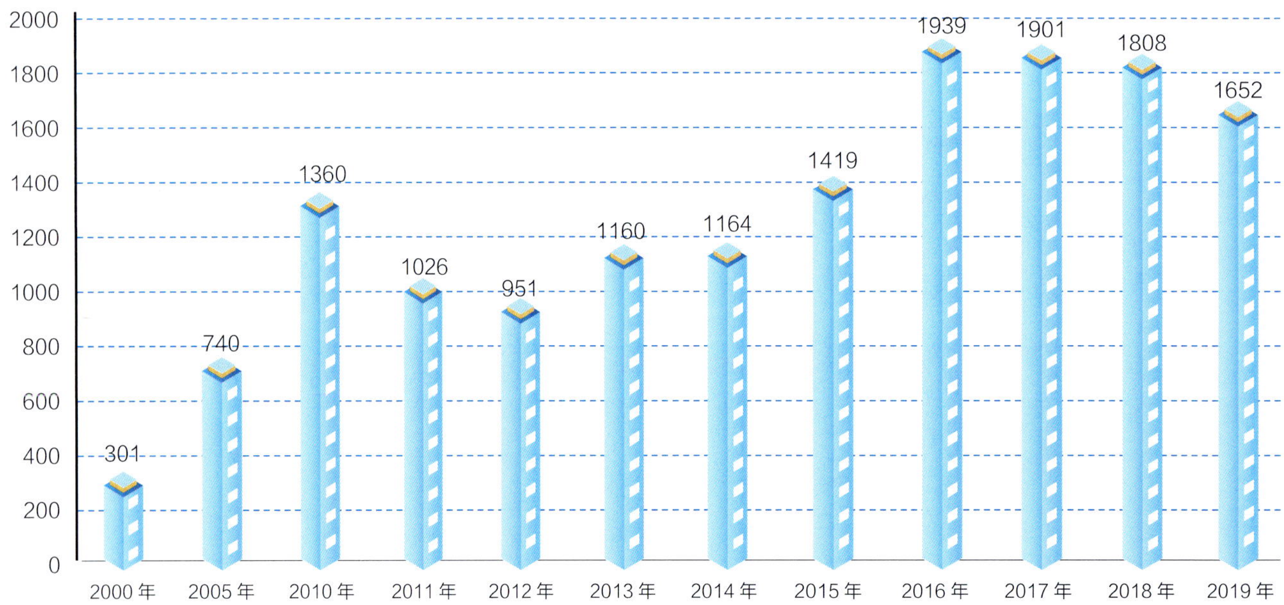

消费构成（%）（2019年）

2019 Composition Of Consumption (%)

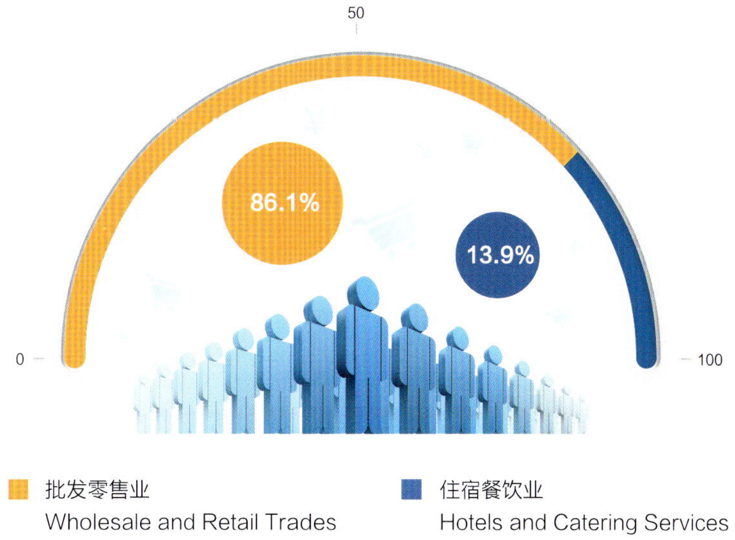

社会消费品零售总额（亿元）

Total Retail Sales Of Consumer Goods (100 million yuan)

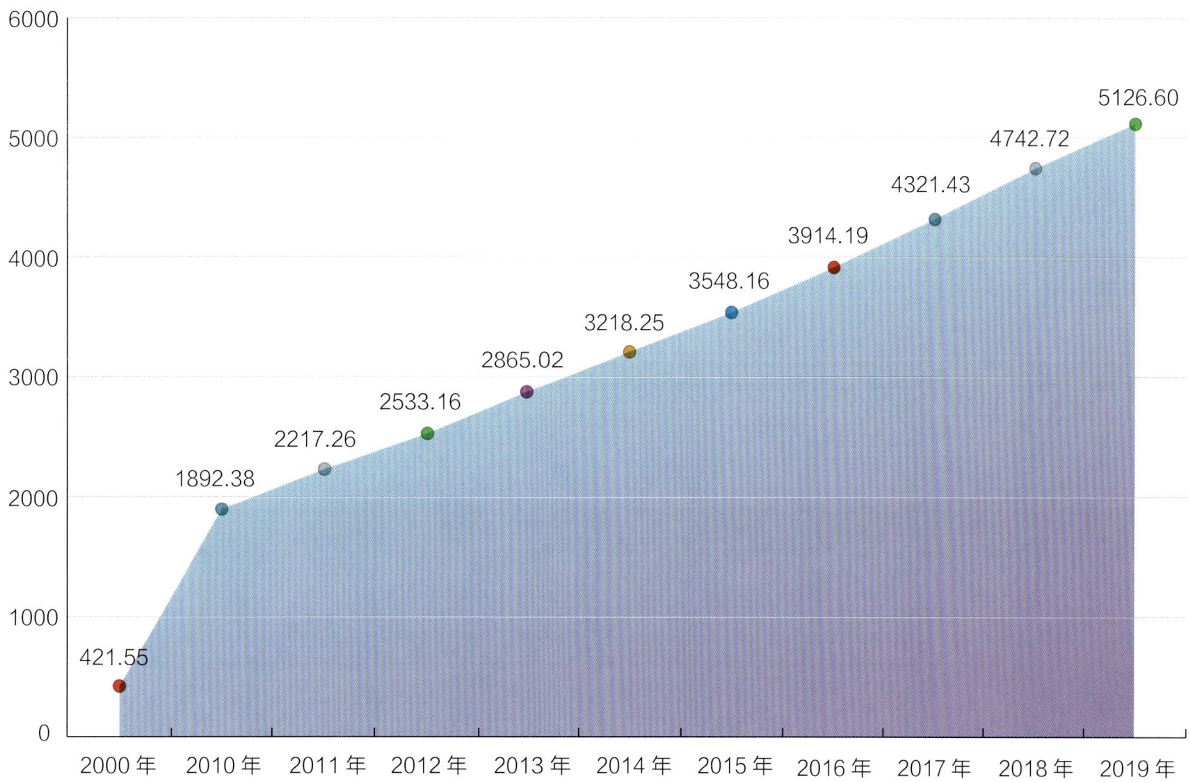

旅游人数（万人次）

Number Of Tourists (10 000 person-times)

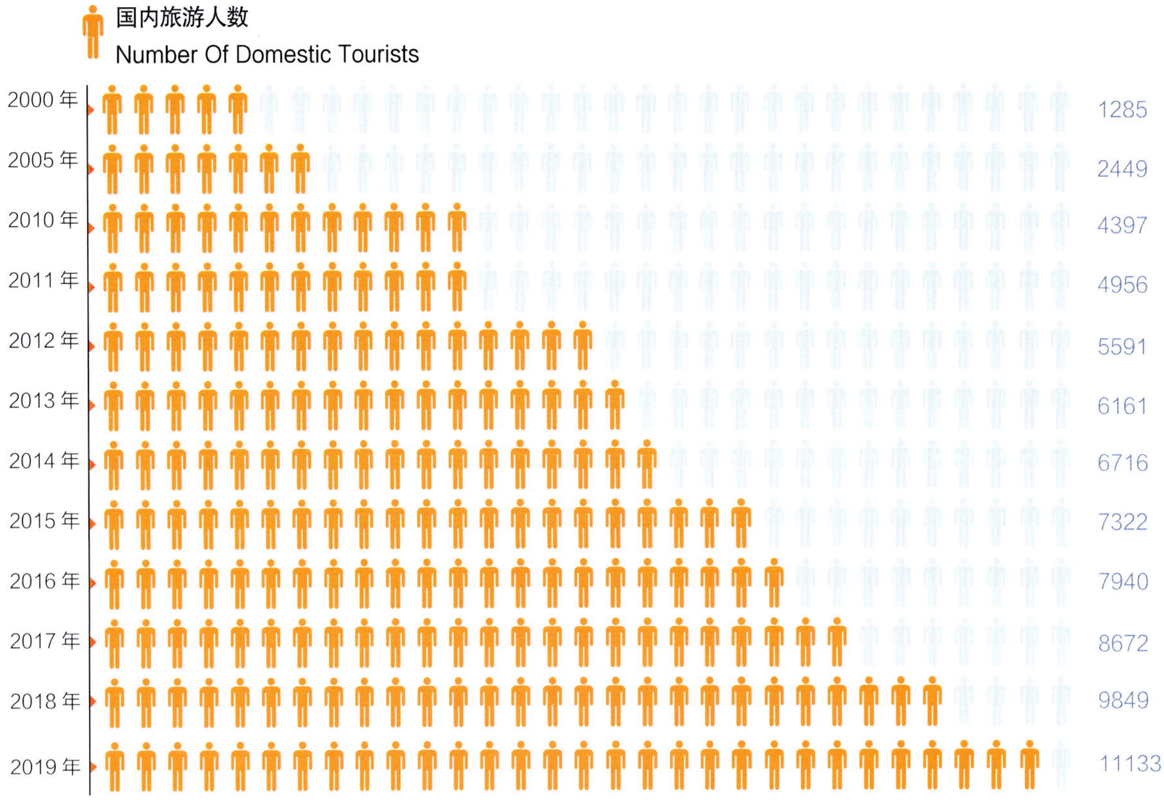

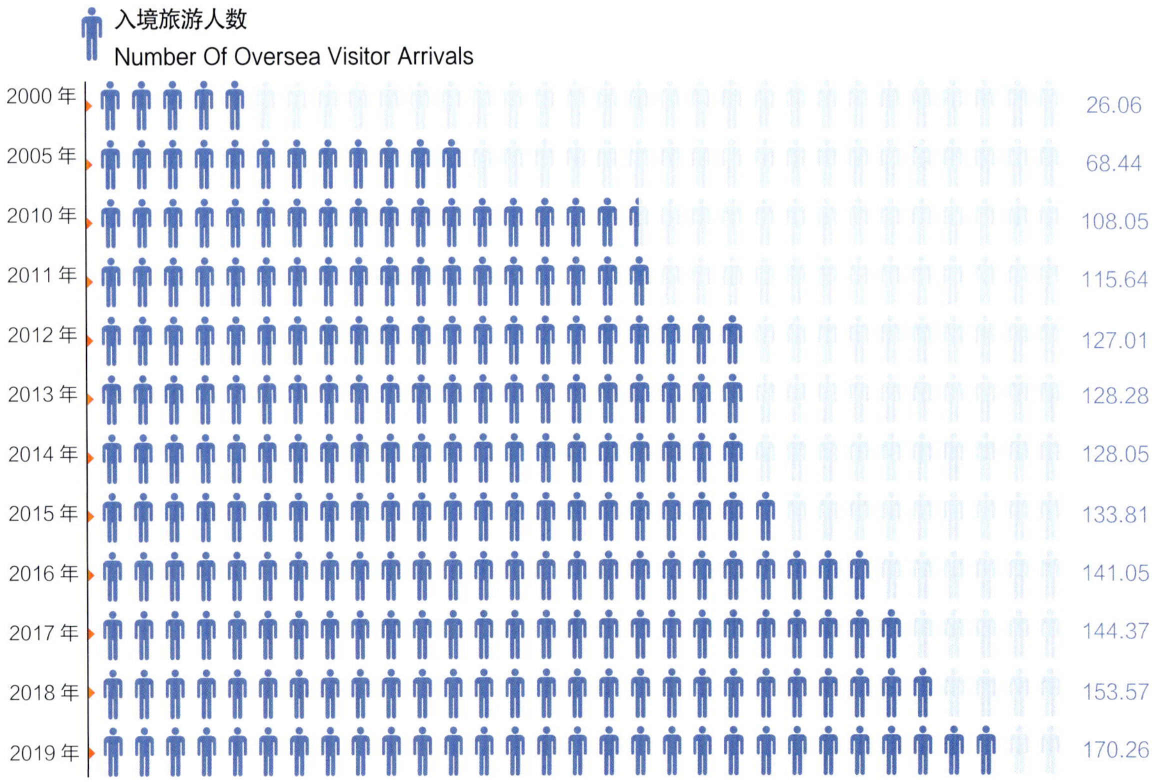

地方财政收入（亿元）

Revenue Of Local Government Finance (100 million yuan)

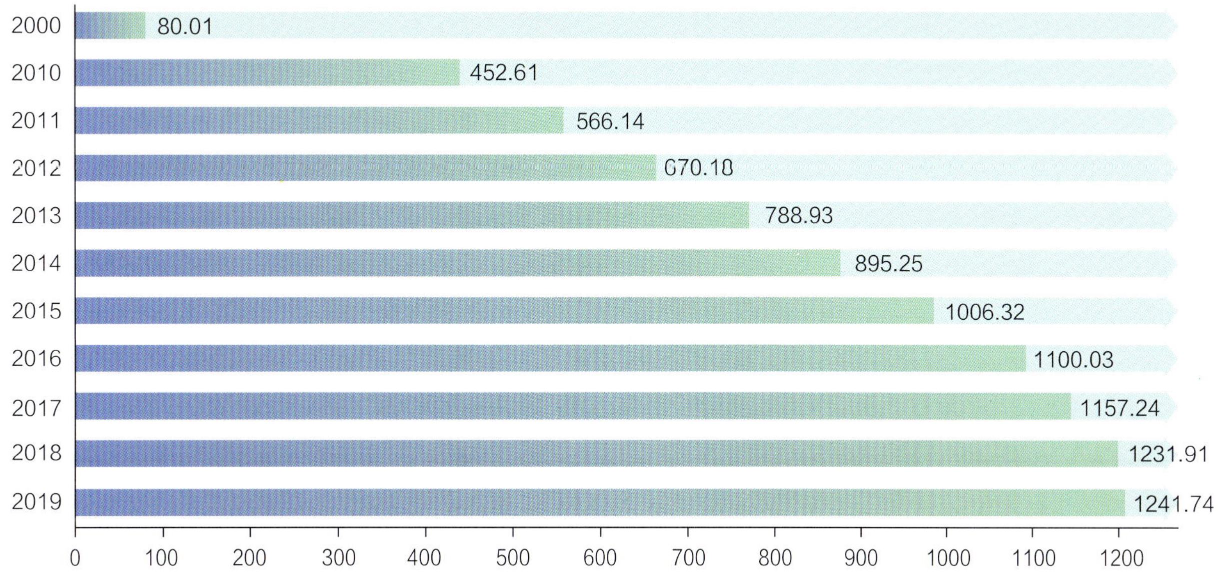

注：2002 年以后财政收入为一般预算收入数。

Note：Since 2002，revenue of government finance refers to general budgetary revenue.

金融机构年末人民币存贷款余额（亿元）

Year-end Savings Deposits And Loans Of Financial Institution (RMB) (100 million yuan)

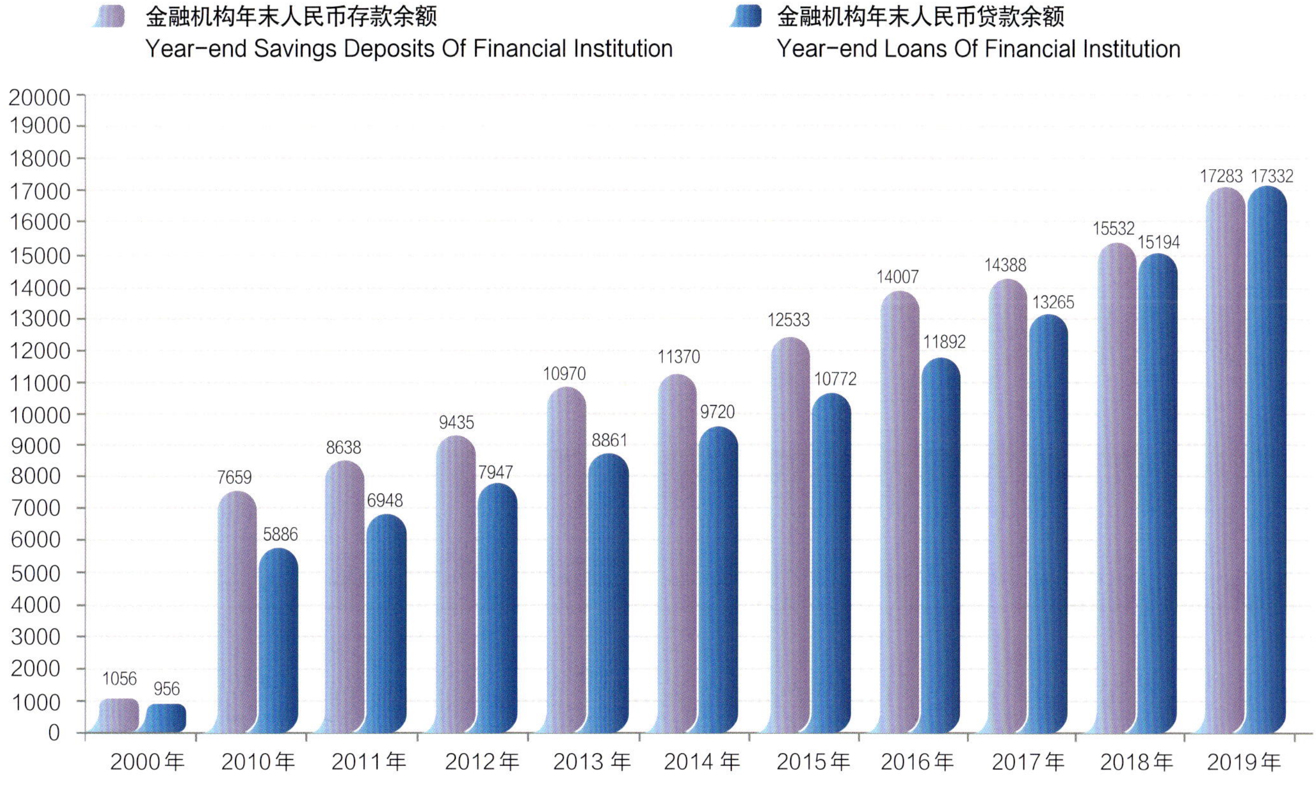

社会从业人数（万人）

Social Employment (10 000 persons)

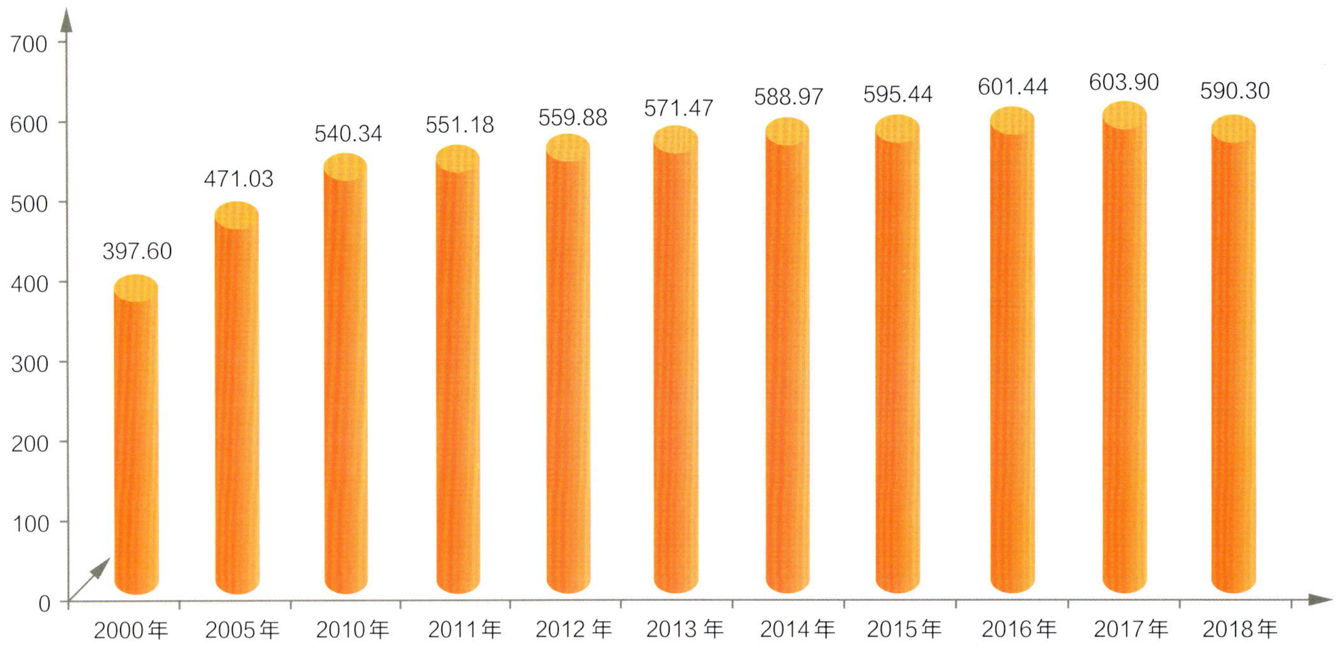

城镇非私营单位平均工资（元）

Average Salary Of Urban Non-Private Units (yuan)

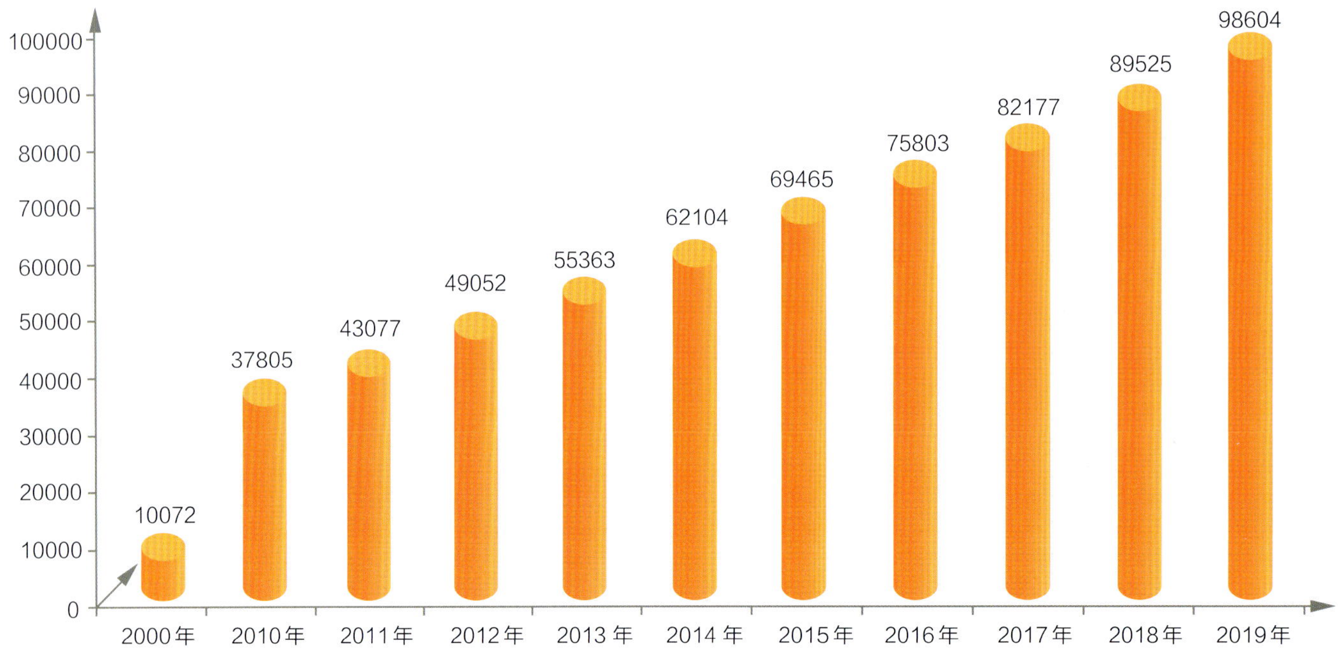

居民消费价格指数（上年=100）
Consumer Price Indices (preceding year = 100)

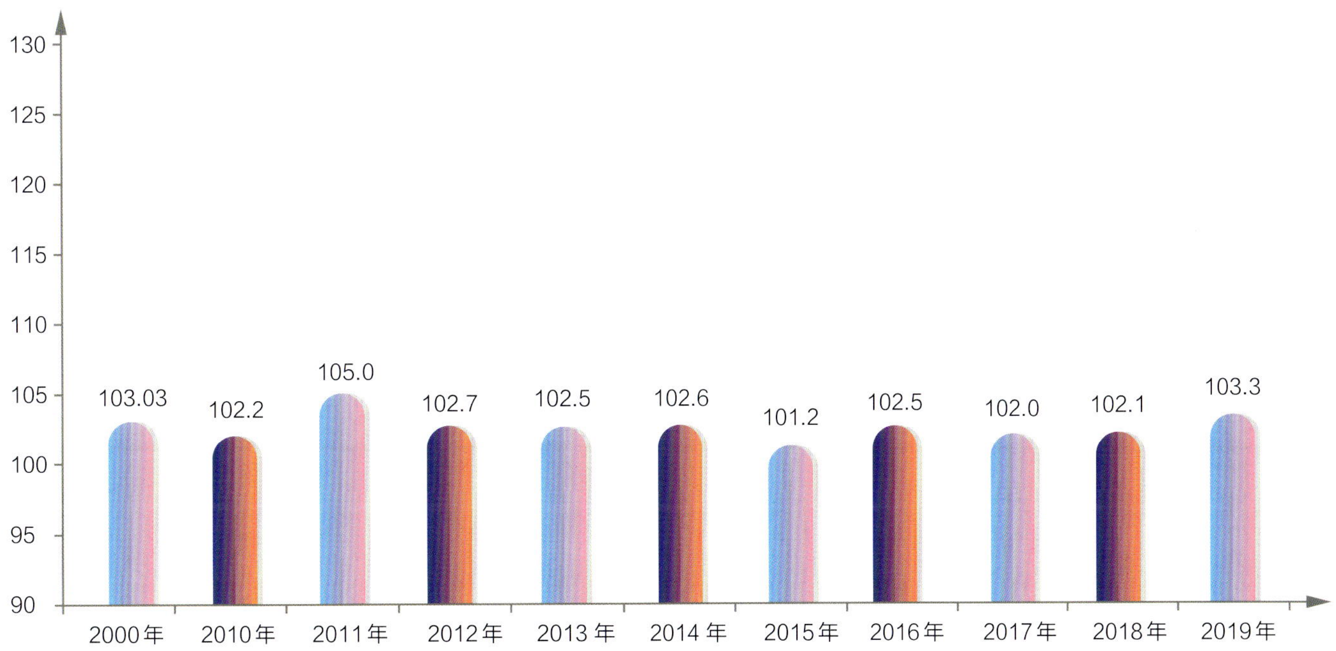

商品零售价格指数（上年=100）
Retail Price Indices (preceding year = 100)

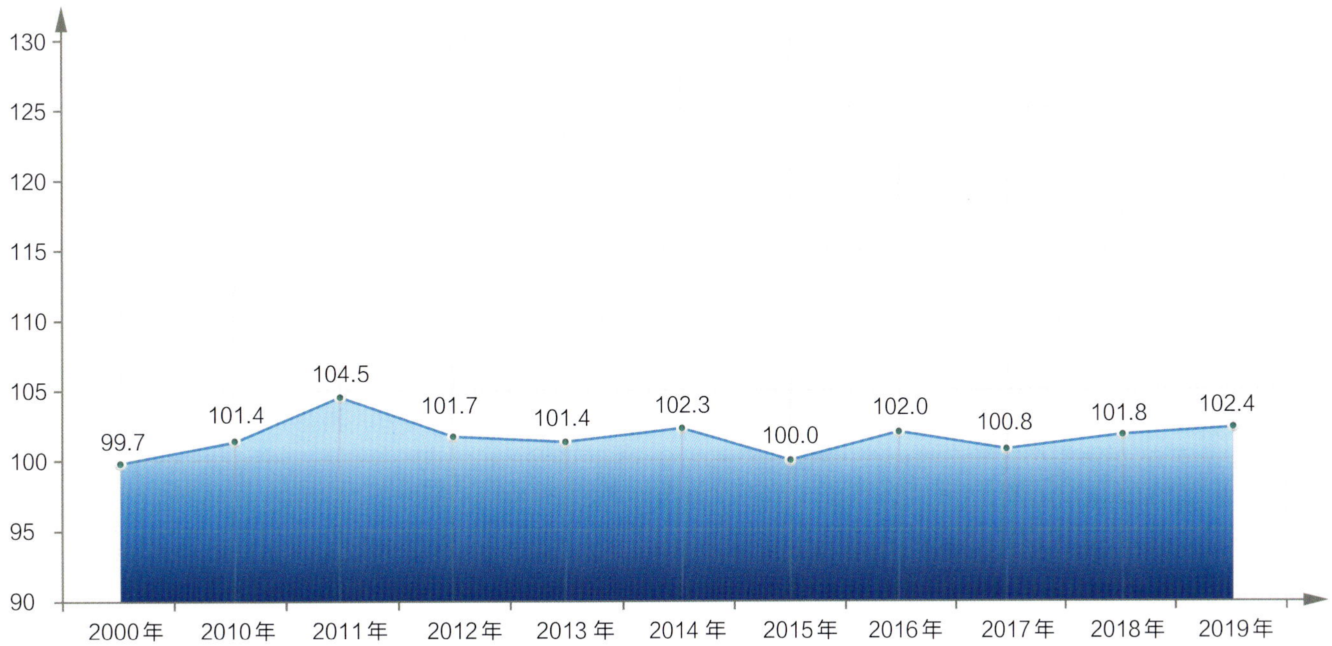

城市建成区面积（平方公里）

Developed Area Of the City (sq.km)

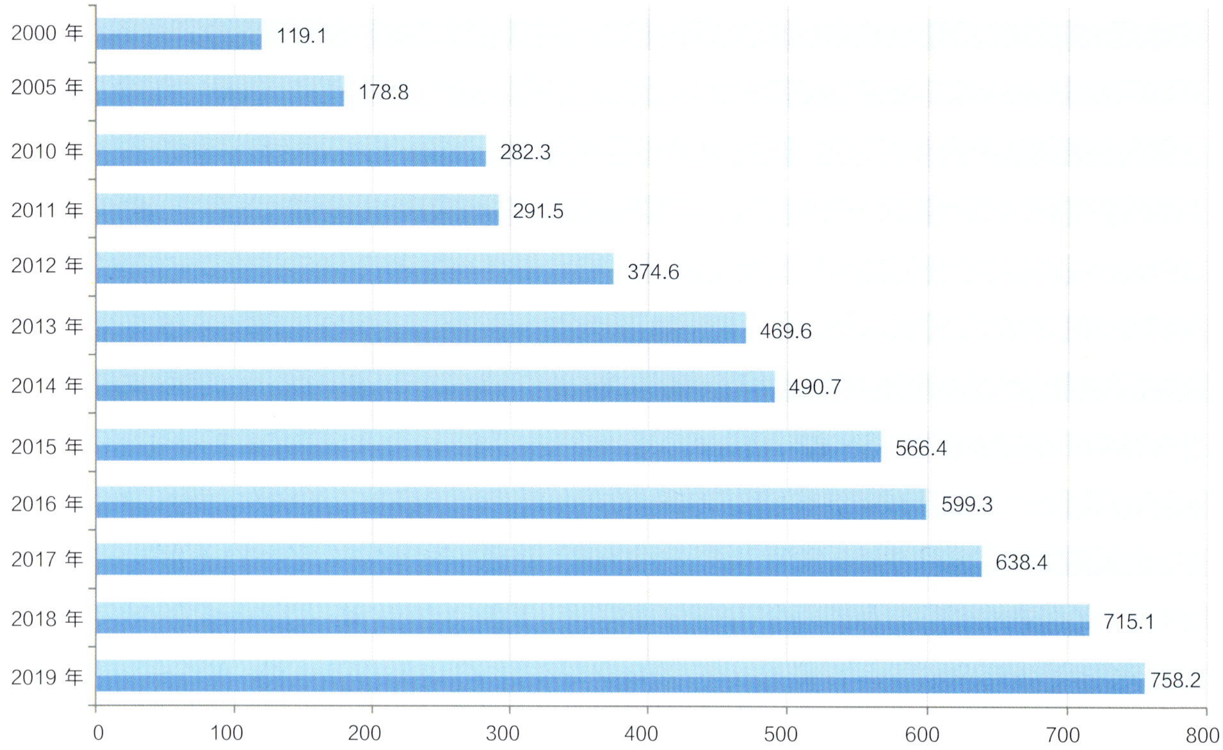

铺装道路面积（万平方米）

Area Of Roads (10 000 sq.m)

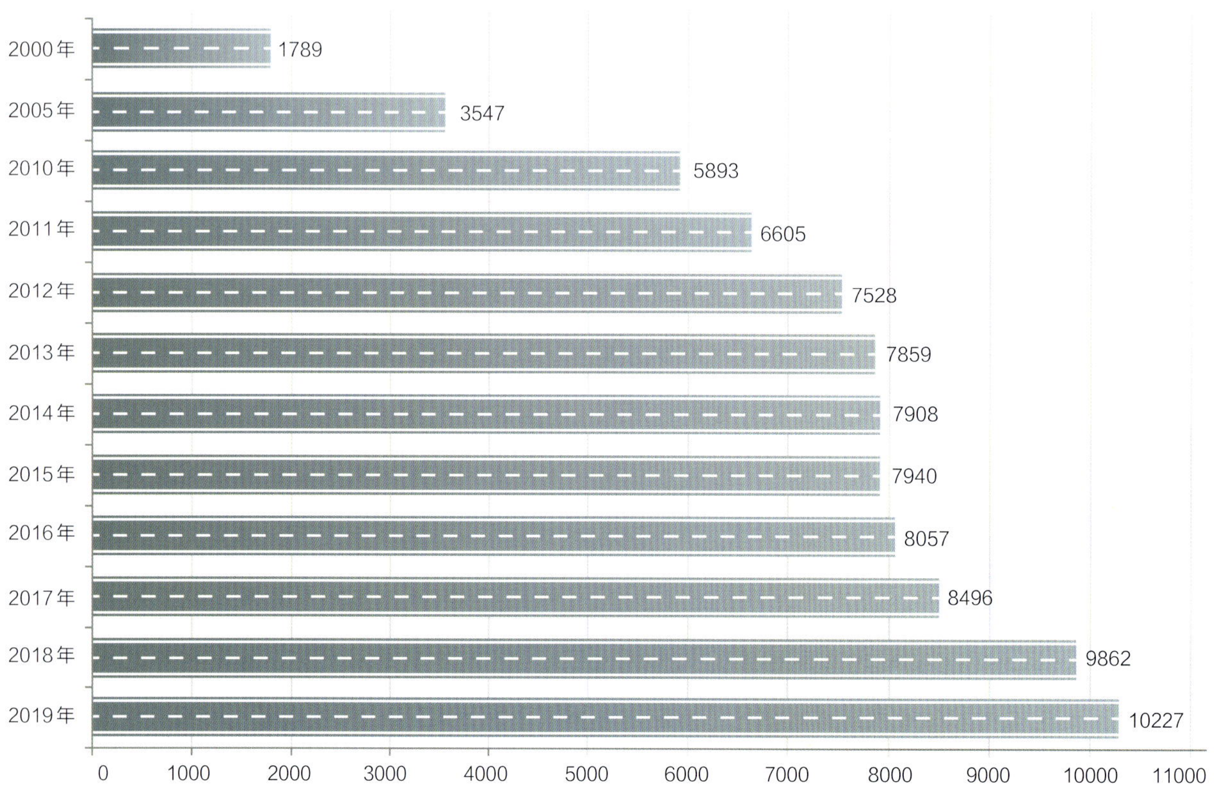

医疗卫生机构（个）

Health Care Institutions (unit)

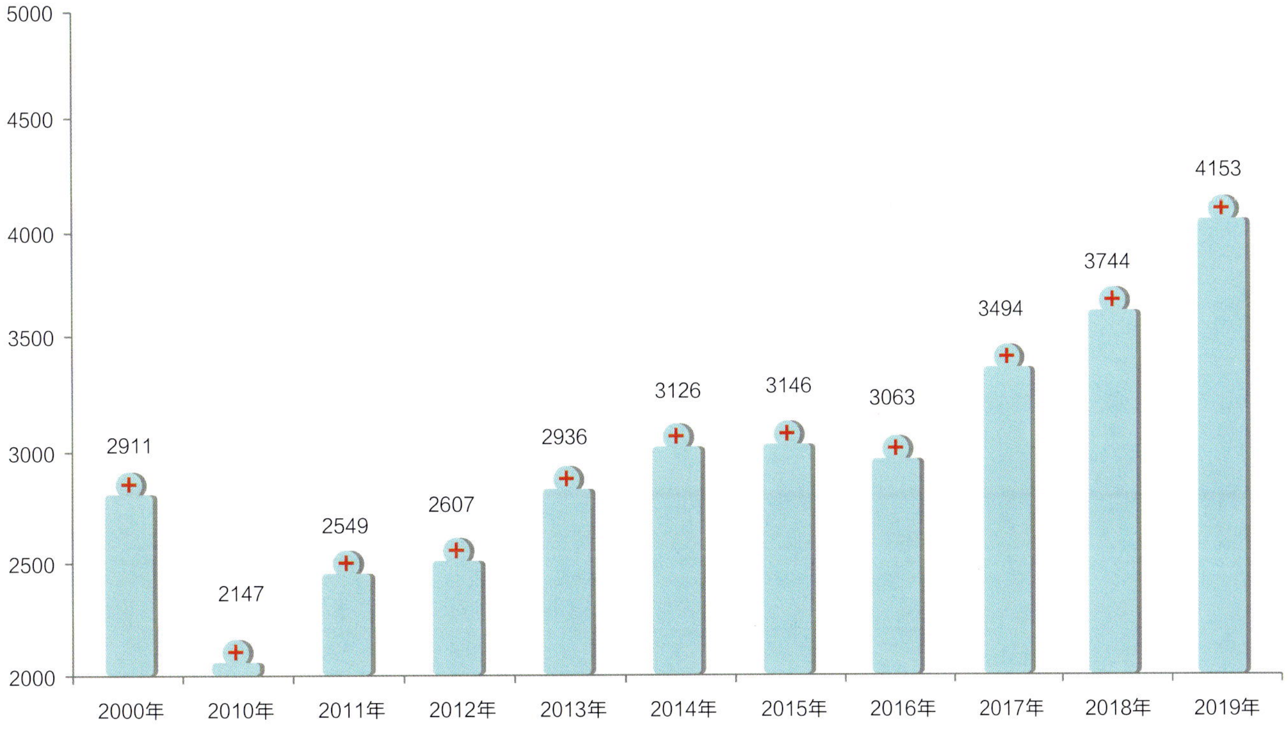

普通高校在校人数（万人）

Students Enrollment Of Regular Institutions Of Higher Education (10 000 persons)

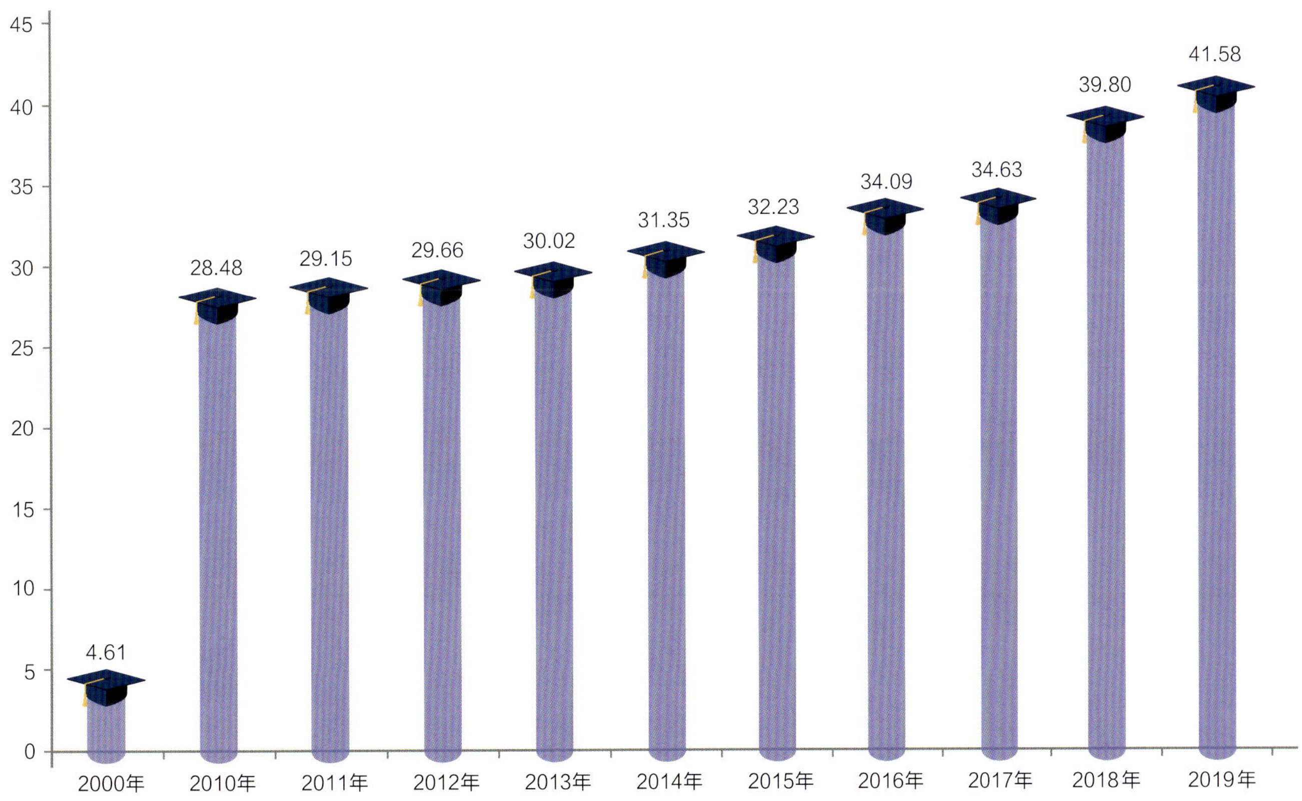

编辑委员会

EDITORIAL BOARD

编者说明

一、《青岛统计年鉴 -2020》是一部全面反映青岛市国民经济和社会发展情况、信息高度密集的资料工具书。

二、《青岛统计年鉴 -2020》共包括发展成果图、统计公报、统计表、附录四大部分。

统计表部分收录了 2019 年青岛市经济和社会等各方面的统计数据，以及建国以来重要年份和改革开放以来的主要统计数据，包括：综合，人口，从业人员及职工工资，固定资产投资，对外经济贸易，城市建设、环境保护，能源消耗，财政金融和保险业，价格指数，人民生活，农业，工业，规模以上服务业，建筑业，运输、邮电，批发和零售业，住宿、餐饮业和旅游，教育、科技和文化，体育、卫生和民政、司法。

为方便读者正确地使用年鉴资料，各篇章前设有《简要说明》，概括介绍各篇主要内容和资料来源；篇末还附有《主要统计指标解释》。

三、本《年鉴》部分历史数据已根据经济普查和农业普查数据进行了修订，在此之前公布的数据凡与本年鉴数字不符的一律以本年鉴为准。

四、部门分区市数据按照所属职能部门提供的区市名称范围划分。

五、本年鉴中的符号说明：年鉴各表中的“空格”表示该项统计指标数据不足本表最小单位数、数据不详或无该项数据；"#" 表示其中的主要项。

六、《青岛统计年鉴》自公开出版以来，受到社会各界的关心和支持，对于年鉴的内容和编辑工作提出了许多宝贵的意见，对此我们深表谢意。限于我们的水平，欢迎读者继续对年鉴的不足之处给予批评和指正，帮助我们进一步改进年鉴编辑工作，以期更好地为广大读者服务。

《青岛统计年鉴》编委会

2020 年 8 月

Editor's Note

Ⅰ. *Qingdao Statistical Yearbook 2020* is a very important reference book, which reflects various aspects of Qingdao's social and economic development and contains High–density information.

Ⅱ.The yearbook contains the following four parts: achievement graphs, statistic gazette, statistics and appendixes.

Statistics contains all kinds of data on Qingdao's social and economic development in 2019, and data in significant year or data since the beginning of reform and opening up, including: General Survey; Population; Employment and Wages; Investment in Fixed Assets; Foreign Trade; City Construction and Environment Protection; Consumption of Energy; Government Finance ,Financial and Insurance; Price Indexes; People's Living Conditions; Agriculture; Industry; Service Enterprises Above Designated Size; Construction; Transport, Postal and Telecommunication Services; Wholesale and Retail Trades; Hotels, Catering Services and Tourism; Education, Science & Technology and Culture; Sports, Public Health and Civil Affairs, Judicial Affairs.

In brief introduction at the beginning of each chapter, main coverage, data sources and statistical coverage are concerned. Meanwhile explanatory notes on major statistical indicators have been attached for readers to use the data correctly.

Ⅲ.Part of the historical data in this book has been revised based on the economic census and agricultural census data. Any data published before that does not match the figures in this book shall be subject to this book.

Ⅳ. Departmental district city data is divided according to the range of district and city names provided by the respective functional departments.

Ⅴ. Marks in this book: “(blank)” indicates that the figure is not large enough to be measured with the smallest unit in the table, the data is not available, or the data is not available; “#” indicates the major items of the total.

Ⅵ. Since the publication of the "Qingdao Statistical Yearbook", it has received concern and support from all walks of life, and has put forward many valuable opinions on the content and editing of the yearbook, for which we are deeply grateful. Limited to our level, readers are welcome to continue to criticize and correct the deficiencies of the yearbook, and to help us further improve the editing of the yearbook in order to better serve the readers.

Editorial Board

August, 2020

目　　录
CONTENTS

一、综　　合
Chapter 1.　GENERAL SURVEY

二、人　口
Chapter 2.　POPULATION

三、从业人员及职工工资
Chapter 3.　EMPLOYMENT AND WAGES

四、固定资产投资
Chapter 4. INVESTMENT IN FIXED ASSETS

五、对外经济贸易
Chapter 5. FOREIGN TRADE

六、城市建设、环境保护
Chapter 6.　CITY CONSTRUCTION AND ENVIRONMENT PROTECTION

七、能源消耗

Chapter 7.　CONSUMPTION OF ENERGY

八、财政、金融和保险业

Chapter 8.　GOVERNMENT FINANCE, FINACIAL AND INSURANCE

九、价格指数
Chapter 9.　PRICE INDEXES

十、人民生活
Chapter 10.　PEOPLE'S LIVING CONDITIONS

十一、农　业
Chapter 11.　AGRICULTURE

十二、工　业
Chapter 12. INDUSTRY

十三、规模以上服务业

Chapter 13. SERVICE ENTERPRISES ABOVE DESIGNATED SIZE

十四、建　筑　业
Chapter 14.　CONSTRUCTION

十五、运输、邮电
Chapter 15.　TRANSPORT, POSTAL AND TELECOMMUNICATION SERVICES

十六、批发和零售业
Chapter 16.　WHOLESALE AND RETAIL TRADES

十七、住宿、餐饮业和旅游
Chapter 17.　HOTELS, CATERING SERVICES AND TOURISM

十八、教育、科技和文化
Chapter 18.　EDUCATION SCIENCE & TECHNOLOGY AND CULTURE

十九、体育、卫生和民政、司法

Chapter 19.　SPORTS, PUBLIC HEALTH AND CIVIL AFFAIRS, JUDICIAL AFFAIRS

附　录
APPENDIX

2019年
青岛市国民经济和社会发展
统　计　公　报

青岛市统计局

国家统计局青岛调查队

（2020年3月27日）

2019年，全市上下坚持以习近平新时代中国特色社会主义思想为指导，认真贯彻落实习近平总书记视察山东、视察青岛的重要讲话、重要指示批示精神，加快推进“中国—上海合作组织地方经贸合作示范区”“军民融合创新示范区”“中国（山东）自由贸易试验区青岛片区”等重大战略实施，在市委、市政府的坚强领导下，抓运行强支撑、提质量增效益、增活力强动力、抓统筹促融合、补短板兜底线，坚持稳中求进工作总基调，全面深化改革，实施创新驱动战略，深入推进乡村振兴，强抓实体经济建设，提升重点区域发展能级，着力保障和改善民生，统筹推进稳增长、促改革、调结构、惠民生、防风险、保稳定，“学深圳、赶深圳”，全面发起15个攻势，全市经济呈现稳中有进、稳中有新、稳中提质发展态势，为加快建设开放现代活力时尚的国际大都市奠定了基础。

一、综　合

山东省统计局首次统一核算并反馈结果显示，2019年全市生产总值11741.31亿元，按可比价格计算，增长6.5%；其中，第一产业增加值409.98亿元，增长1.6%；第二产业增加值4182.76亿元，增长4.7%；第三产业增加值7148.57亿元，增长8.0%。三次产业比例为3.5:35.6:60.9。人均GDP达到124282元。

年末，全市常住总人口949.98万人，增长1.12%。其中，市区常住人口645.20万人，增长1.57%。

表1：2019年全市及区市常住人口情况

区　市	常住人口（万人）
全　市	949.98
市南区	58.88
市北区	111.1
李沧区	58.92
崂山区	45.59
西海岸新区	160.82
城阳区	74.49
即墨区	124.89
胶州市	90.75
平度市	137.79
莱西市	76.24
红岛经济区	10.51

全年财政总收入 4089.5 亿元，增长 10.4%。一般公共预算收入 1241.7 亿元，增长 0.8%。其中，税收收入 901.7 亿元，下降 0.5%；增值税 361.2 亿元，增长 10.2%；企业所得税 148.5 亿元，下降 2.6%；个人所得税 35.1 亿元，下降 28.1%；城市维护建设税 57.2 亿元，下降 0.9%。一般公共预算支出 1576.6 亿元，增长 1.1%。其中，一般公共服务支出 184.5 亿元，增长 13.4%；教育支出 275.4 亿元，增长 4.7%；科学技术支出 66.8 亿元，增长 48.0%；社会保障和就业支出 194.5 亿元，增长 24.6%；城乡社区事务支出 279.5 亿元，下降 15.8%。全年税务系统组织税收收入（含海关代征）2441.2 亿元，增长 1.3%。其中，国内税收 1764.1 亿元，增长 2.6%。

全年居民消费价格指数为 103.3，工业生产者出厂价格指数为 100.0，工业生产者购进价格指数为 98.4。12 月新建商品住宅销售同比价格指数为 104.2，二手住宅同比价格指数为 94.6。

表 2：2019 年全市居民消费价格指数

指标名称	全年（上年同期 =100）
居民消费价格总指数	103.3
非食品价格指数	101.3
服务价格指数	101.7
消费品价格指数	104.3
一、食品烟酒	108.6
食品	111.6
# 粮食	103.2
鲜菜	103.0
猪肉	156.1
鸡蛋	102.4
二、衣着	100.6
三、居住	100.5
四、生活用品及服务	100.5
五、交通和通信	97.3
六、教育文化和娱乐	104.7
七、医疗保健	102.8
八、其他用品和服务	105.3

供给侧结构性改革继续深化。全市规模以上工业每百元营业收入中的费用 11.09 元，比上年减少 0.82 元，规上服务业企业管理运营费用支出在可控区间合理增长，均低于营业收入增速。年末，商品房待售面积 459.1 万平方米，总量接近于 2014 年年初水平。其中，住宅待售 164.1 万平方米。投资项目建设成效显著。2019 年，全市共有在建投资项目 5649 个，是 2018 年项目总量的 1.5 倍。全市计划投资亿元以上产业类大项目 1622 个，比 2018 年增加 453 个。

“三大攻坚战”稳步推进。全市不良贷款率降至 1.43%，较年初下降 0.44 个百分点。市级安排财政扶贫资金 2.4 亿元，实施贫困人口动态调整机制，年末“脱贫享受政策”建档立卡贫困户人口为 25731 人。全市主要污染物细颗粒物（PM2.5）、二氧化硫、氮氧化物年均值分别为 37、8、32 微克 / 立方米，蓝天保卫战提速加力，大气污染防治工作取得积极进展。

发起高效青岛建设攻势。深度再造政务服务流程，企业开办时间压缩至 1 个工作日，工程建设项目审批控制在 85 个工作日以内。在全省率先推行“秒批”改革，申请人提交申请后，系统即时出具审查结果。公积金提取、社保缴纳、无犯罪记录证明等 12 个领域、89 项业务均可通过“秒批”系统办理。

二、新动能与创新

“新产业”稳步发展。全年全市高技术产业实现增加值增长 11.7%，占 GDP 比重为 6.4%。其中，高技术制造业增加值增长 1.7%，占 GDP 比重为 2.1%；高技术服务业增加值增长 17.5%，占 GDP 比重为 4.2%。战略性新兴产业实现增加值增长 5.2%，占 GDP 比重为 8.8%。其中，工业战略性新兴产业增加值增长 4.6%，占 GDP 比重为 5.8%；服务业战略性新兴产业增加值增长 7.1%，占 GDP 比重为 3.0%。

“新业态”“新模式”显现活力。全市电子商务交易平台实现交易额 1.1 万亿元，增长 6.5%；限额以上批发和零售业企业网络销售额增长 13.2%。“新技术”发展迅速。全市规模以上软件和信息技术服务业营业收入 233.2 亿元，增长 28.8%；规模以上高技术服务业中，信息服务增长 17.3%，检验检测服务增长 20.7%，专业技术服务业的高技术服务增长 11.3%，知识产权及相关法律服务增长 15.2%。“新产品”产量增速较快。城市轨道车辆 1770 辆，增长 15.8%；智能电视 1441.9 万台，增长 25.5%。

初步统计，全市共取得重要科技成果 588 项，获得国家级科技奖励 11 项。其中，技术发明奖 3 项，科技进步奖 8 项。获得省级科技奖励 100 项。其中，自然科学奖 9 项，技术发明奖 9 项，科技进步奖 80 项，国际合作奖 2 项。技术合同交易额 170.58 亿元，增长 9.5%。涉海技术合同成交额 20.99 亿元，增长 15.5%。全年有效发明专利 31929 件，增长 21.6%。每万人有效发明专利拥有量 34.37 件，PCT 国际专利申请 1381 件。国家知识产权示范企业 12 家，国家知识产权优势企业 108 家，高新技术企业总数达到 3829 家。研发力量加快聚集，现有国家重点实验室 9 家，国家级工程技术研究中心 10 家，省级工程技术研究中心 82 家。

三、农　业

全年农业增加值 436.2 亿元，增长 2.0%。其中，种植业增加值 212.6 亿元，增长 4.2%；林业增加值 2.7 亿元，增长 18.5%；畜牧业增加值 78.6 亿元，下降 1.3%；渔业增加值 116.1 亿元，下降 0.1%。农林牧渔专业及辅助性活动增加值 26.2 亿元，增长 9.2%。

全年粮食播种面积 47.5 万公顷，蔬菜播种面积 10.8 万公顷，花生播种面积 7.5 万公顷。粮食总产量 302.6 万吨，减产 2.4%；蔬菜及食用菌总产量 626.2 万吨，下降 2.8%；花生总产量 34.2 万吨，下降 11.0%；水果（含果用瓜）总产量 118.6 万吨，增长 8.6%。现代农业园区 1028 个，新增 135 个；认证“三品一标”（无公害农产品、绿色食品、有机农产品和农产品地理标志）产品 1042 个，其中国家地理标志保护产品 52 个。

全年实际完成造林（更新）面积 1 万公顷。

全年肉类总产量 52.8 万吨，增长 1.1%；禽蛋产量 20.0 万吨，增长 10.1%；奶类产量 28.9 万吨，下降 3.0%。

全年水产品产量（不包括远洋捕捞）100.8 万吨，下降 2.6%。海、淡水养殖面积 3.4 万公顷，下降 2.3%。远洋捕捞量 14.5 万吨，基本持平。

农机总动力 740 万千瓦，增加 8 万千瓦。农作物生产综合机械化水平达到 88.5%。农田有效灌溉面积 33.1 万公顷。其中，节水灌溉面积 19.1 万公顷。

表 3：2019 年主要种植业产品产量及增速

指标	单位	产量	增长（%）
粮食	万吨	302.6	−2.4
夏粮	万吨	142.6	3.6
秋粮	万吨	160.0	−7.2
油料	万吨	34.2	−11.0
蔬菜及食用菌	万吨	626.2	−2.8
水果	万吨	118.6	8.6
园林水果	万吨	74.5	4.6

四、工业与建筑业

全市全部工业增加值 3159.86 亿元，增长 2.8%。其中，规模以上工业实现增加值增长 0.6%。分经济类型看，国有控股企业实现增加值增长 1.8%，集体企业实现增加值下降 10.6%，股份制企业实现增加值增长 1.4%，外商及港澳台商投资企业实现增加值下降 1.3%。分门类看，采矿业实现增加值增长 10.4%，制造业实现增加值增长 0.4%，电力、热力、燃气及水生产和供应业实现增加值增长 5.9%。全年规模以上工业企业产销率达到 99.6%。规模以上工业企业实现出口交货值增长 5.4%，比上年提升 2.6 个百分点。工业重点行业中，电气机械和器材制造业实现增加值增长 10.1%，铁路、船舶、航空航天和其他运输设备制造业实现增加值增长 18.1%，石油加工、炼焦和核燃料加工业实现增加值下降 17.6%，汽车制造业实现增加值增长 7.2%，计算机、通信和其他电子设备制造业实现增加值下降 5.8%。

表4：2019年规模以上工业主要产品产量及增速

产品名称	单位	产量	增长（%）
彩色电视机	万台	1580.4	20.8
其中：智能电视	万台	1441.9	25.5
家用电冰箱	万台	731.8	0.6
家用洗衣机	万台	513.7	-7.9
房间空气调节器	万台	874.4	-17.4
智能手机	万台	667.2	-43.6
啤酒	万千升	172.7	7.6
橡胶轮胎外胎	万条	4388.1	6.4
平板玻璃	万重量箱	393.6	-30.1
粗钢	万吨	319.3	3.1
汽车	万辆	3.0	-67.5
动车组	辆	1098.0	-10.7
城市轨道车辆	辆	1770.0	15.8
金属集装箱	万立方米	1094.4	-21.0

规模以上工业利润下降0.6%。其中，国有控股企业下降5.4%，集体企业下降4.9%，股份制企业下降1.6%，外商及港澳台商投资企业增长3.4%。

表5：2019年规模以上工业利润增速

指标	增长（%）
规模以上工业利润	-0.6
其中：国有控股	-5.4
集体企业	-4.9
股份制企业	-1.6
外商及港澳台投资企业	3.4

资质内总承包专业承包建筑业企业790家，实现增加值1042.24亿元，增长13.7%；完成建筑业总产值2809.9亿元，增长21.7%；签订合同6014亿元，增长25.9%；实现利税总额115.7亿元，增长9.6%。

五、服务业

全市服务业实现增加值 7148.57 亿元，增长 8.0%，占 GDP 比重为 60.9%，比上年提高 1.3 个百分点，对经济增长的贡献率为 70.4%。

全市规模以上服务业总体较快增长，营业收入比上年增长 9.9%。生产性服务业中，规模以上互联网和相关服务营业收入比上年增长 55.3%，商务服务业增长 21.4%，研究和试验发展服务业增长 14.2%，专业技术服务业增长 11.1%。生活性服务业中，规模以上房地产租赁经营营业收入比上年增长 19.6%，旅行社及相关服务增长 17.6%，职业技能培训增长 16.6%，文化艺术业增长 11.0%，居民服务业增长 14.6%，新闻和出版业增长 8.0%。2019 年全市现代服务业增加值 3697.4 亿元，增长 7.1%，占 GDP 比重为 31.5%。

全年港口吞吐量 5.77 亿吨，增长 6.6%；外贸吞吐量 4.20 亿吨，增长 7.5%；集装箱吞吐量 2101 万标准箱，增长 8.8%。年末，拥有国内航线 166 条，国际航线 34 条，港澳台地区航线 3 条，全年航空旅客吞吐量达到 2556 万人次，增长 4.2%；航空货邮吞吐量 26 万吨，增长 14.2%。年末，全市机动车保有量 306 万辆，增长 8.3%。其中，私人汽车 253 万辆，增长 9.2%。全年地铁开行列车 47 万列次，总运营里程 1516 万列公里，总客运量 18753 万人次。全年完成邮电业务总量 915.63 亿元，增长 40.7%。其中，邮政业务总量 103.55 亿元，增长 25%；电信业务总量 812.08 亿元，增长 43%。快递业务量 4.53 亿件，增长 18.3%。固定宽带互联网用户 440.4 万户，增长 10.6%。全市移动电话 1246 万户。其中，3G、4G 和 5G 用户 1084 万户，下降 3.9%。

表 6：2019 年主要运输方式完成的运输量及增速

运输方式	单位	运输量	增长（%）
客运周转量	亿人公里	196.73	7.8
铁路	亿人公里	121.36	15.2
公路	亿人公里	75.18	-2.3
水运	亿人公里	0.19	17.4
货运周转量	亿吨公里	1749.83	6.2
铁路	亿吨公里	185.91	-2.6
公路	亿吨公里	589.87	10.8
水运	亿吨公里	974.05	5.4

金融业健康发展。年末，金融机构本外币存款余额 17876.3 亿元，比年初增加 1752.0 亿元；人民币存款余额 17283.0 亿元，比年初增加 1747.8 亿元。其中，住户存款 6755.2 亿元，比年初增加 838.9 亿元。本外币贷款余额 18209.9 亿元，比年初增加 2071.1 亿元；人民币贷款余额 17331.8 亿元，比年初增加 2097.0 亿元，其中住户贷款 5691.5 亿元，比年初增加 859.7 亿元。保险业实现保费收入 486.9 亿元，增长 10.8%。其中，产险公司实现保费收入 132.8 亿元，同比下降 0.04%；寿险公司实现保费收入 354.1 亿元，增长 15.5%。青岛辖区全口径证券经营机构代理买卖证券交易额 69736.5 亿元，增长 41.2%。在中基协登记的私募基金管理人 271 家，管理基金规模 821.2 亿元，增长 28.2%。境内上市公司累计 39 家，比上年增加 9 家。

旅游业快速发展。初步统计，全年全市接待游客总人数 1.09 亿人次，增长 9%；实现旅游总收入 1955.9 亿元，增长 13%。年末，拥有 A 级旅游景区 110 处。其中，5A 级旅游景区 1 处，4A 级旅游景区 26 处，3A 级旅游景区 67 处。拥有星级酒店 98 个。其中，5 星级酒店 9 个，4 星级酒店 24 个，3 星级酒店 62 个。拥有旅行社 575 个。其中，经营出境旅游业务旅行社 60 个，经营入境和国内旅游业务旅行社 515 个。

六、固定资产投资

全市固定资产投资增长 21.6%。其中，第一产业投资增长 3.5%，第二产业投资增长 18.2%，第三产业投资增长 22.7%。亿元以上新开工项目（含房地产）1190 个，较 2018 年增加 702 个，完成投资增长 40.2%，占全市固定资产投资的比重为 38.2%。

以“双招双引”推动全市新旧动能转换。全市“十强”产业投资项目 3059 个，投资增长 28.3%；新动能投资拉动明显，装备制造业投资增长 16.8%；战略新兴产业投资增长 26.5%；高技术制造业投资增长 26.8%；工业技改投资增长 29.7%。全面发起“15 个攻势”，推动高质量发展。经略海洋攻势，“蓝色药库”等重大工程顺利实施，全市涉及海洋产业投资项目 128 个，海洋产业投资增长 56.5%。交通基础设施建设攻势，交通基础设施投资项目 271 个，投资增长 12.3%，胶东机场建设基本完成，济青高速改扩建、新机场高速公路建成通车。全市以军民融合示范区为主的军民融合发展投资表现优异，在建投资项目 90 个，投资增长 43.2%；乡村振兴投资项目 966 个，投资增长 25.5%；民营经济发展活力增强，民间投资在建项目 3504 个，完成投资增长 20.9%；科技引领城建设加快，科技领域相关投资项目 206 个，投资增长 133.5%。

全年房地产开发完成投资 1803.8 亿元，增长 21.5%。其中，住宅投资 1239.1 亿元，增长 19.7%。商品房销售面积 1651.8 万平方米，下降 8.6%。其中，住宅销售面积 1475.6 万平方米，下降 6.5%。

表 7：2019 年全市房地产开发投资、商品房销售面积及增速

分 类	房地产开发投资（亿元）	增长（%）	商品房销售面积（万平方米）	增长（%）
总计	1803.8	21.5	1651.8	-8.6
住宅	1239.1	19.7	1475.6	-6.5
办公楼	127.6	29.6	71.2	-7.2
商业营业用房	178.6	16.2	87.9	-26.7
其他	258.6	30.4	17.2	-48.0

全年保障性住房基本建成 3788 套。其中，公共租赁住房 1076 套，经济适用住房 953 套，限价商品住房 1759 套。截至年底，全市正在享受租赁补贴家庭共 9937 户，全年发放租赁补贴 5151.76 万元。

七、国内贸易

全年社会消费品零售总额比上年增长 8.1%。按经营地统计，城镇消费品零售额增长 7.6%；乡村消费品零售额增长 10.3%。按消费类型统计，商品零售额增长 7.1%；餐饮收入额增长 14.7%。

在限额以上单位商品零售额中，粮油、食品类零售额比上年增长 3.2%，饮料类增长 94.7%，烟酒类增长 15.8%，服装、鞋帽、针纺织品类增长 0.2%，化妆品类增长 1.3%，金银珠宝类下降 2.7%，日用品类下降 1.8%，家用电器和音像器材类增长 4.3%，中西药品类增长 1.8%，文化办公用品类增长 11.7%，电子出版物及音像制品类增长 35.9%，家具类增长 64.1%，通讯器材类增长 6.1%，智能手机类增长 27.2%，建筑及装潢材料类下降 4.0%，石油及制品类下降 2.3%，汽车类增长 1.8%。

八、对外经济

全市实现外贸货物进出口总额 5925.6 亿元，增长 11.2%。其中，出口额 3411.9 亿元，增长 7.4%；进口额 2513.7 亿元，增长 16.9%。对“一带一路”沿线国家市场进出口总额 1563.1 亿元，增长 30%。其中，出口 928.6 亿元，增长 32.9%；进口 634.5 亿元，增长 26.1%。对上合组织国家进出口 422.7 亿元，增长 17%；出口 254.5 亿元，增长 26.4%，进口 168.2 亿元，增长 5.2%。

按省商务厅统计口径，2019 年全市服务进出口 839.9 亿元，增长 8.4%。其中，出口 446.3 亿元，增长 13%；进口 393.5 亿元，增长 3.6%。全市承接服务外包合同 8941 份，增长 3.3%；合同额 71.5 亿美元，增长 26.1%；执行额 47.1 亿美元，增长 6.3%。其中，离岸服务外包合同 7617 份，增长 4.7%；合同额 61.5 亿美元，增长 34.3%；执行额 39.5 亿美元，增长 9.6%。

青岛口岸对外贸易进出口总额 12718.4 亿元，增长 4.0%。其中，出口额 6944.5 亿元，增长 2.6%；进口额 5773.9 亿元，增长 5.7%。

表 8：2019 年全市主要商品进出口情况

项目	进出口		出 口		进 口	
	金 额（亿元）	增 长（%）	金 额（亿元）	增 长（%）	金 额（亿元）	增 长（%）
纺织服装	502.2	−1.8	477.2	−1.0	25.0	−14.4
农产品	931.6	16.8	407.4	5.2	524.2	27.7
机电产品	1915.6	7.1	1444.9	6.7	470.7	8.3
高新技术产品	521.4	−0.7	279.1	−11.7	242.4	15.9

表 9：2019 年对主要国家和地区货物进出口额及增速

国别（地区）	出口额（亿美元）	增 长（%）	进口额（亿美元）	增 长（%）
亚洲	231.1	10.7	146.2	14.2
香港	14.6	−23.8	1.0	−10.8
台湾	4.9	18.5	11.5	−3.6
日本	58.0	2.9	18.5	−0.4
韩国	43.3	−2.6	35.3	3.0
东盟	62.4	34.2	44.6	17.6
南亚	18.8	16.5	6.8	75.0
中东	25.3	33.4	22.1	62.7
非洲	22.2	14.9	27.0	3.4
南非	4.5	0.2	1.9	−28.6
欧洲	105.2	3.2	60.4	19.1
欧盟	89.2	1.2	40.5	39.5
英国	14.5	3.0	7.3	20.6
德国	16.9	11.5	12.5	46.0
法国	8.9	4.3	3.5	−4.4
意大利	7.8	−8.4	2.4	15.4
独联体及东欧	13.6	13.1	16.1	−12.4
俄罗斯	9.9	9.6	14.9	−14.9
南美洲	32.7	3.1	70.6	32.7
巴西	6.3	14.6	52.4	39.8
北美洲	89.0	−15.0	26.6	−16.1
美国	78.9	−15.2	19.2	−24.9
加拿大	10.1	−8.2	6.7	25.6
大洋洲	13.8	1.9	33.2	−6.1
澳大利亚	11.3	−0.1	27.0	−9.5

注：本表非全口径。

2019年，全市新批外商投资项目954个，下降0.2%；合同外资133.6亿美元，增长36.3%。全市实际使用外资58.4亿美元，增长0.7%。

全市企业对“一带一路”沿线国家和地区投资项目53个，中方协议投资额14.5亿美元，增长642%；中方实际投资额2.4亿美元，下降65.5%。

全市对外承包工程业务新承揽项目86个，新签合同额33.6亿美元，下降31.9%；完成营业额41.8亿美元，下降3%。对外劳务合作业务派出各类劳务人员19181人。

九、社会事业

年末，全市共有各类大专院校(含民办高校)26所。其中，普通高校24所；全年研究生招生1.7万人，在学研究生5.0万人，毕业生1.1万人(不含驻青科研院所研究生)。普通本专科招生10.9万人，在校生36.6万人，毕业生9.3万人。中等职业教育招生3.7万人，在校生11.3万人，毕业生3.5万人。接受中等职业教育的学生占高中阶段在校生的47.2%。普通高中招生4.9万人，在校生12.7万人，毕业生4万人。初中招生9.6万人，在校生28.2万人，毕业生8.1万人。普通小学招生10.7万人，在校生58.4万人，毕业生9.5万人。特殊教育招生0.04万人，在校生0.2万人，毕业生0.02万人。幼儿园在园幼儿23.6万人。

全市共有影剧院90处，文化馆(站)148处，博物馆100处，公共图书馆12处，艺术表演团体9个，广播电台6座、374套节目，电视台6座、129套节目。全市共有档案馆12处。

年末，全市共有卫生机构(不含村卫生室)4152处。其中，医院、卫生院427处，疾病预防控制中心11处，妇幼保健机构12处，门诊部(所)、诊所、卫生所、医务室3315处。年末，各类卫生技术人员9.04万人。其中，医生3.78万人。全市拥有医疗床位6.05万张。其中，医院、卫生院床位5.85万张。

全市运动员在各项比赛中共获得金牌604.5枚、银牌436枚、铜牌467枚。重点体校1所，学员2236人；业余体校10所，学员1702人。

十、城市建设

年末，全市常住人口城镇化率达到74.12%，比上年提高0.45个百分点。

年末，市区常规公交8488辆，线路635条，年客运量108338万人次，日均客运量297万人次。市区巡游出租汽车10866辆，年客运量23686万人次，日均客运量65万人次。地铁运营线路4条，年客运量18753万人次，日均客运量51万人次。

十一、能源、环境和安全生产

全年全市规模以上工业综合能源消费量1412万吨标准煤，下降5.1%。其中，煤炭消费量1319万吨，下降3.2%；石油消费量1537万吨，下降18.7%；天然气消费量10.9亿立方米，增长9.5%。全社会用电量458亿千瓦时，增长6%。其中，工业用电量245亿千瓦时，增长2.9%；城乡居民生活用电量82亿千瓦时，增长5.9%。

全年全市能源生产量2422万吨标准煤，下降14.5%。其中，原油加工量1219万吨，下降20.9%；汽油生产量375

万吨，下降21%；柴油生产量305万吨，下降20.2%；发电量180.6亿千瓦时，下降6.5%。新能源发电量17亿千瓦时，增长2.6%。其中，风力发电量增长1.5%，垃圾焚烧发电量增长7.4%，太阳能发电量增长38.4%。新能源发电量占全市发电总量比重为9.3%，提高0.8个百分点。

全市年平均气温13.9℃，平均年降水量为431.9毫米。市区空气质量优良天数达287天，占全年的78.6%。近岸海域水质状况总体良好，98.8%的海域符合第一、二类海水水质标准，同比提升0.2个百分点。市区区域环境噪声平均值56.5分贝，市区交通干线噪声平均值68.3分贝。

全市七个行业（领域）发生各类生产安全事故87起，死亡63人，分别下降8.4%和6%。亿元GDP生产安全事故死亡率0.005，十万工矿商贸企业就业人员生产安全事故死亡率0.89，道路交通事故万车死亡1.03人。

十二、人民生活和社会保障

全年全市居民人均可支配收入45452元，增长8.2%。按常住地分，城镇居民人均可支配收入54484元，增长7.2%；农村居民人均可支配收入22573元，增长8.4%。全市居民人均消费支出29501元，增长8.0%，恩格尔系数为28.2%。按常住地分，城镇居民人均消费支出35266元，增长7.2%；农村居民人均消费支出14899元，增长7.3%。

表10：2019年城乡居民人均可支配收入构成情况

指标名称	全体居民		城镇居民		农村居民	
	绝对值（元）	增长（%）	绝对值（元）	增长（%）	绝对值（元）	增长（%）
可支配收入	45452	8.2	54484	7.2	22573	8.4
工资性收入	27164	7.4	32921	6.4	12580	7.7
经营净收入	8685	8.2	8455	7.9	9270	9.2
财产净收入	3850	10.8	5234	9.3	344	11.1
转移净收入	5753	10.3	7874	8.8	379	12.0

表 11：2019 年城乡居民人均消费支出情况

指标名称	全体居民		城镇居民		农村居民	
	绝对值（元）	增长（%）	绝对值（元）	增长（%）	绝对值（元）	增长（%）
消费支出	29501	8.0	35266	7.2	14899	7.3
食品烟酒	8325	6.9	9877	6.0	4393	7.2
衣着	2657	4.7	3276	3.4	1091	6.9
居住	6969	9.5	8449	9.0	3222	6.5
生活用品及服务	1957	6.5	2333	5.7	1004	6.3
交通和通信	4369	7.0	5062	6.3	2611	6.8
教育文化娱乐	2904	12.9	3503	12.2	1389	11.5
医疗保健	1600	8.1	1893	7.3	856	7.9
其他用品和服务	720	10.2	873	9.9	333	6.0

表 12：2019 年每百户居民家庭主要耐用消费品拥有量

指标名称	单位	数　量		
		全体居民	城镇居民	农村居民
家用汽车	辆	57	64	40
摩托车	辆	28	14	64
电冰箱（柜）	台	110	111	108
洗衣机	台	99	100	98
热水器	台	98	99	96
空调	台	118	126	98
彩色电视机	台	108	110	104
计算机	台	75	89	42
移动电话	部	231	233	227

据抽样调查，年末城镇居民人均现住房建筑面积 31.9 平方米，农村居民人均现住房建筑面积 37.0 平方米。

2019 年城镇新增就业 75.1 万人，增长 5.4%。其中，本市劳动者就业增长 6.4%，外来劳动者来青就业增长 4.3%。服务业吸纳就业 50.52 万人，增长 9.6%。民营经济吸纳就业 60.96 万人，增长 4.1%。

年末，全市城镇居民最低生活保障人数 19311 人，城镇居民最低生活保障资金 18546.1 万元；农村五保供养人数 6300 人，农村五保供养支出 8538.5 万元。

年末，全市城镇职工基本养老保险参保缴费人数为 291.44 万人，参加失业保险人数为 239.34 万人，全年累计领取失业保险金的人数为 7.54 万人。全市城镇登记失业率为 2.97%，上升 0.03 个百分点。

注：

1. 公报中统计数据均为初步统计数。

2. 全市生产总值（GDP）及各产业增加值绝对数按现价计算，增长速度按可比价计算。

3. 常住人口包括：①住本户、户口在本乡镇街道的人（含户口在本户，外出不满半年的人）；②住本户半年以上，户口在外乡镇街道的人；③住本户不满半年，户口在外乡镇街道，离开户口登记地半年以上的人；④住本户，户口待定的人。

4. PCT(Patent Cooperation Treaty）是《专利合作条约》的英文缩写。PCT 国际专利是指我国专利申请人根据 PCT 规定，可以向中国专利局或向世界知识产权组织提交国际专利申请，是反映地区外向型经济发展水平和地区国际技术竞争能力的重要指标。

5. 战略性新兴产业根据国家规划，现阶段主要包括节能环保、新一代信息技术、生物、高端装备制造、新能源、新材料、新能源汽车等七个产业领域。

6. 按照《高技术产业（制造业）分类（2017）》，包括：医药制造，航空、航天器及设备制造，电子及通信设备制造，计算机及办公设备制造，医疗仪器设备及仪器仪表制造，信息化学品制造等6大类。按照《高技术产业（服务业）分类（2018）》，包括信息服务、电子商务服务、检验检测服务、专业技术服务业的高技术服务、研发与设计服务、科技成果转化服务、知识产权及相关法律服务、环境监测及治理服务和其他高技术服务等 9 大类。

7. 规模以上工业企业为年主营业务收入 2000 万元及以上企业。限额以上贸易企业为批发业年主营业务收入在 2000 万元及以上、零售业 500 万元及以上、住宿和餐饮业 200 万元及以上的法人企业。固定资产投资项目统计的起点标准为计划总投资额 500 万元。规模以上服务业企业，一是指年营业收入 1000 万元及以上或年末从业人员 50 人及以上服务业法人单位。包括：交通运输、仓储和邮政业，信息传输、软件和信息技术服务业，租赁和商务服务业，科学研究和技术服务业，水利、环境和公共设施管理业，教育，卫生和社会工作；以及物业管理、房地产中介服务、自有房地产经营活动和其他房地产业等行业。二是指年营业收入 500 万元及以上或年末从业人员 50 人及以上服务业法人单位。包括：居民服务、修理和其他服务业，文化、体育和娱乐业。

8. 电子商务交易平台统计范围：辖区内规模以上工业、有资质的建筑业、限额以上批发和零售业、限额以上住宿和餐饮业、有开发经营活动的全部房地产开发经营业、规模以上服务业法人单位拥有的电子商务交易平台，以及年交易额 1000 万元及以上的其他电子商务交易平台。

9. 各类生产安全事故起数、死亡人数统计范围包括生产经营性道路交通、水上交通、铁路交通、民航飞行、农业机械、渔业船舶和工矿商贸七个行业（领域）发生的事故，不再包括森林火灾、火灾事故和非生产经营性道路交通。

10. 资料来源：本公报中财政数据来自市财政局；人才、登记失业率、社会保障数据来自市人力资源和社会保障局；银行数据来自人民银行青岛市中心支行；证券保险数据来自青岛证监局、青岛银保监局；水产品数据来自市海洋发展局；林业数据来自市园林和林业局；“三品一标”、农机等数据来自市农业农村局；灌溉面积数据来自市水务管理局；交通运输数据来自市交通运输局；邮政数据来自市邮政管理局；固定电话、宽带、移动电话等数据来自市通信管理局；进出口、外资、对外承包工程、对外劳务合作等数据来自市商务局；旅游数据来自市文化和旅游局；教育数据来自市教育局；科技数据来自市科技局；专利数据来自市场监管局；低保数据来自市民政局；体育数据来自市体育局；卫生数据来自市卫生健康委；环境数据来自市生态环境局；用电量数据来自青岛供电公司；气象数据来自市气象局；安全生产数据来自市应急局；扶贫数据来自市扶贫开发办；汽车保有量来自市公安局；居民收支、价格、城乡居民住房面积等数据来自国家统计局青岛调查队；其他数据来自市统计局。

STATISTICS COMMUNIQUE QINGDAO'S ECONOMIC AND SOCIAL DEVELOPMENT IN THE YEAR OF 2019

QINGDAO MUNICIPAL STATISTICS BUREAU

NBS SURVEY OFFICE IN QINGDAO

(March 27, 2020)

In 2019, the city takes Xi Jinping's new era of socialism with Chinese characteristics as the guide, in-depth implementation of General Secretary Xi Jinping's inspection of Shandong, inspection of Qingdao's important speech and important instructions, accelerate the implementation of major strategies such as the "China-Shanghai Cooperation Organization Local Economic and Trade Cooperation Demonstration Zone", "Military-Civilian Integration Innovation Demonstration Zone", "China(Shandong) Free Trade Zone Qingdao Area", etc., and under the strong leadership of the municipal government of the Communist Party of China, grasp the implementation and strengthen support, improve quality and increase efficiency, enhance vitality and strengthen motivation, pay close attention to coordination and promote integration, make up for the shortcomings and keep the bottom line, adhere to the general tone of working forward in a steady way, comprehensively deepen reform, implement an innovation-driven strategy, deepen the promotion of rural revitalization, strengthen the construction of the real economy, improve the development level of key areas, focus on safeguarding and improving people's livelihood, and promote the steady growth, promote reform, adjust the structure, benefit the people's livelihood, prevent risks, keep the steady, "Learn Shenzhen, catch Shenzhen", fifteen offensives were launched in an all-round way, and the city's economy showed steady development, new development, and stable quality improvement, laying a foundation for accelerating the construction of an open, modern and fashionable international metropolis.

Ⅰ. General

Shandong Statistics Bureau for the first time unified accounting and feedback results show, the city's GDP in 2019 is 1,174.131 billion yuan, calculated at comparable prices, with an increase of 6.5%. Therein, the 40.998 billion yuan of added value of the first industry increased by 1.6%. The value-added 418.276 billion yuan of the second industry increased by 4.7%. The value-added 714.857 billion yuan of the tertiary industry increased by 8.0%. The proportion of three industries is 3.5:35.6:60.9. GDP per capita reached 124,282 yuan.

At the end of the year, the total population of the city is 9.4998 million, increased by 1.12%. Therein, the urban resident population is 6.4520 million, increased by 1.57%.

Table 1: City resident population in 2019

Region	Resident Population(10 000 persons)
Total	949.98
Shinan District	58.88
Shibei District	111.1
Licang District	58.92
Laoshan District	45.59
West Coast New Area	160.82
Chengyang District	74.49
Jimo District	124.89
Jiaozhou	90.75
Pingdu	137.79
Laixi	76.24
Hongdao Economic Zone	10.51

The total annual financial income was 408.95 billion yuan, increased by 10.4%. The general public budget income 124.17 billion yuan, increased by 0.8%. Therein, the total price was 90.17 billion yuan, down by 0.5%. The VAT was 36.12 billion yuan, increased by 10.2%. The corporate income tax was 14.85 billion yuan, down by 2.6%. The personal income tax was 3.51 billion yuan, down by 28.1%. The urban maintenance and construction tax was 5.72 billion yuan, down by 0.9%.The general public budget expenditure was 157.66 billion yuan, increased by 1.1%. Therein, the general public service expenditure was 18.45 billion yuan, increased by 13.4%. The educational expenditure was 27.54 billion yuan, increased by 4.7%. The scientific and technological expenditure was 6.68 billion yuan, increased by 48%. The social security and employment expenditure was 19.45 billion yuan, increased by 24.6%. The urban and rural community affairs expenditure was 27.95 billion yuan, down by 15.8%. The tax system organized tax revenue (including customs collection) for the year was 244.12 billion yuan, increased by 1.3%. Among them, domestic tax revenue was 176.41 billion yuan, increased by 2.6%.

The annual consumer price index was 103.3, the industrial producer ex-factory price index was 100.0, and the industrial producer purchase price index was 98.4. The year-on-year price index for new commercial residential sales in December was 104.2, and the second-hand residential year-on-year price index was 94.6.

Table 2: Consumer Price Index of the City in 2019

Name	The whole year(the same period last year=100)
General Consumer Price Index	103.3
Non-Food Price Index	101.3
Service Price Index	101.7
Consumer Price Index	104.3
1. Food, Tobacco and Liquor	108.6
Food	111.6
#Grain	103.2
Vegetables	103.0
Pork	156.1
Egg	102.4
2. Clothing	100.6
3. Residence	100.5
4. Supplies and Services	100.5
5. Transportation and Communication	97.3
6. Education, Culture and Recreation	104.7
7. Medical Care	102.8
8. Others	105.3

Supply-side structural reforms continued to deepen. The cost per 100 yuan of operating income of industries above designated size in the city was 11.09 yuan, a decrease of 0.82 yuan from the previous year, the management and operation expenditures of service enterprises in the regulation industry have increased reasonably within a controllable range, both of which are lower than the growth rate of operating income. At the end of the year, the floor space of commercial housing for sale was 4.591 million square meters, which was close to the level at the beginning of 2014. Among them, 1.641 million square meters of residential properties were for sale. The construction of investment projects has achieved remarkable results. In 2019, the city has a total of 5,649 investment projects under construction, 1.5 times the total number of projects in 2018. The city plans to invest 1,622 large industrial projects with a total investment of over 100 million yuan, an increase of 453 from 2018.

The "three major battles" have steadily advanced. The non-performing loan ratio of the city's banks fell to 1.43%, a decrease of 0.44 percentage points from the beginning of the year. The municipal level allocated 240 million yuan in poverty alleviation funds, implemented a dynamic adjustment mechanism for the poor, and established a poverty-stricken population with 25,731 people at the end of the year through the "Poverty Free Enjoyment Policy". The annual average values of fine particulate matter (PM2.5), sulfur dioxide and nitrogen dioxide of main pollutants were 37, 8, and 32 $\mu g/m^3$ respectively. The blue sky defense war accelerated and the air pollution prevention work made positive progress.

Launched an efficient Qingdao construction offensive. Once again, the government affairs service process was deeply created. The start-up time of enterprises was reduced to 1 working day, and the approval of engineering construction projects was controlled within 85 working days. The "second approval" reform was first implemented in the province. After the applicant submitted the application, the system immediately issued the review result. 89 businesses including 12 areas such as provident fund withdrawal, social security payment, and proof of no criminal record can be handled through the "second approve" system.

Ⅱ. New Kinetic Energy and Innovation

"New industry" is developing steadily. In the whole year, the city's high-tech industry realized an increase of 11.7% in value added, accounting for 6.4% of GDP. Therein the added value of high-tech manufacturing increased by 1.7%, accounting for 2.1% of GDP. The added value of the high-tech service industry increased by 17.5%, accounting for 4.2% of GDP. The value added of strategic emerging industries increased by 5.2%, accounting for 8.8% of GDP. Therein, the added value of industrial strategic emerging industries increased by 4.6%, accounting for 5.8% of GDP, the added value of strategic emerging industries of service industries increased by 7.1%, accounting for 3.0% of GDP.

"New business" "new model" shows vitality. The city's e-commerce transaction platform achieved a transaction volume of 1.1 trillion yuan, an increase of 6.5%, and the retail sales of wholesale and retail units above designated size increased by 13.2%. The "new technology" has developed rapidly. The city's above-scale software and information technology service industry's operating income was 23.32 billion yuan, an increase of 28.8%, among the above-scale high-tech service industry, information service increased by 17.3%, inspection and testing service increased by 20.7%, and professional technical service industry increased by 11.3 %, intellectual property and related legal services increased by 15.2%. The output of "new products" increased rapidly. 1,770 urban rail vehicles, an increase of 15.8%, 14.419 million smart TVs, an increase of 25.5%.

According to preliminary statistics, the city has achieved 588 important scientific and technological achievements and 11 state-level scientific and technological awards. Among them, 3 technical invention awards and 8 scientific and technological progress awards. Received 100 provincial science and technology awards. Among them, there are 9 natural science awards, 9 technical invention awards, 80 scientific and technological progress awards, and 2 international cooperation awards. The transaction volume of technology contracts was 17.058 billion yuan, an increase of 9.5%. The turnover of sea-related technical contracts was 2.099 billion yuan, an increase of 15.5%. There were 31,929 effective invention patents throughout the year, an increase of 21.6%. There are 34.37 effective invention patents per 10,000 people and 1,381 PCT international patent applications. There are 12 national intellectual property demonstration enterprises, 108 national intellectual property advantage enterprises, and a total of 3,829 high-tech enterprises. R&D forces are accelerating, and there are currently 9 national key laboratories, 10 national engineering technology research centers, and 82 provincial engineering technology research centers.

Ⅲ. Agriculture

The annual agricultural added value was 43.62 billion yuan, an increase of 2.0%. Therein, the added value for the plating industry amounted to 21.26 billion yuan, an increase of 4.2%, the added value of animal husbandry was 270 million yuan, an increase of 18.5%, the added value of animal husbandry was 7.86 billion yuan, down by1.3%, the added value of fishery was 11.61 billion yuan, down by 0.1%. The added value of agriculture, forestry, animal husbandry and fishery and auxiliary activities was 2.62 billion yuan, an increase of 9.2%.

The grain sowing area stands at 475,000 hectares throughout the year, the vegetables sowing area stands at 108,000 hectares, the peanuts sowing area stands at 75,000 hectares. The total output of peanuts stands at 3,026,000 tons, declined by 2.4%. The total output of vegetables and edible fungi stands at 6,262,000 tons, declined by 2.8%. The total output of peanuts stands at 342,000 tons, declined by11%. The total output of fruit(including the fruits-purpose melons) stands at 1,186,000 tons, increased by 8.6%. The modern agricultural parks amount to 1,028 , added 135. Those certified with "three products and one mark" (pollution-free agricultural products, green food, organic agricultural products and agricultural products geographical indication) amounts to 1,042, including 52 national geographical mark protected products.

The area of afforestation (renewal) actually completed was 10,000 hectares throughout the year.

The total meat output was 528,000 tons in the whole year, increased by 1.1%. The output of poultry eggs weighs 200,000 tons, increased by 10.1%. The output of dairy stands at 289,000 tons, declined by 3.0%.

The annual output of aquatic products (excluding for ocean fishing) was 1.008 million tons, decreased by 2.6%. The ocean and fresh water cultivation area stands at 34,000 hectares, declined by 2.3%. The ocean fishing volume stands at 145,000 tons, which is basically the same.

The total power of agricultural machinery is 7.4 million kW, increasing by 80,000 kW. The mechanization level of crop production reached 88.5%. The effective irrigation area of farmland stands at 331,000 hectares. Among them, the water-saving irrigation area stands at 191,000 hectares.

Table 3 : Production and Growth of Major Plantation Products in 2019

Indicators	Unit	Yield	Growth(%)
Grain	10 000 tons	302.6	-2.4
Summer grain	10 000 tons	142.6	3.6
Autumn grain	10 000 tons	160.0	-7.2
Oilseed	10 000 tons	34.2	-11.0
Vegetable and edible fungi	10 000 tons	626.2	-2.8
Fruit	10 000 tons	118.6	8.6
Garden fruit	10 000 tons	74.5	4.6

Ⅳ. Industry and Construction

The added value of all industries in the city was 315.986 billion yuan, an increase of 2.8%. Among them, the value added of industries above designated size increased by 0.6%. In terms of economic types, state-owned holding companies realized a 1.8% increase in added value, collective enterprises realized a 10.6% decrease in value added, joint-stock enterprises realized a 1.4% increase in value added, and foreign and Hong Kong, Macao, and Taiwan-invested enterprises realized a 1.3% decrease in added value. In terms of categories, the value-added of the mining industry increased by 10.4%, the value-added of the manufacturing industry increased by 0.4%, and the value-added of the power, heat, gas and water production and supply industries increased by 5.9%. The annual sales rate of industrial enterprises above designated size reached 99.6%. The export delivery value of industrial enterprises above designated size increased by 5.4%, an increase of 2.6 percentage points over the previous year. Among the key industrial industries, the value added of electrical machinery and equipment manufacturing increased by 10.1%, the value added of railway, shipping, aerospace and other transportation equipment manufacturing increased by 18.1%, and the value added of petroleum processing, coking and nuclear fuel processing industries decreased by 17.6 %, the added value of the automobile manufacturing industry increased by 7.2%, and the added value of the computer, communications and other electronic equipment manufacturing industry decreased by 5.8%.

Table 4: The Output and Growth Rate of the Main Products of Industries above Designated Size in 2019

Description	Unit	Output	Growth(%)
Color TV sets	10 000 sets	1580.4	20.8
Of which: Smart TV	10 000 sets	1441.9	25.5
Household refrigerators	10 000 sets	731.8	0.6
Household washing machine	10 000 sets	513.7	–7.9
Room air conditioners	10 000 sets	874.4	–17.4
Smart phone	10 000 sets	667.2	–43.6
Beer	10 000 KL	172.7	7.6
Rubber tire casing	10 000 tires	4388.1	6.4
Plate glass	10 000 weight cases	393.6	–30.1
Crude steel	10 000 tons	319.3	3.1
Automobile	10 000 vehicle	3.0	–67.5
Motor train units	vehicle	1098.0	–10.7
Urban rail vehicle	vehicle	1770.0	15.8
Metal shipping containers	10 000 cu.m	1094.4	–21.0

The above–scale industrial profits fell by 0.6%. Therein, the state–owned holding enterprises fell by 5.4%, the collective enterprises fell by 4.9%, the shareholding enterprises fell by 1.6%, and foreign merchants and Hong Kong, Macao, and Taiwan merchants increased by 3.4%.

Table 5: Above–scale industrial profit growth in 2019

Indicators	Growth(%)
Industrial profits above the scale	–0.6
Of which: State–owned holding	–5.4
Collective businesses	–4.9
Shareholder businesses	–1.6
Businesses invested by foreigner or by compatriots from Hong Kong, Macao and Taiwan	3.4

There were 790 contracted construction enterprises in the general contracting industry, achieving an added value of 104.224 billion yuan, an increase of 13.7%. The total output value of the construction industry was 280.99 billion yuan, an increase of 21.7%. The contract value was 601.4 billion yuan, an increase of 25.9%. The total profit and tax was 11.57 billion yuan, an increase of 9.6%.

V. Service enterprises

The city's service industry realized an added value of 714.857 billion yuan, an increase of 8.0%, accounting for 60.9% of GDP, an increase of 1.3 percentage points from the previous year, and a contribution rate of 70.4% to economic growth.

The service enterprises above designated size in the city has grown rapidly, with operating income up 9.9% over the previous year. In the productive services industry, the operating income of Internet and related services above designated size increased by 55.3% over the previous year, business services increased by 21.4%, research and experimental development services increased by 14.2%, and professional technology services increased by 11.1%. In the life service industry, the operating income of the above-scale real estate leasing operations increased by 19.6% over the previous year, travel agencies and related services increased by 17.6%, vocational skills training increased by 16.6%, culture and art industry increased by 11.0%, and the residents service industry increased by 14.6%. News And the publishing industry grew by 8.0%. In 2019, the city's modern service industry added value of 369.74 billion yuan, an increase of 7.1%, accounting for 31.5% of GDP.

The port throughput for the year was 577 million tons, an increase of 6.6%. The foreign trade throughput was 420 million tons, an increase of 7.5%. The container throughput was 21.01 million TEUs, an increase of 8.8%. At the end of the year, it had 166 domestic routes, 34 international routes, and 3 routes in Hong Kong, Macao and Taiwan, the annual air passenger throughput reached 25.56 million, an increase of 4.2%. The throughput of air cargo and mail was 260,000 tons, an increase of 14.2%. At the end of the year, the city had 3.06 million motor vehicles, an increase of 8.3%. Among them, 2.53 million private cars, an increase of 9.2%. In the whole year, the number of subway trains was 470,000 with a total operating mileage of 15.16 million kilometers and a total passenger volume of 187.53 million. The total amount of postal and telecommunication services completed was 91.563 billion yuan, an increase of 40.7%. Among them, the total amount of postal services was 10.355 billion yuan, an increase of 25%, the total amount of telecommunications services was 81.208 billion yuan, an increase of 43%. The express delivery business volume was 453 million pieces, an increase of 18.3%. There were 4.404 million fixed broadband Internet users, an increase of 10.6%. There were 12.46 million mobile phones in the city. Among them, 10.84 million 3G, 4G and 5G subscribers, down by 3.9%.

Table 6: Volume and Growth Rate Completed by transportation in 2019

Transportation	Unit	Traffic volume	Growth(%)
Passenger volume	100 billion person-km	196.73	7.8
Railways	100 billion person-km	121.36	15.2
Highways	100 billion person-km	75.18	-2.3
Waterways	100 billion person-km	0.19	17.4
Cargo volumes	100 billion ton-km	1749.83	6.2
Railways	100 billion ton-km	185.91	-2.6
Highways	100 billion ton-km	589.87	10.8
Waterways	100 billion ton-km	974.05	5.4

The financial industry is development healthily. The foreign currency deposits balance of financial institutions at the end of the year stands at the 1787.63 billion yuan, increased by 175.20 billion yuan over the beginning of the year. The RMB deposits balance stands at 1728.30 billion yuan, increased by 174.78 billion yuan over the beginning of the year. Therein, the residents savings amounts to 675.52 billion yuan, increased by 83.89 billion yuan over the beginning of the year. The foreign currency loans balance stands at 1820.99 billion yuan, increased by 207.11 billion yuan from the beginning of the year. The RMB loans balance stands at 1733.18 billion yuan, increased by 209.70 billion yuan from the beginning of the year, of which household loans stands at 569.15 billion yuan, increased by 85.97 billion yuan from the beginning of the year. The insurance industry realized the 48.69 billion yuan of premium income, increased by 10.8%. Among them, the insurance company realized the 13.28 billion yuan of premium income, decreased by 0.04%. Life insurance company realized the 35.41 billion yuan of premium income, increased by 15.5%. The trading volume of securities trading agencies in Qingdao under the jurisdiction of the agency was 6973.65 billion yuan, increased by 41.2%. There was 271 private equity fund managers registered with the China Foundation Association, with a managed fund size of 82.12 billion yuan, increased by 28.2%. There are a total of 39 domestic listed companies, increased by 9 from the previous year.

The tourism industry is developing rapidly. According to preliminary statistics, the total tourism consumption stands at 109 million, increased by 9%. The total tourism revenue stands at 195.59 billion yuan, increased by 13%. At the end of the year, there were 110 A-level tourist tourist scenic spots, including 1 5A-level tourist scenic spots, 26 4A-level tourist tourist scenic spots, and 67 3A-level tourist tourist scenic spots. There are 98 star-rated hotels. Among them, there are 9 5-star hotels, 24 4-star hotels and 62 3-star hotels. It has 575 travel agencies. Among them, there are 60 outbound travel business travel agencies and 515 travel and domestic travel business travel agencies.

Ⅵ. Fixed Investment

The city's fixed asset investment increased by 21.6%. Among them, the investment in the primary industry increased by 3.5%, the investment in the secondary industry increased by 18.2%, and the investment in the tertiary industry increased by 22.7%. There were 1,190 new projects (including real estate) with a total investment of over 100 million yuan, an increase of 702 compared with 2018, and the completed investment increased by 40.2%, accounting for 38.2% of the city's fixed asset investment.

Promote the conversion of old and new kinetic energy in the city with "double strokes and double citations" The city's "Top Ten" industrial investment projects were 3,059, with an investment growth of 28.3%. New kinetic energy investment was significantly driven, and equipment manufacturing investment increased by 16.8%. Strategic emerging industry investment increased by 26.5%. High-tech manufacturing investment increased by 26.8%. Industrial technological transformation Investment increased by 29.7%. Fully launch "15 Offensives" to promote high-quality development. After a brief marine offensive, major projects such as the "Blue Medicine Depot" were successfully implemented. The city involved 128 marine industry investment projects, and marine industry investment increased by 56.5%. The construction of transportation infrastructure is offensive. There are 271 transportation infrastructure investment projects, with an investment growth of 12.3%. The construction of Jiaodong airport is basically completed. The reconstruction and expansion of Jinan to Qingdao expressway and the opening of the new airport expressway are completed. The city's military-civilian integration demonstration area, with a focus on military-civilian integration demonstration areas, has excellent performance, with 90 investment projects under construction, an increase of 43.2%. Rural revitalization investment projects with 966, an increase of 25.5%. The development of private economic development, with private investment under construction. There were 3,504 projects with a 20.9% increase in completed investment. The construction of a technology-led city accelerated, and 206 related investment projects in the field of science and technology, an increase of 133.5%.

An investment of 180.38 billion yuan has been accomplished for the real estate development, increased by 21.5%. Therein, the residential investment stands at 123.91 billion yuan, increased by 19.7%. The sales area of Commercial House was 16.518 million square meters, decreased by 8.6%. Therein, the residential sales area stands at 14.756 million square meters, decreased by 6.5%.

Table 7 : Real Estate Development Investment, Sales Area of Commodity House and Speed Increase in 2019

Category	Real Estate Development Investment (100 million yuan)	Growth (%)	Sales Area of Commodity House(10 000 m^2)	Growth (%)
Total	1803.8	21.5	1651.8	-8.6
Residential	1239.1	19.7	1475.6	-6.5
Office building	127.6	29.6	71.2	-7.2
Commercial operation house	178.6	16.2	87.9	-26.7
Other	258.6	30.4	17.2	-48.0

Throughout the year, the guaranteed housing basically established stands at 3,788 sets. Among them, there were 1,076 sets of public rental housing, 953 sets of affordable housing, and 1,759 sets of commodity housing. By the end of the year, a total of 9,937 households were enjoying rental subsidies throughout the city, and the rental subsidies 51.5176 million yuan was distributed throughout the year.

Ⅶ. Domestic Trade

The total retail sales of social consumer goods increased by 8.1% over the previous year. According to the statistics of the place of operation, the retail sales of urban consumer goods increased by 7.6%. The retail sales of rural consumer goods increased by 10.3%. According to consumption patterns, retail sales of goods increased by 7.1%. The catering revenue increased by 14.7%.

Among the retail sales of units above designated size, the retail sales of grains, oils and foods increased by 3.2% over the previous year, beverages increased by 94.7%, tobacco and alcohol increased by 15.8%, clothing, shoes, hats, needle textiles increased by 0.2%, and cosmetics increased 1.3%, gold and silver jewelry decreased by 2.7%, daily necessities decreased by 1.8%, household appliances and audio–visual equipment increased by 4.3%, Chinese and Western medicines increased by 1.8%, cultural and office supplies increased by 11.7%, electronic publications and audio–visual products increased 35.9%, furniture increased 64.1%, communications equipment increased 6.1%, smart phones increased 27.2%, construction and decoration materials decreased 4.0%, petroleum and products decreased 2.3%, and automotive increased 1.8%.

Ⅷ. Foreign Trade

The city's total import and export of foreign trade goods reached 592.56 billion yuan, an increase of 11.2%. Among them, the export value was 341.19 billion yuan, increased by 7.4%, the import value was 251.37 billion yuan, increased by 16.9%. The total value of imports and exports to countries along the "Belt and Road" was 156.31 billion yuan, increased by 30%. Among them, exports were 92.86 billion yuan, increased by 32.9%. Imports were 63.45 billion yuan, increased by 26.1%. Imports and exports to the SCO countries were 42.27 billion yuan, increased by 17%. The exports were 25.45 billion yuan, increased by 26.4%, and imports were 16.82 billion yuan, increased by 5.2%.

According to the statistics of the Provincial Department of Commerce, the city's service imports and exports stands at 83.99 billion yuan in 2019, increased by 8.4%. Among them, exports were 44.63 billion yuan, increased by 13%, imports were 39.35 billion yuan, increased by 3.6%. The city undertook 8,941 service outsourcing contracts, increased by 3.3%, the contract value was US$7.15 billion, increased by 26.1%, the execution value was US$4.71 billion, increased by 6.3%. Among them, 7,617 offshore service outsourcing contracts, increased by 4.7%, the contract value was US$ 6.15 billion, increased by 34.3%, the execution value was US$ 3.95 billion. increased by 9.6%.

Qingdao Port's total foreign trade imports and exports totaled 1271.84 billion yuan, increased by 4.0%. Among them, the export value was 694.45 billion yuan, increased by 2.6%, the import value was 577.39 billion yuan, increased by 5.7%.

Table8 : Import & Export of Main Commodities in Qingdao in 2019

Project	Import & Export		Export		Import	
	Amount (100 million yuan)	Growth (%)	Amount (100 million yuan)	Growth (%)	Amount (100 million yuan)	Growth (%)
Textiles and garments	502.2	−1.8	477.2	−1.0	25.0	−14.4
Agricultural products	931.6	16.8	407.4	5.2	524.2	27.7
Elextrical and mechanical	1915.6	7.1	1444.9	6.7	470.7	8.3
High–tech products	521.4	−0.7	279.1	−11.7	242.4	15.9

Table 9: Import and Export Volume and Growth Rate of Goods to Major Countries and Regions in 2019

Country (Region)	Export Amount (100 million USD)	Growth (%)	Import Amount (100 million USD)	Growth (%)
Asia	231.1	10.7	146.2	14.2
Hong Kong	14.6	–23.8	1.0	–10.8
Taiwan	4.9	18.5	11.5	–3.6
Japan	58.0	2.9	18.5	–0.4
Korea	43.3	–2.6	35.3	3.0
ASEAN	62.4	34.2	44.6	17.6
South Asia	18.8	16.5	6.8	75.0
Middle East	25.3	33.4	22.1	62.7
Africa	22.2	14.9	27.0	3.4
South Africa	4.5	0.2	1.9	–28.6
Europe	105.2	3.2	60.4	19.1
EU	89.2	1.2	40.5	39.5
UK	14.5	3.0	7.3	20.6
Germany	16.9	11.5	12.5	46.0
France	8.9	4.3	3.5	–4.4
Italy	7.8	–8.4	2.4	15.4
CIS and Eastern Europe	13.6	13.1	16.1	–12.4
Russia	9.9	9.6	14.9	–14.9
South America	32.7	3.1	70.6	32.7
Brazil	6.3	14.6	52.4	39.8
North America	89.0	–15.0	26.6	–16.1
USA	78.9	–15.2	19.2	–24.9
Canada	10.1	–8.2	6.7	25.6
Oceania	13.8	1.9	33.2	–6.1
Australia	11.3	–0.1	27.0	–9.5

Note: This table is not full caliber.

In 2019, the city approved 954 newly foreign investment projects, a decrease of 0.2%. The contractual foreign investment was US$ 13.36 billion, an increase of 36.3%. The actual use of foreign capital in the city was US$ 5.84 billion, an increase of 0.7%.

The city's enterprises have invested in 53 projects in countries and regions along the "Belt and Road" . The agreed investment by China was US$1.45 billion, an increase of 642%. The actual investment by China was US$240 million, a decrease of 65.5%.

The city's foreign contracted engineering business newly contracted 86 projects, with a newly signed contract value of US$3.36 billion, a decrease of 31.9%. And a completed turnover of US$4.18 billion, a decrease of 3%. 19,181 laborers of various types were dispatched for foreign labor cooperation business.

Ⅸ. Society enterprise

At the end of the year, there were 26 colleges and universities of various types (including private colleges and universities) in the city. Among them, 24 colleges and universities, 17,000 graduate students enrolled in the whole year, 50,000 graduate students, and 11,000 graduates (excluding the postgraduates stationed Qingdao research institutes). The general undergraduate and junior college enrolled 109,000 students, 366,000 students and 93,000 graduates. Secondary vocational education enrolled 37,000 students, 113,000 students and 35,000 graduates. Students receiving secondary vocational education accounted for 47.2% of the high school students. Regular high schools enroll 49,000 students, with 127,000 students and 40,000 graduates. The junior high school enrolled 96,000 students, 282,000 students and 81,000 graduates. Regular primary schools enrolled 107,000 students, with 584,000 students and 95,000 graduates. Special education enrolled 400 students, 2,000 students, and 200 graduates. There are 236,000 children in kindergartens.

The city has 90 theaters, 148 cultural centers (stations), 100 museums, 12 public libraries, 9 art performance groups, 6 radio stations and 374 programs, and 6 television stations and 129 programs. There are 12 archives in the city.

At the end of the year, there were 4,152 health institutions (excluding the clinics in village) in the city. Among them, there are 427 hospitals and health centers, 11 disease prevention and control centers, 12 maternal and child health care institutions, and 3,315 outpatient departments (offices), clinics, health centers, and medical offices. At the end of the year, there were 90,400 various types of health technicians. Among them, 37,800 doctors. The city has 60,500 medical beds. Among them, there are 58,500 beds in hospitals and health centers.

The city's athletes won 604.5 gold medals, 436 silver medals, and 467 bronze medals in various competitions. There is 1 key sports universities with 2,236 students. The amateur sports schools amounted to 10, with 1,702 students.

Ⅹ. Urban construction

At the end of the year, the urbanization rate of the city's permanent population reached 74.12%, an increase of 0.45 percentage points over the previous year.

At the end of the year, there were 8,488 conventional buses and 635 lines in the urban area, with an annual passenger volume of 1083.38 million passengers and an average daily passenger volume of 2.97 million passengers. There are 10,866 urban cruise taxis, with an annual passenger volume of 236.86 million passengers and an average daily passenger volume of 650,000. There are 4 subway operating lines, with an annual passenger volume of 187.53 million passengers and an average daily passenger volume of 510,000.

XI. Energy, Environment and Work Safety

In the whole year, the city's industrial comprehensive energy consumption above designated size was 14.12 million tons of standard coal, down by 5.1%. Among them, coal consumption was 13.19 million tons, down by 3.2%. The oil consumption was 15.37 million tons, down by 18.7%. The natural gas consumption was 1.09 billion cubic meters, increased by 9.5%. The electricity consumption of the whole society was 45.8 billion kWh, increased by 6%. Among them, industrial electricity consumption was 24.5 billion kWh, increased by 2.9%. The urban and rural residents' daily consumption of 8.2 billion kWh, increased by 5.9%.

The city's energy production output was 24.22 million tons of standard coal, down by 14.5%. Among them, crude oil processing volume was 12.19 million tons, down by 20.9%. The gasoline production volume was 3.75 million tons, down by 21%. The diesel production volume was 3.05 million tons, down by 20.2%. The power generation volume was 18.06 billion kWh, down by 6.5%. New energy power generation was 1.7 billion kWh, increased by 2.6%. Among them, wind power generation increased by 1.5%, waste incineration power generation increased by 7.4%, and solar power generation increased by 38.4%. New energy power generation accounted for 9.3% of the city's total power generation, increased by 0.8%.

The city's annual average temperature was 13.9℃, and the average annual precipitation was 431.9 mm. The number of days with good air quality in the urban area reached 287 days, accounting for 78.6% of the total. The water quality of the coastal waters was generally good. 98.8% of the waters meet the first and second categories of sea water quality standards, an increase of 0.2% year–on–year. The average value of environmental noise in the urban area was 56.5 decibels, and the average value of noise in urban arterial traffic was 68.3 decibels.

There were 87 production safety accidents of various types in seven industries (fields) of the city, with 63 deaths, a decrease of 8.4% and 6% respectively. The death rate of production safety accidents per 100 million yuan of GDP was 0.005, the death rate of production safety accidents of 100,000 employees in industrial, mining and commercial enterprises was 0.89, and the death rate of road traffic accidents was 1.03 for 10,000 vehicles.

XII. Living Conditions and Social Security

The annual per capita disposable income of residents in the city was 45,452 yuan, an increase of 8.2%. In terms of permanent residence, the per capita disposable income of urban residents was 54484 yuan, an increase of 7.2%. The per capita disposable income of rural residents was 22573 yuan, an increase of 8.4%. The per capita consumption expenditure of residents in the city was 29,501 yuan, an increase of 8.0%, and the Engel coefficient was 28.2%. In terms of permanent residence, the per capita consumption expenditure of urban residents was 35,266 yuan, an increase of 7.2%. The per capita consumption expenditure of rural residents was 14,899 yuan, an increase of 7.3%.

Table 10 : Per Capita Disposable Income of Urban and Rural Residents in 2019

Description of indicators	Residents		Urban Residents		Rural Residents	
	Absolute Value (yuan)	Growth (%)	Absolute Value (yuan)	Growth (%)	Absolute Value (yuan)	Growth (%)
Disposable income	45452	8.2	54484	7.2	22573	8.4
Salary income	27164	7.4	32921	6.4	12580	7.7
Operating net income	8685	8.2	8455	7.9	9270	9.2
Property net income	3850	10.8	5234	9.3	344	11.1
Transfer net income	5753	10.3	7874	8.8	379	12.0

Table 11: Per Capita Disposable Expense of Urban and Rural Residents in 2019

Description of indicators	Residents		Urban Residents		Rural Residents	
	Absolute Value (yuan)	Growth (%)	Absolute Value (yuan)	Growth (%)	Absolute Value (yuan)	Growth (%)
Consumption expense	29501	8.0	35266	7.2	14899	7.3
Tobacco and liquor	8325	6.9	9877	6.0	4393	7.2
Clothing	2657	4.7	3276	3.4	1091	6.9
Housing Living	6969	9.5	8449	9.0	3222	6.5
Product and services	1957	6.5	2333	5.7	1004	6.3
Transportation and communication	4369	7.0	5062	6.3	2611	6.8
Education, culture and entertainment	2904	12.9	3503	12.2	1389	11.5
Medical and health care	1600	8.1	1893	7.3	856	7.9
Other product and services	720	10.2	873	9.9	333	6.0

Table 12: Amount of Major Consumer Durable Owned by every 100 Households in 2019

Description of indicators	Unit	Quantity		
		Residents	Urban Residents	Rural Residents
Household automobiles	vehicle	57	64	40
Motorcycles	vehicle	28	14	64
Refrigerators	set	110	111	108
Washing machines	set	99	100	98
Water heaters	set	98	99	96
Air-conditioners	set	118	126	98
Color TV	set	108	110	104
Computers	set	75	89	42
Mobile telephones	set	231	233	227

According to a sample survey, at the end of the year, the current housing area per capita of urban residents was 31.9 square meters, and that of rural residents was 37.0 square meters.

In 2019, there were 751,000 new jobs in urban areas, increased by 5.4%. Among them, the employment of laborers in this city increased by 6.4%, and the employment of foreign laborers in youth increased by 4.3%. The service industry absorbed 505,200 jobs, increased by 9.6%. The private economy absorbed 609,600 jobs, increased by 4.1%.

At the end of the year, the city's urban residents had a minimum living guarantee of 19,311, and urban residents had a minimum living guarantee of 185.461 million yuan. The number of rural residents was 6,300, and the rural five–guarantee expenditure was 85.385 million yuan.

At the end of the year, the number of people participating in the basic pension insurance for urban employees in the city was 2,914,400, and the number of people participating in unemployment insurance was 2,393,400. The cumulative number of people receiving unemployment insurance benefits throughout the year was 75,400. The registered unemployment rate in cities and towns in the city was 2.97%, an increase of 0.03 percentage points.

Note：

1. Figures reported herein are preliminary statistics.

2. The absolute figures of gross domestic product (GDP) and added value of each industry are calculated according to the current price, and the growth rate is calculated according to the current price.

3. The resident population includes: ① the people who lives in the household and the household registration in the township of this town (including the people whose household registration is in the household and who has been out for less than half a year). ② the people who has lived in the household for more than half a year, the household registration is in the street outside the township. ③ The household registration is in the street of the foreign township, and the person who has left the household registration for more than half a year. ④ who lives in the household and whose household registration is pending.

4. PCT is an English abbreviation for "Patent Cooperation Treaty". The PCT international patent refers to Chinese patent application people can submit international patent application to the China Patent Office or to the World Intellectual Property Organization according to the PCT regulations, and is an important index to reflect the development level of export–oriented economic development in the region and the competitiveness of international technology in the region.

5. The strategic emerging industry, according to the national planning, mainly includes seven industrial fields such as energy conservation, environmental protection, new generation of information technology, biology, high–end equipment manufacturing, new energy, new materials and new energy automobile.

6. According to the "High–tech Industry (Manufacturing) Classification (2017)", including: pharmaceutical manufacturing, aviation, spacecraft and equipment manufacturing, electronic and communication equipment manufacturing, computer and office equipment manufacturing, medical equipment and instrumentation manufacturing, 6 categories including information chemical manufacturing. According to the "High–tech Industry (Service Industry) Classification (2018)", including information services, e–commerce services, inspection and testing services, high–tech services for professional technical services, R&D and design services, scientific and technological achievements transformation services, intellectual property rights and related 9 categories including legal services, environmental monitoring and governance services, and other high–tech services.

7. The industrial enterprises above the scale are the annual main business income 20 million yuan and the above enterprises. Trade enterprises above designated size are units with a main business income of 20 million yuan or more in the wholesale industry, 5 million yuan or more in the retail industry, and 2 million yuan and above in the accommodation and catering industry. The starting point standard of the fixed asset investment project statistics is the planned total investment 5 million yuan. For service enterprises above designated size, the first refers to service companies with an annual business income of 10 million yuan or more or 50 or more employees at the end of the year. Including transport, storage and postal services, information transmission, software and information technology services, rental and business services, scientific research and technology services, water resources, environmental and public facilities management, education, health and social work. As well as property management, real estate brokerage services, self–owned real estate business activities and other real estate industry. Second, it refers to a service legal entity with an annual operating income of 5 million yuan or more or 50 or more employees at the end of the year. Including: resident services, repairs and other services, cultures, sports and recreation.

8. E–commerce trading platform statistics scope: industries above designated size, qualified construction industry, wholesale and retail businesses above designated size, accommodation and catering industry above designated size, all real estate development and operation industries with development and operation activities, and service industries above designated size within the jurisdiction E–commerce trading platforms owned by legal entities and other e–commerce trading platforms with an annual transaction volume of 10 million yuan and above.

9. The statistics range of the number of production safety accidents and the number of deaths include the accidents that occur in the seven industries (areas) of production and business road traffic, water transportation, railway transportation, civil aviation flight, agricultural machinery, fishery ship and maritime trade and commerce, and no longer includes forest fire, Real–time and non–production operational road traffic.

10. Data source: The fiscal data in this bulletin comes from the Municipal Finance Bureau. The talent, registered unemployment rate, and social security data comes from the Municipal Human Resources and Social Security Bureau. The bank data comes from the Qingdao City Center Branch of the People's Bank of China. The securities insurance data comes from the Qingdao Securities Regulatory Bureau , Qingdao Banking and Insurance Regulatory Bureau. The aquatic product data from the Municipal Ocean Development Bureau. The forestry data from the Municipal Gardens and Forestry Bureau. "Three products and one standard", agricultural machinery and other data from the Municipal Agriculture and Rural Bureau. The irrigation area data from the Municipal Water Affairs Administration. The transportation data comes from the Municipal Transportation Bureau; postal data comes from the Municipal Postal Administration. The fixed telephone, broadband, mobile phone and other data come from the Municipal Communications Administration. The import and export, foreign investment, foreign contracted projects, foreign labor cooperation and other data come from the Municipal Bureau of Commerce. The tourism data comes from the Municipal Bureau of Culture and Tourism. The education data comes from the Municipal Education Bureau. The scientific and technological data comes from the Municipal Science and Technology Bureau; patent data comes from the Market Supervision Bureau. The subsistence allowance data comes from the Civil Affairs Bureau. The sports data comes from the Municipal Sports Bureau. The health data comes from the Municipal Health Commission. The environmental data from the Municipal Ecological Environment Bureau. The electricity consumption data from Qingdao Power Supply Company. The meteorological data from the Municipal Meteorological Bureau. The safety production data from the Municipal Emergency Bureau. The poverty alleviation data from the Municipal Poverty Alleviation Development Office. The car ownership from the Municipal Public Security Bureau. The Resident income and expenditure, prices, and housing area of urban and rural residents are from the Qingdao Survey Office of the National Bureau of Statistics. The other data comes from the Municipal Bureau of Statistics.

综合 1

GENERAL SURVEY

简要说明

一、本篇资料的主要内容

本篇资料是对我市行政区划、气象情况、分行业法人单位数、各部门机构数和国民经济、社会发展的综合反映，主要包括行政区划、气象情况、分行业法人单位数、各部门机构数、国民经济主要比例关系、国民经济和社会发展主要指标占全国全省比重、国民经济和社会发展主要指标及其增长速度等资料。

二、本篇资料的来源

1.“行政区划”主要包括2019年底各区（市）街道办事处（乡镇）、社区居委会（村民委员会）区划资料，数据来源于市民政局。

2.“气象情况”包括分区市、市区分月气象资料，数据来源于市气象局。

3.“全市生产总值”来源于国民经济核算统计报表，由市统计局国民经济核算处整理提供。

4. 国民经济和社会发展综合部分来源于本年鉴各篇章中的资料，由市统计局国民经济综合统计处加工整理。

Brief Introduction

I. Main Content

The information in this article is a comprehensive reflection of Qingdao′s administrative divisions, meteorological conditions, the number of legal entities by industry, the number of various departments and institutions, and the national economic and social development, including administrative divisions, meteorological conditions, the number of legal entities by industry, the number of agencies, the main proportions of the national economy, the proportion of the main indicators of national economic and social development in the province, the main indicators of national economic and social development and their increase speed and other information.

II. Source of Data

1. "Administrative divisions" mainly include the division data of district (city) sub-district offices (townships) and community neighborhood committees (village committees) at the end of 2019. The data comes from Qingdao Civil Affairs Bureau.

2. "Meteorological conditions" includes monthly meteorological data of district cities and cities, and the data comes from Qingdao Meteorological Bureau.

3. The "Gross Product of the City" comes from the national economic accounting statistical report, which is compiled and provided by the National Economic Accounting Office of Qingdao Statistics Bureau.

4. The comprehensive part of the national economy and social development is derived from the data in each chapter of this yearbook, processed and compiled by the National Economic Comprehensive Statistics Division of Qingdao Bureau of Statistics.

1-1　行政区划（2019 年底）
ADMINISTRATIVE DIVISION (END OF 2019)

单位：个 (unit)

市区名称	Region	街道办事处 Street Offices	社区居委会 Community Residents' Committees	镇 Town	村民委员会 Villagers' Committees
全　市	**Whole Municipality**	**104**	**1207**	**41**	**5419**
市南区	Shinan District	14	50		
市北区	Shibei District	30	137		
李沧区	Licang District	11	118		
崂山区	Laoshan District	5	162		
黄岛区	Huangdao District	12	267	10	961
城阳区	Chengyang District	8	248		
即墨区	Jimo District	8	65	7	1028
胶州市	Jiaozhou	8	79	4	786
平度市	Pingdu	5	48	12	1783
莱西市	Laixi	3	33	8	861

1-2　气象情况(2019年)
METEOROLOGY (2019)

市区名称	Region	平均气温(摄氏度) Average Temperature (℃)	极端气温 Extreme Temperature (centigrade)		降水量(毫米/年) Precipitation (millimeter/year)	日照时数(小时/年) Sunshine Hours (hour/year)	平均气压(百帕) Average Atmospheric Pressure(100 pa)
			最高(摄氏度) Maximum(℃)	最低(摄氏度) Minimum(℃)			
市　区	Urban Area	14.1	33.6	-7	479.5	2234.7	1008.1
崂山区	Laoshan District	13.9	33.7	-7.3	408.4	2237.7	1010.8
黄岛区	Huangdao District	14.2	37.8	-8.1	504.3	2248.6	1016.1
即墨区	Jimo District	14.1	36.6	-10.2	396.8	2376.4	1011.6
胶州市	Jiaozhou	14.1	39	-8.8	272.9	2240.4	1007.2
平度市	Pingdu	13.7	37.7	-9.9	485.2	2433.2	1009.9
莱西市	Laixi	13	37.5	-11.2	476.3	2369.8	1008.1

注：以上为7个国家基准站或基本站。
Note：These are 7 national reference or base stations.

1-3　市区分月气象情况(2019年)
MONTHLY METEOROLOGY OF URBAN AREA (2019)

月　份	Month	平均气温(摄氏度) Average Temperature (℃)	降水量(毫米) Precipitation (millimeter)	日照时数(小时) Sunshine Hours (hour)
一月	Jan.	1.2	5.4	155.8
二月	Feb.	1.9	9.6	104
三月	Mar.	8.4	25.4	215
四月	Apr.	11.7	42.1	167.2
五月	May	18.6	46.6	272.7
六月	June	20.8	44.7	204.6
七月	July	25.5	123.4	204
八月	Aug.	26	120.7	196.7
九月	Sep.	23.5	8.3	224.2
十月	Oct.	17	19.1	184.6
十一月	Nov.	10.9	15.1	159.4
十二月	Dec.	4.2	19.1	146.5
全　年	Annual Total	14.1	479.5	2234.7

1-4 各部门机构数（2019 年底）

GRASS-ROOTS UNITS IN VARIOUS SECTORS (END OF 2019)

项目	Item	单位	Unit	机构数 Grass-roots Units
农村基层单位	**Rural Grass-roots Units**			
镇政府	Town Governments	个	unit	41
乡村户数	Number of Rural Households	万户	10 000 households	127.4
规模以上工业企业单位	**Industrial enterprises above designated size**	个	**unit**	3536
# 国有企业	State-owned Enterprises	个	unit	175
集体企业	Collective-owned Enterprises	个	unit	5
外商及港澳台商投资企业	Enterprises with Funds from Hong Kong, Macao, Taiwan and Foreign Countries	个	unit	868
交通运输业	**Transportation**			
铁路	Railway	个	unit	1
公路	Highway	个	unit	286
水运	Waterway	个	unit	20
邮电业	**Post and Telecommunication Services**			
邮政局（所）	Post Offices	处	unit	265
电信营业网点（自有）	Telecom business outlets	个	unit	438
建筑业企业	**Construction Enterprises**	个		760
国有企业	State-owned Enterprises	个	unit	18
集体企业	Collective-owned Enterprises	个	unit	7
其他	Others	个	unit	735
批发和零售业、住宿和餐饮业	Wholesale & Retail Trades, Hotels and Catering Services			
限额以上批发业	Wholesale Trade above Designated Size	个	unit	1752
限额以上零售业	Retail Trade above Designated Size	个	unit	706
限额以上住宿业	Hotel above Designated Size	个	unit	232
限额以上餐饮业	Catering Service above Designated Size	个	unit	219

1-4 续表
Continued

项目	Item	单位	Unit	机构数 Grass-roots Units
教育事业	Education			
普通高等学校	Regular Institutions of Higher Education	所	unit	24
中等专业学校	Specialized Secondary Schools	所	unit	6
普通中学	Regular Secondary Schools	所	unit	327
普通小学	Regular Primary Schools	所	unit	720
幼儿园	Kindergartens	所	unit	2352
科研机构	Science and Technology Institutions			
中央属	Central Level	个	unit	22
地方属	Local	个	unit	36
文化及相关产业	Culture and Related Industry			
公共图书馆	Public Libraries	个	unit	12
影剧院	Theater	个	unit	
卫生事业	Public Health			
# 医院	Hospitals	个	unit	427
民政行政单位	Civil Affairs Departments			
# 提供住宿的社会服务机构	Social service agencies that provide accommodation	个	unit	245

1-5 按行业分法人单位数
NUMBER OF CORPORATE UNITS BY SECTOR

单位：个 (unit)

行　业	Sector	2019 年
总　计	Total	433193
农、林、牧、渔业	Agriculture, Forestry, Animal Husbandry and Fishery	6941
采矿业	Mining	180
制造业	Manufacturing	66385
电力、热力、燃气及水生产和供应业	Electricity, heat, gas, water production and supply industry	606
建筑业	Construction	33716
批发和零售业	Wholesale and Retail Trades	145298
交通运输、仓储和邮政业	Transport, Storage and Post	17752
住宿和餐饮业	Hotels and Catering Services	6737
信息传输、软件和信息技术服务业	Information Transmission, Computer Services and Software	19439
金融业	Financial Industry	2603
房地产业	Real Estate	11723
租赁和商务服务业	Leasing and Business Services	56902
科学研究和技术服务业	Scientific Research and Technical Services	25073
水利、环境和公共设施管理业	Management of Water, Conservancy Environment and Public Facilities	2709
居民服务、修理和其他服务业	Resident Services, Repairs and Other Services	7905
教育	Education	7359
卫生和社会工作	Health Social Security and Social Welfare	3201
文化、体育和娱乐业	Culture, Sports and Entertainment Industry	7942
公共管理、社会保障和社会组织	Public Administration, Social Security and Social Organization	10722

1-6 国民经济主要平均指标
AVERAGE INDICATORS ON NATIONAL ECONOMY

指 标	Indicator	单位	Unit	2000年	2005年
人口密度	Density of Population	人/平方公里	person/sq.km	664	695
每户年平均人口	Average Household Size	人	person	3.14	3.12
城镇非私营单位在岗职工年平均工资	The Average Annual Wage of Staff and Workers in the Post in Non-Private Units in Towns and Cities	元	yuan	10 072	19086
城市居民人均年可支配收入	Annual Per Capita Net Income of urban Households	元	yuan	8 016	12920
农民人均年纯收入	Annual Per Capita Net Income of Rural Households	元	yuan	3 637	5806
每一播亩平均粮食产量	Output of Grain Per Mu of Sowing Area	千克	kg	411	421
每亩蔬菜平均产量	Average Output of Vegetables Per Mu	千克	kg	2 735	2985
每亩茶叶平均产量	Average Output of tea Per Mu	千克	kg	8.1	16.5
每亩花生平均产量	Average Output of Peanut Per Mu	千克	kg	298	327
每亩棉花平均产量	Average Output of Cotton Per Mu	千克	kg	83	74
每台拖拉机负担耕地面积	Cultivated Area Ploughed by Per Tractor	亩/台	mu/unit	56	39
每亩耕地施用化肥量（折纯）	Chemical Fertilizer Consumption Per Mu (convert to pure amount)	千克	kg	45	52
每人平均消费品零售额	Per Capita Retail Sales of Consumer Goods	元	yuan	5965	11445
城市每天平均生活用水量	Daily Residential Consumption of Water	万吨	10 000 tons	33.33	34.35
城市每人平均公园绿地面积	Per Capita Public Green Areas	平方米	sq.m	8.50	11.82
每万人拥有医疗床位	Number of Hospital Beds Per 10000 Population	张	bed	34.5	41.3
每万人拥有医生数	Number of Doctors per 10000 Population	人	person	21.0	20.3
每万人中高等学校学生数	Students Enrollment of Institutions of Higher Education per 10000 Population	人	person	65	324
每万人中中等学校学生数	Students Enrollment of Secondary Schools per 10000 Population	人	person	704	768
每万人中小学学生数	Students Enrollment of primary Schools per 10000 Population	人	person	757	648

注：1. 自2015年开始，全市城乡住户调查统一使用一体化改革后的数据，与原数据相比，城乡居民收支指标的调查范围和口径均存较大变化。原“城市居民人均可支配收入”调整为“城镇居民人均可支配收入”；原“农民人均纯收入”调整为“农村居民人均可支配收入”。
2.2008年–2017年农作物数据为根据第三次农业普查结果核定修正后数据。

Note: 1. Since 2015, the urban and rural households investigation unified the data after the integrated reform, compared with the original data, the investigation scope and the caliber of urban and rural residents' income and expenditure indicators have changed greatly.
The original “ per capita disposable income of urban residents” is adjusted to be a “ per capita disposable income of urban residents”. The original “ per capita net income of farmers” is adjusted to “ per capita disposable income of rural residents”.
2. Crop data from 2008 to 2017 are revised based on the results of the third agricultural census.

2008 年	2009 年	2010 年	2011 年	2012 年	2013 年	2014 年	2015 年	2016 年	2017 年	2018 年	2019 年
715	676	677	679	682							
3.13	3.12	3.10	3.09	3.09							
29404	32507	37501	43077	49052	55363	62104	69465	76616	83539	90840	103108
20464	22368	24998	28567	32145	35227	38294	40370	43598	47176	50817	54484
8509	9249	10550	12370	13990	15731	17461	16730	17969	19364	20820	22573
408	411	399	407	411	407	396	400	404	414	430	430
3551	3624	3689	3867	3887	3957	3963	3889	3760	3931	3796	3883
39	38	44	47	51	49	52	57	74	75	80	75
316	315	306	316	326	314	305	287	294	319	321	305
70	71	62	74	81	81	89	86	82	85	110	105
36	35	32	31			38	38	37	36	36	36
50	48	47	47			37	36	36	36	35	34
18982	21927	24781	28932	32917	37032	41226	45309	49360	53722	57991	70125
30.96	33.56	34.31	27.53	33.21	32.50	40.60	42.10	67.60	50.3	50.6	54.3
14.53	14.50	14.58	14.58	14.60	14.60	14.60	14.60	18.60	17.4	16.0	16.9
42.5	43.0	47.2	52.2	61.4	58.0	60.3	62.0	63.9	69.4	68.2	72.8
21.4	21.9	23.2	23.9	28.1	31.2	32.0	33.5	34.9	38.4	42.3	45.5
354	361	373	380	386	388	402	411.0	430.0	431.0	486.6	500.3
765	740	701	659	635	626	614	596.0	593.0	611.0	612.5	627.8
627	610	606	626	630	642	662	685.0	690.0	685.3	696.9	702.4

1-7　主要年份社会经济主要指标

MAJOR YEAR´S INDICATORS ON SOCIETY AND ECONOMY

指　标	Indicator	单位	Unit	2000 年	2005 年	2008 年
人口	**Population**					
总人口（年末）	Population at Year-end	万人	10 000 persons	706.65	740.91	761.56
男性人口	Male	万人	10 000 persons	357.74	374.03	382.46
女性人口	Female	万人	10 000 persons	348.91	366.87	379.10
市区人口	Urban Area	万人	10 000 persons	234.60	265.43	276.25
就业	**Employment**					
社会从业人员	Employment	万人	10 000 persons	397.6	471.0	513.8
#单位从业人员	Employed Persons in Units	万人	10 000 persons	118.3	224.3	254.1
经济总量	**Gross Economic Amount**					
全市生产总值（当年价）	GDP (at current price)	亿元	100 million yuan	1183.14	2576.95	4141.9
第一产业增加值	Primary Industry	亿元	100 million yuan	135.81	168.06	210.53
第二产业增加值	Secondary Industry	亿元	100 million yuan	546.12	1292.49	2007.89
第三产业增加值	Tertiary Industry	亿元	100 million yuan	501.21	1116.4	1923.49
人均生产总值	Per Capita GDP	元	yuan	15900	31725	49183
农林牧渔业总产值（当年价）	Gross Output Value of Farming, Forestry, Animal Husbandry and Fishery (at current price)	亿元	100 million yuan	248.33	320.51	399.5
工业总产值（当年价）	Gross Industrial Output Value (at current price)	亿元	100 million yuan	1940.83	5001.78	8946.73

注：1. 单位从业人员 2004 年以前为职工人数（不含私营企业）。
　　2. 规模以上固定资产投资数据 2003 年以前为城镇以上统计范围。
　　3. 2002 年以前地方财政一般预算收支数据为地方财政收支口径。
　　4. 2008 年 -2017 年农林牧渔业总产值为根据第三次农业普查结果核定修正后数据。
　　5. 全国第四次经济普查后，对 2000 年至 2018 年历年 GDP 数据进行了修订（以下相关表同）。

Note: 1. Before 2004, the data of employed persons in units refers to the number of staff and workers (excluding private enterprises) .
2. Before 2003, the data of investment in fixed assets above designated size refers to urban investment.
3. Before 2002, the data of general budgetary revenue and expenditure of local government finance refers to revenue and expenditure of local government finance.
4. Gross output value of farming, forestry, animal husbandry and fishery from 2008 to 2017 is revised according to the results of the third agricultural census.
5. After the fourth national economic census, the GDP data from 2000 to 2018 was revised (the following related tables are the same) .

2009年	2010年	2011年	2012年	2013年	2014年	2015年	2016年	2017年	2018年	2019年
762.92	763.64	766.36	769.56							
382.35	381.92	382.69	383.82							
380.56	381.72	383.67	385.74							
275.47	275.50	277.09	279.57							
525.7	540.3	551.2	559.9	571.5	589.0	595.4	601.4	603.9	590.3	
260.5	269.4	275.9	283.2	293.7	303.0	309.2	315.6	321.4	330.4	
4534.2	5350.69	6248.48	6869.61	7508.7	8120.66	8658.57	9283.17	10136.96	10949.38	11741.31
216.99	261.03	288.73	305.72	332.1	341.68	356.19	357.4	367.71	386.91	409.98
2146.53	2482.6	2823.7	3010.6	3225.9	3389.1	3503.4	3592.80	3849.18	4033.33	4182.76
2170.7	2607.08	3136.06	3553.33	3950.68	4389.87	4798.98	5332.96	5920.06	6529.14	7148.57
53481	62148	71354	77783	84213	90178	95447	101450	109621	117198	124282
407.1	480.2	534.6	567.3	610.6	627.9	612.4	669.1	697.9	737.0	778.1
10255.62	11614.83	13277.96	15306.32	16897.18	17444.21	18019.43	17416.71	13019.73	11389.78	

1-7　续表 1
Continued

指　标	Indicator	单位	Unit	2000 年	2005 年
财政	**Government Finance**				
公共财政预算收入	Public Budget Revenue	亿元	100 million yuan	80.01	176.34
公共财政预算支出	Public Budget Expenditure	亿元	100 million yuan	87.87	203.06
规模以上固定资产投资额	**Investment in Fixed Assets above Designated Size**	亿元	**100 million yuan**	**242.68**	**1403.30**
社会消费品零售额	**Total Retail Sales of Consumer Goods**	亿元	**100 million yuan**	**421.55**	**847.97**
港口货物吞吐量	**Volume of Freight Handled in Ports**	万吨	**10 000 tons**	**8661**	**18727**
集装箱吞吐量	**Volume of Containers Handled**	万标箱	**Ten Thousand TEUs**	**212.0**	**630.7**
航空货邮吞吐量	**Air cargo and mail throughput**	万吨	**10 000 tons**	**3.44**	**8.91**
对外贸易	**Foreign Trade**				
外贸进出口总额	Imports and Exports（excluding central and provincial companies）	亿美元	100 million USD	108.31	304.55
#出口总额	Exports	亿美元	100 million USD	61.14	175.88
教育、卫生、文化	**Education, Public Health and Culture**				
小学在校学生数	Students Enrollment in Primary Schools	万人	10 000 persons	53.49	47.98
普通中学在校学生	Students Enrollment in Regular Secondary Schools	万人	10 000 persons	39.85	39.11

注：根据市交通运输局提供民航货邮吞吐量数据，对历史数据进行了修正。

Note: According to the air cargo and mail throughput data provided by the Municipal Transportation Bureau, the historical data has been revised.

2008年	2009年	2010年	2011年	2012年	2013年	2014年	2015年	2016年	2017年	2018年	2019年
342.44	376.99	452.61	566.14	670.18	788.93	895.25	1006.26	1100.03	1157.24	1231.91	1241.74
369.41	433.58	532.39	658.06	765.98	1014.23	1074.71	1222.87	1352.85	1403.03	1561.23	1575.97
2019.01	**2458.89**	**3022.48**	**3502.54**	**4153.91**	**5027.86**	**5766.03**	**6555.70**	**7454.70**	**7777.09**		
1445.62	**1672.88**	**1892.38**	**2217.26**	**2533.16**	**2865.02**	**3218.25**	**3548.16**	**3914.19**	**4321.43**	**4742.72**	**5126.6**
30029	**31668**	**35012**	**37971**	**41465**	**45782**	**47701**	**49749**	**51463**	**51314**	**54250**	**57736**
1037.7	**1027.7**	**1201**	**1302**	**1450**	**1552**	**1658**	**1743**	**1805**	**1831**	**1932**	**2101**
13.05	**13.54**	**16.37**	**16.65**	**17.19**	**18.62**	**20.44**	**20.81**	**23.69**	**23.21**	**22.45**	**25.63**
521.59	439.86	561.49	712.63	732.08	779.12	798.88	702.22	4350.67（亿元）	5033.50（亿元）	5321.26（亿元）	5925.58（亿元）
314.62	269.22	333.51	400.56	408.20	419.86	457.77	453.50	2821.91（亿元）	3031.81（亿元）	3172.22（亿元）	3411.90（亿元）
47.72	46.50	46.27	47.95	49.50	49.63	51.65	53.65	54.72	55.05	56.99	58.38
37.39	37.74	38.00	37.32	36.96	36.51	36.26	35.54	35.61	37.22	38.54	40.9

1-7 续表 2
Continued

指 标	Indicator	单位	Unit	2000 年	2005 年
高等学校在校学生	Students Enrollment in Institutions of Higher Education	万人	10 000 persons	4.61	23.98
小学专任教师	Full-time Teachers in Primary Schools	万人	10 000 persons	3.17	3.17
普通中学专任教师	Full-time Teachers in Regular Secondary Schools	万人	10 000 persons	2.63	2.97
医生总数	Doctors	万人	10 000 persons	1.49	1.50
医院床位数	Hospital Beds	万张	10 000 beds	2.01	2.86
人民生活	**People's Living Conditions**				
就业人员工资总额	Total wages of Employed Persons	亿元	100 million yuan	120.4	359.5
城市居民人均可支配收入	Per Capita Disposable Income of Urban Households	元	yuan	8016	12920
农民人均纯收入	Per Capita Net Income of Rural Households	元	yuan	3637	5806
城乡人民币储蓄存款余额	Savings Deposit of Urban and Rural Households	亿元	100 million yuan	535.32	1343.10
物价指数	**Price Indexes**				
商品零售价格指数（以 1950 年价格为 100）	Retail Price Index（1950=100）	%	%	520.5	495.0
居民消费价格指数（以 1950 年价格为 100）	Consumer Price Index（1950=100）	%	%	711.9	753.1
#食品价格指数（以 1950 年价格为 100）	Food Price Index（1950=100）	%	%	800.1	871.8

注：1. 就业人员工资总额 2005 年前统计范围为全部职工不含私营企业，2015 年及以前为在岗职工工资总额；
2. 2015 年“城乡人民币储蓄存款余额”改为“住户存款”。

Note: 1. The total wages of the Full-Time Employees on duty were before 2005, the statistics ranged from all employees to private enterprises, total wages for staff and workers in 2015 and before.
2. In 2015, “balance of RMB deposits in urban and rural areas” changed to “household deposits.”

2008年	2009年	2010年	2011年	2012年	2013年	2014年	2015年	2016年	2017年	2018年	2019年
26.93	27.52	28.49	29.15	29.66	30.02	31.35	32.23	34.09	34.62	39.8	41.58
3.24	3.22	3.20	3.16	3.17	3.28	3.22	3.45	3.42	3.47	3.69	3.53
2.99	3.06	3.08	3.14	3.20	3.18	3.20	3.29	3.39	3.47	3.60	3.98
1.63	1.67	1.77	1.83	2.16	2.41	2.50	2.63	2.76	3.09	3.46	3.78
2.99	3.05	3.34	3.56	4.12	3.97	4.30	4.51	4.73	4.63	5.08	5.85
578.7	638.1	738.0	877.5	1044.3	1251.7	1456.0	1644.4	1852.7	2034.7	2251.7	
20464	22368	24998	28567	32145	35227	38294	40370	43598	47176	50817	54484
8509	9249	10550	12370	13990	15731	17461	16730	17969	19364	20820	22573
2123.36	2527.88	2912.33	3198.51	3757.60	4141	4436	5024	5326	5394	5914	6755
526.6	519.2	526.5	550.2	559.6	567.4	580.5	580.5	592.1	596.8	607.6	622.2
831.4	835.6	854.0	896.7	920.9	943.9	968.4	980.0	1004.5	1024.6	1046.1	1080.6
1105.3	1123.0	1194.9	1327.5	1384.6	1458.0	1522.2	1548.1	1625.5	1619.0	1669.2	1862.8

1-8 国民经济主要结构指标
COMPOSITION INDICATORS ON NATIONAL ECONOMY

指　标	Indicator	2000 年	2005 年	2008 年	2009 年	2010 年
社会从业人员	**Employment**					
产业结构	Industrial Composition					
第一产业	Primary Industry	36.4	22.2	19.9	20.1	19.5
第二产业	Secondary Industry	33.9	41.8	43.0	41.9	41.4
第三产业	Tertiary Industry	29.7	36.0	37.1	38.0	39.1
全市生产总值	**GDP**					
产业结构	Industrial Composition					
第一产业	Primary Industry	11.5	6.5	5.1	4.8	4.9
第二产业	Secondary Industry	46.1	50.2	48.5	47.3	46.4
第三产业	Tertiary Industry	42.4	43.3	46.4	47.9	48.7
农业	**Agriculture**					
农林牧渔业产值结构	Composition of Farming, Forestry, Animal Husbandry and Fishery					
#农业	Farming	45.0	39.5	43.2	43.5	45.8
林业	Forestry	0.8	0.8	0.6	0.5	0.4
牧业	Animal Husbandry	27.9	33.4	29.9	27.9	25.5
渔业	Fishery	26.4	26.3	22.7	24.1	24.6
工业	**Industy**					
轻重工业产值结构	Composition of Output Value of Light and Heavy Industry					
轻工业	Light Industry	64.1	49.4	42.3	41.7	38.7
重工业	Heavy Industry	35.9	50.6	57.7	58.3	61.3
固定资产投资	**Investment in Fixed Assets**					
投资结构	Composition of Investment					
生产性	Productive	54.0	65.4	61.6	56.3	53.6
非生产性	Non-productive	46.0	34.6	38.4	43.7	46.4

注：2008 年 -2017 年农业数据为根据第三次农业普查结果核定修正后数据。
Note: Agricultural data from 2008 to 2017 are revised according to the results of the third agricultural census.

2011年	2012年	2013年	2014年	2015年	2016年	2017年	2018年	2019年
19.2	18.8	18.8	18.4	18.1	17.8	16.9	16.3	
41.2	41.0	40.6	39.0	38.5	38.0	37.8	36.4	
39.6	40.2	40.6	42.6	43.3	44.2	45.3	47.4	
4.6	4.5	4.4	4.2	4.1	3.9	3.6	3.5	3.5
45.2	43.8	43.0	41.7	40.5	38.7	38.0	36.9	35.6
50.2	51.7	52.6	54.1	55.4	57.4	58.4	59.6	60.9
40.9	40.0	41.7	42.1	40.3	42.5	43.0	44.7	46.3
0.4	0.4	0.4	0.4	0.4	0.4	0.4	0.5	0.6
28.1	26.6	25.5	24.8	25.0	24.2	23.8	22.1	21.5
26.7	28.8	28.0	27.7	29.6	26.6	26.2	26.1	24.9
38.3	39.5	39.5	38.8	39.5	39.4	37.6	34.3	
61.7	60.5	60.5	61.2	60.5	60.6	62.4	65.7	
53.2	58.4	61.65	57.08	63.16	59.81	53.64		
46.8	41.6	38.35	42.92	36.84	40.19	46.36		

1-9　平均每天主要社会经济活动

SELECTED INDICATORS ON AVERAGE DAILY SOCIAL AND ECONOMIC ACTIVITIES

指　标	Indicator	单位	Unit	2000 年	2005 年	2008 年
全市生产总值	GDP	万元	10 000 yuan	32415	70601	113477
工业总产值	Gross Industrial Output Value	万元	10 000 yuan	53174	137035	245116
农林牧渔业总产值	Gross Output Value of Farming, Forestry, Animal Husbandry and Fishery	万元	10 000 yuan	6803	8781	10945
主要工业产品产量	Output of Major Industrial Products					
发电量	Electricity	万千瓦时	10 000 kW · h	2489	2701	4509
钢材	Rolled-steel	吨	ton	2558	9049	9593
纱	Yarn	吨	ton	191	198	118
布	Cloth	万米	10 000 m	114	141	133
家用电冰箱	Refrigerator	台	unit	8523	24899	19813
彩色电视机	Color TV set	台	unit	10395	36282	22922
社会消费品零售总额	Total Retail Sales of Consumer Goods	万元	10 000 yuan	11549	23232	39606
固定资产投资	Investment in Fixed Assets above Designated Size	万元	10 000 yuan	6649	38446	55315
外贸进出口总额	Imports and Exports	万美元	10 000 USD	3707	9047	14695
港口吞吐量	Volume of Freight Handled in Ports	万吨	10 000 tons	23.73	51.31	82.27

注：1. 固定资产投资包括城镇、农村 500 万元以上投资项目。
　　2. 一年按照 365 天计算。
　　3. 2008 年 -2017 年农林牧渔业总产值为根据第三次农业普查结果核定修正后数据。

Note :1. Investment in fixed assets includes construction projects involving an urban or rural investment of 5,000,00 yuan and over.
　　2. A year is computed according to 365 days.
　　3. Gross output value of farming, forestry, animal husbandry and fishery from 2008 to 2017 is revised according to the results of the third agricultural census.

2009年	2010年	2011年	2012年	2013年	2014年	2015年	2016年	2017年	2018年	2019年
124225	146594	171191	188208	205718	222484	237221	254333	277725	299983	321680
280976	318215	363780	419351	462936	477924	493683	477143	356705	312048	
11153	13157	14646	15541	16728	17203	16777	18331	19120	20192	21318
4730	4984	4759	4787	4935	4885	4754	4805	4981	5271	4947
9579	9136	9101	7525	6312	5830	3853	5243	7996	8764	9211
106	97	53	53	92	89	76	92	73	79	111
85	48	120	134	141	122	77	68	65	127	31
22663	21951	19686	15754	14366	16714	23893	24170	22429	24290	20050
29170	30444	31622	39452	41426	46984	37704	57855	46658	46443	43299
45832	51846	60747	69402	78494	88171	97210	107238	118395	129938	140455
67367	82808	95960	113806	137751	157973	179608	204238	213071		
12288	15633	19768	20057	21346	21887	19239	119196（万元）	137904（万元）	145787（万元）	162345（万元）
86.76	96	104	114	125	131	136	141	141	149	158

1-10 主要指标占全国全省比重（2019 年）

PERCENTAGE OF MAIN INDICATORS TO CHINA AND SHANDONG (2019)

指　标	Indicator	单位	Unit
一、生产总值	**GDP**	亿元	100 million yuan
第一产业	Primary Industry	亿元	100 million yuan
第二产业	Secondary Industry	亿元	100 million yuan
第三产业	Tertiary Industry	亿元	100 million yuan
二、年末总人口（常住人口）	**The Total Population (Resident Population)at the End of the Year**	万人	10 000 persons
三、主要工业产品产量	**Output of Major Industrial Products**		
发电量	Electricity	亿千瓦小时	100 million kW・h
房间空气调节器	Air Conditioner	万台	10 000 units
家用电冰箱	Refrigerator	万台	10 000 units
彩色电视机	Color TV Set	万台	10 000 units
钢材	Rolled-steel	万吨	10 000 tons
水泥	Cement	万吨	10 000 tons
四、主要农产品产量	**Output of Major Farm Products**		
粮食	Grain	万吨	10 000 tons
油料	Oil Plants	万吨	10 000 tons
肉类产量	Meat	万吨	10 000 tons
水产品	Aquatic Products	万吨	10 000 tons
五、房地产开发投资	**Investment In Real Estate Development**	亿元	100 million yuan
六、货物进出口总额	**Imports and Exports**	亿元	100 million yuan
其中：出口	Export	亿元	100 million yuan
进口	Import	亿元	100 million yuan

注：1. 本表全国、全省均为公报数。
　　2. 青岛市主要工业产品产量数据为本地口径。

Note：1. The number of the country and province in the table are obtained from the statistical report.
　　2. The output of main industrial products of Qingdao are at local calibre.

全国 China	全省 Shandong	青岛市 Qingdao	青岛市占全国比重（%） Qingdao/China	青岛市占全省比重（%） Qingdao/Shandong
990865	71067.5	11741.31	1.18	16.52
70467	5116.4	409.98	0.58	8.01
386165	28310.9	4182.76	1.08	14.77
534233	37640.2	7148.57	1.34	18.99
140005	10070.21	949.98	0.68	9.43
75034.3	5586.7	180.6	0.24	3.23
21866.2	876.4	874.43	4.00	99.78
7904.3	732.5	731.81	9.26	99.91
18999.1	1580.6	1580.42	8.32	99.99
120477.4	9289.4	336.19	0.28	3.62
235000	14357.1	442.47	0.19	3.08
66384	5357.0	302.6	0.46	5.65
3495	289.0	34.2	0.98	11.83
7649	698.6	52.8	0.69	7.56
6450	781.9	100.8	1.56	12.89
132194	8614.9	1803.8	1.36	20.94
315505	20420.9	5925.58	1.88	29.02
172342	11130.4	3411.90	1.98	30.65
143162	9290.6	2513.7	1.76	27.06

1-11 主要年份全市生产总值（按当年价格计算）
MAJOR YEAR´S GROSS DOMESTIC PRODUCT(AT CURRENT PRICE)

单位：亿元 (100 million yuan)

年份 Year	全市生产总值 GDP	第一产业 Primary Industry	第二产业 Secondary Industry	#工 业 Industry	第三产业 Tertiary Industry	人均生产总值（元） Per Capita GDP (yuan)
1949	2.87	1.19	1.10		0.58	71
1952	6.74	1.76	3.25	2.95	1.73	163
1957	10.82	2.00	5.76	5.39	3.06	239
1962	9.69	1.11	4.68	4.27	3.90	205
1965	15.50	1.80	8.96	8.48	4.74	325
1970	23.23	3.15	14.46	13.86	5.62	451
1975	29.07	6.93	15.39	14.67	6.75	522
1978	38.43	8.23	20.16	19.15	10.04	663
1980	48.65	9.61	26.15	24.28	12.90	819
1985	82.28	20.06	37.37	34.03	24.84	1311
1988	142.87	30.84	69.99	63.42	42.04	2199
1990	180.77	37.00	86.36	78.94	57.41	2714
1991	205.65	40.56	98.48	89.64	66.61	3053
1992	261.35	41.39	129.67	117.61	90.29	3856
1993	371.90	58.62	182.50	164.35	130.79	5455
1994	510.81	80.21	243.17	218.87	187.43	7436
1995	631.45	106.04	293.07	263.98	232.34	9089
1996	713.60	125.59	320.84	289.87	267.17	10130
1997	802.59	110.71	376.50	342.80	315.39	11235
1998	901.19	132.56	407.70	369.89	360.93	12443
1999	1018.97	133.27	466.50	424.15	419.20	13884
2000	1183.14	135.81	546.12	497.34	501.21	15900

1-11 续表 1
Continued

单位：亿元 (100 million yuan)

年份 Year	全市生产总值 GDP	第一产业 Primary Industry	第二产业 Secondary Industry	#工　业 Industry	第三产业 Tertiary Industry	人均生产总值（元） Per Capita GDP (yuan)
2001	1349.98	139.14	625.59	566.71	585.24	17882
2002	1551.42	141.89	728.77	658.00	680.76	20236
2003	1819.03	143.51	877.95	786.49	797.58	23340
2004	2193.60	157.52	1080.95	961.94	955.13	27577
2005	2576.95	168.06	1292.49	1156.53	1116.40	31725
2006	3029.40	173.35	1528.60	1374.12	1327.45	36743
2007	3545.48	191.86	1752.63	1577.15	1600.99	42509
2008	4141.91	210.53	2007.89	1795.88	1923.49	49183
2009	4534.22	216.99	2146.53	1887.38	2170.70	53481
2010	5350.69	261.03	2482.57	2155.73	2607.08	62148
2011	6248.48	288.73	2823.69	2430.66	3136.06	71354
2012	6869.61	305.72	3010.56	2608.44	3553.33	77783
2013	7508.70	332.10	3225.92	2752.90	3950.68	84213
2014	8120.66	341.68	3389.11	2878.71	4389.87	90178
2015	8658.57	356.19	3503.40	2944.80	4798.98	95447
2016	9283.17	357.40	3592.80	2989.24	5332.96	101450
2017	10136.96	367.71	3849.18	3133.78	5920.06	109621
2018	10949.38	386.91	4033.33	3161.34	6529.14	117198
2019	11741.31	409.98	4182.76	3159.86	7148.57	124282

注：1. 人均生产总值按常住人口计算。
2. 三次产业分类采用《国民经济行业分类》（GB/T 4754—2017）和《三次产业划分规定》（国统字 [2012]108 号），将农林牧渔业中的农、林、牧、渔专业及辅助性活动以及工业中的开采专业及辅助性活动和金属制品、机械和设备修理业归入第三产业。
3. 全国第四次经济普查后，对 2000 年至 2018 年历年 GDP 数据进行了修订（以下相关表同）。
4. 2019 年 GDP 数据为初步核算数（以下相关表同）。

Note: 1. Per capita GDP are calculated at permanent population.
2. The classification of the three industries adopts the "Classification of National Economic Industries" (GB/T 4754–2017) and the "Regulations on the Classification of the Three Industries" (Guo Tong Zi [2012] No. 108), which classifies the agricultural, forestry, animal husbandry and fishery Professional and ancillary activities, mining professional and ancillary activities in industry, and metal products, machinery and equipment repair businesses are included in the tertiary industry.
3. After the fourth national economic census, the GDP data from 2000 to 2018 was revised (the following related tables are the same).
4. GDP data for 2019 are preliminary accounting figures(The same applies to tables following).

1-12 主要年份全市生产总值构成（以全市生产总值为 100）

COMPOSITION OF MAJOR YEAR'S GROSS DOMESTIC PRODUCT
(GROSS DOMESTIC PRODUCT=100)

单位：%

年份 Year	全市生产总值 GDP	第一产业 Primary Industry	第二产业 Secondary Industry	#工　业 Industry	第三产业 Tertiary Industry
1952	100	26.1	48.2	43.8	25.7
1957	100	18.5	53.3	49.8	28.2
1962	100	11.4	48.3	44.1	40.3
1965	100	11.6	57.8	54.7	30.6
1970	100	13.6	62.2	59.7	24.2
1975	100	23.9	52.9	50.5	23.2
1978	100	21.4	52.5	49.8	26.1
1980	100	19.8	53.7	49.9	26.5
1985	100	24.4	45.4	41.4	30.2
1988	100	21.6	49.0	44.4	29.4
1990	100	20.5	47.8	43.7	31.7
1991	100	19.7	47.9	43.6	32.4
1992	100	15.8	49.6	45.0	34.6
1993	100	15.7	49.1	44.2	35.2
1994	100	15.7	47.6	42.8	36.7
1995	100	16.8	46.4	41.8	36.8
1996	100	17.6	45.0	40.6	37.4
1997	100	13.8	46.9	42.7	39.3
1998	100	14.7	45.2	41.0	40.1
1999	100	13.1	45.8	41.6	41.1
2000	100	11.5	46.1	42.0	42.4
2001	100	10.3	46.3	42.0	43.4
2002	100	9.1	47.0	42.4	43.9
2003	100	7.9	48.3	43.2	43.8
2004	100	7.2	49.3	43.9	43.5
2005	100	6.5	50.2	44.9	43.3
2006	100	5.7	50.5	45.4	43.8
2007	100	5.4	49.4	44.5	45.2
2008	100	5.1	48.5	43.4	46.4
2009	100	4.8	47.3	41.6	47.9
2010	100	4.9	46.4	40.3	48.7
2011	100	4.6	45.2	38.9	50.2
2012	100	4.5	43.8	38.0	51.7
2013	100	4.4	43.0	36.7	52.6
2014	100	4.2	41.7	35.4	54.1
2015	100	4.1	40.5	34.0	55.4
2016	100	3.9	38.7	32.2	57.4
2017	100	3.6	38.0	30.9	58.4
2018	100	3.5	36.9	28.9	59.6
2019	100	3.5	35.6	26.9	60.9

1-13 主要年份全市生产总值增长速度（以上年为 100）

GROWTH RATE OF MAJOR YEAR 'S GROSS DOMESTIC PRODUCT (PRECEDING YEAR=100)

单位：%

年份 Year	全市生产总值 GDP	第一产业 Primary Industry	第二产业 Secondary Industry	第三产业 Tertiary Industry	人均生产总值（元） Per Capita GDP (yuan)
1979	12.0	10.6	12.9	11.4	10.4
1980	10.4	4.3	13.1	10.3	9.4
1981	-2.0	-3.6	-1.9	-1.0	-3.2
1982	4.1	5.5	-0.2	11.9	2.6
1983	16.9	42.8	9.3	12.7	15.3
1984	13.0	18.9	11.5	10.3	12.0
1985	9.9	5.4	5.8	21.3	9.3
1986	9.2	2.6	12.1	10.0	8.3
1987	12.0	3.6	16.0	12.0	10.6
1988	13.8	-0.3	21.5	11.2	12.1
1990	9.3	9.8	7.3	12.2	8.0
1991	10.6	16.6	11.6	5.4	9.4
1992	18.2	-1.6	22.9	24.7	17.4
1993	22.4	20.4	21.1	25.5	21.7
1994	14.4	3.7	14.7	19.7	13.5
1995	12.0	10.9	12.1	12.3	10.8
1996	7.2	7.6	7.6	6.5	5.7
1997	11.5	-10.7	16.8	14.1	9.9
1998	12.9	17.6	11.3	13.4	11.3
1999	13.9	4.0	15.5	15.2	12.4
2000	14.3	6.4	14.9	16.0	12.7
2001	13.0	1.8	14.9	13.9	11.3
2002	13.7	3.1	15.5	14.2	11.9

1-13 续表 1
Continued

单位：%

年份 Year	全市生产总值 GDP	第一产业 Primary Industry	第二产业 Secondary Industry	第三产业 Tertiary Industry	人均生产总值（元） Per Capita GDP (yuan)
2003	15.4	2.4	18.8	14.5	13.5
2004	15.8	2.7	18.8	14.9	13.5
2005	15.6	0.4	18.1	15.3	13.2
2006	14.5	0.5	15.3	15.6	12.8
2007	14.6	-2.6	13.8	17.8	13.3
2008	12.5	1.4	10.0	16.6	11.4
2009	11.3	3.0	11.3	12.0	10.5
2010	12.1	1.4	11.2	14.0	10.4
2011	11.0	4.5	11.0	11.8	9.2
2012	9.9	3.2	10.0	10.4	9.0
2013	9.4	2.1	8.5	10.9	8.3
2014	7.8	3.9	7.2	8.6	6.7
2015	7.9	3.6	7.0	9.0	7.1
2016	7.7	2.9	5.7	9.4	6.7
2017	7.4	3.1	5.8	8.7	6.2
2018	7.3	3.4	6.8	7.8	6.2
2019	6.5	1.6	4.7	8.0	5.3
1978-2010 平均每年增长 1978-2010 Average Increase Rate	12.1	5.5	12.6	13.4	10.7
1991-2010 平均每年增长 1991-2010 Average Increase Rate	13.7	4.2	14.8	15.0	12.3
1996-2010 平均每年增长 1996-2010 Average Increase Rate	13.2	2.4	14.2	14.2	11.6
2001-2010 平均每年增长 2001-2010 Average Increase Rate	13.8	1.4	14.7	14.9	12.2
2006-2010 平均每年增长 2006-2010 Average Increase Rate	13.0	0.7	12.3	15.2	11.7
2010-2015 平均每年增长 2010-2015 Average Increase Rate	9.7	3.1	9.1	10.8	8.4

1-14　分市、区生产总值（2019 年）
GROSS DOMESTIC PRODUCT BY REGION (2019)

单位：亿元 (100 million yuan)

市、区名称	Region	地区生产总值 GDP	第一产业 Primary Industry	第二产业 Secondary Industry	第三产业 Tertiary Industry
市南区	Shinan District	1217.47		131.09	1086.38
市北区	Shibei District	912.75		171.17	741.58
李沧区	Licang District	518.03		153.05	364.98
崂山区	Laoshan District	818.14	6.63	255.82	555.69
西海岸新区	West Coast New Area	3554.44	78.58	1355.64	2120.22
黄岛区	Huangdao District	3418.68	78.58	1320.67	2019.43
保税港区	Qingdao Free Trade Port Area of China	135.76		34.97	100.79
城阳区	Chengyang District	1121.83	17.23	556.25	548.35
城阳区（不含高新区）	Chengyang District (Excluding High tech District)				
高新区	High tech District				
即墨区	Jimo District	1201.05	74.63	586.67	539.75
胶州市	Jiaozhou	1147.59	56.49	534.29	556.81
平度市	Pingdu	684.67	109.55	246.21	328.91
莱西市	Laixi	526.35	66.88	193.01	266.46

注：表中所列“城阳区（不含高新区）、高新区”口径无 2019 年核算数据。

Note: The caliber of "Chengyang District (excluding High-tech District) and High-tech District " listed in the table does not have 2019 accounting data.

1-15 按支出法计算的全市生产总值（2019 年）
GROSS DOMESTIC PRODUCT BY EXPENDITURE APPROACH (2019)

单位：亿元 (100 million yuan)

项目	Item	2019 年	2019 年为 2018 年 % 2019/2018 (%)
支出法计算的全市生产总值	**Gross Domestic Product by Expenditure Approach**	**11741.31**	**106.5**
（一）最终消费	Final Consumption Expenditures	4764.07	107.1
1. 居民消费	Household Consumption Expenditures	3466.43	108.0
农村居民	Rural Household	580.75	107.8
城镇居民	Urban Household	2885.68	108.1
2. 政府消费	Government Consumption Expenditures	1297.64	104.9
（二）资本形成总额	Gross Capital Formation	6723.59	106.1
1. 固定资产形成总额	Gross Fixed Capital Formation	6481.88	106.3
2. 存货增加	Change in Inventories	241.71	99.9
（三）货物和服务净流出	Net Exports of Goods and Services	253.65	104.3

注：1. 绝对额按当年价格计算，速度按可比价格计算。
　　2. 此表为初步测算数据，未经省局认定。

Note：1. The absolute numbers are calculated at current price, their growth are calculated at constant price.
　　2. This table is preliminary calculation data and has not been confirmed by the provincial bureau.

1-16 全市生产总值构成（2019 年）

COMPOSITION OF GROSS DOMESTIC PRODUCT（2019）

指标	Indicator	增加值（亿元） Added Value (10 000 million yuan)	2019 年为 2018 年 % 2019/2018 (%)
地区生产总值	**GDP**	**11741.31**	**106.5**
农林牧渔业	Farming, Forestry, Animal Husbandry and Fishery	436.21	102.0
#农林牧渔服务业	Agriculture, Forestry, Animal Husbandry and Fishery Service Industry	26.23	109.2
工业	Industry	3159.86	102.8
#开采辅助活动	#Mining Auxiliary Activities	0.77	102.4
#金属制品、机械和设备修理业	#Metal Products, Machinery and Equipment Repair Industries	18.57	102.8
建筑业	Construction	1042.24	113.7
批发和零售业	Wholesale and Retail Trade	1823.22	109.6
批发业	Wholesale	1201.25	110.5
零售业	Retail Trade	621.97	108.0
交通运输、仓储和邮政业	Transport, Storage and Post	790.76	108.4
住宿和餐饮业	Hotels and Catering Services	226.88	107.0
住宿业	Hotels	42.62	106.2
餐饮业	Catering Services	184.26	107.2
金融业	Financial Industry	754.31	109.7
房地产业	Real Estate	838.55	100.1
房地产业（K 门类）	Real Estate (K category)	708.31	98.4
自有房地产经营活动	Self-Owned Real Estate Business Activities	130.24	105.0
其他服务业	Other Services	2669.28	108.4
营利性服务业	For-Profit Services	1094.60	112.4
非营利性服务业	Non-Profit Services	1574.68	105.8
第一产业	Primary Industry	409.98	101.6
第二产业	Secondary Industry	4182.76	104.7
第三产业	Tertiary Industry	7148.57	108.0

主要统计指标解释

国内生产总值（GDP）　指按市场价格计算的一个国家（或地区）所有常住单位在一定时期内生产活动的最终成果。国内生产总值有三种表现形态，即价值形态、收入形态和产品形态。从价值形态看，它是所有常住单位在一定时期内生产的全部货物和服务价值超过同期中间投入的全部非固定资产货物和服务价值的差额，即所有常住单位的增加值之和；从收入形态看，它是所有常住单位在一定时期内创造并分配给常住单位和非常住单位的初次收入分配之和；从产品形态看，它是所有常住单位在一定时期内最终使用的货物和服务价值与货物和服务净出口价值之和。在实际核算中，国内生产总值有三种计算方法，即生产法、收入法和支出法。三种方法分别从不同的方面反映国内生产总值及其构成。对于一个地区来说，称为地区生产总值或地区 GDP。

人均 GDP　人均 GDP 是一定时期内 GDP 与同期人口平均数的比值。按照国际标准，人口平均数应该是同期平均常住人口。我国在核算制度中也规定，无论是国家还是地区，人口数都采用常住人口。国家统计局规定从 2004 年开始，过去采用户籍人口计算人均 GDP 的地区，作为过渡性措施，可在两年内同时计算两种口径的人均 GDP（数据后面必须注明是什么口径），两年后取消按户籍人口计算的人均 GDP。我市采用常住人口计算人均 GDP。

三次产业　是根据社会生产活动历史发展的顺序对产业结构的划分，产品直接取自自然界的部门称为第一产业，对初级产品进行再加工的部门称为第二产业，为生产和消费提供各种服务的部门称为第三产业。它是世界上通用的产业结构分类，但各国的划分不尽一致。我国的三次产业划分是：

第一产业：是指农业、林业、畜牧业、渔业和农林牧渔服务业。

第二产业：是指采矿业，制造业，电力、燃气及水的生产和供应业；建筑业。

第三产业：除第一、第二产业以外的其他行业。

支出法国内生产总值　是从最终使用角度反映一个国家（或地区）一定时期内生产活动最终成果的一种方法，包括最终消费支出，资本形成总额及货物和服务净出口三部分。对于地区，名称为“支出法地区生产总值”。

最终消费　指常住单位为满足物质、文化和精神生活的需要，从本国经济领土和国外购买的货物和服务的支出；不包括非常住单位在本国经济领土内的消费支出。最终消费分为居民消费和政府消费。

居民消费　指常住住户在一定时期内对货物和服务的全部最终消费支出。居民消费支出除了直接以货币形式购买货物和服务的消费之外，还包括以其他方式获得的货物和服务的消费支出，即所谓的虚拟消费支出。居民虚拟消费支出包括以下几种类型：单位以实物报酬及实物转移的形式提供给劳动者的货物和服务；住户生产并由本住户消费了的货物和服务，其中的服务仅指住户的自有住房服务和付酬的家庭雇员提供的家庭和个人服务；金融机构提供的金融媒介服务。

政府消费　指政府部门为全社会提供公共服务的消费支出和免费或以较低价格向居民住户提供的货物和服务的净支出。前者等于政府服务的产出价值减去政府单位所获得的经营收入的价值；后者等于政府部门免费或以较低价格向居民住户提供的货物和服务的市场价值减去向住户收取的价值。

资本形成总额　指常住单位在一定时期内获得的减去处置的固定资产和存货的净额，包括固定资本形成总额和存货增加。

固定资本形成总额　指常住单位在一定时期内获得的固定资产减处置的固定资产的价值总额。固定资产是通过生产活动生产出来的，且使用年限在一年以上、单位价值在规定标准以上的资产，不包括自然资产。分有形固定资产形成总额和无形固定资产形成总额。有形固定资产形成总额包括一定时期内完成的建筑工程、安装工程和设备工器具购置（减处置）价值，以及土地改良、新增役、种、奶、毛、娱乐用牲畜和新增经济林木价值。无形固定资产形成总额包括矿藏的勘探、计算机软件等获得减处置。

存货增加　指常住单位在一定时期内存货实物量变动的市场价值，即期末价值减期初价值的差额，再扣除当期由于价格变动而产生的持有收益。存货增加可以是正值，也可以是负值；正值表示存货上升，负值表示存货下降。它包括生产单位购进的原材料、燃料和储备物资等存货，以及生产单位生产的产成品、在制品和半成品等存货。

货物和服务净出口　指货物和服务出口减货物和服务进口的差额。出口包括常住单位向非常住单位出售或无偿转让的各种货物和服务的价值；进口包括常住单位从非常住单位购买或无偿得到的各种货物和服务的价值。由于服务活动的提供与使用同时发生，一般把常住单位从国外得到的服务作为进口，非常住单位从本国得到的服务作为出口。货物的出口和进口都按离岸价格计算。

气候　指地球与大气之间长期能量交换与质量交换所形成的一种自然环境状态，它是多种因素综合作用的结果。气候既是人类生活和生产的环境要素之一，又是供给人类生活和生产的重要资源。气温、降水、湿度等气象要素的多年平均值是用来描述一个地区气候状况的主要参数，而各种气象要素某年、某月的平均值（或总量）则可以反映出该时期天气气候状况的重要特征。

气温　指空气的温度，我国一般以摄氏度（℃）为单位表示。气象观测的温度表是放在离地面约 1.5 米处通风良好的百叶箱里测量的，因此，通常说的气温指的是离地面 1.5 米处百叶箱中的温度。其统计计算方法为：月平均气温是将全月各日的平均气温相加，除以该月的天数而得。

年平均气温　是将 12 个月的月平均气温累加后除以 12 而得。

降水量　指从天空降落到地面的液态或固态（经融化后）水，未经蒸发、渗透、流失而在地面上积聚的深度。其统计计算方法为：月降水量是将全月各日的降水量累加而得。年降水量是将 12 个月的月降水量累加而得。

Explanatory Notes on Main Statistical Indicators

Gross Domestic Product (GDP)　refers to the final products at market prices produced by all resident units in a country(or a region)during a certain period of time.Gross domestic product is expressed in three different perspectives, namely value, income, and products respectively. GDP in its value perspective refers to the total value of all goods and services produced by all resident units during a certain period of time, minus the total value of input of goods and services of the nature of non-fixed assets, in other words, it is the sum of the value-added of all resident units. GDP from the perspective of products refers to the value of all goods and services for final consumption by all resident units minus the net exports of goods and services during a given period of time. In the practice of national accounting, gross domestic product is calculated from three approaches,namely production approach, income approach and expenditure approach, which reflect gross domestic product and its composition from different angles. For a certain region, it refers region gross product or region GDP.

Per Capita GDP　refers to the ratio of GDP in a certain term and average population in the same term. According to the international standard, average population should be average permanent population in the same term.In the account regulation,population of both the country and the region should be permanent population.In the after two years since 2004, per capita GDP can be calculated at two coverage.i.e. at permanent population and household registered population(the note of coverage should follow the data). The per capita GDP calculated with household registered population will be abolished after two years. Per capita GDP of Qingdao is calculated at permanent population.

Three Strata of Industries　has been classified according to the historical sequence of development. Primary industry refers to extraction of natural resources, secondary industry involves processing of primary products, and tertiary industry provides services of various kinds for production and consumption. The above classification is universal although it varies to some extent from country to country. In China economic activities are categorized into the following three strata of industry:

Primary industry refers to farming, forestry, animal husbandry, fishery and services in support of these industries.

Secondary industry refers to mining and quarrying, manufacturing, production and supply of electricity, water and gas, and construction.

Tertiary industry refers to all other economic activities not included in primary or secondary industries.

GDP by Expenditure Approach refers to the method of measuring the final results of production activities of a country (region) during a given period from the perspective of final use. It includes final consumption, total capital formation and net export of goods and services.It reflects use and composition of gross domestic product. For a certain region,it refers region gross product by expenditure approach.

Final Consumption refers to the total expenditure of resident units for purchases of goods and services from both the domestic economic territory and abroad to meet the needs of material, cultural and spiritual life. It does not include the expenditure of non–resident units on consumption in the economic territory of the country. The final consumption is broken down into household consumption and government consumption.

Household Consumption refers to the total expenditure of resident households on the final consumption of goods and services. In addition to the consumption of goods and services bought by the households directly with money, the household consumption also includes expenditure on goods and services obtained by the households in other ways, i.e. the so–called imputed consumption, which includes the following: The goods and services provided to households by employers in the form of payment in kind and transfer in kind, goods and services produced and consumed by the households themselves, in which the services refer to the owner–occupied housing and services offered by payed family employees, financial intermediate services provided by financial institution.

Government Consumption refers to the consumption expenditure spent for the provision of public services provided by the government to the whole country and the net expenditure on the goods and services provided by the government to households free of charge or at reduced prices. The former equals to the output value of the government services minus the value of operating income obtained by the government departments. The latter equals to the market value of the goods and services provided by the government free of charge or at reduced prices to the households minus the value received by the government from the households.

Gross Capital Formation refers to the fixed assets acquired less disposal and the net value of inventory, thus including the gross fixed capital formation and charges in inventories.

Gross Fixed Capital Formation refers to the value of acquisitions less those disposals of fixed assets during a given period. Fixed assets are the assets produced through production activities with unit value above a specified amount and which could be used for over one year. Natural assets are not included. Gross fixed capital formation can be categorized into total tangible fixed capital formation and total intangible fixed capital formation. Total tangible fixed capital formation includes the value of the construction projects and installation projects completed and the equipment, apparatus and instruments purchased (less those disposed) as well as the value of land improved, the value of draught animals, breeding stock and animals for milk, for wool and for recreational purposes and the newly increased forest with economic value. Total intangible fixed capital formation includes the prospecting of minerals and the acquisition of computer software minus the disposal of them.

Charges in Inventories refers to the market value of the change in the physical volume of inventory of resident units during a given period, i.e. the difference between the values at the beginning and at the end of the period minus the gains due to the change in prices. The changes in inventories can have a positive or a negative value. A positive value indicates an increase in inventory while a negative value indicates a decrease in inventory. The inventory includes raw materials, fuels and reserve materials purchased by the production units as well as the inventory of finished products, semi–finished products and work–in–progress.

Net Export of Goods and Services　refers to the exports of goods and services subtracting the imports of goods and services. Exports include the value of various goods and services sold or gratuitously transferred by resident units to non–resident units. Imports include the value of various goods and services purchased or gratuitously acquired resident units from non–resident units. Because the provision of services and the use of them happen simultaneously, the acquisition of services by resident units from abroad is usually treated as import while the acquisition of services by non–resident units in this country is usually treated as export. The exports and imports of goods are calculated at FOB.

Climate　refers to the natural environmental status formed by the long–term exchange of energy and mass between the earth and the air, and is the results of interaction of many factors. Climate is both one of the environment factors and the important resources for the living and production activities of the human being. The average values across several years of meteorological factors such as temperature, rainfall and humidity are used as important parameters to describe the climate of a region, while the average values (or total values) of a given year or month of meteorological factors reflect the key characteristics of climate for that period of time.

Temperature　refers to the air temperature. China uses centigrade as the unit. The thermometry used for weather observation is put in a breezy shutter, which is 1.5 meters high from the ground. Therefore, the commonly used temperature refers to the temperature in the breezy shutter 1.5 meters away from the ground. The calculation method is as follows: Monthly average temperature is the summation of average daily temperature of one month divided by the actual days of that particular month.

Annual average temperature　is the summation of monthly average of a year divided by 12 months.

Volume of Precipitation　refers to the deepness of liquid state or solid state (thawed) water falling from the sky to the ground that has not been evaporated, infiltrated or run off. The calculation method is as follows: Monthly precipitation is the summation of daily precipitation of a month. Annual precipitation is the summation of 12 months precipitation of a year.

人口 2

POPULATION

简要说明

一、本篇资料的主要内容

本篇资料主要反映了全市人口方面的基本情况，包括全市主要年份和区（市）的户数、人口数、人口密度、土地面积数据、人口出生率、死亡率、自然增长率、计划生育等数据。另外还对建国以来开展的六次人口普查主要数据进行了比较。

二、本篇资料的来源

本篇资料分别来源于国家开展的人口普查、人口抽样调查和市公安局的户籍登记资料，由市统计局人口和社会科技统计处整理提供。

Brief Introduction

I. Main Content

The information in this article mainly reflects the basic demographic situation of the city, including the number of households, population, population density, land area data, birth rate, death rate, natural growth rate, family planning, etc. in main years and districts (cities) of the city data. In addition, the main data of the six census conducted since the founding of the People´s Republic of China were compared.

II. Source of Data

The data in this article are derived from the national population census, population sample survey and household registration data of the Municipal Public Security Bureau, which are compiled and provided by the Population and Social Science and Technology Statistics Division of Qingdao Statistics Bureau.

2-1 主要年份全市户籍人口数
MAJOR YEAR'S TOTAL REGISTERED POPULATION

单位：人 (person)

年份 Year	总人口 Total Population	按性别分 Grouped by Gender		平均人口 Average Population
		男 Male	女 Female	
1949	4056550	1997293	2059257	4054431
1952	4233586	2125392	2108194	4203428
1957	4822756	2424729	2398027	4773862
1962	4627432	2319658	2307774	4578313
1965	4901670	2461629	2440041	4859712
1970	5391852	2720633	2671219	5337282
1975	5742206	2904347	2837859	5717456
1978	5853321	2959800	2893521	5841638
1980	5961129	3015357	2945772	5937187
1985	6267223	3185409	3081814	6253157
1988	6516920	3319534	3197386	6474541
1989	6571597	3348454	3223143	6544259
1990	6666482	3392253	3274229	6619040
1991	6709277	3411776	3297501	6687880
1992	6731072	3420886	3310186	6720175
1993	6753497	3431149	3322348	6742285
1994	6785291	3446019	3339272	6769394
1995	6846346	3476300	3370046	6815819
1996	6902677	3502600	3400077	6874512
1997	6954391	3527588	3426803	6928534
1998	6995666	3545403	3450263	6975029
1999	7029707	3561061	3468646	7012687
2000	7066481	3577367	3489114	7048094
2001	7104875	3595652	3509223	7085678
2002	7156537	3619778	3536759	7130706
2003	7206806	3644032	3562774	7181672
2004	7311228	3692991	3618237	7259017
2005	7409052	3740309	3668743	7360140
2006	7493812	3779891	3713921	7451432
2007	7579910	3816620	3763290	7536861
2008	7615647	3824665	3790982	7597779
2009	7629161	3823534	3805627	7622404
2010	7636392	3819240	3817152	7632777
2011	7663612	3826931	3836681	7650002
2012	7695585	3838205	3857380	7679599

注：截止出书前，未获得公安部门青岛市 2013 年 –2019 年户籍人口信息。
Note：Data come from the Qingdao Municipal Public Security Bureau, and the data of 2013–2019 are absent.

2-2　主要年份全市户数、人口数、人口密度（户籍）

MAJOR YEAR´S HOUSEHOLDS, POPULATION AND DENSITY OF POPULATION (WITH PERMANENT RESIDENCE)

年份 Year	总户数（万户） Total Households (10000 households)		总人口（万人） Total Population (10000 persons)		平均每户人口（人） Average Persons Per Household(person)		人口密度（人/平方公里） Density of Population (person/sq.km)	
	全市 Whole Municipality	市区 Urban Area	全市 Whole Municipality	市区 Urban Area	全市 Whole Municipality	市区 Urban Area	全市 Whole Municipality	市区 Urban Area
1949	90.64	21.68	405.66	103.69	4.48	4.78	381	941
1952	93.96	22.70	423.36	107.62	4.51	4.74	397	977
1957	102.56	27.41	482.28	134.76	4.70	4.92	453	1223
1962	106.11	29.29	462.74	137.86	4.36	4.71	434	1251
1965	105.31	29.64	490.17	146.74	4.65	4.95	460	1332
1970	113.07	32.14	539.19	150.81	4.77	4.69	506	1369
1975	123.18	36.56	574.22	161.13	4.66	4.41	539	1462
1978	131.27	40.08	585.33	168.00	4.46	4.19	549	1525
1980	138.44	43.03	596.11	175.27	4.31	4.07	560	1591
1985	157.06	53.43	626.72	190.87	3.99	3.57	588	1732
1988	169.72	58.95	651.69	201.38	3.84	3.42	612	1827
1989	177.47	61.57	657.16	203.63	3.70	3.31	617	1848
1990	186.79	63.94	666.65	205.78	3.57	3.22	626	1867
1991	192.46	67.15	670.93	207.22	3.49	3.09	630	1880
1992	199.08	68.94	673.11	209.28	3.38	3.04	632	1899
1993	201.36	70.13	675.35	212.06	3.35	3.02	634	1924
1994	204.05	71.24	678.53	214.97	3.33	3.02	637	1951
1995	208.13	72.53	684.63	218.38	3.29	3.01	643	1982
1996	212.40	75.11	690.27	223.86	3.25	2.98	648	2032
1997	215.12	76.39	695.44	227.22	3.23	2.97	653	2062
1998	218.59	77.90	699.57	229.58	3.20	2.95	657	2084
1999	222.61	79.27	702.97	231.94	3.16	2.93	660	2105
2000	224.73	80.46	706.65	234.60	3.14	2.92	664	2129
2001	227.43	81.41	710.49	237.60	3.12	2.92	667	2156
2002	229.67	82.85	715.65	241.74	3.12	2.92	672	2194
2003	232.26	84.15	720.68	246.77	3.10	2.93	677	2240
2004	235.29	86.93	731.12	258.40	3.11	2.97	686	2229
2005	237.35	87.99	740.91	265.43	3.12	3.02	695	2290
2006	239.33	89.12	749.38	271	3.13	3.04	703	2338
2007	241.55	90.21	757.99	275.55	3.14	3.05	711	2377
2008	243.18	91.22	761.56	276.25	3.13	3.03	715	2384
2009	244.74	92.15	762.92	275.47	3.12	2.99	676	1873
2010	246.11	93.30	763.64	275.50	3.10	2.95	677	1873
2011	247.94	94.69	766.36	277.09	3.09	2.93	679	1884
2012	249.27	95.87	769.56	279.57	3.09	2.92	682	1901

2-3 主要年份全市常住人口数
MAJOR YESR´S TOTAL RESIDENT POPULATION

单位：万人 (10 000 persons)

年份 Year	总人口 Total population
2005	819.55
2006	829.42
2007	838.67
2008	845.61
2009	850.03
2010	871.51
2011	879.51
2012	886.85
2013	896.41
2014	904.62
2015	909.70
2016	920.40
2017	929.05
2018	939.48
2019	949.98

2-4 青岛市常住人口
TOTAL RESIDENT POPULATION

单位：万人 (10 000 person)

市、区名称	Region	2019 年	2018 年	2019 年比 2018 年 ± 2019/2018 (±)
全市	**Whole Municipality**	**949.98**	**939.48**	**1.12**
市南区	Shinan District	58.88	58.83	0.08
市北区	Shibei District	111.10	110.11	0.90
李沧区	Licang District	58.92	57.74	2.04
崂山区	Laoshan District	45.59	44.59	2.24
西海岸新区	West Coast New Area	160.82	157.73	1.96
城阳区	Chengyang District	85.00	82.42	3.13
城阳区(不含高新区)	Chengyang District (Excluding High tech District)	74.49	72.05	3.39
高新区	High tech District	10.51	10.37	1.35
即墨区	Jimo District	124.89	123.83	0.86
胶州市	Jiaozhou	90.75	90.05	0.78
平度市	Pingdu	137.79	137.89	-0.07
莱西市	Laixi	76.24	76.29	-0.07

2-5 主要年份常住人口城镇化率
THE URBANIZATION RATE OF THE MAIN YEAR PERMANENT RESIDENTS

单位：%(%)

年份 Year	城镇化率 Urbanization rate
2005	63.20
2006	63.59
2007	63.90
2008	64.31
2009	64.68
2010	65.81
2011	66.52
2012	67.14
2013	67.72
2014	68.41
2015	69.99
2016	71.53
2017	72.57
2018	73.67
2019	74.12

注：城镇化率为城镇区域常住人口数量与全市常住总人口的比值。

Note: The urbanization rate is the ratio of the number of permanent urban residents to the total resident population of the city.

2-6　分市、区土地面积（2019 年底）
LAND AREA (END OF 2019)

市、区名称	Region	土地面积（平方公里）Land Area (aq.km)
全　市	**Whole Municipality**	**11293.36**
市南区	Shinan District	32.21
市北区	Shibei District	65.85
李沧区	Licang District	99.10
崂山区	Laoshan District	395.79
黄岛区	Huangdao District	2128.31
城阳区	Chengyang District	583.68
即墨区	Jimo District	1920.90
胶州市	Jiaozhou	1323.65
平度市	Pingdu	3175.65
莱西市	Laixi	1568.22

注：2018 年度土地变更调查结果。
Note：Survey results of land quality change in 2018.

2-7 第一、二、三、四、五、六次人口普查主要数据

MAIN DATA OF THE FIRST, SECOND, THIRD, FOURTH, FIFTH AND SIXTH CENSUSES

项目	Item	第一次人口普查 1st National Population Census	第二次人口普查 2nd National Population Census	第三次人口普查 3rd National Population Census	第四次人口普查 4th National Population Census	第五次人口普查 5th National Population Census	第六次人口普查 6th National Population Census
一、总人口（万人）	**Total Population (10000 persons)**	**91.68**	**138.34**	**422.76**	**666.40**	**749.42**	**871.51**
按性别分	By Gender						
男（万人）	Male(10000 persons)	48.44	69.64	214.09	338.86	375.74	439.18
女（万人）	Female(10000 persons)	43.24	68.71	208.67	327.54	373.68	432.33
二、总户数（万户）	**Total Household (10000 Household)**	**19.27**	**28.01**	**101.41**	**186.61**	**241.62**	**296.64**
家庭户（万户）	Family Household (10000 Household)			101.09	185.56	232.70	282.43
平均家庭户规模（人）	Average Family Household Size(person)			4.07	3.49	2.97	2.79
三、民　族	**Ethnicity**						
民族个数（个）	Number of Ethnic Groups (unit)	14	16	25	41	51	53
汉族人口（万人）	Population of Han (10000 persons)	91.33	137.76	422.09	665.58	746.12	863.84
少数民族人口（万人）	Population of Ethnic Minorities(10000 persons)	0.36	0.58	0.67	0.82	3.30	7.67
四、各种文化程度人口	**Population with Various Education Attainments**						
大　学（万人）	College(10000 persons)		1.51	3.62	12.39	41.64	129.54
高　中（万人）	Senior Secondary School (10000 persons)		4.86	34.82	68.42	111.40	150.82
初　中（万人）	Junior Secondary School (10000 persons)		13.72	102.28	195.10	281.91	334.22
小　学（万人）	Primary School (10000 persons)		51.25	144.52	236.34	206.91	170.77

2-8 计划生育情况（1978-2019 年）
FAMILY PLANNING SITUATION (1978-2019)

年份 Year	已婚有生育能力的人数（人） Married and Fertile Persons (person)	节育人数（人） Persons under Birth Control (person)	节育率（%） Contraceptive Prevalence Rate (%)	四项手术人数（人） Persons Performed Four-operation (person)	#放环人数 Persons Set Rings
1978	694292	571077	82.25	125913	68475
1980	**763226**	**673069**	**88.19**	**180979**	**70927**
1985	1017649	929284	91.32	146742	67234
1990	**1258232**	**1165216**	**92.61**	**149327**	**70964**
1991	1319722	1219795	92.43	153970	77406
1992	1348503	1256271	93.16	90107	56226
1993	1380717	1271884	92.12	76783	45492
1994	1400425	1268378	90.57	73169	41482
1995	1427442	1285264	90.04	84099	52716
1996	1459465	1316516	90.21	84370	57648
1997	1482204	1340399	90.43	76579	55285
1998	1505499	1367648	90.84	74199	50526
1999	1523471	1378131	90.46	73663	44976
2000	**1521331**	**1371447**	**90.15**	**74285**	**45999**
2001	1514274	1360543	89.85	70205	43601
2002	1541855	1400145	90.81	50575	45453
2003	1518448	1354917	89.23	57458	47953
2004	1540706	1357703	88.04	52934	42859
2005	1590476	1417755	89.14	58097	49716
2006	1604665	1427785	88.98	51864	42457
2007	1595390	1426787	89.43	50074	41198
2008	1587344	1410426	88.85	120539	93291
2009	1623969	1418178	87.33	111084	100193
2010	**1591103**	**1377726**	**86.59**	**78721**	**51794**
2011	1581231	1355808	85.74	70823	48210
2012	1575996	1349572	85.63	62880	43021
2013	1527731	1293810	84.69	53252	30851
2014	1506274	1275142	84.66	34008	12827
2015	1475887	1226439	83.10	34879	9108
2016	1456953	1183221	81.21	36449	4474
2017	1439008	1188307	82.58	20905	4669
2018	1406047	1159775	82.48	17786	5097
2019	1375598	1141584	82.92	12582	3959

2-9 分市、区计划生育情况（2019 年）
FAMILY PLANNING SITUATION BY REGION (2019)

市、区名称	Region	计划生育率（%）Fertility Rate (%)	计划内出生（人）Birth within the Plan (person)		计划外出生（人）Birth without the Plan (person)		多胎（人）Third Birth and Above (person)
			一胎 First Birth	二胎 Second Birth	一胎 First Birth	二胎 Second Birth	
全市	**Whole Municipality**	**98.07**	**39939**	**45739**	**107**	**34**	**3029**
市南区	Shinan District	99.92	3079	1636			57
市北区	Shibei District	99.78	4924	3283	1	1	94
李沧区	Licang District	99.88	3285	3213	1		64
崂山区	Laoshan District	99.73	1701	1606	1		56
西海岸新区	West Coast New Area	97.44	7252	9020	24	8	736
城阳区	Chengyang District	98.73	3615	4083	7	3	194
即墨区	Jimo District	97.60	4896	6942	7	3	529
胶州市	Jiaozhou	97.12	3537	5051	14	5	430
平度市	Pingdu	96.92	4956	7166	34	7	557
莱西市	Laixi	97.22	2694	3739	18	7	312

主要统计指标解释

人口数 指一定时点、一定地区范围内有生命的个人总和。

出生率（又称粗出生率） 指在一定时期内（通常为一年）一定地区的出生人数与同期内平均人数（或期中人数）之比，用千分率表示。本资料中的出生率指年出生率，其计算公式为：

$$出生率=\frac{年出生人数}{年平均人数}\times 1000‰$$

式中：出生人数指活产婴儿，即胎儿脱离母体时（不管怀孕月数），有过呼吸或其他生命现象。

死亡率（又称粗死亡率） 指在一定时期内（通常为一年）一定地区的死亡人数与同期内平均人数（或期中人数）之比，用千分率表示。本资料中的死亡率指年死亡率，其计算公式为：

$$死亡率=\frac{年死亡人数}{年平均人数}\times 1000‰$$

人口自然增长率 指在一定时期内（通常为一年）人口自然增加数（出生人数减死亡人数）与该时期内平均人数（或期中人数）之比，用千分率表示。计算公式为：

$$人口自然增长率=\frac{本年出生人数-本年死亡人数}{年平均人数}\times 1000‰$$
$$=人口出生率-人口死亡率$$

Explanatory Notes on Main Statistical Indicators

Total Population to the total number of people alive at a certain point of time within a given area.

Birth Rate (or Crude Birth Rate) refers to the ratio of the number of births to the average population (or mid-period population) during a certain period of time (usually a year), expressed in ‰. Birth rate in the chapter refers to annual birth rate. The following formula is used:

Birth Rate=(Number of Births/Average Number of Population) × 1000‰

Number of births in the formula refers to live births, i.e. when a baby has breathed or showed any vital phenomena regardless of the length of pregnancy.

Death Rate (or Crude Death Rate) refers to the ratio of the number of deaths to the average population (or mid-period population) during a certain period of time (usually a year), expressed in ‰. Death rate in the chapter refers to annual death rate. The following formula is used:

Death Rate=(Number of Deaths/Annual Average Number of Population) × 1000‰

Natural Growth Rate of Population refers to the ratio of natural increase in population (number of births minus number of deaths) in a certain period of time (usually a year) to the average population (or mid-period population) of the same period, expressed in ‰. The following formula is applied:

Natural Growth Rate of Population=[(Number of Births−Number of Deaths)/Average Number of Population] × 1000‰

Natural Growth Rate of Population=Birth Rate−Death Rate

从业人员及职工工资 3

EMPLOYMENT AND WAGES

简要说明

一、本篇资料的主要内容

本篇资料主要反映了全市从业人员和职工工资方面的基本情况，主要包括全市社会从业人数及各区（市）单位从业人数、在岗职工工资总额和平均工资等方面的资料。

二、本篇资料的来源

单位从业人员和职工工资来源于劳动统计年报，全市从业人员根据劳动统计年报、农村年报和市工商行政管理局、市人力资源和社会保障局、市交通委相关资料测算。由市统计局人口和社会科技统计处整理提供。

Brief Introduction

I. Main Content

The data in this chapter mainly reflects the basic situation of employees and wages in the city, mainly including the number of employees in the city, the number of employees in each district (city) unit, the total wages and average wages of employees on the job, etc.

II. Source of Data

The wages of employees and employees of the unit are derived from the annual labor statistics. The employees in the city are calculated based on the annual labor statistics, rural annual reports, Qingdao Administration for Industry and Commerce, Qingdao Human Resources and Social Security Bureau, and Qingdao Transportation Commission. Provided by the Population and Social Science and Technology Statistics Department of Qingdao Municipal Statistics Bureau.

3-1 社会就业人数（1978-2018年）
SOCIAL EMPLOYMENT (1978-2018)

单位：万人 (10 000 persons)

年份 Year	合计 Total	第一产业 Primary Industry	第二产业 Secondary Industry	第三产业 Tertiary Industry
1978	256.70	157.40	65.60	33.70
1979	265.60	156.10	72.20	37.30
1980	270.10	153.00	77.30	39.80
1981	278.90	153.60	82.10	43.20
1982	282.70	151.10	86.20	45.40
1983	289.60	156.40	85.00	48.10
1984	304.20	149.20	97.70	57.40
1985	315.30	149.20	104.50	61.70
1986	326.40	149.60	112.10	64.60
1987	334.80	149.90	120.20	64.70
1988	336.50	147.60	123.20	65.70
1989	344.20	152.50	122.10	69.60
1990	352.80	156.50	123.30	73.10
1991	361.20	161.90	124.30	74.90
1992	370.30	161.70	127.80	80.80
1993	365.70	160.50	128.80	76.40
1994	367.60	157.10	129.40	81.20
1995	374.20	155.40	132.40	86.40
1996	381.50	152.20	137.10	92.20
1997	388.70	155.20	138.10	95.30
1998	393.10	154.80	138.60	99.70
1999	396.10	150.30	142.00	103.80
2000	397.60	144.70	134.91	117.99
2001	400.50	133.90	142.30	124.30
2002	413.31	121.38	153.85	138.08
2003	438.96	119.91	163.93	155.12
2004	458.81	113.98	180.63	164.20
2005	471.03	104.48	196.80	169.75
2006	490.10	102.97	209.83	177.30
2007	505.80	102.30	217.80	185.70
2008	513.80	102.40	220.80	190.60
2009	525.71	105.65	220.33	199.73
2010	540.34	105.16	223.85	211.33
2011	551.18	106.02	227.08	218.08
2012	559.88	104.95	229.79	225.14
2013	571.47	107.59	232.17	231.71
2014	588.97	108.45	229.91	250.61
2015	595.44	107.92	229.51	258.01
2016	601.44	107.30	228.44	265.70
2017	603.90	101.86	228.14	273.90
2018	590.30	96.10	214.60	279.60

3-2 主要年份全市单位就业人员人数

MAJOR YEAR´S NUMBER OF EMPLOYEES IN THE CITY

单位：万人 (10 000 persons)

年份 Year	合计 Total	#市区 Urban Area	#国有单位 State-owned Units	#集体单位 Collective-owned Units	其他所有制单位 Other Ownership Units
1949	14.8	13.4	9.3	5.5	
1952	23.4	20.1	18.3	5.1	
1957	29.7	24.5	24.1	5.6	
1962	32.3	26.8	24.5	7.8	
1965	36.7	30.6	26.8	9.9	
1970	45.6	37.4	32.2	13.4	
1975	53.4	43.5	38.0	15.4	
1978	70.7	54.5	49.2	21.5	
1980	79.2	61.5	55.0	24.2	
1985	88.8	66.7	59.8	28.9	0.1
1988	98.2	70.0	66.7	31.2	0.3
1990	103.2	70.6	69.5	32.9	0.8
1991	105.4	78.4	71.5	32.5	1.4
1992	108.2	80.4	73.6	32.8	1.8
1993	109.4	80.8	75.3	29.5	4.6
1994	110.1	80.2	72.4	28.3	9.4
1995	111.6	80.2	72.4	27.5	11.7
1996	118.4	81.1	71.6	26.0	20.8
1997	117.1	78.1	69.0	22.6	25.5
1998	116.2	75.6	64.2	19.0	33.0
1999	119.0	78.3	60.4	16.6	42.0
2000	118.3	76.6	57.6	14.2	46.5
2001	117.5	75.1	53.2	12.2	52.1
2002	119.1	75.2	49.5	10.3	59.3
2003	118.0	74.3	47.2	8.9	61.9
2004	207.1	111.1	43.7	18.0	145.4
2005	224.3	122.3	43.9	18.2	162.2
2006	243.2	133.7	41.7	16.2	185.3
2007	249.8	137.3	45.1	17.9	186.8
2008	254.1	140.9	44.4	15.4	194.3
2009	260.5	145.6	44.4	14.6	201.5
2010	269.4	151.1	44.6	15.1	209.7
2011	275.9	156.5	44.3	14.7	216.9
2012	283.2	162.1	44.0	13.8	225.4
2013	293.7	184.1	37.8	5.4	250.5
2014	303.0	191.4	36.7	4.9	261.4
2015	309.2	192.4	35.8	4.6	268.8
2016	315.6	196.4	35.5	4.7	275.4
2017	321.4	249.1	35.1	4.6	281.7
2018	330.4	258.3	34.7	2.0	293.7
2019	146.6	118.5	34.1	1.1	111.4

注：1. 2004 年以前为城镇单位职工人数。
2. 2013 年统计口径变化，国有单位、集体单位数据与上年不可比。
3. 2019 年统计口径变化，全市单位就业人员人数为全市城镇非私营口径。

Note：1. Before 2004, the data refer to number of staff and workers in urban units.
2. Because of the adjustment about the statistics system, the data of State-owned Units and Collective-owned Units since 2013 are not fully comparable with historical statistics.
3. Because of the adjustment about the statistics system, the number of employed persons in all units of the city is the urban non-private caliber of the city.

3-3 全市城镇非私营单位国民经济各行业就业人员人数（2019 年）

NUMBER OF EMPLOYED PERSONS IN NON-PRIVATE UNITS OF THE CITY BY SECTOR (2019)

单位：万人 (10 000 persons)

		2019 年		2018 年	
		合计 Total	女性 Female	合计 Total	女性 Female
总计	**Total**	**146.6**	**60.8**	**144.9**	**57.9**
1. 农、林、牧、渔业	Farming, Forestry, Animal Husbandry and Fishery	0.0	0.0	0.1	0.0
2. 采矿业	Mining	0.0	0.0	0.0	0.0
3. 制造业	Manufacturing	43.7	16.2	52.1	20.3
4. 电力、热力、燃气及水生产和供应业	Electricity, Heat, Gas and Water Production and Supply Industry	2.0	0.5	1.8	0.6
5. 建筑业	Construction	16.3	2.1	16.0	1.8
6. 批发和零售业	Wholesale and Retail Trade	9.3	5.5	8.7	5.4
7. 交通运输、仓储和邮政业	Transport, Storage and Post	8.9	2.5	9.8	2.8
8. 住宿和餐饮业	Hotels and Catering Services	2.8	1.4	2.5	1.4
9. 信息传输、软件和信息技术服务业	Information Transmission Computer Services and Software	2.3	1.0	2.0	0.8
10. 金融业	Financial Industry	12.0	7.6	5.8	3.3
11. 房地产业	Real Estate	4.7	1.9	4.4	1.7
12. 租赁和商务服务业	Leasing and Business Services	3.6	1.5	3.1	1.3
13. 科学研究和技术服务业	Scientific Research and Technical Services	3.9	1.2	3.5	1.1
14. 水利、环境和公共设施管理业	Management of Water Conservancy, Environment and Public Facilities	1.7	0.6	2.0	0.7
15. 居民服务、修理和其他服务业	Residents Service, Repair and Other Services	0.6	0.3	0.4	0.1
16. 教育	Education	13.3	8.6	13.5	8.1
17. 卫生和社会工作	Health and Social Welfare	7.4	5.3	6.7	4.7
18. 文化、体育和娱乐业	Culture, Sports and Entertainment	1.2	0.5	1.2	0.6
19. 公共管理、社会保障和社会组织	Public Management, Social Security and Social Organization	12.9	4.1	11.3	3.2

3-4 全市城镇非私营单位分市、区国民经济各部门就业人员人数（2019年）
NUMBER OF EMPLOYED PERSONS IN NON-PRIVATE UNITS OF THE CITY BY REGION AND SECTOR OF NATIONAL ECONOMY (2019)

市、区名称	Region	合计 Total	农林牧渔业 Farming, Forestry, Animal Husbandry and Fishery	采矿业 Mining	制造业 Manufacturing	电力热力燃气及水生产和供应业 Electricity, Heat, Gas and Water Production and Supply Industry
全市	**Whole Municipality**	**146.6**			**43.7**	**2.0**
市直	Municipal Government	1.0			1.0	
市南区	Shinan District	26.0			0.1	0.3
市北区	Shibei District	12.4			0.8	0.4
李沧区	Licang District	6.0			0.8	0.1
崂山区	Laoshan District	15.4			2.1	0.1
西海岸新区	West Coast New Area	31.7			13.4	0.5
黄岛区	Huangdao District	29.2			12.0	0.5
保税港区	Qingdao Free Trade Port Area of China	2.5			1.4	
城阳区	Chengyang District	17.0			9.8	0.1
城阳区（不含高新区）	Chengyang District (Excluding High tech District)	14.9			8.4	0.1
高新区	High tech District	2.1			1.4	
即墨区	Jimo District	10.0			5.4	0.1
胶州市	Jiaozhou	10.6			4.8	0.1
平度市	Pingdu	7.1			3.1	0.1
莱西市	Laixi	9.6			2.6	0.1

注：表中的合计数不等于分项数之和均系四舍五入导致。

Note: The total number in the table is not equal to the sum of the number of items, which is caused by rounding.

单位：万人 (10 000 persons)

建筑业 Construction	批发和零售业 Wholesale and Retail Trade	交通运输仓储和邮政业 Transport, Storage and Post	住宿和餐饮业 Hotels and Catering Services	信息传输软件和信息技术服务业 Information Transmission Computer Services and Software
16.3	**9.3**	**8.9**	**2.8**	**2.3**
1.1	2.8	1.3	1.6	1.2
1.6	1.5	1.9	0.1	0.1
0.6	0.6	0.3	0.1	
1.8	1.0	1.2	0.2	0.5
5.7	1.2	2.6	0.4	0.2
5.7	0.8	2.0	0.4	0.2
	0.4	0.6		
0.4	0.7	1.2	0.1	
0.2	0.7	1.1	0.1	
0.2	0.0	0.1	0.0	
0.1	0.2	0.0	0.1	
0.7	0.7	0.2	0.1	
0.2	0.2			
4.0	0.1	0.1		

3-4 续表
Continued

市、区名称	Region	金融业 Financial Industry	房地产业 Real Estate	租赁和商务服务业 Leasing and Business Services	科学研究和技术服务业 Scientific Research and Technical Services	水利环境和公共设施管理业 Management of Water Conservancy, Environment and Public Facilities
全市	**Whole Municipality**	**12.0**	**4.7**	**3.6**	**3.9**	**1.7**
市直	Municipal Government					
市南区	Shinan District	9.0	0.6	1.5	0.9	0.4
市北区	Shibei District	0.3	0.8	0.3	0.4	0.2
李沧区	Licang District		0.4	0.2	0.2	0.4
崂山区	Laoshan District	2.6	0.4	0.3	1.6	0.2
西海岸新区	West Coast New Area		1.1	0.4	0.3	0.1
黄岛区	Huangdao District		1.1	0.4	0.3	0.1
保税港区	Qingdao Free Trade Port Area of China					
城阳区	Chengyang District		0.5	0.3	0.1	0.2
城阳区（不含高新区）	Chengyang District (Excluding High tech District)		0.4	0.3	0.1	0.2
高新区	High tech District		0.1			
即墨区	Jimo District		0.2	0.1	0.1	0.1
胶州市	Jiaozhou		0.4	0.2	0.1	
平度市	Pingdu		0.2			0.1
莱西市	Laixi			0.1		0.2

注：表中的合计数不等于分项数之和均系四舍五入导致。
Note: The total number in the table is not equal to the sum of the number of items, which is caused by rounding.

单位：万人 (10 000 persons)

居民服务修理和其他服务业 Services to Households and Other Services	教育 Education	卫生和社会工作 Health and Social Welfare	文化体育和娱乐业 Culture, Sports and Entertainment	公共管理社会保障和社会组织 Public Management, Social Security and Social Organization	国际组织 International Organization
0.6	**13.3**	**7.4**	**1.2**	**12.9**	
0.2	1.2	1.3	0.5	2.1	
	1.1	1.8	0.1	0.8	
	0.9	0.6	0.1	0.6	
0.2	1.7	0.2	0.2	1.1	
	2.4	0.9	0.1	2.1	
	2.4	0.9	0.1	2.0	
				0.1	
0.1	1.4	0.5	0.2	1.2	
0.1	1.4	0.5	0.1	1.1	
			0.1	0.1	
	1.1	0.6	0.1	1.6	
	1.2	0.6	0.1	1.3	
	1.4	0.5		1.2	
	0.8	0.4		1.0	

3-5 全市城镇非私营单位分市、区就业人员人数（2019 年底）

NUMBER OF EMPLOYED PERSONS IN NON-PRIVATE UNITS OF THE CITY BY REGION AND SECTOR (END OF 2019)

单位：万人 (10 000 persons)

市、区名称	Region	年末人数 Year-end Population	国有单位 State-owned Units	集体单位 Collective-owned Units	其他经济类型单位 Units in Other Types of Economy
全市	**Whole Municipality**	**146.6**	**34.1**	**1.1**	**111.4**
市直	Municipal Government	1.0		0.2	1.0
市南区	Shinan District	26.0	6.4	0.1	19.4
市北区	Shibei District	12.4	3.4	0.1	8.8
李沧区	Licang District	6.0	1.9	0.1	4.0
崂山区	Laoshan District	15.4	3.1	0.1	12.2
西海岸新区	West Coast New Area	31.7	5.1	0.1	26.6
黄岛区	Huangdao District	29.2	5.0		24.1
保税港区	Qingdao Free Trade Port Area of China	2.5	0.1	0.2	2.5
城阳区	Chengyang District	17.0	2.8	0.2	14.1
城阳区（不含高新区）	Chengyang District (Excluding High tech District)	14.9	2.6		12.1
高新区	High tech District	2.1	0.2	0.1	2.0
即墨区	Jimo District	10.0	3.2	0.1	6.7
胶州市	Jiaozhou	10.6	2.6	0.1	7.9
平度市	Pingdu	7.1	3.2	0.2	3.8
莱西市	Laixi	9.6	2.3		7.1

注：表中的合计数不等于分项数之和均系四舍五入导致。

Note: The total number in the table is not equal to the sum of the number of items, which is caused by rounding.

3-6 全市就业人员工资总额、平均工资(1978-2019年)

TOTAL WAGES AND AVERAGE WAGE OF CITYWIDE FULL-TIME EMPLOYEES (1978-2019)

年份 Year	工资总额(亿元) Total Wage Bill (100 million yuan)		平均工资(元) Average Wage (yuan)	
	全社会单位 All Units	其中：非私营单位 of which：Non-private Units	全社会单位 All Units	其中：非私营单位 of which：Non-private Units
1978		4.0		584
1979		4.8		662
1980		6.0		782
1981		6.3		778
1982		6.6		785
1983		6.9		809
1984		9.0		1041
1985		9.6		1103
1986		11.8		1311
1987		14.2		1519
1988		18.0		1862
1989		20.7		2120
1990		24.4		2400
1991		26.4		2553
1992		31.8		2970
1993		40.4		3694
1994		59.5		5455
1995		68.3		6164
1996		78.2		6640
1997		82.5		7030
1998		87.2		7518
1999		100.1		8405
2000		120.4		10072
2001		135.8		11426
2002		153.8		12839
2003	225.6	160.3	12597	15335
2004	280.5	193.4	13932	17190
2005	359.5	242.8	16015	20022
2006	445.6	292.0	18574	23457
2007	518.1	338.6	21419	27083
2008	578.7	371.9	23296	30233
2009	638.1	393.2	25396	33258
2010	738.0	446.8	28549	37805
2011	877.5	522.0	32763	43077
2012	1044.3	613.1	37399	49052
2013	1251.7	785.7	42688	55363
2014	1456.0	890.5	48453	62104
2015	1644.4	993.0	53715	69465
2016	1852.7	1088.5	58551	75803
2017	2034.7	1193.6	63047	82177
2018	2251.7	1290.8	68197	89525
2019		1438.3		98604

注：1. 2003年以前为职工工资总额、平均工资。
2. 2015年以前为在岗职工工资总额、平均工资。
3. 2019年统计口径变化，无全部单位工资数据。

Note：1. The data before 2003 refer to the total wage bill and average wage of stall and workers.
2. It was the total salary and average salary of the on-spot staff before 2015.
3. The statistical caliber changes in 2019, and there is no wage data for all units.

3-7 全市就业人员工资总额、平均工资指数（1978-2019 年）
INDEXES OF TOTAL WAGES AND AVERAGE WAGE OF CITYWIDE FULL-TIME EMPLOYEES (1978-2019)

年份 Year	工资总额指数 Total Wage Bill Indexed		平均工资指数 Average Wage Indexes	
	全社会单位 All Units	其中：非私营单位 of which：Non-private Units	全社会单位 All Units	其中：非私营单位 of which：Non-private Units
1978		120.80		104.66
1979		119.53		113.36
1980		123.95		118.13
1981		106.71		99.49
1982		103.80		100.90
1983		104.14		103.06
1984		130.64		128.68
1985		107.11		105.96
1986		123.22		118.86
1987		120.10		115.87
1988		126.48		122.58
1989		115.29		113.86
1990		117.66		113.21
1991		108.28		106.38
1992		120.26		116.33
1993		127.09		124.38
1994		147.46		147.67
1995		114.76		113.00
1996		114.54		107.72
1997		105.50		105.87
1998		105.64		106.94
1999		114.81		111.80
2000		120.29		119.83
2001		112.77		113.44
2002		113.31		112.37
2003		108.84		110.30
2004	124.34	120.65	110.60	112.10
2005	128.16	125.54	114.95	116.47
2006	123.95	120.26	115.98	117.16
2007	116.27	115.96	115.32	115.46
2008	111.70	109.83	108.76	111.63
2009	110.26	105.73	109.01	110.01
2010	115.66	113.63	112.42	113.67
2011	118.90	116.83	114.76	113.95
2012	119.01	117.45	114.15	113.87
2013	119.86	128.15	114.14	112.87
2014	116.32	113.34	113.50	112.18
2015	112.94	111.51	110.86	111.85
2016	110.25	106.49	109.71	110.33
2017	109.82	109.66	107.68	108.41
2018	110.66	108.14	108.17	108.94
2019		111.43		110.14

注：1. 2004 年以前为职工工资总额、平均工资指数。
2. 2015 年以前为在岗职工工资总额、平均工资。
3. 2019 年统计口径变化，无全部单位工资数据。

Note：1. The data before 2004 refer to the indexes of total wage of stall and workers.
2. It was the total salary and average salary of the on-spot staff before 2015.
3. The statistical caliber changes in 2019, and there is no wage data for all units.

3-8 城镇非私营和城镇私营单位分行业就业人员平均工资（2019 年）

AVERAGE WAGES OF EMPLOYED PERSONS IN URBAN NON-PRIVATE AND URBAN PRIVATE UNITS BY SECTOR (2019)

行业	Sector	非私营单位（元）Non-private Units (yuan)	私营单位（元）Private Units (yuan)
总计	**Total**	**98604**	**57988**
（一）农、林、牧、渔业	Farming, Forestry, Animal Husbandry and Fishery	60236	46638
（二）采矿业	Mining	45977	53466
（三）制造业	Manufacturing	80549	56461
（四）电力、热力、燃气及水生产和供应业	Electricity, Heat, Gas and Water Production and Supply Industry	91660	53661
（五）建筑业	Construction	82553	56714
（六）批发和零售业	Wholesale and Retail Trade	76437	52000
（七）交通运输、仓储和邮政业	Transport, Storage and Post	94071	58498
（八）住宿和餐饮业	Hotels and Catering Services	60741	46013
（九）信息传输、软件和信息技术服务业	Information Transmission, Computer Services and Software	126342	67238
（十）金融业	Financial Industry	96098	62190
（十一）房地产业	Real Estate	105076	55883
（十二）租赁和商务服务业	Leasing and Business Services	96426	73962
（十三）科学研究和技术服务业	Scientific Research and Technical Services	129845	70782
（十四）水利、环境和公共设施管理业	Management of Water Conservancy, Environment and Public Facilities	61056	36705
（十五）居民服务、修理和其他服务业	Residents Service, Repair and Other Services	76287	48722
（十六）教育	Education	133697	53089
（十七）卫生和社会工作	Health and Social Welfare	143704	65419
（十八）文化、体育和娱乐业	Culture, Sports and Entertainment	105602	57640
（十九）公共管理、社会保障和社会组织	Public Management, Social Security and Social Organization	138701	

3-9 分市、区城镇非私营单位就业人员工资总额（2019 年）

TOTAL WAGES OF FULL-TIME EMPLOYEES IN NON-PRIVATE UNITS OF THE CITY BY REGION AND SECTOR (2019)

单位：亿元 (100 million yuan)

市、区名称	Region	合计 Total	国有单位 State-owned Units	集体单位 Collective-owned Units	其他所有制单位 Other Ownership Units
全市	**Whole Municipality**	**1438.3**	**469.3**	**8.9**	**960.1**
市直	Municipal Government	9.9			9.9
市南区	Shinan District	267.1	99.5	1.3	166.3
市北区	Shibei District	128.4	53.9	0.7	73.8
李沧区	Licang District	55.2	24.6	0.3	30.3
崂山区	Laoshan District	200.9	49.8	1.0	150.1
西海岸新区	West Coast New Area	296.1	69.9	0.5	225.7
黄岛区	Huangdao District	273.5	68.6	0.5	204.4
保税港区	Qingdao Free Trade Port Area of China	22.6	1.3		21.3
城阳区	Chengyang District	167.5	39.2	1.3	127.3
城阳区（不含高新区）	Chengyang District (Excluding High tech District)	146.6	37.6	1.3	107.9
高新区	High tech District	20.9	1.6		19.4
即墨区	Jimo District	84.6	39.0	0.6	44.9
胶州市	Jiaozhou	86.0	33.3	0.7	52.0
平度市	Pingdu	61.2	36.5	0.6	24.0
莱西市	Laixi	81.4	23.7	1.9	55.8

注：表中的合计数不等于分项数之和均系四舍五入导致。

Note: The total number in the table is not equal to the sum of the number of items, which is caused by rounding.

3-10 分市、区城镇非私营单位就业人员平均工资（2019 年）

AVERAGE WAGE OF FULL-TIME EMPLOYEES IN NON-PRIVATE UNITS OF THE CITY BY REGION AND SECTOR (2019)

单位：元 / 年 (yuan/year)

市、区名称	Region	合计 Total	国有单位 State-owned Units	集体单位 Collective-owned Units	其他所有制单位 Other Ownership Units
全市	**Whole Municipality**	**98604**	**138817**	**79002**	**86547**
市直	Municipal Government	114246			114246
市南区	Shinan District	99902	156804	72278	82290
市北区	Shibei District	106603	157527	48892	87063
李沧区	Licang District	96268	129631	47208	75291
崂山区	Laoshan District	131820	162826	94599	124287
西海岸新区	West Coast New Area	95475	138828	66989	87129
黄岛区	Huangdao District	92159	138175	66989	87455
保税港区	Qingdao Free Trade Port Area of China	86071	186808		84117
城阳区	Chengyang District	99483	145397	83187	90839
城阳区（不含高新区）	Chengyang District (Excluding High tech District)	99574	147598	83187	89724
高新区	High tech District	85767	107483		97606
即墨区	Jimo District	85065	122978	84569	67098
胶州市	Jiaozhou	98291	126357	107888	65854
平度市	Pingdu	86787	111334	61765	64027
莱西市	Laixi	81157	104228	115435	79516

主要统计指标解释

单位从业人员 指报告期末最后一日24时在本单位中工作，并取得工资或其他形式劳动报酬的人员数。该指标为时点指标，不包括最后一日当天及以前已经与单位解除劳动合同关系的人员，是在岗职工、劳务派遣人员及其他就业人员之和。就业人员不包括：

（1）离开本单位仍保留劳动关系，并定期领取生活费的人员；

（2）利用课余时间打工的学生及在本单位实习的各类在校学生；

（3）本单位因劳务外包而使用的人员。

在岗职工 指在本单位工作且与本单位签订劳动合同，并由单位支付各项工资和社会保险、住房公积金的人员，以及上述人员中由于学习、病伤、产假等原因暂未工作仍由单位支付工资的人员。在岗职工还包括：

（1）应订立劳动合同而未订立劳动合同人员（如使用的农村户籍人员）；

（2）处于试用期人员；

（3）编制外招用的人员；

（4）派往外单位工作，但工资仍由本单位发放的人员（如挂职锻炼、外派工作等情况）。

工资总额 指根据《关于工资总额组成的规定》（1990年1月1日国家统计局发布的一号令）进行修订，在报告期内（季度或年度）直接支付给本单位全部就业人员的劳动报酬总额。包括计时工资、计件工资、奖金、津贴和补贴、加班加点工资、特殊情况下支付的工资，是在岗职工工资总额、劳务派遣人员工资总额和其他就业人员工资总额之和。

工资总额是税前工资，包括单位从个人工资中直接为其代扣或代缴的房费、水费、电费、住房公积金和社会保险基金个人缴纳部分等。

工资总额不论是计入成本的还是不计入成本的，不论是以货币形式支付的还是以实物形式支付的，均应列入工资总额的计算范围。

平均工资 指单位就业人员在一定时期内平均每人所得的工资额。它表明一定时期工资收入的高低程度，是反映就业人员工资水平的主要指标。

Explanatory Notes on Main Statistical Indicators

Jobholders refers to the number of employees who works in the institution or company and gets salary or other form of labor reward at 24:00 of the last day of the report period. This is a time-point indicator which is the total of on-spot staff, labor dispatched personnel and other employees, excluding persons that have released the employment contract with the institution or company on the last day or before. The following are not deemed as Jobholders:

1. Persons that keep the employment relations and get regular living expenses after leaving the institution or company.
2. Various students who work part time or as internship.
3. Personnel that uses by the institution or company in labour outsourcing.

On-spot staff refers to the employees that works for and signs the employment contract with the institution or company, and relevant salary, social insurance and house funding are paid by the institution or company, and the persons of the previous employees that are not working but still gets salary from the institution or company due to the reason of learning, injury, maternity leave, etc. It also includes the following:

1. Employees who shall sign the employment contract with institution or company but not signed (for example, employees of rural household registration).

2. Employees that are still in probation period.

3. Employees that are recruited outside the authorized size.

4. Employees that are sent to other institution or company but the salaries are still paid by the institution or company (such as onsite training and labour dispatching).

Total salary refers to total payment for labour made directly to all jobholders of the institution or company within the report period (quarterly or annually) revised according to Regulations on Constitution of Total Salary, Order No. 1 released by National Bureau of Statistics on January 1, 1990, including hourly wage, piece wage, bonus, allowance and subsidy, overtime wage, and wages paid under special situations. It is also the total volume of on–spot staff, labour dispatching staff and other employment.

Total salary is the pre–tax salary, including the expenses of housing, water, power and the personal part of house funding and social insurance funds, which has been withheld and paid by the institution or company from personal salaries.

No matter it is credited into cost or not, no matter it is paid in currency or in kind, all total salary shall be categorized as total salary.

Average salary refers to the total salary per capita of employees of the institution or company within the certain period, which is the major indicator of the salary level of employees and the level of salary income of the certain salary.

固定资产投资 4

INVESTMENT IN FIXED ASSETS

简要说明

一、本篇资料的主要内容

本篇资料主要反映了全市固定资产投资及房地产开发方面的情况，主要包括固定资产投资的规模、结构、资金来源和房地产开发投资、施竣工及销售情况等方面的资料。

二、本篇资料的来源

本篇资料来源于固定资产投资及房地产开发投资统计年报，由市统计局固定资产投资统计处整理提供。

Brief Introduction

I. Main Content

Data in this chapter show the basic conditions of investment in fixed assets and real estate development of the whole city, mainly including the total investment in fixed assets, the structure of investment, the resources of investment and investment in real estate development, construction, completion and sales, etc.

II. Source of Data

Data in this chapter are based on the annual report on investment in fixed assets and real estate development, and provided by the Division of Investment and Construction Statistics of Qingdao Municipal Bureau of Statistics.

4-1 主要年份固定资产投资
MAJOR YEAR'S INVESTMENT IN FIXED ASSETS

单位：万元 (10 000 yuan)

年份 Year	规模以上固定资产投资总额 Investment in Fixed Assets above Designated Size	按用途分 Grouped by Use		
		生产性投资 Productive Investment	非生产性投资 Non-Productive Investment	#住宅投资 Investment in Residential Buildings
1949	16	12	4	3
1952	3097	1368	1729	1007
1957	5923	3947	1976	1151
1962	2747	2049	698	192
1965	5481	4155	1326	375
1970	6100	5813	287	154
1975	15839	13548	2381	1064
1978	29660	23499	6161	3203
1980	47499	33865	13634	9335
1985	107421	60643	73424	19058
1990	284576	210453	74123	38898
1991	349031	256633	92398	51898
1992	583068	420748	162320	83844
1993	953274	511684	441590	162419
1994	1329716	728532	601184	324094
1995	1648281	925194	723087	390206
1996	1610562	972398	638164	285412
1997	1611902	932207	679695	278951
1998	1909711	1125821	783890	316999
1999	2205891	1246328	959563	421151
2000	2426820	1311538	1115282	470963
2001	2934728	1487762	1446966	729181
2002	3683623	1962588	1721035	765030
2003	5475526	3023930	2451596	1038304
2004	9845646	6336279	3509367	1608738
2005	14032960	9172206	4860754	1841644
2006	14856894	9214578	5642316	2222733
2007	16353636	10231673	6121963	2720970
2008	20190098	12443179	7746919	3315538
2009	24588889	13852653	10736236	3831976
2010	30224785	16207885	14016900	5609189
2011	35025382	18622819	16402563	5707625
2012	41539146	24246803	17292343	6689114
2013	50278649	30996768	19281881	7220432
2014	57660308	32913906	24746402	7311090
2015	65556685	41402714	24153971	7569123
2016	74547006	44588200	29958806	9561782
2017	77770902	41719893	36051009	9255095

注：1. 规模以上固定资产投资数据 2003 年以前为城镇以上统计范围。
2. 因 2004 年以来数据有调整，故表中数据不可比。

Note： 1. The data of investment above designated size refer to investment above city and town level before 2003.
2. The data since 2004 are not comparable with other data because of the adjustment.

4-1 续表
Continued

单位：万元 (10 000 yuan)

年份 Year	按构成分 Grouped by Composition of Funds			按资金来源分 Grouped by Sources of Funds			
	建筑安装工程 Construction and Installation	设备工器具购置 Purchase of Equipment and Instruments	其他费用 Others	国家投资 State Investment	国内贷款 Domestic Loans	利用外资 Foreign Investment	自筹及其他 Self-raising Fund and Others
1949	11	3	2	16			
1952	2146	870	81	1512			1585
1957	2853	2773	297	3816			2107
1962	1631	984	132	2205			542
1965	3346	1859	276	4451			1030
1970	3136	2835	129	2721			3379
1975	7489	8133	217	9378	1362		5099
1978	19968	9124	568	16828	1601		11231
1980	30993	15541	965	10371	12925	1420	22783
1985	64665	35100	7656	17377	35888	1136	53020
1990	167731	91305	25540	24687	91895	23688	144306
1991	196212	108929	43890	22615	131676	38325	156415
1992	304060	208384	70624	22660	213217	89130	258061
1993	600011	225555	127708	23736	208672	94469	626397
1994	842809	272126	214781	26062	318334	221265	764055
1995	1020484	385934	241863	25683	379198	328124	915276
1996	929735	458284	222543	35639	444443	310722	819758
1997	875057	485122	251723	27928	297089	363789	923096
1998	1034500	574852	300359	67762	491812	170709	1179428
1999	1456473	459596	289822	128603	584120	145589	1347579
2000	1476397	652640	297783	75978	489697	164175	1806238
2001	1781235	744549	408944	93491	620562	217526	2157787
2002	2328492	796685	558446	78775	719677	411704	2831288
2003	3544790	1133333	797403	127861	989178	722644	4237643
2004	6413046	2312139	1120461	85549	1100297	1016145	8245272
2005	8949231	3141732	1941997	136632	1250343	1850921	11540604
2006	8818614	3668191	2370089	391315	2126523	1662897	11856506
2007	9981666	4171878	2200092	215649	2427031	1788056	13109824
2008	11795435	5907195	2487468	322484	3309471	1951468	15855082
2009	14911874	5869214	3807801	778090	4217265	1593287	21555685
2010	18725922	6362880	5135983	1305737	5881886	2135736	27898294
2011	22865421	7521441	4638520	1640702	5871709	1766278	33579182
2012	26080239	8601282	6857625	1324159	5484459	1561597	37356847
2013	33237368	9969777	7071504	1959340	8154829	1528585	49552883
2014	39006113	11640126	7014069	1404667	7452983	1181541	55024776
2015	42893643	15972153	6690889	2067396	7249574	1098178	62458544
2016	45915827	16425993	8789790	1788103	14203650	903773	66069945
2017	55647641	10977494	11145767	2257927	14569701	641216	65055089

4-2 主要年份固定资产投资构成（以投资总额为 100）

COMPOSITION OF MAJOR YEAR´S INVESTMENT IN FIXED ASSETS (TOTAL INVESTMENT=100)

年份 Year	按用途分 Grouped by Use		
	生产性投资 Productive Investment	非生产性投资 Non-Productive Investment	# 住宅投资占非生产性比重 Percentage of Investment in Residential Buildings to Non-Productive Investment
1949	75.00	25.00	75.00
1952	44.17	55.83	58.24
1957	66.64	33.36	58.25
1962	74.59	25.41	27.51
1965	75.81	24.19	28.28
1970	95.30	4.70	53.66
1975	84.97	15.03	44.69
1978	79.23	20.77	51.99
1980	71.30	28.70	68.47
1985	56.45	43.55	40.74
1990	73.95	26.05	52.50
1991	73.53	26.47	56.17
1992	72.16	27.84	51.65
1993	53.68	46.32	36.78
1994	54.79	45.21	53.91
1995	56.10	43.90	54.00
1996	60.40	39.60	44.70
1997	57.80	42.20	41.00
1998	59.00	41.00	16.60
1999	56.50	43.50	19.10
2000	54.00	46.00	19.40
2001	50.70	49.30	50.40
2002	53.30	46.70	44.50
2003	55.20	44.80	42.40
2004	64.40	35.60	45.80
2005	65.40	34.60	37.90
2006	62.00	38.00	39.40
2007	62.60	37.40	44.40
2008	61.60	38.40	42.80
2009	56.30	43.70	35.70
2010	53.62	46.38	40.02
2011	53.17	46.83	34.80
2012	58.37	41.63	38.68
2013	61.65	38.35	37.45
2014	57.08	42.92	29.54
2015	63.16	36.84	31.34
2016	59.81	40.19	31.92
2017	53.64	46.36	25.67

4-2 续表
Continued

年份 Year	按构成分 Grouped by Composition of Funds			按资金来源分 Grouped by Sources of Funds			
	建筑安装工程 Construction and Installation	设备工器具购置 Purchase of Equipment and Instruments	其他费用 Others	国家投资 State Investment	国内贷款 Domestic Loans	利用外资 Foreign Investment	自筹及其他 Self-raising Fund and Others
1949	68.75	18.75	12.5	100			
1952	69.29	28.09	2.62	48.82			51.18
1957	48.17	46.82	5.01	64.43			35.57
1962	59.37	35.82	4.81	80.27			19.73
1965	61.05	33.92	5.03	81.21			18.79
1970	51.41	46.48	2.11	44.61			55.39
1975	47.28	51.35	1.37	59.21	8.60		32.19
1978	67.32	30.76	1.92	56.74	5.40		37.86
1980	65.25	32.72	2.03	21.83	27.21	2.99	47.97
1985	60.2	32.68	7.12	16.18	33.41	1.06	49.35
1990	58.94	32.08	8.98	8.68	32.29	8.32	50.71
1991	56.22	31.21	12.57	6.48	37.73	10.98	44.81
1992	52.15	35.74	12.11	3.89	36.56	15.29	44.26
1993	62.94	23.66	13.4	2.49	21.89	9.91	65.71
1994	63.38	20.46	16.16	1.96	23.94	16.64	57.46
1995	61.9	23.4	14.7	1.6	23.0	19.9	55.5
1996	57.7	28.5	13.8	2.2	27.6	19.3	50.9
1997	54.3	30.1	15.6	1.7	18.4	22.6	57.3
1998	54.2	20.8	15.7	3.5	25.8	8.9	61.8
1999	66.0	20.8	13.2	5.8	26.5	6.6	61.1
2000	60.8	26.9	12.3	3.1	20.2	6.8	74.4
2001	60.7	25.4	13.9	3.0	20.1	7.0	69.9
2002	63.2	21.6	15.2	1.9	17.8	10.2	70.1
2003	64.7	20.7	14.6	2.1	16.3	11.9	69.7
2004	65.1	23.5	11.4	0.8	10.6	9.7	78.9
2005	63.8	22.4	13.8	0.9	8.5	12.5	78.1
2006	59.4	24.7	15.9	2.4	13.3	10.4	73.9
2007	61.0	25.5	13.5	1.2	13.8	10.2	74.8
2008	58.4	29.3	12.3	1.5	15.4	9.1	74.0
2009	60.6	23.9	15.5	2.8	15.0	5.6	76.6
2010	62.0	21.0	17.0	3.5	15.8	5.7	75.0
2011	65.3	21.5	13.3	3.8	13.7	4.1	78.4
2012	62.8	20.7	16.5	2.9	12.0	3.4	81.7
2013	66.1	19.8	14.1	3.2	13.3	2.5	81.0
2014	67.6	20.2	12.2	2.2	11.5	1.8	84.6
2015	65.4	24.4	10.2	2.8	10.0	1.5	85.7
2016	61.6	22.0	11.8	2.2	17.1	1.1	79.6
2017	71.6	14.1	14.3	2.7	17.7	0.8	78.8
2018	68.8	7.8	23.4	2.9	15.2	0.4	81.5
2019	65.3	7.0	27.7	1.8	16.2	1.3	80.7

4-3 按三次产业分规模以上固定资产投资增速（2019年）

GROWTH RATE OF INVESTMENT IN FIXED ASSETS ABOVE DESIGNATED SIZE BY THREE STRATA OF INDUSTRY(2019)

单位：%

指标	Indicator	2019年
总　计	**Total**	**21.6**
第一产业	Primary Industry	3.5
第二产业	Secondary Industry	18.2
#工业	Industry	20.2
第三产业	Tertiary Industry	22.7

4-4 分市、区规模以上固定资产投资增速（2019年）

GROWTH RATE OF FIXED ASSET INVESTMENT ABOVE DESIGNATED SIZE BY CITY AND DISTRICT (2019)

单位：%

市、区名称	Region	规模以上固定资产投资增速 Growth Rate Of Investment In Fixed Assets Above Designated Size	#房地产开发投资增速 Real Estate Development Investment Growth Rate
		21.6	**21.5**
市南区	Shinan District	15.2	69.9
市北区	Shibei District	15.4	11.3
李沧区	Licang District	26.8	1.4
崂山区	Laoshan District	26.6	6.6
西海岸新区	West Coast New Area	32.1	51.2
黄岛区	Huangdao District	32.2	51.2
保税港区	Qingdao Free Trade Port Area of China	23.8	–
城阳区	Chengyang District	25.3	-1.3
城阳区（不含高新区）	Chengyang District (Excluding High tech District)	35.5	-1.6
高新区	High tech District	10.1	-0.4
即墨区	Jimo District	23.1	38.1
胶州市	Jiaozhou	25.8	53.6
平度市	Pingdu	16.1	9.9
莱西市	Laixi	31.3	15.4

4-5 规模以上固定资产投资（2019 年）
INVESTMENT IN FIXED ASSETS ABOVE DESIGNATED SIZE (2019)

单位：%

项目	Item	合计 Total	# 房地产开发 Investment in Real Estate Development
一、本年施工项目（个）	**Projects Under Construction This Year (unit)**	**5649**	**1436**
# 本年新开工（个）	of which： Newly Started (unit)	3101	311
二、本年建成投产项目（个）	**Projects Completed and Put into Use This Year (unit)**	**1582**	
三、本年完成投资增速（%）	**Complete Investment Growth Rate This Year （%）**	**21.6**	**21.5**
1. 按构成分	**Grouped by Composition**		
# 建筑安装工程	Construction installation project	15.4	15.9
设备工器具购置	Purchase of Equipment and Instruments	9.1	-9.9
2. 按建设性质分	Grouped by Type of Construction		
# 新建	New Construction	12.1	
扩建	Expansion	84.4	
改建和技术改造	Reconstruction	54	
3. 按国民经济行业分	Grouped by Economic Sector		
（1）农、林、牧、渔业	Farming, Forestry, Animal Husbandry and Fishery	9.7	
农业	Farming	-19.6	
林业	Forestry	113.3	
畜牧业	Animal Husbandry	4.7	
渔业	Fishery	113.8	
农、林、牧、渔服务业	Farming, Forestry, Animal Husbandry and Fishery Services	69.3	
（2）采矿业	Mining	-53.2	
煤炭开采和洗选业	Mining and Washing of Coal		
石油和天然气开采业	Extraction of Petroleum and Natural Gas	-37.3	
黑色金属矿采选业	Mining of Ferrous Metal Ores		
有色金属矿采选业	Mining of Non-ferrous Metal Ores	-72.3	
非金属矿采选业	Mining and Processing of Nonmetal Ores		
开采辅助活动	Auxiliary Activities of Mining		
其他采矿业	Mining of Other Ores		

4-5 续表 1
Continued

单位：%

项目	Item	合计 Total	#房地产开发 Investment in Real Estate Development
（3）制造业	Manufacturing	16.6	
农副食品加工业	Processing of Food from Agricultural Products	19.1	
食品制造业	Manufacture of Foods	47.7	
酒、饮料和精制茶制造业	Manufacture of Liquor, Beverage and Refined Tea	-63.6	
烟草制品业	Manufacture of Tobacco		
纺织业	Manufacture of Textile	-30.3	
纺织服装、服饰业	Manufacture of Textile Wearing Apparel	-26.8	
皮革、毛皮、羽毛及其制品和制鞋业	Manufacture of Leather, Fur, Feather & Its Products Footwear	-66.7	
木材加工和木、竹、藤、棕、草制品业	Processing of Timbers, Manufacture of Wood, Bamboo, Rattan, Palm and Straw Products	-73.7	
家具制造业	Manufacture of Furniture	-77.3	
造纸和纸制品业	Manufacture of Paper and Paper Products	124.1	
印刷和记录媒介复制业	Printing, Reproduction of Recording Media	296.4	
文教、工美、体育和娱乐用品制造业	Manufacture of Articles for Culture, Arts & Crafts, Sports and Entertainment	37.3	
石油加工、炼焦和核燃料加工业	Processing of Petroleum, Coking, Processing of Nucleus Fuel	4601.0	
化学原料和化学制品制造业	Manufacture of Chemical Raw Material and Chemical Products	70.9	
医药制造业	Manufacture of Medicines	135.6	
化学纤维制造业	Manufacture of Chemical Fiber	304.2	
橡胶和塑料制品业	Manufacture of Rubber and Plastic	-0.8	
非金属矿物制品业	Manufacture of Non-metallic Mineral Products	15.6	
黑色金属冶炼和压延加工业	Smelting and Pressing of Ferrous Metals	266.0	
有色金属冶炼和压延加工业	Smelting and Pressing of Non-ferrous Metals	3282.0	
金属制品业	Manufacture of Metal Products	51.8	
通用设备制造业	Manufacture of General Purpose Machinery	12.3	
专用设备制造业	Manufacture of Special Purpose Machinery	15.4	
汽车制造业	Manufacture of Vehicle	-31.2	
铁路、船舶、航空航天和其他运输设备制造业	Manufacture of Transport Equipment for Railway, Shipping, Aerospace and other uses	57.0	
电气机械和器材制造业	Manufacture of Electrical Machinery & Equipment	23.9	
计算机、通信和其他电子设备制造业	Manufacture of Computer, Communication Equipment and Other Electronic Equipment	39.8	
仪器仪表制造业	Manufacture of Measuring Instrument	173.7	
其他制造业	Manufacture of Other Products	61.8	
废弃资源综合利用业	Recycling and Disposal of Waste Resources	137.0	
金属制品、机械和设备修理业	Maintenance of Metal Products, Machinery and Equipment	-97.5	

4-5 续表 2
Continued

单位：%

项目	Item	合计 Total	# 房地产开发 Investment in Real Estate Development
(4) 电力、燃气及水的生产和供应业	Electricity, Gas and Water Production and Supply Industry	80.2	
电力、热力的生产和供应业	Electricity and Heat Production and Supply Industry	103.0	
燃气生产和供应业	Gas Production and Supply Industry	244.2	
水的生产和供应业	Water Production and Supply Industry	14.4	
(5) 建筑业	Construction	-86.1	
(6) 交通运输、仓储及邮政业	Transport Storage and Post	15.2	
铁路运输业	Railway Transport	-36.4	
道路运输业	Road Transport	26.0	
水上运输业	Water Transport	-44.8	
航空运输业	Air Transport	97.5	
管道运输业	Pipeline Transport	-12.9	
装卸搬运和运输代理业	Handing, Carrying and Transportation Agent	-49.5	
仓储业	Ware houses and Storage	35.5	
邮政业	Post		
(7) 信息传输、软件和信息技术服务业	Information Transmission, Software and Information Technology Service Industry	46.6	
(8) 批发和零售业	Wholesale and Retail Trade	-38.9	
(9) 住宿和餐饮业	Hotels and Catering Services	61.0	
(10) 金融业	Financial Industry	96.4	
(11) 房地产业	Real Estate Industry	33.3	21.5

4-5 续表 3
Continued

单位：%

项目	Item	合计 Total	#房地产开发 Investment in Real Estate Development
(12) 租赁和商务服务业	Leasing and Business Services	-4.4	
(13) 科学研究和技术服务业	Scientific Research, Technical Service and Geologic Prospecting	137.7	
(14) 水利、环境和公共设施管理业	Management of Water Conservancy, Environment and Pubic Facilities	-19.4	
水利管理业	Management of Water Conservancy	-25.4	
环境管理业	Environmental Management	157.3	
公共设施管理业	Management of Public Facilities	-22.4	
(15) 居民服务和其他服务业	Services to Households and Other Services	127.9	
居民服务业	Services to Households	673.6	
机动车、电子产品和日用产品修理业	Maintenance of Vehicle, Electronic Products and Daily Articles	70.3	
其他服务业	Other Services	-100.0	
(16) 教育	Education	57.3	
(17) 卫生和社会工作	Health and Social Work	47.4	
卫生	Health	53.0	
(18) 文化、体育和娱乐业	Culture, Sports and Entertainment	87.2	
新闻出版业	Journalism and Publishing Activities	-99.4	
广播、电视、体育和音像业	Broadcasting, Movies, Televisions and Audiovisual Activities	185.2	
文化艺术业	Cultural and Art Activities	107.6	
体育	Sports Activities	543.9	
娱乐业	Entertainment	1.9	
(19) 公共管理、社会保障和社会组织	Public Management, Social Security and Social Organization	-62.5	
中国共产党机关	Communist Party of China	1764.4	
国家机构	Government Agencies	-64.2	
人民政协、民主党派	People' s Political Consultative Conference, Democratic Party	-100.0	
社会保障	Social Security		
群众团体、社会团体和其他成员组织	Non-Governmental Institutions, Social Organizations and Other Organizations	99.7	
基层群众自治组织	Local People Self-government Organization	-65.3	
(20) 国际组织	International Organization		

4-5 续表 4
Continued

单位：%

项目	Item	合计 Total	#房地产开发 Investment in Real Estate Development
四、本年资金来源合计	**Total Funds This Year**	**17.7**	**21**
上年末结余资金	Balance of Last Year	17	15.8
本年资金来源小计	Sub-total Funds This Year	17.8	22.9
国家预算内资金	State Budget	-28.4	
国内贷款	Domestic Loans	25	58.1
债券	State Treasury Bond		
利用外资	Foreign Investment	313.8	10419.1
自筹资金	Self-raising Funds	16.3	52.8
其他资金来源	Others	17.2	0.4

4-6 主要年份房地产开发投资
MAJOR YEAR´S INVESTMENT IN REAL ESTATE DEVELOPMENT

单位：万元、万平方米 (10 000 yuan, 10 000 sq.m)

年份 Year	房地产开发投资额 Investment in Real Estate Development	房屋施工面积 Floor Space Under Construction	房屋竣工面积 Floor Space Completed	房屋实际销售面积 Floor Space of Buildings Sold	房屋实际销售额 Sale of Buildings
1995	562861	1008	240	103	185384
1996	455765	748	203	80	125150
1997	426570	675	237	113	216311
1998	438059	742	259	178	351805
1999	629717	900	474	240	430123
2000	675142	1047	352	301	550401
2001	925153	1374	532	406	802364
2002	1036476	1417	537	427	933031
2003	1277969	1765	552	469	1121885
2004	1626965	2101	635	516	1530964
2005	2238370	2363	811	740	2666 738
2006	2683631	2751	654	719	3054907
2007	3223547	3224	641	833	4333566
2008	3805652	3773	672	770	3924175
2009	4594829	4310	814	1262	7036744
2010	6024387	5058	1020	1360	8952942
2011	7827193	5693	925	1026	7702379
2012	9301099	6474	1212	951	7660684
2013	10485229	7073	957	1160	9786176
2014	11177297	8171	1136	1164	9708984
2015	11223458	8971	1523	1419	12628568
2016	13691425	9101	1426	1939	17899532
2017	13305432	9533	1487	1901	19992012
2018	14852089	10390	1625	1808	22824618
2019	18038081	11580	1602	1652	22469992

4-7 房地产开发投资情况（2019 年）
INVESTMENT IN REAL ESTATE DEVELOPMENT（2019）

单位：万元（10 000 yuan）

指标名称	Indicator	合计 Total	按经济类型分 Grouped by Economic Types 国有经济 State-owned	集体经济 Collective-owned	其他经济 Others
本年完成投资额	**Investment Completed This Year**	**18038081**	**1490209**	**178353**	**16369519**
1. 住宅	Residential Buildings	12390688	935076	105725	11349887
2. 办公楼	Office Buildings	1275940	139133	9175	1127632
3. 商业营业用房	Houses for Business Use	1785846	155952	2939	1626955
4. 其他	Others	2585607	260048	60514	2265045

4-7 续表
Continued

单位：万元（10 000 yuan）

指标名称	Indicator	按资质等级分 Grouped by Qualification Criteria 一级 First Grade	二级 Second Grade	三级 Third Grade	四级 Fourth Grade	暂定 Provisional	其他 Others
本年完成投资额	**Investment Completed This Year**	**458497**	**383239**	**668840**	**142566**	**13303304**	**3081635**
1. 住宅	Residential Buildings	329082	302287	514646	74763	8961566	2208344
2. 办公楼	Office Buildings	34830	1362	51857	2316	1025668	159907
3. 商业营业用房	Houses for Business Use	72247	35964	66582	60436	1343912	206705
4. 其他	Others	22338	43626	35755	5051	1972158	506679

4-8 房地产施工、竣工面积及竣工价值（2019 年）
FLOOR SPACE UNDER CONSTRUCTION AND COMPLETED AND COMPLETED VALUE OF REAL ESTATE (2019)

单位：万平方米 (10 000 sq.m)

施工、竣工房屋面积及竣工价值	Indicator	施工面积 Floor Space Under Construction	#新开工 Newly Started	竣工房屋 Floor Space Completed	竣工房屋价值（万元） Completed Value（10 000 yuan）
房屋建筑面积总计	**Floor Space of Buildings**	**11580**	**3473**	**1602**	**5214667**
住宅	Residential Buildings	7588	2278	1063	3513880
办公楼	Office Buildings	837	276	136	520829
商业营业用房	Houses for Business Use	1021	251	149	470594
其他	Others	2134	668	254	709364

4-9 商品房屋销售情况（2019 年）
BASIC STATISTICS ON SALES OF COMMERCIALIZED BUILDINGS (2019)

单位：万平方米 (10 000 sq.m)

商品房屋销售情况	Sales and Rental of Commercialized Buildings	实际销售 Actual Sales	实际销售额（万元） Actual Sales Volume (10 000 yuan)	待售面积 Area for Sale
房屋面积总计	**Floor Space of Buildings**	**1652**	**22469992**	**459**
住宅	Residential Buildings	1476	20177235	164
办公楼	Office Buildings	71	939998	91
商业营业用房	Houses for Business Use	88	1228402	166
其他	Others	17	124357	38

主要统计指标解释

固定资产投资 是以货币形式表现的在一定时期内建造和购置固定资产的工作量以及与此有关的费用的总称。

房地产开发投资 指各种登记注册类型的房地产开发法人单位统一开发的住宅、厂房、仓库、饭店、宾馆、度假村、写字楼、办公楼等房屋建筑物，配套的服务设施，土地开发工程（如道路、给水、排水、供电、供热、通讯、平整场地等基础设施工程）和土地购置的投资；不包括单纯的土地开发和交易活动。

固定资产投资的资金来源 根据固定资产投资的资金来源不同，分为国家预算资金、国内贷款、利用外资、自筹资金和其他资金。

固定资产投资 按建设性质分建设项目的性质一般分为新建、扩建、改建和技术改造、单纯建造生活设施、迁建、恢复、单纯购置。

固定资产投资 按构成分固定资产投资活动按其工作内容和实现方式分为建筑安装工程，设备、工具、器具购置，其他费用三个部分。

新增生产能力（或工程效益） 指建成投产项目或工程新增生产能力（或工程效益）的名称。

房屋施工面积 是指报告期内施工的全部房屋建筑面积。包括本期新开工的面积和上期开工跨入本期继续施工的房屋面积，以及上期已停缓建在本期恢复施工的房屋面积。本期竣工和本期施工后又停缓建的房屋，其建筑面积仍计入本期房屋施工面积中。

房屋竣工面积 是指在报告期内房屋建筑按照设计要求全部完工，达到住人和使用条件，经验收鉴定合格（或达到竣工验收标准），正式移交使用单位的各栋房屋建筑面积的总和。

本年新增固定资产 指在报告期已经完成建造和购置过程，并已交付生产或使用单位的固定资产的价值，包括已经建成投入生产或交付使用的工程投资和达到固定资产标准的设备、工具、器具的投资及有关应摊入的费用。

Explanatory Notes on Main Statistical Indicators

Fixed investment is a generic term of quantity of work from building and acquiring of fixed assets over a period of time and any relevant expenses incurred thereby in the form of currency.

Real estate development investment means investments in all kinds of registered housing & building, including residences, plants, warehouses, restaurants, hotels, resorts, office buildings and administrative buildings which are developed uniformly by real estate development corporation, supporting service facilities and land development projects (such as road, water supply & drainage, power supply, heat supply, telecommunication and ground leveling and other infrastructure projects) and land acquisition, excludes simple land development and transaction activities.

Source of funds for fixed-asset investment can be divided into national budget funds, domestic loans, utilization of foreign capital, self-raised funds and other funds in accordance with the different sources.

Construction items of fixed–asset investment can be divided into new construction, extension, reconstruction, technical reform, simply–constructed living facilities, relocation, restoration and simple acquisition by property of construction.

Fixed–asset investment activities can be divided into three parts, namely construction and installation project, acquisition of equipement, tools and appliances and other expenses by working content and method of achieving.

New productive capacity (or project benefit) means the completed projects or new productive capacity (or projevt benefit) of project.

Construction area means total areas of all buildings which are under construction in the report period, including the area which is newly constructed in this period and the areas of buildings which commence in the last period and carry forward to this period for continuing construction. and the areas of buildings which stop constructing in the last period and resume to be constructed in this period. The areas of the buildings which are completed in this period and stop constructing after this period' s construction are still reckoned in floor space under construction in this period.

Completed ares means the sum total of areas of housings & buildings which are completed according to design requirements in the report period, reach conditions of living and using and are transferred to building users formally after checked and accepted (or reach the standards of completion and acceptance) .

New fixed assets in this year means the value of fixed assets which are completed and acquired in the report period and delivered for production or use, including investment in constructions which are put into production or service, investment in equipment, tools and appliances which reach the standards of fixed asset, and the expenses which should be added into fixed assets.

对外经济贸易 5

FOREIGN TRADE

简 要 说 明

一、本篇资料的主要内容

本篇资料主要反映了全市外经外贸和外资企业的基本情况，主要包括外贸进出口、利用外资、对外投资与经济合作等方面的资料。

二、本篇资料的来源

1. 口岸进出口数据来源于青岛市海关。

2. 进出口、利用外资等资料、对外投资与经济合作来源于市商务局。

本篇资料由市统计局外经贸易统计处整理提供。

Brief Introduction

I. Main Content

Data in this chapter show the basic conditions of foreign trade and foreign-funded enterprises, mainly including imports and exports, utilization of foreign capitals, production and operation condition of foreign-funded enterprises, etc.

II. Source of Data

1. Data on imports and exports of Qingdao port are provided by Office of Qingdao Port Administration.

2. Data on imports & exports and utilization of foreign capitals are provided by Qingdao Municipal Commerce Bureau.

Data in this chapter are prepared and compiled by the Division of Trade and External Economic Relations Statistics of Qingdao Municipal Bureau of Statistics.

5-1 青岛口岸进出口总额(1985-2019年)

TOTAL VALUE OF IMPORTS AND EXPORTS OF QINGDAO PORT (1985-2019)

单位：万美元(10 000 USD)、万元(10 000 yuan)

年份 Year	青岛口岸进出口总额 Total Value of Imports and Exports Qingdao Port	出口 Exports	进口 Imports
1985	414448	234652	179796
1986	382840	191926	190914
1987	445090	259458	185632
1988	474516	259176	215340
1989	506152	268397	237755
1990	477117	304011	173106
1991	519273	332949	186324
1992	581495	350163	231332
1993	678013	360297	317716
1994	888574	510760	377814
1995	1307508	705245	602263
1996	1391323	760566	629757
1997	1542284	936142	609142
1998	1463718	933392	530326
1999	1696514	1063768	632746
2000	2520420	1423266	1097154
2001	2797085	1636888	1160197
2002	3128048	1889612	1238436
2003	4088096	2366046	1722050
2004	5677570	3197697	2479873
2005	6932944	3959947	2972997
2006	8019198	4495731	3523467
2007	9257099	5263539	3993560
2008	11558079	5953501	5604578
2009	9049699	4694832	4354867
2010	11912702	5988254	5924448
2011	15095088	7294226	7800862
2012	14888716	7120813	7767903
2013	15662732	7696141	7966591
2014	16489966	8736358	7753608
2015	14448349	8776286	5672063
2016	94927180	56513317	38413863
2017	111024375	63298062	47726314
2018	121968146	67385279	54582867
2019	127239314	69443761	57795553

注：2016年起，统计单位为人民币万元。
Note : Statistic unit is RMB ten thousand Yuan as from 2016.

5-2 进出口总额（1988-2019年）
TOTAL VALUE OF IMPORTS AND EXPORTS (1988-2019)

单位：万美元 (10 000 USD)、万元 (10 000 yuan)

年份 Year	进出口总额（含中央、省驻青公司） Total Value of Imports and Exports (including central and provincial companies)	出口 Exports	进口 Imports	进出口总额（不含中央、省驻青公司） Total Value of Imports and Exports (including central and provincial companies)	出口 Exports	进口 Imports
1988				28097	21731	6366
1989				39327	27797	11530
1990				41649	33529	8120
1991				54624	44746	9878
1992				88600	66291	22309
1993	517643	346288	171355	139048	100201	38847
1994	633213	434102	199111	234978	164135	70843
1995	858560	536386	322174	376372	245072	131300
1996	863521	516317	347204	461950	287123	174827
1997	916269	579261	377008	521967	338535	183432
1998	882042	573020	309022	595826	382657	213169
1999	1009885	631072	378813	775565	446260	329305
2000	1353222	826891	526331	1083133	611426	471707
2001	1541564	950160	591404	1235781	712024	523757
2002	1692567	1057141	635426	1409598	850420	559178
2003	2065912	1239199	826713	1784556	1035528	749028
2004	2698781	1578167	1120614	2433188	1391171	1042017
2005	3302230	1942242	1359988	3045542	1758834	1286708
2006	3911543	2346552	1564991	3655737	2164541	1491196
2007	4572534	2831004	1741530	4360499	2677596	1682903
2008	5363659	3262476	2101183	5215886	3146246	2069640
2009	4485115	2729865	1755250	4398639	2692197	1706442
2010	5705963	3391560	2314403	5614928	3335141	2279787
2011	7215217	4061309	3153908	7126310	4005572	3120738
2012				7320781	4081968	3238813
2013				7791217	4198605	3592612
2014				7988833	4577696	3411137
2015				7022243	4535015	2487228
2016				43506659	28219059	15287600
2017				50334973	30318103	20016870
2018				53212551	31722209	21490342
2019				59255880	34119000	25136880

注：1. 2012年起，中央、省驻青公司外贸统计划归青岛，取消含中央、省驻青公司统计口径；
2. 2016年起，统计单位为人民币万元。

Note：1. Since 2012, the statistical calibre including central and provincial companies has been cancelled.
2. Statistic unit is RMB ten thousand Yuan as from 2016.

5-3 分国别外贸出口总额

TOTAL VALUE OF EXPORTS BY COUNTRIES OR REGIONS

单位：万美元 (10 000 USD)

国别（地区）	Country (Region)	2019 年	2019 年比 2018 年 ±% 2019/2018（±%）	占比 %
亚洲	Asia	2311053	10.7	46.8
香港	Hong Kong	146185	-23.8	3.0
日本	Japan	579647	2.9	11.7
韩国	Korea	432683	-2.6	8.8
东盟	ASEAN	624240	34.2	12.6
非洲	Africa	221785	14.9	4.5
南非	South Africa	45308	0.2	0.9
欧洲	Europe	1052299	3.2	21.3
欧盟	EU	892359	1.2	18.1
南美洲	South America	327150	3.1	6.6
北美洲	North America	889947	-15.0	18.0
美国	USA	788683	-15.2	16.0
大洋洲	Oceania	138399	1.9	2.8
澳大利亚	Australia	113291	-0.1	2.3

5-4 外贸出口商品分类
EXPORT COMMODITIES BY CATEGORY

单位：万元 (10 000 yuan)

项目	Item	2019 年	2019 年比 2018 ± % 2019/2018 (± %)	占比 %
合计	**Total**	**34119000**	**7.4**	**100.0**
按企业性质划分	By Enterprises Nature			
国有企业	State-owned Enterprises	2989178	7.0	8.8
外商投资企业	Foreign Funded Enterprises	9307581	-8.0	27.3
其他企业	Other Enterprises	21822241	15.7	63.9
# 集体企业	#Collective-owned Enterprises	865611	-3.5	2.5
私营企业	Private Enterprises	20904922	16.5	61.2
按贸易方式划分	By Customs Regime			
一般贸易	Ordinary Trade	24169954	9.9	70.8
加工贸易	Processing Trade	8605845	-3.6	25.3
其他贸易	Others	1343201	59.6	3.9
按大类商品划分	By Category of Commodities			
纺织服装	Textile Garments	4771872	-1.0	14.0
农产品	Agricultural Products	4074444	5.2	11.9
机电产品	Mechanical and Electrical Products	14449354	6.7	42.4
高新技术产品	High-tech Products	2790725	-11.7	8.2

5-5 外贸进口商品分类
IMPORT COMMODITIES BY CATEGORY

单位：万元（10 000 yuan）

项目	Item	2019 年	2019 年比 2018 ± % 2019/2018 (± %)	占比 %
合计	**Total**	**25136880**	**16.9**	**100.0**
按企业性质划分	By Enterprises Nature			
国有企业	State-owned Enterprises	4857038	-2.2	19.3
外商投资企业	Foreign Funded Enterprises	6535127	5.4	26.0
其他企业	Other Enterprises	13744715	33.0	54.7
# 集体企业	#Collective-owned Enterprises	60980	-71.7	0.2
私营企业	Private Enterprises	13500171	34.4	53.7
按贸易方式划分	By Customs Regime			
一般贸易	Ordinary Trade	13171318	16.6	52.4
加工贸易	Processing Trade	3079140	-4.0	12.2
其他贸易	Others	8886422	26.9	35.4
按大类商品划分	By Category of Commodities			
纺织服装	Textile Garments	249993	-14.4	1.0
农产品	Agricultural Products	5241895	27.7	20.9
机电产品	Mechanical and Electrical Products	4707130	8.3	18.7
高新技术产品	High-tech Products	2423683	15.9	9.6

5-6 二十大出口商品出口情况
INFORMATION ON THE EXPORTATION OF TOP 20 PRODUCTS

单位：万美元 (10 000 USD)

商品名称	Name	2019 年	2019 年比 2018 年 ± % 2019/2018 (± %)	占比 %
合计	**Total**	**4003502**	**−4.2**	**100.0**
机械设备	Machinery and Equipment	748006	13.0	18.7
电器及电子类产品	Electric Appliance and Electronic Products	498558	−12.9	12.5
服装	Garments	439316	−5.3	11.0
计算机与通信技术	Computer and Communication Technology	272964	−27.6	6.8
运输工具	Transport Tools	418507	−3.8	10.5
纺织品	Textile Products	252933	−5.0	6.3
金属制品	Metal Products	269441	11.8	6.7
轮胎	Tyre	167206	7.1	4.2
电话机	Telephone Sets	83394	−48.2	2.1
水海产品	Aquatic and Seawater Products	137707	4.6	3.4
蔬菜	Vegetables	106525	−11.8	2.7
家具及其零件	Furniture	107535	3.7	2.7
钢材	Rolled Steel	129488	−4.0	3.2
鞋类	Shoes	100019	2.3	2.5
塑料制品	Plastic Articles	97686	17.6	2.4
箱包	Luggage and Bags	62676	3.6	1.6
汽车零件	Parts of Motor Vehicles	73127	0.5	1.8
空调	Air Conditioner	38008	−6.7	0.9
游戏机	Game Console	362	1102.4	
铁合金	Ferroalloy	42	−41.1	

5-7 二十大进口商品进口情况
INFORMATION ON THE IMPORTATION OF TOP 20 PRODUCTS

单位：万美元 (10 000 USD)

商品名称	Name	2019 年	2019 年比 2018 年 ± % 2019/2018 (± %)	占比 %
合计	**Total**	**1995726**	**4.8**	**100.0**
铁矿砂	Machinery and Equipment	364064	13.0	18.2
电器及电子产品	Electric Appliance and Electronic Products	248769	3.3	12.5
机械设备	Machinery and Equipment	216428	9.0	10.8
粮食	Grain	144273	5.1	7.2
合成橡胶	Synthetic Rubber	118476	5.0	5.9
天然橡胶	Natural Rubber	93100	16.9	4.7
仪器仪表	Instruments and Meters	137320	0.8	6.9
集成电路	Integrated Circuits	110844	8.6	5.6
塑料原料	Plastic Raw Materials	112023	-8.1	5.6
冻鱼	Frozen Fish	114165	3.0	5.7
液晶显示板	Liquid Crystal Display	42379	-31.4	2.1
棉花	Cotton	68885	-14.9	3.5
纺织品	Textile Products	34230	-16.2	1.7
运输工具	Means of Conveyance	48778	-7.6	2.4
钢材	Rolled Steel	39246	-4.4	2.0
塑料制品	Plastic Articles	9276	-12.8	0.5
铝锭及铝材	Aluminum Ingots and Aluminum Products	4233	-50.9	0.2
成品油	Refined Petroleum Products	81663	118.1	4.1
氧化铝	Alumina	3796	31.8	0.2
钻石	Diamonds	3777	-4.6	0.2

5-8 利用外资情况（2000-2019 年）
UTILIZATION OF FOREIGN CAPITAL（2000-2019）

项目	Item	单位	Unit	2000 年	2005 年
批准企业（项目）个数	**Number of Enterprises (Projects) Approved**	**个**	**unit**	**1132**	**2530**
一、外商直接投资	Foreign Direct Investments	个	unit	1128	2530
中外合资企业	Sino-foreign Joint Ventures	个	unit	303	274
中外合作企业	Sino-foreign Cooperative Enterprises	个	unit	57	18
外商独资企业	Foreign-owned Enterprises	个	unit	76	2236
外商投资股份制	Foreign-invested joint-stock system	个	unit	1	2
合伙企业	Partnership	个	unit		
二、外商其他投资	Other Foreign Investments	个	unit	4	
合同外资金额	**Total Amount of Contracted Foreign Investment**	**万美元**	**10000 USD**	**269081**	**954486**
一、外商直接投资	Foreign Direct Investments	万美元	10000 USD	266221	954486
中外合资企业	Sino-foreign Joint Ventures	万美元	10000 USD	69889	112777
中外合作企业	Sino-foreign Cooperative Enterprises	万美元	10000 USD	26835	17588
外商独资企业	Foreign-owned Enterprises	万美元	10000 USD	169370	813485
外商投资股份制	Foreign-invested joint-stock system	万美元	10000 USD	127	10636
合伙企业	Partnership	万美元	10000 USD		
二、外商其他投资	Other Foreign Investments	万美元	10000 USD	2860	
实际利用外资金额	**Total Amount of Foreign Investment Actually Utilized**	**万美元**	**10000 USD**	**128171**	**365625**
一、外商直接投资	Foreign Direct Investments	万美元	10000 USD	126132	365625
中外合资企业	Sino-foreign Joint Ventures	万美元	10000 USD	39224	77636
中外合作企业	Sino-foreign Cooperative Enterprises	万美元	10000 USD	3886	5654
外商独资企业	Foreign-owned Enterprises	万美元	10000 USD	82992	280130
外商投资股份制	Foreign-invested joint-stock system	万美元	10000 USD	30	2205
合伙企业	Partnership	万美元	10000 USD		
二、外商其他投资	Other Foreign Investments	万美元	10000 USD	2039	

单位：万美元 (10 000 USD)

2008 年	2009 年	2010 年	2011 年	2012 年	2013 年	2014 年	2015 年	2016 年	2017 年	2018 年	2019 年
640	**647**	**731**	**707**	**553**	**645**	**619**	**763**	**680**	**650**	**956**	**954**
640	647	731	707	553	645	619	763	680	650	956	954
99	99	153	158	113	165	140	162	154	188	294	358
4	2	4	4	2	2	1	2		1	8	1
537	545	574	544	438	478	475	597	523	457	653	586
	1		1			3	2	3	4	1	2
											7
304505	**271504**	**475723**	**528501**	**600231**	**758063**	**638637**	**827357**	**769101**	**909629**	**980231**	**1335551**
304505	271504	475723	528501	600231	758063	638637	827357	769101	909629	980231	1335551
81796	61734	124148	142535	102252	191172	126878	116013	207933	246280	195336	415708
367	4531	9179	15173	122	4765	-849	1731	28	327	34333	1010
221759	204187	341977	369425	490764	562208	506271	706172	554073	655377	756426	794686
583	1052	419	1368	7093	-82	6337	3441	7067	7645	-5864	93315
											30832
264295	**186397**	**284281**	**363350**	**460027**	**552227**	**608100**	**669062**	**700273**	**773500**	**869257**	**584193**
264295	186397	284281	363350	460027	552227	608100	669062	700273	773500	869257	584193
43810	46856	84920	100699	169469	159424	172180	135671	171051	195189	191040	215914
2945	3971	3567	2759	6262	2355	128	1570	251	220	19032	68
217540	135026	194500	255763	275579	390210	435102	531544	520052	569461	658368	299610
	544	1294	4129	8717	238	690	277	8918	8325	817	68585
											16

5-9 当年外商直接投资项目数和投资额（2019年）
NUMBER OF PROJECTS AND TOTAL AMOUNT OF FOREIGN DIRECT INVESTMENT (2019)

单位：万美元 (10 000 USD)

项目	Item	批准企业项目数（个）Number of Projects Approved (unit)	实际利用外资金额（万美元）Total Amount of Foreign Investment Actually Utilized (10000 USD)
外商直接投资	**Foreign Direct Investments**		
一、按投资方式分	**Grouped by Investment Form**		
# 中外合资企业	Sino-foreign Joint Ventures	358	215914
中外合作企业	Sino-foreign Cooperative Enterprises	1	68
外商独资企业	Foreign-owned Enterprises	586	299610
二、按主要行业分	**Grouped by Sector**		
# 农、林、牧、渔业	Farming, Forestry, Animal Husbandry and Fishery	8	10979
制造业	Manufacturing	140	99283
电力、燃气及水的生产和供应业	Production and Supply of Electricity, Gas and Water	5	2858
建筑业	Construction	9	2257
信息传输、计算机服务和软件业	Information transmission, computer services and software industry	2	6180
批发和零售业	Wholesale and Retail Trades	289	16634
房地产业	Real estate industry	74	245956
租赁和商务服务业	Leasing and Business Services	135	79631
科学研究、技术服务和地质勘查业	Scientific Research, Technical Service and Geological Survey	72	18376
三、按主要国别（地区）分	**Grouped by Countries (Regions)**		
# 香港	Hong Kong	326	468994
韩国	Korea	269	8146
美国	USA	46	13722
日本	Japan	27	6753
德国	Germany	14	34034
澳大利亚	Australia	14	1699
新加坡	Singapore	18	6189

5-10 对外投资与经济合作
OUTBOUND INVESTMENT AND INTERNATIONAL ECONOMIC COOPERATION

名称	Name	单位	Unit	2019 年	2019 年比 2018 年 ± % 2019/2018 (± %)
对外投资项目数	Number of Outbound Investment Projects	个	unit	113	19.0
对外投资中方投资额	The Amount of Investment by Chinese Sides in Outbound Investment	万美元	10000 USD	266355.81	-47.2
对外承包工程新签合同额	The Amount of New Contracts for Foreign Contracted Projects	万美元	10000 USD	335980	-31.9
对外承包工程完成营业额	The Completed Turnover of Foreign Contracted Projects	万美元	10000 USD	418315	-3.0
对外劳务合作	Number of Persons Sent Overseas for International Labor Service Cooperation	人	Person	19181	50.9

5-11 对外投资分国别（地区）情况表（2019 年）
TABLE OF FOREIGN INVESTMENT BY COUNTRY (REGION) (2019)

国别（地区）	Country (Region)	项目数量（个） Number of Projects (unit)	2019 年比 2018 年 ± % 2019/2018 (± %)	中方投资额（万美元） Amount of Investment by Chinese Sides (10000 USD)	2019 年比 2018 年 ± % 2019/2018 (± %)
总计	**Total**	113	19.0	266356	-47.2
亚洲	Asia	72	50.0	119340	-40.9
韩国	Korea	11	-15.4	8300	-88.4
中国香港	Hong Kong, China	10	-16.7	1182	-99.0
越南	Vietnam	3	-62.5	23125	376.6
乌兹别克斯坦	Uzbekistan	2	-33.3	247	70.3
泰国	Thailand	7	250.0	27832	2653.7
柬埔寨	Cambodia	5	150.0	7488	545.5
巴基斯坦	Pakistan	2	100.0	130	-99.4
老挝	Laos				
马来西亚	Malaysia	4	300.0	2436	-133.6
日本	Japan	4	300.0	1452	-122.8
缅甸	Myanmar	4	300.0	2529	166.2

5-11 续表 4
Continued

国别（地区）	Country (Region)	项目数量（个）Number of Projects (unit)	2019 年比 2018 年 ± % 2019/2018 (± %)	中方投资额（万美元）Amount of Investment by Chinese Sides (10000 USD)	2019 年比 2018 年 ± % 2019/2018 (± %)
哈萨克斯坦	Kazakhstan				
新加坡	Singapore	4	300.0	10710	1095.3
印度	India	5	400.0	10084	33512.5
欧洲	Europe	14	100.0	41323	-35.0
英国	UK	增资	-100.0	276	84.6
荷兰	Holland	1	-50.0	1350	-10.7
德国	Germany	7	600.0	1940	16268.7
葡萄牙	Portugal				
意大利	Italy	增资	-100.0	1439	-97.7
俄罗斯联邦	Russia	3		1335	203.5
拉丁美洲	Latin America	4	-33.3	4806	-64.3
英属维尔京群岛	British Virgin Islands	1	-50.0	5	-100.0
墨西哥	Mexico	1	-50.0	4251	687.7
阿根廷	Argentina	1		550	2335.8
玻利维亚	Bolivia				
巴拿马	Panama				
北美洲	North America	14	-22.2	7646	-96.2
美国	USA	13	-7.1	7115	-92.3
加拿大	Canada	1	-75.0	531	-99.5
百慕大群岛	Bermuda				
大洋洲	Oceania	3	-57.1	92371	213.6
澳大利亚	Australia	1	-85.7	1027	-96.5
新西兰	New Zealand	2		91344	16691.2

主要统计指标解释

批准企业（项目）个数 是指外商直接投资中批准设立的外商投资企业个数、批准的合作开发项目个数。

合同外资金额 是指批准外商投资企业的合同、章程中规定的外国投资者认缴的出资额和企业投资总额内的应由外方投资者以自己的境外自有资金直接向企业提供的贷款。包括新批准企业合同外资和原有企业的增资减资，增资减资不对企业（项目）个数进行调整。

实际使用外资金额 是指合同外资金额的实际执行金额。

外商直接投资 是指外国企业和经济组织或个人（包括华侨、港澳台胞以及我国在境外注册的企业）按我国有关政策、法规，用现汇、实物、技术等在我国境内开办外商独资企业、与我国境内的企业或经济组织共同举办中外合资经营企业、合作经营企业或合作开发资源的投资（包括外商投资收益的再投资）以及经政府有关部门批准的项目投资总额内，企业从境外借入的资金。

外商其它投资 是指除外商直接投资以外其他方式吸收的外资。

进出口总额 指实际进出我国国境的货物总金额。包括对外贸易实际进出口货物，来料加工装配进出口货物，国家间、联合国及国际组织无偿援助物资和赠送品，华侨、港澳台同胞和外籍华人捐赠品，租赁期满归承租人所有的租赁货物，进料加工进出口货物，边境地方贸易及边境地区小额贸易进出口货物（边民互市贸易除外），中外合资企业、中外合作经营企业、外商独资经营企业进出口货物和公用物品，到、离岸价格在规定限额以上的进出口货样和广告品（无商业价值、无使用价值和免费提供出口的除外），从保税仓库提取在中国境内销售的进口货物，以及其他进出口货物。

Explanatory Notes on Main Statistical Indicators

Enterprises (Projects) Permitted refers to number of foreign invested enterprises and developed projects under cooperation through the permission.

Contracted Foreign Investment refers to expenditure promised by the foreign investor and loan stemmed from broad innate fund of the foreign investor, according to the contract and regulation approved of enterprise invested by foreigner. Including the newly approved enterprise contract foreign investment and the capital increase and decrease of the original enterprise, the capital increase and decrease do not adjust the number of enterprises (projects) .

Actual Utilization of Foreign Investment refers to actual usage of contracted foreign investment, including cash, investment in kind and incorporeal agreed by the both sides as part of the investment, such as services and technology.

Foreign Direct Investment refers to the investments by foreign enterprises and economic organizations or individuals (including overseas Chinese, compatriots from Hong Kong, Macao and Taiwan and Chinese enterprises registered abroad) , following the relevant policies and laws of China, for the establishment of ventures and cooperative enterprises or cooperative exploration of resources with enterprises or economic organizations in China. It includes the reinvestment of the foreign entrepreneurs with the profits gained from the investment and the funds that enterprises borrow from aboard in the total investment of projects which are approved by the relevant department of the government.

Other Investment by Foreign Entrepreneurs refers to all forms of utilization of foreign capitals other than foreign direct investment.

Total Imports and Exports refers to the real value of commodities imported into and exported from the boundary of China. They include the actual imports and exports through foreign trade, imported and exported goods under the processing and assembling trades and materials, supplies and gifts as aid given gratis between governments and by the United Nations and other international organizations, and contributions donated by overseas Chinese, compatriots in Hong Kong, Macao and Chinese with foreign citizenship, leasing commodities owned by tenant at the expiration of leasing period, the imported and exported commodities processed with imported materials, commodities trading in border areas (excluding mutual exchange goods) , the imported and exported commodities and articles for public use of the Sino–foreign joint ventures, cooperative enterprises and ventures exclusively with foreign own investment. Also included are import or export of samples and advertising goods for whose CIF or FOB value are beyond the permitted ceiling (excluding goods of no trading or use value and free commodities for export) , imported goods sold in China from bonded warehouses and other imported or exported goods.

6 城市建设、环境保护

CITY CONSTRUCTION AND ENVIRONMENT PROTECTION

简要说明

一、本篇资料的主要内容

本篇资料主要反映了全市城市基础设施基本情况，包括市政设施、供水、供电、公共交通、园林绿化、燃气供热、城市环卫、环境保护及工业“三废”排放情况等方面的资料。

二、本篇资料的来源

1. 本篇资料中市政设施、供水、公共交通、园林绿化、燃气供热、城市环卫相关资料来源于市建设委员会的城市建设统计年报，由市统计局固定资产投资统计处整理提供。

2. 本篇资料中供电资料来源于青岛供电公司，由市统计局能源统计处整理提供。

3. 本篇资料中环境保护、环境质量及工业“三废”排放情况来源于市环境保护局，由市统计局能源统计处整理提供。

Brief Introduction

I. Main Content

Data in this chapter show the basic conditions of public facilities of the whole city, including urban construction and infrastructure, water supply, electricity supply, public communications, urban greenery, gas and heating, urban sanitation, environmental protection and discharge conditions of industrial waste water, waste gas and solid waste, etc.

II. Source of Data

1. Data on conditions of urban construction and infrastructure, water supply, public communications, urban greenery, gas and heating, urban sanitation are based on the annual report of city construction provided by Qingdao Municipal Construction Commission, and compiled by the Division of Investment and Construction Statistics of Qingdao Municipal Bureau of Statistics.

2. Data on electricity supply are provided by Qingdao Power Corporation, and compiled by the Division of Energy Statistics of Qingdao Municipal Bureau of Statistics.

3. Data on environmental protection, environmental conditions and discharge conditions of industrial waste water, waste gas and solid waste are provided by Qingdao Municipal Bureau of Environmental Protection, and compiled by the Division of Energy Statistics of Qingdao Municipal Bureau of Statistics.

6-1 主要年份城市建设和公用事业
MAJOR YEAR´S CITY CONSTRUCTION AND PUBLIC UTILITIES

年份 Year	建成区面积 （平方公里） Developed Areas (sq.km)	年末道路长度 （公里） Length of Roads at Year-end (km)	年末道路面积 （万平方米） Area of Roads at Year-end (10 000 sq.m)	公共汽车、电车线路网长度 （公里） Network Length of Bus and Trolley Bus (km)
1949	27	243	206	26.4
1952	29	245	213	124.4
1957	36	248	217	232.3
1962	55	266	235	252.8
1965	57	266	235	308.1
1970	59	374	346	358.5
1975	63	392	355	389.3
1978	66	408	368	422.1
1980	72	408	377	474.1
1985	79	462	464	611.3
1990	94.3	667	786	777
1991	94.7	673	826	922
1992	95.4	683	840	988
1993	99.9	764	944	1094
1994	103.9	811	985	1372
1995	106	936	1177	1101
1996	110	991	1339	1211
1997	112	1047	1436	1492
1998	114	1106	1436	1859
1999	116	1171	1698	2339
2000	119.1	1192	1789	2711
2001	123	1248	2169	2521
2002	133	1426	2594	896
2003	145.9	1595	2816	973
2004	154.8	1755	3254	1185
2005	178.8	1862	3547	1159
2006	227.5	3160	5218	1362
2007	250.7	3288	5411	1480
2008	267.1	3318	5596	1470
2009	272.9	3402	5763	1216
2010	282.3	3409	5893	1383
2011	291.5	3705	6605	1719
2012	374.6	4281	7528	1978
2013	469.6	4334	7859	2002
2014	490.7	4393	7908	2023
2015	566.4	4375	7940	2106
2016	599.3	4484	8057	2116
2017	638.4	4865	8496	2220
2018	715.1	5770	9862	2400
2019	758.2	6315	10227	3973

6-1 续表 1
Continued

年份 Year	自来水供水管道长度（公里） Length of Tap Water Pipelines (km)	全年供水总量（万立方米） Annual Volume of Tap Water Supply (10 000 cu.m)	#全年售水量（万立方米） Annual Volume of Tap Water Sale (10 000 cu.m)	#居民家庭用水 of which: Consumption for Residential Use	用水普及率（%） Coverage Rate of Population with Access to Tap Water (%)	排水管道长度（公里） Length of Sewage Pipes (km)	全年用电量（亿千瓦时） Annual Volume of Electricity Supply (100 million kW·h)	#居民生活用电 of which: Consumption for Residential Use
1949	308	721	456	331	89	200	0.88	0.14
1952	341	778	612	310	90	227	1.85	0.14
1957	412	1392	1 296	606	93	273	2.61	0.26
1962	483	2700	2 512	937	98	290	3.77	0.57
1965	500	3220	2 979	929	98	295	5.92	0.68
1970	521	4503	4106	1085	99	350	9.83	1.02
1975	564	6726	6302	1950	99	361	12.41	1.43
1978	572	5334	4975	1314	99	382	16.34	1.62
1980	588	8224	7874	2577	99	394	21.48	2.78
1985	685	7557	7038	2628	99.9	505	26.39	2.87
1990	873	11896	10211	4270	96.9	645	41.08	4.32
1991	908	13865	11760	4990	96.6	649	44.51	5.34
1992	1035	16385	13070	5931	96.5	672	51.78	6.84
1993	1123	16137	14027	6124	99.1	734	55.02	7.66
1994	1124	17367	14716	6405	100	811	60.74	8.78
1995	1046	22513	15810	7050	100	990	67.23	10.16
1996	1182	23277	16566	7731	100	1051	72.87	12.23
1997	1266	24130	17215	8787	100	1167	77.82	13.73
1998	1390	23845	17271	9115	100	1210	79.65	14.28
1999	1471	23849	18558	10032	100	1301	88.12	15.31
2000	1524	25414	20642	11405	100	1460	106.80	16
2001	1665	22225	18556	10555	100	1539	116.10	17.62
2002	1781	27662	21684	10129	100	1641	131.44	18.31
2003	2060	27594	21483	10142	100	1884	147.68	19.88
2004	2566	30877	23864	11695	100	2002	167.95	23.63
2005	2876	33265	25874	12536	100	2309	193.81	33.76
2006	3984	30524	25572	10682	100	3994	215.35	34.87
2007	4187	31533	26454	11408	100	4079	236.42	37.40
2008	4642	32675	27396	11301	100	4229	250.07	40.31
2009	4767	33490	28274	12250	100	4555	259.42	43.29
2010	4926	34909	29617	12524	100	4708	292.97	49.50
2011	5121	34109	28837	10049	100	5187	313.44	50.13
2012	5243	38945	33039	12121	100	6814	318.36	51.64
2013	5522	38331	32418	11851	100	6536	339.27	57.52
2014	6177	46649	40612	14834	100	6840	337.82	59.95
2015	6142	46203	40202	15381	100	6993	342.29	64.71
2016	6132	43033	36748	14430	100	7146	367.26	69.52
2017	6498	45991	38963	17439	100	7367	401.06	74.84
2018	7531	53235	43298	18473	100	8854	431.82	77.39
2019	7997	52203	44597	19809	100	9350	457.90	81.95

6-1 续表 2
Continued

年份 Year	公共汽车、电车营运车辆（辆） Number of Bus and Trolley Bus under Operation (unit)	全年客运量（万人次） Annual Passenger Traffic (10 000 person-times)	出租汽车（辆） Number of Taxi (unit)	使用液化气、煤气、天然气人数（万人） Population with Access to Gas (10 000 person)	液化气 Liquefied Petroleum	煤气 Coal Gas	天然气 Natural Gas	液化气供气量（吨） Volume of Liquefied Petroleum Supply (ton)
1949	32	298						
1952	76	932						
1957	112	4110						
1962	127	4747						
1965	173	6092						
1970	224	13002						
1975	324	14426		2	2			184.9
1978	409	27351		17	17			3246
1980	485	38981	48	24	24			4345
1985	621	48852	219	42.1	42.1			10619
1990	801	63495	832	75.0	57.4	17.6		17512
1991	1372	67552	1070	76.2	57.4	18.8		17963
1992	1470	73529	1828	82.8	62.0	20.8		19565
1993	1875	72427	4874	88.4	64.6	23.8		22224
1994	1850	78231	5806	103.6	77.4	26.2		24684
1995	1891	71867	5887	116.2	82.9	33.3		32443
1996	2012	49077	6660	126.0	88.0	38.0		4065
1997	2148	55642	6861	133.6	92.9	40.7		38717
1998	2184	51042	7469	146.8	97.8	49.0		45381
1999	2470	55414	7839	154.9	98.3	56.6		40537
2000	3141	59879	7933	164.1	93.3	70.8		46951
2001	3453	60167	8110	168.8	87.5	81.3		45295
2002	3681	61713	8376	224.2	133.8	90.4		60123
2003	3648	58792	8109	246.7	138.3	93.1	15.3	67803
2004	3848	66463	8144	258.4	140.6	78.8	39.0	58548
2005	4039	68776	8121	265.0	132.6	45.7	86.7	78000
2006	4167	73726	8146	271.0	112.5	49.5	109.0	97343
2007	4524	78702	8221	275.6	104.1	12.1	159.4	79715
2008	4701	82460	9241	276.3	91.9	10.5	173.9	81987
2009	4288	81768	9316	276.1	59.8	12.3	204.0	96721
2010	4664	85251	9539	276.3	36.7	12.6	227.0	80073
2011	5419	89614	9683	277.1	25.8	12.6	238.7	79812
2012	5640	97922	9693	313.7	36.7	13.1	263.9	54341
2013	6179	101108	9826	318.9	33.0	0.0	285.9	41302
2014	6515	105592	9720	325.4	33.0	0.0	292.4	39255
2015	6748	102402	10033	338.3	28.9	0.0	309.4	35255
2016	7210	99596	10048	441.6	29.0	0.0	412.6	32291
2017	7420	104898	10875	445.8	26.2	0.0	419.6	28309
2018	7795	104782	10867	512.7	29.9	0.0	482.8	30427
2019	8489	108339	10877	529.5	27.0	0.0	502.5	30210

注：1990 年以前公共营运车辆不包括系统外及个体。
Note： Vehicles not belonging to system and individual vehicles are not contained in public operating vehicles before 1990.

6-1 续表 3
Continued

年份 Year	煤气供气量（万立方米）Volume of Coal Gas Supply (10 000 cu.m)	天然气供气量（万立方米）Volume of Natural Gas Supply (10 000 cu.m)	燃气普及率(%) Coverage Rate of Population with Access to Gas (%)	绿地面积（公顷）Area of Green Areas (Hectate)	公园绿地面积（公顷）Park Green Areas (hectare)	人均公园绿地面积(平方米) Per Capita Park Green Areas (sq.m)	建成区绿化覆盖率(%) Green Coverage Rate of Developed Areas (%)	公园(个) Number of Parks and Zoos (unit)	公园面积（公顷）Area of Parks and Zoos (hectare)
1949				133	42	0.7	4.9	3	43
1952				134	43	0.7	4.4	4	45
1957				245	132	1.7	6.9	10	122
1962				771	184	2.2	14.0	12	174
1965				777	184	2.1	13.7	12	174
1970				772	184	2.1	13.0	6	117
1975			2.3	465	162	1.8	7.6	5	134
1978			18.6	469	162	1.7	7.6	6	165
1980			24.5	625	206	2.1	10.4	6	152
1985			36.3	1072	255	2.3	17.3	7	153
1990	3073		56.2	2120	492	3.7	22.8	26	404
1991	3439		56.5	2318	500	3.7	24.4	28	443
1992	3824		60.0	2471	515	3.7	25.9	28	417
1993	4215		63.1	2488	543	3.9	26.5	31	453
1994	4116		63.1	2866	572	4.0	27.9	31	463
1995	4734		79.2	4547	771	5.3	30.1	33	675
1996	5447		83.9	4679	836	5.6	30.4	33	675
1997	5920		87.3	4717	924	6.0	31.3	34	730
1998	5959		92.5	6812	1047	6.6	35.0	35	775
1999	7319		96.0	7007	1186	7.4	35.9	36	791
2000	9567		98.0	7439	1423	8.5	37.0	37	790
2001	11814		99.0	7688	1588	9.3	37.5	39	832
2002	13500		99.5	7967	1791	8.1	36.4	43	926
2003	14826	1181	100	8829	2305	9.3	37.5	45	1034
2004	15503	2710	100	10047	2842	11.0	38.0	48	1421
2005	16573	7456	100	11137	3132	11.8	38.8	47	1110
2006	9821	13876	100	11756	3198	11.8	39.2	47	1188
2007	9516	18103	100	15369	3661	13.3	37.8	73	1268
2008	8691	21780	100	15630	4014	14.5	41.5	77	1815
2009	7523	26948	100	16003	4003	14.5	43.4	71	1897
2010	9153	35681	100	16619	4027	14.6	43.4	72	1917
2011	9137	46147	100	18013	4041	14.6	44.7	74	1931
2012	8148	68397	100	21471	4573	14.6	44.7	78	2112
2013	0	70918	100	28007	4649	14.6	44.7	87	2698
2014	0	74823	100	28805	4741	14.6	44.7	91	2988
2015	0	70311	100	29117	4802	14.6	44.7	87	3163
2016	0	70586	100	34851	8194	18.6	38.6	151	4460
2017	0	91572	100	36209	7763	17.4	39.1	175	4727
2018	0	120089	100	39229	8587	16	39	191	5767
2019	0	131867	100	40844	8922	17	40	192	5773

注：1. 自 2002 年起人均公共绿地面积按辖区内全部人口计算。
2. 2005 年以前所用园林绿地面积；公共绿地面积；人均公共绿地面积；公园、动物园个数；公园、动物园面积指标分别改为现在的绿地面积；公共绿地面积；人均公园绿地面积；公园个数；公园面积。
3. 由于城阳区绿化指标进行了调整，部分绿地属性发生变化。导致 2017 年公园绿地面积及人均公园绿地面积的数据小于 2016 年。

Note: 1. Per capita public green areas is calculated at total population in the area under jurisdiction since 2002.
2. Before 2005, the corresponding indicators of greenbelt area, public greenbelt area, public greenbelt area, per capita public greenbelt area, coverage rate of green, number of parks and zoos, area of parks and zoos.
3. As the green index of Chengyang District has been adjusted, some green space properties have changed. As a result, the data of park green area and per capita park green area in 2017 are smaller than 2016.

6-2 全年供电（2019 年）

ANNUAL ELECTRICITY SUPPLY (2019)

全年供电项目	Item	单位	Unit	2019 年
发电设备总容量	Total Capacity of Generation Equipment	万千瓦	10 000 kW	376.30
#青岛电厂	Qingdao Power Plant	万千瓦	10 000 kW	127.00
黄岛电厂	Huangdao Power Plant	万千瓦	10 000 kW	156.50
全年发电量	Annual Electricity Generation	亿千瓦时	100 million kw · h	180.58
#青岛电厂	Qingdao Power Plant	亿千瓦时	100 million kw · h	55.96
黄岛电厂	Huangdao Power Plant	亿千瓦时	100 million kw · h	70.30
全年实际用电量	Annual Electricity Consumption	亿千瓦时	100 million kw · h	457.90
#工业	Industrial Consumption	亿千瓦时	100 million kw · h	244.66
农业	Agricultural Consumption	亿千瓦时	100 million kw · h	9.93
生活	Residential Consumption	亿千瓦时	100 million kw · h	81.95
平均每日用电量	Average Daily Consumption	万千瓦时	100 million kw · h	12545.18

6-3 分行业用电（2019年）
ELECTRICITY CONSUMPTION BY SECTOR (2019)

单位：万千瓦时 (10 000 kW · h)

行业	Sector	2019年	2019年比2018年增长（%）Growth Rate in 2019 over 2018 (%)
全社会用电总计	**Total Electricity Consumption**	**4578992**	**6.04**
一、农、林、牧、渔业	Farming, Forestry, Animal Husbandry and Fishery	99330	19.44
二、工业	Industry	2446626	2.89
三、建筑业	Construction	97311	11.73
四、交通运输、仓储和邮政业	Transport, Storage and Post	195092	20.99
五、信息传输、计算机服务和软件业	Information Transmission, Computer Services and Software	62583	3.72
六、商业、住宿和餐饮业	Trade, Hotels and Catering Services	260775	11.07
七、金融、房地产、商务及居民服务业	Finance, Real Estate, Business and Residential Services	256327	14.43
八、公共事业及管理组织	Public Management and Social Organization	341446	8.13
九、城乡居民生活用电	Household Consumption	819501	5.90
城镇居民	Urban Area	516704	6.60
乡村居民	Rural Area	302798	4.72

6-4 城市供水
URBAN WATER SUPPLY

项目	Item	单位	Unit	2019 年
自来水供水管道长度	Length of Tap Water Pipelines	公里	km	7997
综合生产能力	Synthesis Production Capacity	万立方米 / 日	10 000 cu.m/day	217
全年供水总量	Annual Volume of Tap Water Supply	万立方米	10 000 cu.m	52203
# 售水量	Volume of Tap Water Supply	万立方米	10 000 cu.m	44597
# 生产运营用水	Consumption for Production Use	万立方米	10 000 cu.m	15469
公共服务用水	Consumption for Public Services Use	万立方米	10 000 cu.m	9144
居民家庭用水	Consumption for Residential Use	万立方米	10 000 cu.m	19809
其他用水	Consumption for Other Uses	万立方米	10 000 cu.m	175
平均每日供水量	Daily Volume of Tap Water Supply	万立方米	10 000 cu.m	143
# 生产用	Consumption for Production Use	万立方米	10 000 cu.m	42
生活用	Consumption for Residential Use	万立方米	10 000 cu.m	54
用水户数	Households with Access to Water	户	household	1904141
用水人口	Population with Access to water	万人	10 000 person	529
工业用水量重复利用率	Recycle Rate of water for Industrial Use	%	%	91

6-5 城市公共交通
URBAN PUBLIC TRAFFIC

项目	Item	单位	Unit	2019 年
公共汽车、电车线路网长度	Network Length of Bus and Trolley Bus	公里	km	3973
轨道交通线路长度	Rail Transit Line Length	公里	km	176
公共汽车、电车营运车辆	Number of Bus and Trolley Bus under Operation	辆	unit	8489
#汽车	Bus	辆	unit	3135
电车	Trolley Bus	辆	unit	3536
公共汽车、电车全年客运量	Annual Passenger Traffic of Bus and Trolley Bus	万人次	10 000 person-times	108339
公共汽车、电车平均每日客运量	Daily Passenger Traffic of Bus and Trolley Bus	万人	10 000 person	297
出租汽车数	Number of Taxi	辆	unit	10877
轮渡运营船数	Number of Ferry Boat under Operation	艘	ship	1
轮渡客运总量	Passenger Traffic of Ferry Boat	万人次	10 000 person-times	16.44
轮渡平均每日客运量	Daily Passenger Traffic of Ferry Boat	万人	10 000 person	0.05
轨道交通客运总量	Total Passenger Traffic Of Rail Transit	万人次	10 000 person-times	18720
轨道交通平均每日客运量	Average Daily Passenger Volume of Rail Transit	万人	10 000 person	51

6-6 城市供气
URBAN GAS SUPPLY

项目	Item	单位	Unit	2019 年
煤气供应总量	Volume of Coal Gas Supply	万立方米	10 000 cu.m	0
#家庭用量	Household Consumption	万立方米	10 000 cu.m	0
煤气用气户数	Households with Access to Coal Gas	户	household	0
#家庭用户	Household Users	户	household	0
液化石油气供应总量	Volume of Liquefied Petroleum Supply	吨	ton	30210
#家庭用量	Household Consumption	吨	ton	16679
液化石油气用气户数	Households with Access to Liquefied Petroleum	户	household	121874
#家庭用户	Household Users	户	household	118522
天然气供应总量	Volume of Natural Gas Supply	万立方米	10 000 cu.m	131867
#家庭用量	Household Consumption	万立方米	10 000 cu.m	30377
天然气用气户数	Households with Access to Natural Gas	户	household	2096932
#家庭用户	Household Users	户	household	2081760
燃气普及率	Coverage Rate of Population with Access to Gas	%	%	100

6-7 城市环境卫生
URBAN ENVIRONMENTAL SANITATION

项目	Item	单位	Unit	2019 年
市容环卫专用车辆总数	Number of Special Vehicles for Environmental Sanitation	辆	unit	5406
生活垃圾清运量	Volume of Garbage Disposal	万吨	10 000 ton	282
生活垃圾无害化处理厂（场）数	Number of Bio-safety Disposal Plant of Garbage	座	unit	8
生活垃圾无害化处理能力	Bio-safety Disposal Capacity of Garbage	吨 / 日	ton/day	11500
生活垃圾无害化处理量	Bio-safety Disposal Volume of Garbage	万吨	10 000 ton	282
道路清扫保洁面积	Area under Cleaning Program	万平方米	10 000 sq.m	8393
#机械化	of which：Mechanization	万平方米	10 000 sq.m	5737
公共厕所	Public Toilets	个	unit	965

6-8 城市道路、下水道及绿化
URBAN ROAD, SEWAGE AND GREEN

项目	Item	单位	Unit	2019 年
道路	**Road**	–	–	–
年末道路长度	Length of Roads at Year-end	公里	km	6315
年末道路面积	Area of Roads at Year-end	万平方米	10 000 sq.m	10227
# 人行道面积	Area of Pavements	万平方米	10 000 sq.m	2198
排水管道长度	Length of Sewage Pipes	公里	km	9350
园林绿化	**Greening**			–
绿化覆盖面积	Area of Green Coverage Areas	公顷	hectare	44169
绿地面积	Area of Green Areas	公顷	hectare	40844
公园绿地面积	Area of Park Green Areas	公顷	hectare	8922
公园数	Number of Parks and Zoos	个	unit	192
公园面积	Area of Parks and Zoos	公顷	hectare	5773
城市每人平均公园绿地面积	Per Capita Park Green Area	平方米	sq.m	16.9
建成区绿化覆盖率	Green Coverage Rate of Developed Areas	%	%	40.22

6-9 环境保护基本情况
BASIC CONDITIONS OF ENVIRONMENTAL PROTECTION

项目	Item	单位	Unit	2019 年	2018 年	2019 年比 2018 年增（+）减（-）% 2019 Compared to 2018 (+/-)
二氧化硫排放总量	Sulphur Dioxide Emission	吨	ton	13916.78	14631.39	-4.88
氮氧化物排放总量	Discharge Amount of Nitrogen Oxides	吨	ton	13923.01	16096.19	-13.50
烟（粉）尘排放总量	Soot (Dust) Emission	吨	ton	12907.66	12981.91	-0.57
工业固体废物排放总量	Industrial Solid Wastes Discharged	吨	ton	0.00	0.00	0.00
化学需氧量排放总量	Discharge Amount of Chemical Oxygen Demand	吨	ton	24414.40	25891.22	-5.70
氨氮排放总量	Discharge Amount of Ammonia and Nitrogen	吨	ton	2391.09	2468.19	-3.12
废水排放总量	Waste Water Discharged	万吨	10 000 tons	63363.91	58731.33	7.89

6-10 环境质量状况
ENVIRONMENT CONDITION

项目	Item	单位	Unit	2019 年	2018 年	2019 年比 2018 年增（+）减（-）% 2019 Compared to 2018 (+/-)
市区空气质量优良率	Urban air quality good rate	%	%	78.60	88.80	-10.20
一、二类海水水质面积比例	The proportion of Grade Ⅰ and Ⅱ waters	%	%	98.80	98.6	0.20
市区区域环境噪声平均等效声级	The Average Equivalent Sound Level of the Urban Regional Environmental Noise	分贝（A）	db(A)	56.50	56.90	-0.70
市区道路交通噪声平均等效声级	The Average Equivalent Sound Level of the Urban Road Traffic Noise	分贝（A）	db(A)	68.30	68.00	0.44

6-11 工业“三废”排放情况
DISCHARGE CONDITIONS OF INDUSTRIAL WASTE WATER, WASTE GAS AND SOLID WASTE

项目	Item	单位	Unit	2019年	2018年	2019年比2018年增（+）减（-）% 2019 Compared to 2018 (+/-)
工业废水排放总量	Industrial Waste Water Discharged	万吨	10 000 tons	5779.99	5536.18	4.40
废水治理设施数	Number of Facilities for Treatment of Waste Water	套	set	424	367	15.53
废水治理设施处理能力	Capacity of Facilities for Treatment of Waste Water	万吨 / 日	10 000 tons/day	39.55	38.16	3.65
进入城市污水处理厂量	Volume Handled by Sewage Treatment Plant	万吨	10 000 tons	5050.93	5039.64	0.22
化学需氧量排放量	Discharge Amount of Chemical Oxygen Demand	吨	ton	1536.06	1622.47	-5.33
氨氮排放量	Discharge Amount of Ammonia and Nitrogen	吨	ton	73.44	76.07	-3.46
工业废气排放总量	Industrial Waste Air Discharged	万标立方米	10 000 cu.m	42925879.90	35407404.02	21.23
废气治理设施数	Number of Facilities for Treatment of Waste Air	套	set	2794	2071	34.91
其中：脱硫设施数	of which： Desulphurization Facilities	套	set	285	268	6.34
废气治理设施处理能力	Capacity of Facilities for Treatment of Waste Air	万标立方米 / 时	10 000 cu.m/hr	14535.82	11986.01	21.27
二氧化硫去除量	Sulphur Dioxide Removed	吨	ton	205242.55	213219.24	-3.74
二氧化硫排放量	Sulphur Dioxide Emission	吨	ton	3511.58	4227.39	-16.93
烟（粉）尘排放量	Soot (Dust) Emission	吨	ton	4744.57	4821.91	-1.60
工业固体废物产生量	Industrial Solid Wastes Produced	万吨	10 000 tons	821.50	793.50	3.53
其中：危险废物	of which: Hazardous Wastes	吨	ton	176843.17	147029.43	20.28
工业固体废物综合利用量	Industrial Solid Wastes Comprehensive Utilized	万吨	10 000 tons	715.53	734.44	-2.58
工业固体废物排放量	Industrial Solid Wastes Discharged	万吨	10 000 tons	0	0	0.00
其中：危险废物	of which: Hazardous Wastes	吨	ton	0	0	0.00
污染治理项目完成投资	Investment in Treatment Projects of Pollution	万元	10 000 yuan	55956.66	41191.94	35.84
污染治理项目数	Number of Treatment Projects of Pollution	个	item	40	31	29.03
当年竣工治理项目数	Number of Completed Treatment Projects in the Year	个	item	30	25	20.00

主要统计指标解释

供水综合生产能力 指按供水设施取水、净化、送水、出厂输水干管等环节设计能力计算的综合生产能力。

年末供水管道长度 指从送水泵至用户水表之间所有管道的长度。不包括新安装尚未使用的管道。

用水普及率 指城市用水人口数与城市人口总数的比率。计算公式：

$$用水普及率=\frac{城市用水人口数}{城市人口总数}\times 100\%$$

全年供水总量 指报告期供水企业（单位）供出的全部水量。包括有效供水量和漏损水量。

全年供气总量 指全年燃气企业（单位）向用户供应的燃气数量。包括销售量和损失量。

用气普及率 指报告期末使用燃气的城市人口数与城市人口总数的比率。计算公式为：

$$用气普及率=\frac{城市用气人口数}{城市人口总数}\times 100\%$$

年末道路长度 指年末道路长度和与道路相通的广场、桥梁、隧道的长度，按车行道中心线计算。在统计时只统计路面宽度在3.5米（含3.5米）以上的各种铺装道路，包括开放型工业区和住宅区道路在内。

工业废气排放量 指报告期内企业厂区内燃料燃烧和生产工艺过程中产生的各种排入大气的含有污染物的气体的总量，以标准状态（273K，101325Pa）计算。

工业废水排放量 指经过企业厂区所有排放口排到企业外部的工业废水量。包括生产废水、外排的直接冷却水、超标排放的矿井地下水和与工业废水混排的厂区生活污水，不包括外排的间接冷却水（清污不分流的间接冷却水应计算在内）。

工业废水排放达标量 指各项指标都达到国家或地方排放标准的外排工业废水量，包括未经处理外排达标的和经过处理后外排达标的和两部分。国家排放标准见GB8978-88。

工业固体废物产生量 指企业在生产过程中产生的固体状、半固体状和高浓度液体状废弃物的总量，包括危险废物、冶炼废渣、粉煤灰、炉渣、煤矸渣、尾矿、放射性废物和其他废物等；不包括矿山开采的剥离废石和掘进废石（煤矸石和呈酸性或碱性的废石除外）酸性或碱性废石是指采掘的废石其流经水、雨淋水的pH值小于4或pH值大于10.5者。

工业粉尘排放量 指企业在生产工艺过程中排放的能在空气中悬浮一定时间的固体颗粒物排放量。如钢铁企业的耐火材料粉尘、焦化企业的筛焦系统粉尘、烧结机的粉尘、石灰窑的粉尘、建材企业的水泥粉尘等。不包括电厂排入大气的烟尘。

化学需氧量（COD） 测量有机和无机物质化学分解所消耗氧的质量浓度的水污染指数。

Explanatory Notes on Main Statistical Indicators

Production Capacity of Water Supply refers to the designed comprehensive production capacity of water facilities, covering the 4 links of water collection, purification, conveyance, and outflow through trunk pipelines.

Length of Water Supply Pipelines at the Year-end refers to the total length of all the pipelines between the water pumps and the user water meters, excluding pipelines newly installed but not used yet.

Coverage Rate of Urban Population with Access to Tap Water refers to the ratio of the urban population with access to tap water to the total urban population. The formula is:

Coverage rate of urban population with access to tap water= (Urban population with access to tap water) / (Urban population) × 100%

Annual Volume of Water Supply refers to the total volume of water supplied by water–works (units) during the reference period, including both the effective water supply and loss during the water supply.

Annual Volume of Gas Supply refers to the total volume of gas provided to users by gas–producing enterprises (units) in a year, including the volume sold and the volume lost.

Coverage Rate of Urban Population with Access to Gas refers to the ratio of the urban population with access to gas to the total urban population at the end of the reference period. The formula is:

Coverage rate of urban population with access to gas= (Urban population with access to gas / Urban population) × 100%

Length of Paved Roads at the Year–end refers to the length of roads with paved surface including squares bridges and tunnels connected with roads by the end of the year.Length of the roads is measured by the central lines for vehicles for paved roads with a width of 3.5 meters and over, including roads in open–ended factory compounds and residential quarters.

Industrial Waste Air Emission refers to discharge into atmosphere of waste air containing pollutants generated from fuel burning and production process in enterprises within a given period of time. It is calculated at standard status (273K, 101,325Pa) .

Waste Water Discharged by Industry refers to the volume of waste water discharged by industrial enterprises through all their outlets, including waste water from production process, directly cooled water, groundwater from mining wells which does not meet discharge standards and sewage from households mixed with waste water produced by industrial activities, but excluding indirectly cooled water discharged (It should be included if the discharge is not separated with waste water) .

Industrial Waste Water Meeting Discharge Standards refers to volume of industrial waste water discharge which, with or without treatment, reaches national or local standards with regard to all pollutants. National Discharge standards query GB8978–88.

Industrial Solid Wastes Produced refers to total volume of solid, semi–solid and high concentration liquid residues produced by industrial enterprises from production process in a given period of time, including hazardous wastes, slag, coal ash, gangue, tailings, radioactive residues and other wastes, but excluding stones stripped or dug out in mining (gangue and acid or alkaline stones not included). A stone is acid or alkaline depending on the pH value of the water below 4 or above 10.5 when the stone is in, or soaked by, the water.

Industrial Dust Emission refers to volume of dust emitted by production process of enterprises and suspended in the air for a given period of time, including dust from refractory material of iron and steel works, dust from coke–screening systems and sintering machines of coke plants, dust from lime kilns and dust from cement production in building material enterprises, but excluding soot and dust emitted from power plants.

Chemical Oxygen Demand (COD) refers to index of water pollution measuring the mass concentration of oxygen consumed by the chemical breakdown of organic and inorganic matter.

能源消耗 7

CONSUMPTION OF ENERGY

简 要 说 明

一、本篇资料的主要内容

本篇资料主要反映了全市规模以上工业主要能源消费与库存情况，主要包括规模以上工业主要能源消费与库存、规模以上工业主要能源分行业消费量、重点耗能工业企业能源加工转换、规模以上工业主要能源工业消费量等方面的资料。

二、本篇资料的来源

本篇资料来源于规模以上工业能源统计年报，由市统计局能源统计处整理提供。

Brief Introduction

I. Main Content

Data in this chapter show the consumption and stock of major energy of industry above designated size, including consumption and stock of major energy of industry above designated size, major energy consumption of industry above designated size grouped by sector, energy conversion of major energy–consuming industrial enterprises and major energy consumption of industry above designated size, etc.

II. Source of Data

Data in this chapter are based on the annual report of energy consumed by industrial enterprises above designated size. The data are provided by the Division of Energy Statistics of Qingdao Municipal Bureau of Statistics.

7-1 规模以上工业主要能源消费与库存（2019 年）
CONSUMPTION AND STOCK OF MAJOR ENERGY OF INDUSTRY ABOVE DESIGNATED SIZE (2019)

名称	Name	计算单位	Unit	年初库存 Stock at Year-beginning	本年消费 Consumption in the Year	#工业 Industry	非工业 Non-industry	年末库存 Stock at Year-end
原　煤	Raw Coal	吨	ton	1512953	10965708	10922838	42870	1249414
焦　炭	Coke	吨	ton	76189	1449099	1449099		2549
焦炉煤气	Coking Gas	万立方米	10 000 cu.m		39518	39518		
高炉煤气	Blast Furnace Gas	万立方米	10 000 cu.m		563439	563439		
原　油	Crude Oil	吨	ton	418902	12201490	12201490		462704
汽　油	Petrol	吨	ton	140	27030	15494	11537	26
煤　油	Kerosene	吨	ton		78	78		
柴　油	Diesel Oil	吨	ton	2370	53565	38308	15258	2343
燃料油	Fuel Oil	吨	ton	9277	68705	68124	581	10976
液化石油气	Liquefied Petroleum Gas	吨	ton	2	83158	83140	18	
炼厂干气	Refinery Dry Gas	吨	ton		368469	368469		
热　力	Heat	百万千焦	million kJ		25212810	24810307	402502	
电　力	Electricity	万千瓦时	10 000kW・h		1846883	1827444	19439	

补充资料：2019 年综合能源消费量 1487.69 万吨标准煤。

Additional Materials：In 2019, comprehensive energy consumption is 14.8769 million tons SCE.

7-2 规模以上工业主要能源分行业消费量(2019年)
MAJOR ENERGY CONSUMPTION OF INDUSTRY ABOVE DESIGNATED SIZE BY SECTOR (2019)

名称	Name	原煤(吨) Raw Coal (ton)	焦炭(吨) Coke (ton)	焦炉煤气(万立方米) Coking Gas (10 000 cu.m)	原油(吨) Crude Oil (ton)	汽油(吨) Petrol (ton)
总　计	**Total**	**10965708**	**1449099**	**39519**	**12201490**	**27030**
采掘业	Mining					
制造业	Manufacturing	1714817	1449099	6686	12201490	26141
电力煤气及水生产供应业	Production and Supply of Electricity, Gas and Water	9250891		32833		889

7-2 续表
Continued

名称	Name	煤油(吨) Kerosene (ton)	柴油(吨) Diesel Oil (ton)	燃料油(吨) Fuel Oil (ton)	液化石油气(吨) Liquefied Petroleum Gas (ton)	热力(百万千焦) Heat (million kJ)	电力(万千瓦时) Electricity (10 000kW·h)
总　计	**Total**	**78**	**53565**	**68705**	**83158**	**25212810**	**1846883**
采掘业	Mining		197				4408
制造业	Manufacturing	78	51805	65574	83158	21874820	1611637
电力煤气及水生产供应业	Production and Supply of Electricity, Gas and Water		1563	3131		3337990	230837

7-3 重点耗能工业企业能源加工转换（2019年）

ENERGY CONVERSION OF MAJOR ENERGY-CONSUMING INDUSTRIAL ENTERPRISES (2019)

名称	Name	单位	Unit	能源消费合计 Total Energy Consumption	#加工转换投入 Conversion Input	火电 Thermal Power	供热 Heating	炼油 Petroleum Refining	制气 Gas Production	能源加工转换产出 Conversion Output of Energy
原　煤	Raw Coal	吨	ton	10307717	9717388	5519381	4172867		25140	
洗精煤	Dressing Coal	吨	ton	2122613	2122613					
煤制品	Coal Products	吨	ton	72822	72822		72822			
焦　炭	Coke	吨	ton	1448188						1552144
其他焦化产品	Other Coking Products	吨	ton	43153						80898
焦炉煤气	Coking Gas	万立方米	10 000 cn.m	32833	32833	31642	1191			39518
高炉煤气	Blast Furnace GAS	万立方米	10 000 cn.m	551339	155517	148422	7094			
原　油	Crude Oil	吨	ton	12201490	12191375			12191375		
汽　油	Petrol	吨	ton	263						3745486
煤　油	Kerosene	吨	ton							1440023
柴　油	Diesel Oil	吨	ton	1505	185	185				3054855
燃料油	Fuel Oil	吨	ton	26854	26744	776	2045	23923		171160
液化石油气	Liquefied Petroleum Gas	吨	ton							974829
炼厂干气	Refinery Dry Gas	吨	ton	368469	2700	270	2430			368469
其他石油制品	Other Petroleum Products	吨	ton	773505	439003			439003		997443
热　力	Heat	百万千焦	million kJ	9535030	2778364	2778364				82493039
电　力	Electricity	万千瓦时	10 000kW·h	548861						1706709
其他燃料	Other Fuel	吨标准煤	ton SCE							
能源合计	**Total**	**吨标准煤**	**ton SCE**	**35050204**	**28731564**	**5067373**	**3524069**	**18099938**	**23702**	**24215815**

7-4 规模以上工业主要能源工业消费量(2019 年)
MAJOR ENERGY CONSUMPTION OF INDUSTRY ABOVE DESIGNATED SIZE (2019)

行业	Sector
总　计	**Total**
煤炭开采和洗选业	Mining and Washing of Coal
石油和天然气开采业	Extraction of Petroleum and Natural Gas
黑色金属矿采选业	Mining of Ferrous Metal Ores
有色金属矿采选业	Mining of Non-ferrous Metal Ores
非金属矿采选业	Mining and Processing of Nonmetal Ores
开采辅助活动	Auxiliary Activities of Mining
其他采矿业	Mining of Other Ores
农副食品加工业	Processing of Food from Agricultural Products
食品制造业	Manufacture of Foods
酒、饮料和精制茶制造业	Manufacture of Liquor, Beverage and Refined Tea
烟草制品业	Manufacture of Tobacco
纺织业	Manufacture of Textile
纺织服装、服饰业	Manufacture of Textile Wearing Apparel
皮革、毛皮、羽毛及其制品和制鞋业	Manufacture of Leather, Fur, Feather &Its Products Footwear
木材加工和木、竹、藤、棕、草制品业	Processing of Timbers, Manufacture of Wood, Bamboo, Rattan, Palm and Straw Products
家具制造业	Manufacture of Furniture
造纸和纸制品业	Manufacture of Paper and Paper Products
印刷和记录媒介复制业	Printing, Reproduction of Recording Media
文教、工美、体育和娱乐用品制造业	Manufacture of Articles for Culture, Arts& Crafts, Sports and Entertainment
石油加工、炼焦和核燃料加工业	Processing of Petroleum, Coking, Processing of Nucleus Fuel
化学原料和化学制品制造业	Manufacture of Chemical Raw Material and Chemical Products
医药制造业	Manufacture of Medicines
化学纤维制造业	Manufacture of Chemical Fiber
橡胶和塑料制品业	Manufacture of Rubber and Plastic
非金属矿物制品业	Manufacture of Non-metallic Mineral Products
黑色金属冶炼和压延加工业	Smelting and Pressing of Ferrous Metals
有色金属冶炼和压延加工业	Smelting and Pressing of Non-ferrous Metals
金属制品业	Manufacture of Metal Products
通用设备制造业	Manufacture of General Purpose Machinery
专用设备制造业	Manufacture of Special Purpose Machinery
汽车制造业	Manufacture of Vehicle
铁路、船舶、航空航天和其他运输设备制造业	Manufacture of Transport Equipment for Railway, Shipping, Aerospace and other uses
电气机械和器材制造业	Manufacture of Electrical Machinery &Equipment
计算机、通信和其他电子设备制造业	Manufacture of Computer, Communication Equipment and Other Electronic Equipment
仪器仪表制造业	Manufacture of Measuring Instrument
其他制造业	Manufacture of Other Products
废弃资源综合利用业	Recycling and Disposal of Waste Resources
金属制品、机械和设备修理业	Manufacture of Metal Products, Machinery and Equipment
电力、热力生产和供应业	Production and Supply of Electric Power and Heat Power
燃气生产和供应业	Production and Supply of Gas
水的生产和供应业	Production and Supply of Water

原煤 （吨） Raw Coal (ton)	洗精煤 （吨） Dressing Coal (ton)	其他洗煤 （吨） Other Dressing Coal (ton)	煤制品 （吨） Coal Products (ton)	焦炭 （吨） Coke (ton)
10965708	**2122613**	**28994**	**73408**	**1449099**
122207				
76977			110	
15325				
1			5	
43				
6				
2			4	
59424			466	
2006				
492167		28994		
122803				
240230			1	
580481	2122613			1448188
1242				
205				375
36				536
406				
806				
433				
18				
9250891			72822	

7-4 续表 1
Continued

行业	Sector
总　　计	**Total**
煤炭开采和洗选业	Mining and Washing of Coal
石油和天然气开采业	Extraction of Petroleum and Natural Gas
黑色金属矿采选业	Mining of Ferrous Metal Ores
有色金属矿采选业	Mining of Non-ferrous Metal Ores
非金属矿采选业	Mining and Processing of Nonmetal Ores
开采辅助活动	Auxiliary Activities of Mining
其他采矿业	Mining of Other Ores
农副食品加工业	Processing of Food from Agricultural Products
食品制造业	Manufacture of Foods
酒、饮料和精制茶制造业	Manufacture of Liquor, Beverage and Refined Tea
烟草制品业	Manufacture of Tobacco
纺织业	Manufacture of Textile
纺织服装、服饰业	Manufacture of Textile Wearing Apparel
皮革、毛皮、羽毛及其制品和制鞋业	Manufacture of Leather, Fur, Feather &Its Products Footwear
木材加工和木、竹、藤、棕、草制品业	Processing of Timbers, Manufacture of Wood, Bamboo, Rattan, Palm and Straw Products
家具制造业	Manufacture of Furniture
造纸和纸制品业	Manufacture of Paper and Paper Products
印刷和记录媒介复制业	Printing, Reproduction of Recording Media
文教、工美、体育和娱乐用品制造业	Manufacture of Articles for Culture, Arts& Crafts, Sports and Entertainment
石油加工、炼焦和核燃料加工业	Processing of Petroleum, Coking, Processing of Nucleus Fuel
化学原料和化学制品制造业	Manufacture of Chemical Raw Material and Chemical Products
医药制造业	Manufacture of Medicines
化学纤维制造业	Manufacture of Chemical Fiber
橡胶和塑料制品业	Manufacture of Rubber and Plastic
非金属矿物制品业	Manufacture of Non-metallic Mineral Products
黑色金属冶炼和压延加工业	Smelting and Pressing of Ferrous Metals
有色金属冶炼和压延加工业	Smelting and Pressing of Non-ferrous Metals
金属制品业	Manufacture of Metal Products
通用设备制造业	Manufacture of General Purpose Machinery
专用设备制造业	Manufacture of Special Purpose Machinery
汽车制造业	Manufacture of Vehicle
铁路、船舶、航空航天和其他运输设备制造业	Manufacture of Transport Equipment for Railway, Shipping, Aerospace and other uses
电气机械和器材制造业	Manufacture of Electrical Machinery &Equipment
计算机、通信和其他电子设备制造业	Manufacture of Computer, Communication Equipment and Other Electronic Equipment
仪器仪表制造业	Manufacture of Measuring Instrument
其他制造业	Manufacture of Other Products
废弃资源综合利用业	Recycling and Disposal of Waste Resources
金属制品、机械和设备修理业	Manufacture of Metal Products, Machinery and Equipment
电力、热力生产和供应业	Production and Supply of Electric Power and Heat Power
燃气生产和供应业	Production and Supply of Gas
水的生产和供应业	Production and Supply of Water

焦炉煤气（万立方米）Coking Gas (10 000 cu.m)	高炉煤气（万立方米）Blast Furnace GAS (10 000 cu.m)	原油（吨）Crude Oil (ton)	汽油（吨）Petrol (ton)	煤油（吨）Kerosene (ton)
39518	**563439**	**12201490**	**27030**	**78**
			2170	
			595	
			196	
			708	
			763	
			231	
			18	
			201	
			393	
			982	
			754	
		12201490	94	
			1253	
			445	
			2225	
6686	12101		851	
	395822		74	
			155	
			1302	6
			2252	67
			1562	
			4458	2
			1478	2
			1447	
			924	
			494	
			116	
32833	155517		130	
			274	
			485	

7-4 续表 2
Continued

行业	Sector
总　　计	**Total**
煤炭开采和洗选业	Mining and Washing of Coal
石油和天然气开采业	Extraction of Petroleum and Natural Gas
黑色金属矿采选业	Mining of Ferrous Metal Ores
有色金属矿采选业	Mining of Non-ferrous Metal Ores
非金属矿采选业	Mining and Processing of Nonmetal Ores
开采辅助活动	Auxiliary Activities of Mining
其他采矿业	Mining of Other Ores
农副食品加工业	Processing of Food from Agricultural Products
食品制造业	Manufacture of Foods
酒、饮料和精制茶制造业	Manufacture of Liquor, Beverage and Refined Tea
烟草制品业	Manufacture of Tobacco
纺织业	Manufacture of Textile
纺织服装、服饰业	Manufacture of Textile Wearing Apparel
皮革、毛皮、羽毛及其制品和制鞋业	Manufacture of Leather, Fur, Feather &Its Products Footwear
木材加工和木、竹、藤、棕、草制品业	Processing of Timbers, Manufacture of Wood, Bamboo, Rattan, Palm and Straw Products
家具制造业	Manufacture of Furniture
造纸和纸制品业	Manufacture of Paper and Paper Products
印刷和记录媒介复制业	Printing, Reproduction of Recording Media
文教、工美、体育和娱乐用品制造业	Manufacture of Articles for Culture, Arts& Crafts, Sports and Entertainment
石油加工、炼焦和核燃料加工业	Processing of Petroleum, Coking, Processing of Nucleus Fuel
化学原料和化学制品制造业	Manufacture of Chemical Raw Material and Chemical Products
医药制造业	Manufacture of Medicines
化学纤维制造业	Manufacture of Chemical Fiber
橡胶和塑料制品业	Manufacture of Rubber and Plastic
非金属矿物制品业	Manufacture of Non-metallic Mineral Products
黑色金属冶炼和压延加工业	Smelting and Pressing of Ferrous Metals
有色金属冶炼和压延加工业	Smelting and Pressing of Non-ferrous Metals
金属制品业	Manufacture of Metal Products
通用设备制造业	Manufacture of General Purpose Machinery
专用设备制造业	Manufacture of Special Purpose Machinery
汽车制造业	Manufacture of Vehicle
铁路、船舶、航空航天和其他运输设备制造业	Manufacture of Transport Equipment for Railway, Shipping, Aerospace and other uses
电气机械和器材制造业	Manufacture of Electrical Machinery &Equipment
计算机、通信和其他电子设备制造业	Manufacture of Computer, Communication Equipment and Other Electronic Equipment
仪器仪表制造业	Manufacture of Measuring Instrument
其他制造业	Manufacture of Other Products
废弃资源综合利用业	Recycling and Disposal of Waste Resources
金属制品、机械和设备修理业	Manufacture of Metal Products, Machinery and Equipment
电力、热力生产和供应业	Production and Supply of Electric Power and Heat Power
燃气生产和供应业	Production and Supply of Gas
水的生产和供应业	Production and Supply of Water

柴油 （吨） Diesel Oil (ton)	燃料油 （吨） Fuel Oil (ton)	液化石油气 （吨） Liquefied Petroleum Gas (ton)	炼厂干气 （吨） Refinery Dry Gas (ton)
53565	**68705**	**83158**	**368469**
197			
2370	395	369	
553			
555		286	
215			
391		320	
490	769		
70			
320			
508			
931	900		
518	12		
228	23923		368469
2408	457	80853	
260			
13			
1983	221	299	
25137	38021	460	
115			
674			
1755	62	309	
1740		40	
494		1	
2198		11	
6001	814	18	
675		177	
1008		13	
15		1	
178			
1279	3131		
51			
233			

7-4 续表 3
Continued

行业	Sector
总　　计	**Total**
煤炭开采和洗选业	Mining and Washing of Coal
石油和天然气开采业	Extraction of Petroleum and Natural Gas
黑色金属矿采选业	Mining of Ferrous Metal Ores
有色金属矿采选业	Mining of Non-ferrous Metal Ores
非金属矿采选业	Mining and Processing of Nonmetal Ores
开采辅助活动	Auxiliary Activities of Mining
其他采矿业	Mining of Other Ores
农副食品加工业	Processing of Food from Agricultural Products
食品制造业	Manufacture of Foods
酒、饮料和精制茶制造业	Manufacture of Liquor, Beverage and Refind Tea
烟草制品业	Manufacture of Tobacco
纺织业	Manufacture of Textile
纺织服装、服饰业	Manufacture of Textil Wearing Apparel
皮革、毛皮、羽毛及其制品和制鞋业	Manufacture of Leather, Fur, Feathre&Its Products Footwear
木材加工和木、竹、藤、棕、草制品业	Processing of Timbers, Manufacture of Wood, Bamboo, Rattan, Palm and Straw Products
家具制造业	Manufacture of Furniture
造纸和纸制品业	Manufacture of Paper and Paper Products
印刷和记录媒介复制业	Printing, Reproduction of Recording Media
文教、工美、体育和娱乐用品制造业	Manufacture of Articles for Culture, Arts& Crafts, Sports and Entertainment
石油加工、炼焦和核燃料加工业	Processing of Petroleum, Coking, Processing of Nucleus Fuel
化学原料和化学制品制造业	Manufacture of Chemical Raw Material and Chemical Products
医药制造业	Manufacture of Medicines
化学纤维制造业	Manufacture of Chemical Fiber
橡胶和塑料制品业	Manufacture of Rubber and Plastic
非金属矿物制品业	Manufacture of Non-metallic Mineral Products
黑色金属冶炼和压延加工业	Smelting and Pressing of Ferrous Metals
有色金属冶炼和压延加工业	Smelting and Pressing of Non-ferrous Metals
金属制品业	Manufacture of Metal Products
通用设备制造业	Manufacture of General Purpose Machinery
专用设备制造业	Manufacture of Special Purpose Machinery
汽车制造业	Manufacture of Vehicle
铁路、船舶、航空航天和其他运输设备制造业	Manufacture of Transport Equipment for Railway, Shipping, Aerospace and other uses
电气机械和器材制造业	Manufacture of Electrical Machinery &Equipment
计算机、通信和其他电子设备制造业	Manufacture of Computer, Communication Equipment and Other Electronic Equipment
仪器仪表制造业	Manufacture of Measuring Instrument
其他制造业	Manufacture of Other Products
废弃资源综合利用业	Recycling and Disposal of Waste Resources
金属制品、机械和设备修理业	Manufacture of Metal Products, Machinery and Equipment
电力、热力生产和供应业	Production and Supply of Electric Power and Heat Power
燃气生产和供应业	Production and Supply of Gas
水的生产和供应业	Production and Supply of Water

其他油制品（吨）Other Petroleum Products (ton)	热力（百万千焦）Heat (million kJ)	电力（万千瓦时）Electricity (10 000kW·h)	其他燃料（吨标准煤）Other Fuel (ton SCE)
774415	**25212810**	**1846883**	**4677**
		2281	
		2127	
	2461216	79770	2325
	438123	35324	
	2204685	21162	
	1853602	42982	314
	525349	16006	783
	89083	10710	203
		3252	
	2104	7649	
	863145	12266	
	16756	14384	
	3161	20408	
718940	5533	109037	
55375	5555524	204953	
	386767	14100	
	18769	5044	
	2958221	156111	
	46427	101885	
	1767774	214755	
	51136	24143	
13	54194	82000	
74	94326	65979	892
	96971	27298	
	610595	117822	
13	953718	67922	
	610448	95412	160
	206583	54201	
		4062	
	608	2492	
		226	
		281	
	3337990	179666	
		10656	
		40515	

主要统计指标解释

工业企业能源消费量 工业企业能源消费包括工业企业在生产过程中作为燃料、动力、原料、辅助材料使用的能源以及工艺用能、非生产用能；作为能源加工转换企业，还要包括能源加工转换的投入量。工业企业能源消费量具体包括：

（1）用于本企业产品生产、工业性作业和其他生产性活动的能源。

（2）用于技术更新改造措施、新技术研究和新产品试制以及科学试验等方面的能源。

（3）用于经营维修、建筑及设备大修理、机电设备和交通运输工具等方面的能源。

（4）用于劳动保护的能源。

（5）其他非生产消费的能源。

不包括：

（1）由仓库发到车间，但在报告期最后一天没有消费的能源。这部分能源应在办理假退料手续后计入库存量。

（2）拨到外单位，委托外单位加工用的能源。

（3）调出本单位或借给外单位的能源。

工业生产能源消费 是指工业企业为进行工业生产活动所使用的能源。主要包括：

1. 用于本企业产品生产、工业性作业的能源，包括用作原料、材料、燃料、动力；作为能源加工转换企业，还包括用作加工转换的能源。

2. 产品生产过程中作为辅助材料使用的能源。

3. 生产工艺过程使用的能源。

4. 新技术研究、新产品试制、科学试验使用的能源。

5. 为了工业生产活动而在进行的各种修理过程中使用的能源。

6. 生产区内的劳动保护用能等。

Explanatory Notes on Main Statistical Indicators

Energy Consumption of Industrial Enterprises include energy in the production process as fuel, power, raw materials, supplementary materials, and for use of technology and non-production. As energy processing and conversion enterprises, also include energy processing and conversion of inputs. These specifically include: 1. Energy for the enterprise product, industrial production operations and other activities. 2. Energy for technical upgrading measures and new technology research and new product production and scientific experiments. 3. Energy for operation maintenance, construction and equipment overhaul, electrical and mechanical equipment and transport, and other aspects. 4. Energy for the protection of labor. 5. Energy for Other non-production and consumption. And these exclude: 1. Energy from the warehouse to the workshop, but out of consumption on the last day of the reporting period. This part of the energy should leave retreat materials handling procedures included stock. 2. Energy transferred to other units, entrusted with the processing. 3. Energy transferred out of the unit or loans to other units.

Energy Consumption for Industrial Production refers to energy for industrial enterprises in industrial production activities. These mainly include: 1. Energy for the enterprise products, industrial operations, including energy as raw materials, materials, fuels, and power. As energy processing and conversion enterprises, also include energy for processing and conversion. 2. Energy as supplementary material in product process. 3. Energy used in production process. 4. Energy for new technologies, new product production, and scientific experiment. 5. Energy in process of repairing for industrial production activities. 6. Energy for labor protection in production areas and so on.

财政、金融和保险业 8

GOVERNMENT FINANCE, FINACIAL AND INSURANCE

简要说明

一、本篇资料的主要内容

本篇资料主要反映了全市财政收支、金融和保险方面的情况，主要包括财政收入、财政支出、金融机构存贷款、保险业务开展等方面的资料。

二、本篇资料的来源

1. 财政部分的资料来源于市财政局。

2. 金融方面的资料来源于中国人民银行青岛市中心支行。

3. 保险方面的资料来源于中国保险监督管理委员会青岛监管局。

本篇资料由市统计局国民经济核算处整理提供。

Brief Introduction

I. Main Content

Data in this chapter show the conditions of local government budgetary finance, banking and insurance, and securities, including government revenue and expenditure, deposits and loans of financial institutions and statistics on insurance companies.

II. Source of Data

1. Data on local government finance are provided by Qingdao Municipal Finance Bureau.

2. Data on banking are provided by Qingdao Branch of the People´s Bank of China.

3. Data on insurance are provide by China Insurance Regulatory Commission of Qingdao Bureau.

Data in this chapter are prepared and compiled by the Division of National Accounts of Qingdao Municipal Bureau of Statistics.

8-1 主要年份地方财政收支

MAJOR YEAR´S REVENUE AND EXPENDITURE OF LOCAL GOVERNMENT FINANCE

单位：万元 (10 000 yuan)

年份 Year	财政收入 Revenue of Government Finance	财政支出 Expenditure of Government Finance
1949	1527	306
1952	19809	2226
1957	29875	3556
1962	32869	4327
1965	47682	6280
1970	95778	7825
1975	90220	11966
1978	130749	19427
1980	124835	20064
1985	165155	41996
1988	201206	93931
1990	242303	133875
1991	259377	137716
1992	275589	155696
1993	182348	211938
1994	227490	277331
1995	294771	376982
1996	379674	469569
1997	476804	564787
1998	580434	678575
1999	680089	740937
2000	800120	878702
2001	987080	1097848
2002	1006616	1243880
2003	1201398	1471747
2004	1305136	1646214
2005	1763412	2030622
2006	2257663	2367875
2007	2925798	3211777
2008	3424359	3694111
2009	3769896	4335754
2010	4526138	5323888
2011	5661400	6580605
2012	6701820	7659801
2013	7889313	10142273
2014	8952450	10747138
2015	10063220	12228664
2016	11000303	13528516
2017	11572389	14030252
2018	12319138	15597764
2019	12417359	15759729

注：1. 1993 年以后实行新制度，财政收入数与历年不可比。
2. 2002 年以后，财政收入、支出为一般预算数。

Note : 1. Since 1993, new regulations have been adopted in calculating revenue of government finance, the figures are not comparable with those over the years.
2. Since 2002, revenue of government finance and expenditure of government finance refer to general budgetary revenue and expenditure.

8-2 分市、区公共财政预算收入(2019年)
PUBLIC FINANCE BUDGET REVENUE BY CITY AND DISTRICT (2019)

单位：万元 (10 000 yuan)

市、区名称	Region	一般公共预算收入 Public Finance Budget Revenue	#增值税 Value-added Tax	#营业税 Business Tax	#企业所得税 Enterprise Income Tax
全　市	**Whole Municipality**	**12417359**	**3612489**		**1485273**
市南区	Shinan District	852382	283543		131090
市北区	Shibei District	966945	306296		119967
李沧区	Licang District	1062595	208966		70387
崂山区	Laoshan District	1571045	442196		282715
西海岸新区	West Coast New Area	2680471	887853		367548
黄岛区	Huangdao District	2547929	830965		328463
保税港区	Qingdao Free Trade Port Area of China	132542	56888		39085
城阳区	Chengyang District	1534000	539065		220170
城阳区（不含高新区）	Chengyang District (Excluding High tech District)	1166757	422990		152345
高新区	High tech District	367243	116075		67825
即墨区	Jimo District	1118727	321766		69758
胶州市	Jiaozhou	1013877	310849		101052
平度市	Pingdu	580550	137275		29136
莱西市	Laixi	509591	174680		27035

8-2 续表
Continued

单位：万元 (10 000 yuan)

市、区名称	Region	#个人所得税 Personal Income Tax	#城市维护建设税 Urban Maintenance and Development Tax	#基金预算收入 Funds Budgetary Revenue
全　市	**Whole Municipality**	**350756**	**571598**	**12051372**
市南区	Shinan District	69884	41151	
市北区	Shibei District	33690	53644	
李沧区	Licang District	13729	34949	
崂山区	Laoshan District	76526	99816	1111307
西海岸新区	West Coast New Area	60428	131513	3178728
黄岛区	Huangdao District	57340	125720	3176409
保税港区	Qingdao Free Trade Port Area of China	3088	5793	2319
城阳区	Chengyang District	40484	78178	2057192
城阳区（不含高新区）	Chengyang District (Excluding High tech District)	30991	59193	997535
高新区	High tech District	9493	18985	1059657
即墨区	Jimo District	15364	46892	1445351
胶州市	Jiaozhou	11071	38881	1323859
平度市	Pingdu	8878	20940	212737
莱西市	Laixi	20702	25634	159298

8-3 分市、区公共财政预算支出（2019年）

PUBLIC FINANCE BUDGET REVENUE BY CITY AND DISTRICT (2019)

单位：万元 (10 000 yuan)

市、区名称	Region	一般公共预算支出 Public Finance Budget Revenue	#一般公共服务支出 General Public Services	#公共安全 Public Security	#教育 Education	#科学技术 Science and Technology	#文化体育与传媒 Culture, Sport and Media
全　市	**Whole Municipality**	**15759729**	**1845286**	**945167**	**2750716**	**668363**	**314960**
市南区	Shinan District	496106	60839	22610	108653	6410	3799
市北区	Shibei District	648843	121766	24912	178289	24172	5377
李沧区	Licang District	837013	75399	24328	147651	62110	8355
崂山区	Laoshan District	1021655	92691	46112	138161	119123	6249
西海岸新区	West Coast New Area	2310526	430748	87924	509555	45456	30553
黄岛区	Huangdao District	2236687	408344	87640	509476	35839	30317
保税港区	Qingdao Free Trade Port Area of China	73839	22404	284	79	9617	236
城阳区	Chengyang District	1203845	132106	39929	273523	70058	13608
城阳区（不含高新区）	Chengyang District (Excluding High tech District)	924764	103481	37073	232323	31412	7815
高新区	High tech District	279081	28625	2856	41200	38646	5793
即墨区	Jimo District	1371321	144192	46332	298061	21674	14721
胶州市	Jiaozhou	1170272	163373	72440	284896	20403	17946
平度市	Pingdu	1020663	98967	43440	280140	13828	7694
莱西市	Laixi	749327	112303	30485	111655	3039	7544

8-3 续表
Continued

单位：万元 (10 000 yuan)

市、区名称	Region	#社会保障和就业 Social Security and Employment	#医疗卫生 Health Care	#节能环保 Environment Protection	#城乡社区事务 Urban and Rural Community Affairs	#农林水事务 Affairs of Agriculture Forest and Irrigation	#基金预算支出 Funds Budgetary Expenditure
全　市	**Whole Municipality**	**1946650**	**920427**	**255949**	**2796878**	**808140**	**13113338**
市南区	Shinan District	67902	23205	7630	136556	5505	2676
市北区	Shibei District	84990	42367	9654	125085	56	64896
李沧区	Licang District	79942	32941	34938	349310	6474	178906
崂山区	Laoshan District	56041	55149	28622	324092	71064	784952
西海岸新区	West Coast New Area	269312	140790	30630	298709	110225	3740050
黄岛区	Huangdao District	267849	140559	30630	284322	110211	3736652
保税港区	Qingdao Free Trade Port Area of China	1463	231		14387	14	3398
城阳区	Chengyang District	85251	59545	10157	289146	60093	2303822
城阳区（不含高新区）	Chengyang District (Excluding High tech District)	66052	51037	5451	221453	54475	1568399
高新区	High tech District	19199	8508	4706	67693	5618	735423
即墨区	Jimo District	160712	72253	8609	413623	85933	1599125
胶州市	Jiaozhou	102144	99305	30109	195647	85448	1584216
平度市	Pingdu	212704	107541	7628	71920	125188	245956
莱西市	Laixi	171543	53737	12187	93449	74329	165880

8-4 主要年份金融系统人民币存贷款(年末余额)
MAJOR YEAR'S DEPOSITS AND LOANS OF FINANCIAL INSTITUTIONS (YEAR-END BALANCE)

单位:万元 (10 000 yuan)

年份 Year	存款合计 Total Deposits	#企业存款 Deposits by Enterprises	#储蓄存款 Savings Deposits	贷款合计 Total Loans
1949	693	239	28	278
1952	9093	4308	1838	3322
1957	10372	3359	4037	30690
1962	20040	8579	3279	73601
1965	27331	11830	6347	64555
1970	38264	13024	7576	126382
1975	60622	22568	15637	207006
1978	66523	21004	21455	297184
1980	120644	38105	38609	379666
1985	344760	99736	155604	452142
1990	1235562	321542	655895	1535751
1991	1553564	411417	824428	1871462
1992	2076667	612868	1044165	2352449
1993	2747294	835617	1372239	2940658
1994	3769019	1399110	1918734	3610564
1995	5324026	2030382	2687888	4777864
1996	6991289	2630958	3499219	5941281
1997	7385092	2885632	4060259	6508776
1998	8183471	3018063	4591012	7239231
1999	9160001	3454570	4978045	8945730
2000	10560624	4386316	5353215	9564293
2001	12323942	4955336	6187409	10798871
2002	15225733	5819655	7449408	13044792
2003	18920868	7027227	9084693	16783917
2004	22462592	7924690	10894941	18472613
2005	26975372	8226661	13431016	20394792
2006	32453583	10144296	15676197	25779442
2007	38915882	13213434	17020383	30970553
2008	47353803	14641948	21233637	37483209
2009	63019764	21001185	25278658	48735326
2010	76592065	27271963	29123256	58862263
2011	86384994	49189415	31985099	69477500
2012	94348924	50978985	37576007	79465532
2013	109695588	60367185	41405946	88607439
2014	113703085	60791933	44358964	97200532
2015	125330268	45526577	50235905	107718528
2016	140071344	50912759	53263262	118916821
2017	143877550	53835435	53941843	132647913
2018	155321863	57270448	59137089	151941934
2019	172829678	66873600	67552370	173318261

注:本表数据来源于人民银行,自2015年起,人民银行报表指标变化,企业存款指标暂用非金融企业存款,储蓄存款指标暂用住户存款,口径与以前年度不一致。

Note: The data in this table comes from the People' s Bank of China. Since 2015, the report index of the People's Bank of China has changed, the enterprise deposit index is temporarily used as the deposit of the enterprise, the savings deposit index is temporarily used for household deposit, the caliber is not consistent with the previous year.

8-5 金融系统人民币存贷款（年末余额）

DEPOSITS AND LOANS OF FINANCIAL INSTITUTIONS (YEAR-END BALANCE)

单位：万元 (10 000 yuan)

项目	Item	2019 年	比年初增减数 Incremental/Reductions Compared to the Beginning of the Year
一、存款总计	Total Deposits	172829678	17478276
住户存款	Household Deposits	67552370	8388811
非金融企业存款	Non-Financial Corporate Deposits	66873600	9606129
广义政府存款	General Government Deposits	31080891	1748368
非银行业金融机构存款	Non-Banking Financial Institutions' s Deposits	6855680	-2274908
二、贷款总计	Total Loans	173318261	20970319
住户贷款	Household Loans	56915003	8596693
# 短期贷款	Short-Term Loans	6278795	1593420
中长期贷款	Medium And Long-Term Loans	50636208	7003274
非金融企业及机关团体贷款	Non-Financial Enterprises And Institutions/ Organizations' Loans	116117942	12426610
# 短期贷款	Short-Term Loans	35733198	1387101
中长期贷款	Medium&Long-term Loans	72407558	9558148
票据融资	Notes Financing	6704941	1179750
非银行业金融机构贷款	Non-Banking Financial Institution' s Loans	19852	-261

注：自 2015 年起，人民银行报表中指标发生变化，本表数据按照新指标提供。

Note: Since 2015, the indexes in the People' s Bank of China' s statements have changed, the data in the table are provided according to the new indexes.

8-6 国内保险业务（2000-2019 年）

DOMESTIC INSURANCE BUSINESS (2000-2019)

项目	Item	2000 年	2005 年	2006 年	2008 年	2009 年	2010 年
风险保障金额	**Total domestic insurance Value**	**38357485**	**91691581**	**119396881**	**276989344**	**293519697**	**309244255**
国内业务收入	**Domestic Business Income**	**220780**	**495701**	**605143**	**1027258**	**1153101**	**1538526**
1. 保费收入	Premium Income	218714	495701	605143	1027258	1153101	1538526
# 财产险	Property Insurance	85161	159746	199213	280008	339314	492190
农业险	Agriculture Insurance	18	12	19	3135	4066	3261
人身险	Personal Insurance	133535	335943	405911	744115	809721	1043075
国内业务支出	**Domestic Business Expenditure**	**94877**	**214148**	**252477**	**423743**	**476377**	**497832**
1 . 赔款支出	Indemnity Expenditure	62275	111385	131321	196318	219546	279019
# 财产险	Property Insurance	58361	92700	115214	164415	188723	250966
农业险	Agriculture Insurance	5	11	3	907	3452	2808
人身险	Personal Insurance	3909	18674	16104	30996	27371	25245
2 . 给付支出	Mature Payment	27955	32739	63144	132621	123056	109318
3 . 退保	Surrender	4647	70024	58012	94804	133775	109496

注：本表由青岛保监局提供，风险保障金额 2012 年之前为国内保险总值。

Note: This table was provided by the Qingdao Insurance Regulatory Bureau. The amount of risk protection before 2012 was the total value of domestic insurance.

单位：万元 (10 000 yuan)

2011 年	2012 年	2013 年	2014 年	2015 年	2016 年	2017 年	2018 年	2019 年
380829634	**447476690**	**491953749**	**611632799**	**836499657**	**1687559828**	**2232390824**	**2337365406**	**2759993215**
1457269	**1602881**	**1789854**	**2031421**	**2441172**	**3359013**	**3967170**	**4393970**	**4868673**
1457269	1602881	1789854	2031421	2441172	3359013	3967170	4393970	4868673
556257	644269	744470	872805	920229	1046908	1062116	1269489	1267684
3587	5046	6824	8395	12100	12734	15670	18043	24523
897425	953566	1038560	1150220	1508843	2299371	2889384	3106438	3600989
463751	**592167**	**757404**	**1031415**	**1236281**	**1522375**	**1704218**	**1919252**	**1882881**
307564	360085	432494	492693	539320	681211	733493	917964	937025
286214	328877	392860	442168	492573	526586	554513	756987	720657
1087	1833	3820	5519	9724	16337	18232	10985	14019
20263	29375	35814	45006	37023	138288	160749	149992	216368
156188	154922	194592	274790	340786	455300	470266	493511	498555
69275	77159	130318	263932	356175	376777	500459	507777	447301

主要统计指标解释

财政收入 指国家财政参与社会产品分配所取得的收入，是实现国家职能的财力保证。财政收入所包括的内容几经变化，目前主要包括：

（1）税收收入：包括增值税、营业税、企业所得税、个人所得税、资源税、城市维护建设税、房产税、印花税、城镇土地使用税、土地增值税、车船税、耕地占用税、契税、烟叶税、其他税收收入。

（2）非税收入：包括专项收入、行政事业性收费收入、罚没收入、国有资本经营收入、国有资源有偿使用收入、其他收入。

财政支出 国家财政将筹集起来的资金进行分配使用，以满足经济建设和各项事业的需要，主要包括：

（1）一般公共服务支出：反映政府提供一般公共服务的支出。

（2）公共安全：反映政府维护社会公共安全方面的支出，有关事务包括武装警察、公安、国家安全、检察、法院、司法行政、监狱、劳教、国家保密、缉私警察等。

（3）教育支出：反映政府教育事务支出。有关具体教育事务包括教育行政管理、学前教育、小学教育、初中教育、普通高中教育、普通高等教育、初等职业教育、中专教育、技校教育、职业高中教育、高等职业教育、广播电视教育、留学生教育、特殊教育、干部继续教育、教育机关服务等。

（4）科学技术：反映政府用于科学技术方面的支出。

（5）文化体育与传媒：反映政府在文化、文物、体育、广播电视、新闻出版等方面的支出。

（6）社会保障和就业：反映政府在社会保障与就业方面的支出。有关事项包括社会保障与就业管理事务、民政管理事务、财政对社会保险基金的补助、补充全国社会保障基金、行政事业单位离退休、企业改革补助、就业补助、抚恤、退役安置、社会福利、残疾人事业、城市居民最低生活保障、其他城镇社会救济、农村社会救济、自然灾害生活补助、红十字事务等。

（7）医疗卫生支出：反映政府医疗卫生方面的支出。具体包括医疗卫生管理事务支出、医疗服务支出、医疗保障支出、疾病预防控制支出、卫生监督支出、妇幼保健支出、农村卫生支出等。

（8）环境保护：反映政府环境保护支出。具体包括：环境保护管理事务支出、环境监测与监察支出、污染治理支出、自然生态保护支出、天然林保护工程支出、退耕还林支出、风沙荒漠治理支出、退牧还草支出、已垦草原退耕还草支出。

（9）城乡社区事务：反映政府城乡社区事务支出。具体包括：城乡社区管理事务支出、城乡社区规划与管理支出、城乡社区公共设施支出、城乡社区住宅支出、城乡社区环境卫生支出、建设市场管理与监督支出等。

（10）农林水事务：反映政府农林水事务方面的支出。具体包括农业、林业、水利、扶贫支出、农业综合开发支出等。

存款 指企业、机关、团体或居民根据资金必须收回的原则，把货币资金存入银行或其他信贷机构保管并取得一定利息的一种信用活动形式。根据存款对象或性质的不同可划分为企业存款、财政存款、机关团体存款、基本建设存款、储蓄存款、农村存款、委托存款、其他存款等科目。它是银行信贷资金的主要来源。

贷款 指银行或其他信贷机构根据资金必须归还的原则，按一定利率，为企业、个人等提供资金的一种信用活动形式。我国银行贷款分为短期贷款、中期流动资金贷款、中长期贷款、信托贷款、融资租赁、委托贷款、票据融资、各项垫款等。

承保额 又叫保险金额，指保险人承担赔偿或者给付保险金责任的最高限额。

保费 指投保人为取得保险人在约定范围内所承担赔偿责任而支付给保险人的费用。

Explanatory Notes on Main Statistical Indicators

Government Revenue refers to the revenue of the government finance by means of participating in the distribution of the social products, which is the financial resources for ensuring the government to function. The contents of government revenue have been changed several times. Now it includes the following main items:

1. Various tax revenues: including value added tax, business tax, enterprise income tax, personal income tax, resources tax, fixed assets investment direction regulating tax, tax on city maintenance and construction, real estate tax, stamp tax, tax on use of urban land, land value added tax, vehicle and vessel tax, tax on occupancy of cultivated land, property tax, tobacco leaf tax, and other tax revenues.

2. Non–tax Revenues: including special revenues, revenues from administrative and institutional fees, penalty and confiscatory revenues, revenues from state–owned capital operating, revenues from paid use of state–owned resources, and other revenues.

Government Expenditure refers to the distribution and use of the funds the government finance has raised, so as to meet the needs of economic construction and various causes. It includes the following main items:

1. Expenditure for general public services: It reflects the expenditure from the government for general public services.

2. Expenditure on public security: It reflects the expenditure from the government towards safeguarding the public security, including the related affairs of armed police, public security, state security, procuratorial administration, law court, judicial administration, jail, reeducation through labor, state confidentiality, anti–smuggling patrol, etc.

3. Expenditure on education: It reflects the expenditure from the government on education, including the related affairs of educational administration management, preschool education, primary education, junior secondary educate, regular senior secondary educate, regular higher education, primary vocational education, specialized secondary educate, technical educate, vocational senior secondary educate, vocational higher education, radio and television education, foreign student educate, special education, cadre continuing education, education institution services, etc.

4. Expenditure on science and technology: It reflects the expenditure from the government on science and technology.

5. Expenditure on culture, sport and media: It reflects the expenditure from the government on culture, cultural relics, sport, radio and television, publication, etc.

6. Expenditure on social security and employment: It reflects the expenditure from the government on social security and employment, including the related affairs of management of social security and employment, civil administration, subsidies to social insurance funds, supplement to national social security funds, retirees of government agencies and institutions, subsidies to enterprises reform, subsidies to employment, pension, settling down demobilized servicemen, social security, disabled person administration, minimum living allowance in urban area, other social relief in urban area, social relief in rural area, subsidies to natural disaster, Red Cross business, etc.

7. Expenditure on health care: It reflects the expenditure from the government on health care, including expenditure on management of health care, medical services, medical security, disease control and prevention, public health supervision, rural health care, etc.

8. Expenditure on environment protection: It reflects the expenditure from the government on environment protection, including expenditure on management of environment protection, environment monitoring and supervisory, pollution government, natural ecological protection, project of natural forest protection, returning farmland to forest, sandstorm and wilderness government, returning grazing land to grassland, returning cultivated grassland to grassland, etc.

9. Expenditure on urban and rural community affairs: It reflects the expenditure from the government on urban and rural community affairs, including expenditure on management of urban and rural community affairs, plan and management of urban and rural community, public utility of urban and rural community, residential buildings of urban and rural community, environmental sanitation of urban and rural community, management and supervision of markets construction, etc.

10. Expenditure on agriculture, forest and irrigation: It reflects the expenditure from the government on agriculture, forest and irrigation, including expenditure on agriculture, forest, irrigation, poverty alleviation, comprehensive development of agriculture, etc.

Deposit is a form of credit by which enterprises, institutions, organizations or households can put money into banks and other credit institutions for safekeeping and interest earning under the principle of free withdrawal. According to different depositors, deposits are divided into enterprise deposits, treasury deposits, deposits of government agencies and organizations, capital construction deposits, savings deposits, rural saving deposits, entrusted deposits and other deposits. Deposits are major sources of the credit funds of banks.

Loan is a form of credit by which banks and other credit institutions provide funds at certain interest rate to enterprises and individuals in the light of the principle of unconditional repayment. Loans from Chinese banks include circulating capital loans, fixed assets loans, loans to urban and rural individuals engaged in industrial and commercial business and agricultural loans.

Amount Covered which also is known as amount Insured, refers to the maximum that the insurant will get for the claim of the case insured.

Premium is the fee paid by the insurant to the insurer to obtain the obligation of compensation from the insurance within the agreed terms.

价格指数 9

PRICE INDEXES

简要说明

一、本篇资料的主要内容

本篇资料主要包括工业生产者出厂、工业生产者购进、固定资产投资、房地产、居民消费、商品零售等价格指数。

二、本篇资料的来源

1. 工业生产者出厂、工业生产者购进、固定资产投资、房地产价格指数分别来源于生产、投资、房地产价格统计调查年报，由国家统计局青岛调查队生产价格调查处整理提供。

2. 居民消费、商品零售价格指数来源于消费价格统计调查年报，由国家统计局青岛调查队消费价格调查处整理提供。

Brief Introduction

I. Main Content

Data in this chapter mainly include producer price indices for manufactured goods, purchasing price indices for industrial producers, price indices of investment in fixed assets, real estate price indices, consumer price indices and retail price indices.

II. Source of Data

1. Data on producer price indices for manufactured goods, purchasing price indices for industrial producers, price indices of investment in fixed assets, real estate price indices are based on annual report of price survey on production, investment, real estate, and provided by the Division of Production Price Survey of Survey Office of the National Bureau of Statistics in Qingdao.

2. Data on consumer price indices and retail price indices are based on annual report of consumer price survey, and provided by the Division of Consumer Price Survey of Survey Office of the National Bureau of Statistics in Qingdao.

9-1 主要年份居民消费和商品零售价格指数
MAJOR YEAR'S CONSUMER AND RETAIL PRICE INDEXES

（上年价格 =100） (preceding year=100)

年份 Year	居民消费价格指数 Consumer Price Index	#食品类 Food	#衣着类 Clothing	#服务项目价格指数 Services Price Index	商品零售价格指数 Retail Price Index
1951	110.5	105.2	112.4		110.5
1952	99.8	99.6	98.7		99.8
1957	101.4	101.3	101.4	99.3	101.4
1962	102.6	102.0	100.2	99.9	102.6
1965	101.2	101.3	98.8	96.9	101.2
1970	98.9	99.7	100.0	99.5	98.9
1975	100.3	100.1	100.0	100.0	100.3
1978	100.5	100.2	99.8	100.0	100.5
1980	105.2	108.5	100.3	100.6	105.5
1985	110.4	115.2	102.3	102.7	110.9
1988	120.7	125.2	117.3	118.3	120.9
1990	104.5	103.4	103.4	118.8	103.6
1991	107.0	107.0	112.1	109.6	106.8
1992	111.4	115.1	108.6	119.9	110.8
1993	123.9	120.9	119.0	158.5	119.8
1994	126.9	135.2	130.1	117.9	122.8
1995	116.2	118.1	122.8	123.2	114.2
1996	112.6	110.1	104.3	130.4	106.0
1997	104.0	101.2	102.3	120.8	100.2
1998	100.0	93.7	94.5	136.2	94.9
1999	100.2	96.7	97.1	115.6	96.6
2000	103.3	100.0	108.3	112.0	99.7
2001	101.0	100.6	98.0	108.7	98.9
2002	98.9	97.8	100.2	101.0	99.5
2003	101.4	104.3	98.4	101.7	98.3
2004	102.1	104.0	103.6	104.7	99.0
2005	102.3	102.1	108.3	101.4	99.3
2006	100.9	101.7	99.4	100.8	99.7
2007	104.5	111.6	99.4	102.4	102.7
2008	104.7	111.7	103.9	99.8	103.9
2009	100.5	101.6	101.4	100.6	98.6
2010	102.2	106.4	101.0	100.4	101.4
2011	105.0	111.1	108.2	103.1	104.5
2012	102.7	104.3	106.3	102.1	101.7
2013	102.5	105.3	104.9	100.7	101.4
2014	102.6	104.4	103.2	101.9	102.3
2015	101.2	101.7	102.8	101.3	100.0
2016	102.5	105.0	100.3	101.8	102.0
2017	102.0	99.6	100.5	103.4	100.8
2018	102.1	103.1	103.8	101.6	101.8
2019	103.3	111.6	100.6	101.7	102.4

注：1. 2016 年起，食品类统计口径有变化，不包括“茶及饮料”和“在外餐饮”两项内容。
2. 2016 年起，统计分类“服务项目价格指数”改为“服务价格指数”，增加“养老服务”和“金融服务”两项内容。

Note: 1. Statistical caliber of food category has changed since 2016. The two sections of "Tea and Drinks" and "Catering Service" are not included.
2. The statistical category of "Price Index of Service Item" has been revised to "Price Index of Service" as of 2016 with two additional sections of "Elderly Care Service" and "Financial Service".

9-2 主要年份居民消费和商品零售价格指数（以1950年价格为100）

MAJOR YEAR'S CONSUMER AND RETAIL PRICE INDEXES (1950=100)

年份 Year	居民消费价格指数 Consumer Price Index	#食品类 Food	#衣着类 Clothing	#服务项目价格指数 Services Price Index	商品零售价格指数 Retail Price Index
1951	110.5	105.2	112.4		110.5
1952	110.3	104.8	110.9		110.3
1957	119.5	120.7	115.3	91.6	119.5
1962	127.4	128.8	115.1	94.2	127.4
1965	133.3	138.7	108.4	81.5	133.3
1970	129.0	137.6	110.3	76.8	129.0
1975	128.8	138.2	110.0	75.7	128.8
1978	129.1	138.7	109.8	75.7	129.1
1980	137.6	154.1	109.3	76.1	138.1
1985	160.8	196.1	103.8	80.5	162.5
1988	223.8	295.2	133.2	100.8	227.6
1990	269.7	333.3	166.8	155.9	269.7
1991	288.6	356.7	187.0	170.9	288.1
1992	321.5	410.5	203.1	204.9	319.2
1993	398.3	496.3	241.7	324.8	382.4
1994	505.4	671.1	314.4	382.9	469.5
1995	587.3	792.5	386.1	471.8	536.2
1996	661.3	872.6	402.7	615.2	568.4
1997	687.8	883.0	412.0	743.1	569.5
1998	687.8	827.4	389.3	1012.1	540.5
1999	689.2	800.1	378.0	1170.0	522.1
2000	711.9	800.1	409.4	1310.4	520.5
2001	719.0	804.9	401.2	1424.4	514.8
2002	711.1	787.2	402.0	1438.7	512.2
2003	721.1	821.0	395.6	1463.1	503.5
2004	736.2	853.9	409.8	1531.9	498.5
2005	753.1	871.8	443.8	1553.4	495.0
2006	759.9	886.6	441.2	1565.8	493.5
2007	794.1	989.5	438.5	1603.4	506.8
2008	831.4	1105.3	455.6	1600.2	526.6
2009	835.6	1123.0	462.0	1609.8	519.2
2010	854.0	1194.9	466.6	1616.2	526.5
2011	896.7	1327.5	504.9	1666.3	550.2
2012	920.9	1384.6	536.7	1701.3	559.6
2013	943.9	1458.0	563.0	1713.2	567.4
2014	968.4	1522.2	581.0	1745.8	580.5
2015	980.0	1548.1	597.3	1768.5	580.5
2016	1004.5	1625.5	599.1	1800.3	592.1
2017	1024.6	1619.0	602.1	1861.5	596.8
2018	1046.1	1669.2	625.0	1891.3	607.6
2019	1080.6	1862.8	628.7	1923.4	622.2

注：1. 2016年起，食品类统计口径有变化，不包括“茶及饮料”和“在外餐饮”两项内容。
2. 2016年起，统计分类“服务项目价格指数”改为“服务价格指数”，增加“养老服务”和“金融服务”两项内容。

Note: 1. Statistical caliber of food category has changed since 2016. The two sections of "Tea and Drinks" and "Catering Service" are not included.
2. The statistical category of "Price Index of Service Item" has been revised to "Price Index of Service" of 2016 with two additional sections of "Elderly Care Service" and "Financial Service" .

9-3 主要年份生产投资价格指数

MAJOR YEAR´S PRICE INDEXES FOR PRODUCTION AND INVESTMENT

（上年价格 =100） (preceding year=100)

年份 Year	工业生产者出厂价格指数 Producer Price Indexes for Industrial Producers	工业生产者购进价格指数 Purchasing Price Indexes for Industrial Producers	房屋销售价格指数 Sales Price Indexes of Houses	房屋租赁价格指数 Renting Price Indexes of Houses	物业管理价格指数 Property Management Price Indexes	固定资产投资价格指数 Price Indexes for Investment in Fixed Assets
1990	104.33	108.64				
1991	101.68	108.10				
1992	105.46	107.13				
1993	115.49	126.91				
1994	121.62	120.30				
1995	112.70	114.25				
1996	103.81	103.25				
1997	100.22	101.93				
1998	94.96	92.77	100.1	94.0		
1999	96.93	95.88	103.7	104.3		
2000	101.89	106.81	102.3	95.8		
2001	98.00	97.81	104.1	107.0		
2002	97.37	96.78	107.6	94.4		
2003	100.97	106.51	114.6	99.4		
2004	102.92	113.62	115.2	98.6		105.8
2005	101.39	106.52	110.9	103.3	100.2	103.1
2006	101.08	105.80	106.9	110.1	99.8	102.6
2007	101.50	106.69	106.5	108.3	100.4	104.1
2008	105.33	115.91	105.1	106.5	102.1	111.0
2009	95.78	90.35	100.3	103.5	100.4	94.6
2010	103.75	112.21		103.0	100.5	104.9
2011	104.90	109.39				107.0
2012	98.61	97.00				100.0
2013	98.82	96.53				100.1
2014	99.20	97.40				99.9
2015	97.04	94.24				97.1
2016	98.77	97.28				99.8
2017	104.40	110.73				107.3
2018	104.22	105.22				106.6
2019	100.0	98.4				

注：2010 年之前工业生产者出厂价格为工业品出厂价格；工业生产者购进价格为主要原材料、燃料、动力购进价格。

Note: Producers Prices at works were the prices of industrial products at words before 2010. Producers purchasing price refers to the purchasing price of main raw materials, fuels and power.

9-4 工业生产者出厂价格指数
PRODUCER PRICE INDEXES FOR INDUSTRIAL PRODUCERS

（上年价格 =100）

类别	Item	2000 年	2005 年	2008 年	2009 年	2010 年
总指数	**General Index**	**101.89**	**101.39**	**105.33**	**95.78**	**103.75**
其中：轻工业	Light Industry	98.50	99.78	102.93	97.21	100.80
重工业	Heavy Industry	105.62	104.32	109.17	93.45	107.57
其中：生产资料	**Means of Production**	**105.03**	**103.24**	**108.76**	**94.25**	**106.43**
采掘	Excavation	95.67	114.74	115.24	93.44	130.94
原料	Raw Materials	113.82	106.91	108.81	90.67	115.24
加工	Processing	97.58	101.45	108.59	95.34	103.50
生活资料	**Means of Livelihood**	**98.25**	**99.13**	**101.72**	**97.45**	**99.61**
食品	Food	96.59	98.80	108.42	98.21	105.06
衣着	Clothing	99.37	101.48	103.36	102.03	101.56
一般日用品	Articles for Daily Use	104.52	101.97	103.03	99.39	99.96
耐用消费品	Durable Consumer Goods	97.70	97.43	97.13	94.52	93.23

(preceding year=100)

2011年	2012年	2013年	2014年	2015年	2016年	2017年	2018年	2019年
104.90	**98.61**	**98.82**	**99.20**	**97.04**	**98.77**	**104.40**	**104.22**	**100.0**
103.46	99.70	99.11	99.62	99.85	98.74	101.13	101.27	101.6
105.89	97.87	98.62	98.91	95.10	98.79	106.46	106.01	98.9
105.54	**97.55**	**98.58**	**98.87**	**95.23**	**98.60**	**106.34**	**105.86**	**99.0**
132.07	93.35	91.72	100.65	95.12				
111.52	99.05	99.26	98.87	88.59	93.92	112.92	114.50	95.8
103.49	97.20	98.50	98.84	97.06	99.60	104.96	103.95	99.8
103.82	**100.42**	**99.21**	**99.76**	**100.07**	**99.12**	**100.69**	**100.95**	**101.8**
109.71	99.91	95.34	98.34	102.53	102.59	100.55	100.55	104.8
107.44	102.03	102.74	100.34	100.39	100.93	101.54	100.14	101.6
108.02	101.64	101.42	101.01	99.59	100.12	101.63	101.54	100.3
94.34	98.79	98.41	99.65	98.26	94.58	99.78	101.32	100.3

9-5 工业生产者购进价格指数
PURCHASING PRICE INDEXES FOR INDUSTRIAL PRODUCERS

（上年价格 =100）

类别	Item	2000 年	2005 年	2008 年	2009 年	2010 年
总指数	**General Index**	**106.81**	**106.52**	**115.91**	**90.35**	**112.21**
燃料、动力类	fuel and Power	113.82	117.34	126.19	90.53	115.43
黑色金属材料类	Ferrous Metals	102.66	107.84	122.19	82.38	111.97
#钢材	Rolled-steel	105.44	106.57	119.10	85.25	108.67
其他	Others	101.1	112.88	132.40	72.73	122.64
有色金属材料及电线类	Nonferrous Metals and Electric Wire	106.75	108.06	93.41	86.24	122.65
化工原料类	Raw Chemical Materials	106.9	112.47	123.00	87.66	111.04
木材及纸浆类	Timber and Paper Pulp	108.98	103.8	103.58	89.16	117.06
建筑材料及非金属矿类	Building Materials and Nonmetals	99.5	115.54	124.52	100.98	107.61
其他工业原材料及半成品	Other Industrial Raw Materials and Semi-finished Goods	105.32	97.87	109.65	92.70	106.41
农副产品	Agricultural Products	92.73	101.55	117.68	88.60	121.30
纺织原料类	Textile Materials	104.03	98.15	101.44	98.69	112.90

(preceding year=100)

2011年	2012年	2013年	2014年	2015年	2016年	2017年	2018年	2019年
109.39	**97.00**	**96.53**	**97.40**	**94.24**	**97.28**	**110.73**	**105.22**	**98.4**
111.29	100.64	95.18	97.65	88.51	89.94	112.91	112.55	95.3
113.08	93.20	93.76	95.81	87.26	97.23	117.41	104.02	100.0
107.95	92.33	92.87	96.87	89.99	96.89	119.10	108.75	99.1
129.01	94.64	96.57	92.49	78.70	98.41	110.30	86.82	103.4
108.45	93.64	96.23	96.24	92.34	96.29	114.82	103.94	97.7
113.79	96.72	96.47	99.51	96.44	101.00	107.63	101.55	94.2
103.78	93.12	98.79	102.42	98.33	99.93	125.23	111.21	89.3
116.71	102.48	100.13	97.36	95.52	100.91	115.06	115.97	107.8
103.31	98.05	96.65	96.25	96.95	97.50	106.42	102.41	100.5
115.04	98.21	98.54	97.62	99.75	101.53	105.92	99.70	103.6
111.11	95.61	99.60	97.38	95.86	99.81	110.09	105.80	97.1

9-6 按工业行业分工业生产者出厂价格指数
PRODUCER PRICE INDEXES FOR INDUSTRIAL PRODUCERS BY SECTOR

（上年价格 =100）

行业	Sector
工业生产者出厂价格指数	**Producer Price Indexes for Manufactured Manufactured Goods**
黑色金属矿采选业	Mining of Ferrous Metal Ores
有色金属矿采选业	Mining of Non-ferrous Metal Ores
非金属矿采选业	Mining and Processing of Nonmetal Ores
农副食品加工业	Processing of Food from Agricultural Products
食品制造业	Manufacture of Foods
酒、饮料和精制茶制造业	Manufacturing Industry of Alcohol, Beverage and Refined Tea
纺织业	Manufacture of Textile
纺织服装、服饰业	Industry of Textile and Garment, and Apparel
皮革、毛皮、羽毛及其制品和制鞋业	Industry of Leather, Furs, Down and Related Products, and Shoes Making
木材加工和木、竹、藤、棕、草制品业	Processing of Timbers, Manufacture of Wood, Bamboo, Rattan, Palm, and Staw Products
家具制造业	Manufacture of Furniture
造纸和纸制品业	Manufacture of Paper and Paper Products
印刷和记录媒介复制业	Printing, Reproduction of Recording Media
文教、工美、体育和娱乐用品制造业	Industry of Culture and Education, Arts and Crafts, and Entertainment Products Manufacturing
石油、煤炭及其他燃料加工业	Processing of Petroleum, Coking, Processing of Nucleus Fuel
化学原料和化学制品制造业	Manufacture of Chemical Raw Material and Chemical Products
医药制造业	Manufacture of Medicines
化学纤维制造业	Manufacture of Chemical Fiber
橡胶和塑料制品业	Industry of Rubber and Plastic Products
非金属矿物制品业	Manufacture of Non-metallic Mineral Products
黑色金属冶炼和压延加工业	Smelting and Pressing of Ferrous Metals
有色金属冶炼和压延加工业	Smelting and Pressing of Non-ferrous Metals
金属制品业	Manufacture of Metal Products
通用设备制造业	Manufacture of General Purpose Machinery
专用设备制造业	Manufacture of Special Purpose Machinery
汽车制造业	Vehicle Manufacturing Industry
铁路、船舶、航空航天和其他运输设备制造业	Manufacturing Industry of Railroads. Vessels, Aerospace and Other Transportation Equipment
电气机械和器材制造业	Manufacture of Electrical Machinery&Equipment
计算机、通信和其他电子设备制造业	Computer. Communications and Other Electronic Equipment Manufacturing
仪器仪表制造业	Instruments Manufacturing Industry
其他制造业	Other Manufacturing Industry
金属制品、机械和设备修理业	Industry of Metal Products, and Repair of Machinery and Equipment
电力、热力生产和供应业	Production and Supply of Electric Power and Heat Power
燃气生产和供应业	Production and Supply of Gas
水的生产和供应业	Production and Supply of Water

注：2019 年国民经济行业分类调整，本表中 2011 年— 2019 年数据采用新国民经济行业分类 GB/T 4754-2017。

Note: Classification of national economic industries was adjusted in 2019. The new national economic industries classification by GB/T 4754-2017 applies to data from 2011 to 2019 in this table.

(preceding year=100)

2011年	2012年	2013年	2014年	2015年	2016年	2017年	2018年	2019年
104.90	**98.61**	**98.82**	**99.20**	**97.04**	**98.77**	**104.40**	**104.22**	**100.0**
104.33	99.93	100.00	99.86	100.00				
111.39	102.48	98.72	95.57	89.94				
145.13	89.33	87.06	102.14	94.85				
111.34	98.69	93.46	97.58	102.47	102.80	101.12	101.41	104.8
112.52	103.11	103.08	101.78	100.66	100.30	101.40	98.67	99.4
104.14	105.89	100.48	98.76	99.01	99.97	99.54	100.85	107.2
105.09	96.15	100.18	100.27	99.41	97.60	103.84	103.58	101.0
105.43	101.66	104.17	101.74	100.84	100.83	102.17	100.28	102.5
104.79	102.59	101.83	98.56	99.72	99.81	100.15	99.82	99.6
108.13	103.21	99.67	100.96	100.35				
101.11	102.00	100.02	100.00	99.91	98.46	98.72	100.48	99.3
105.71	95.59	96.13	101.96	99.78	99.58	115.83	104.86	96.7
110.06	107.10	108.65	96.97	95.96	98.45	101.11	102.77	97.5
100.61	101.47	100.47	100.00	99.96	99.88	101.90	100.54	101.2
114.95	104.26	99.49	97.38	76.03	91.60	114.48	121.44	97.8
114.60	89.61	98.04	99.70	96.53	95.20	119.17	113.72	94.2
107.33	95.05	105.08	127.56	100.73	104.83	101.06	100.95	102.6
123.72	92.56	95.65	96.69	90.31	89.56	117.03	98.53	96.4
114.68	99.67	95.40	95.50	94.93	97.60	100.62	100.10	99.4
108.19	98.39	99.82	100.91	101.62	99.08	114.14	120.19	100.1
111.00	86.47	93.52	94.45	83.44	99.13	117.16	108.23	99.7
108.26	89.14	93.87	94.43	87.95	95.29	125.17	102.35	98.0
99.79	99.82	104.14	96.62	96.59	103.64	106.15	105.34	99.4
101.39	100.07	103.87	101.02	100.37	98.78	103.45	104.80	103.4
101.69	101.26	99.99	99.81	99.72	98.36	100.00	101.23	101.0
99.27	98.97	98.59	102.49	101.04	101.46	100.93	99.83	100.9
99.17	99.66	97.65	100.96	100.03	99.29	100.16	99.79	97.3
103.10	98.40	98.82	99.24	98.61	98.96	102.82	102.36	99.8
84.65	95.43	94.31	98.88	96.31	90.16	102.17	100.06	97.7
102.01	98.72	98.01	98.43	97.05	100.00	100.09	100.15	100.2
95.16	98.52	99.94	100.12	99.89	100.87	104.20	105.84	108.8
102.17	98.43	88.75	91.69	90.21				
101.49	104.36	99.81	99.15	98.10	97.59	97.05	97.83	96.6
107.34	103.32	102.54	109.38	98.88	101.26	96.32	108.74	104.7
100.15	100.25	100.05	100.34	103.46	108.78	100.00	113.81	100.0

9-7 固定资产投资价格指数
PRICE INDEXES FOR INVESTMENT IN FIXED ASSETS

（上年价格 =100） (preceding year=100)

项目名称	Item	2005	2008	2009	2010	2011	2012	2013	2014	2015	2016	2017	2018
总计	**Total**	**103.1**	**111.0**	**94.6**	**104.9**	**107.0**	**100.0**	**100.1**	**99.9**	**97.1**	**99.8**	**107.3**	**106.6**
建筑安装、装饰工程	Construction and Installation Project	103.7	115.5	92.1	107.5	110.1	99.8	100.0	99.6	95.5	99.6	110.7	109.5
其中：人工费	Of which : Labor Cost	112.7	112.7	104.9	112.0	115.9	110.4	107.8	104.8	103.1	101.6	103.0	104.9
材料费	Materials Expenses	101.0	120.5	87.5	107.0	109.6	96.7	97.6	97.7	92	98.8	114.9	112.4
机械使用费	Expenses on Machinery Use	104.2	106.9	100.0	104.3	105.0	102.3	101.0	100.8	100.9	100.1	101.2	102.0
设备、工器具购置	Purchase of Equipment, Tools and Instruments	99.7	102.5	98.0	100.2	101.8	99.2	99.3	99.9	99.2	98.7	100.6	101.5
其他费用	Others	105.5	105.9	98.5	102.2	103.0	102.0	101.4	101.4	101.2	102.2	102.0	99.9

注：根据国家制度规定 2019 年起不编制固定资产投资价格指数。

Note: According to national regulations, starting from 2019, no fixed asset investment price index will be compiled.

9-8 住宅销售价格指数（2019 年）
SALES PRICE INDEXES FOR RESIDENCE（2019）

（上年价格 =100） (preceding year=100)

项目	Item	2019
新建住宅销售价格指数	**Sales Price Indexes for Newly Constucted Residence**	
一月	January	113.9
二月	February	114.2
三月	March	114.3
四月	April	114.7
五月	May	113.2
六月	June	110.8
七月	July	109.3
八月	August	108.1
九月	September	107.8
十月	October	107.0
十一月	November	105.1
十二月	December	104.2
二手住宅销售价格指数	**Sales Price Indexes for Second-hand Residence**	
一月	January	111.0
二月	February	110.3
三月	March	108.4
四月	April	106.8
五月	May	105.5
六月	June	104.2
七月	July	101.3
八月	August	98.9
九月	September	97.5
十月	October	96.0
十一月	November	94.6
十二月	December	94.6

9-9 居民消费价格分类指数（2019 年）
CONSUMER PRICE INDEXES BY CATEGORY (2019)

（上年价格 =100） (preceding year=100)

项目	Item	指数 Indexes
居民消费价格总指数	**Consumer Price Index**	**103.3**
非食品烟酒价格指数	Price index of non food cigarettes and alcohol	101.1
服务价格指数	Price index of services	101.7
鲜活食品价格指数	Price index of fresh food	117.6
消费品价格指数	Consumer Goods Price Index	104.3
扣除鲜菜鲜果价格指数	Price Index Without Fresh Vegetables and Fresh Fruits	102.9
一、食品烟酒	**Food, cigarettes and liquor**	**108.6**
1. 食品	Food	111.6
（1）粮食	Grain	103.2
（2）薯类	Potatoes	103.4
（3）豆类	Beans	100.0
（4）食用油	Cooking Oil	104.7
（5）菜	Vegetables	102.8
（6）畜肉类	Livestock Products	137.4
（7）禽肉类	Poultry Products	114.6
（8）水产品	Aquatic Products	102.5
（9）蛋类	Eggs	103.2
（10）奶类	Dairy Products	100.2
（11）干鲜瓜果类	Dried and Fresh Melons and Fruits	117.8
（12）糖果糕点类	Candy and Pastry	100.0
（13）调味品	Flavoring	99.0
（14）其他食品类	Other foods	98.5
2. 茶及饮料	Tea and Beverages	99.0
3. 烟酒	Tobacco Liquor	102.1
4. 在外餐饮	Catering service	103.5

注：2016 年起，居民消费价格调查目录进行了调整，新调查目录与国际标准更为接近。

Note: Since 2016, the consumption price investigation directory has been adjusted, and the new investigation directory is basically consistent with the household consumption expenditure catalogue.

9-9 续表
Continued

项目	Item	指数 Indexes
二、衣着	**Clothing**	**100.6**
1. 服装	Garments	101.2
2. 服装材料	Clothing material	100.5
3. 其他衣着及配件	Other clothing an accessories	99.9
4. 衣着加工服务费	Service charge of clothing processing	100.4
5. 鞋类	Shoes	98.7
三、居住	**Residence**	**100.5**
1. 租赁房房租	Rents	101.3
2. 住房保养维修及管理	Maintenance and management of house	99.8
3. 水电燃料	Water, Electricity and Fuels	100.6
4. 自有住房	Private Housing	100.6
四、生活用品及服务	**Article of daily use and service**	**100.5**
1. 家具及室内装饰品	Furniture and interior decoration	101.5
2. 家用器具	Home appliances	97.7
3. 家用纺织品	Home textile	101.2
4. 家庭日用杂品	Daily Use Household Articles	99.8
5. 个人护理用品	Personal-care supply	99.8
6. 家庭服务	Household Services	107.7
五、交通和通信	**Transportation and Communication**	**97.3**
1. 交通	Transportation	96.5
2. 通信	Communication	98.9
六、教育文化和娱乐	**Education, culture and entertainment**	**104.7**
1. 教育	Education	105.2
2. 文化娱乐	Culture and Entertainment	104.2
七、医疗保健	**Health Care**	**102.8**
1. 药品及医疗器具	Medicine and medical apparatus	105.6
2. 医疗服务	Medical service	99.4
八、其他用品和服务	**Other articles and services**	**105.3**
1. 其他用品类	Other articles	105.4
2. 其他服务类	Other services	105.2

9-10 商品零售价格分类指数（2019年）
RETAIL PRICE INDEXES BY CATEGORY (2019)

（上年=100） (preceding year=100)

项目	Item	指数 Indexes
商品零售价格总指数	**Retail Price Indexes**	**102.4**
一、食品	**Food**	**110.2**
1. 粮食	Grain	103.2
2. 薯类	Potatoes	103.4
3. 豆类	Beans	100.0
4. 食用油	Edible oil	104.7
5. 菜	vegetables	102.8
6. 畜肉类	Stock rneat	137.4
7. 禽肉类	Poultry meat	114.6
8. 水产品	Aquatic Products	102.5
9. 蛋类	Eggs	103.2
10. 奶类	Dairy	100.2
11. 干鲜瓜果类	Dried and Fresh Melon, and Fruits	117.8
12. 糖果糕点类	Sweets and cakes	100.0
13. 调味品	Flavoring	99.0
14. 其他食品类	Other food	98.5
15. 在外餐饮	Catering service	103.5
二、饮料、烟酒	**Beverages, Tobacco and Liquor**	**101.0**
1. 茶及饮料	Tea and Beverages	99.0
2. 烟草	Tobacco	100.4
3. 酒类	Liquor	103.7
三、服装、鞋帽	**Clothing**	**100.6**
1. 服装	Garments	101.2
2. 鞋帽袜	Footgear and Hats	98.8
3. 其他衣着配件	Other clothing and accessories	101.2
四、纺织品	**Textiles**	**101.3**
1. 服装材料	Clothing material	100.5
2. 床上用品	Blend Cloth	101.5
五、家用电器及音像器材	**Household Appliances, Music and Video Equipment**	**97.9**
1. 家庭设备	Household Facilities	97.7
2. 文娱用耐用消费品	Durable Consumer Goods for Cultural and Recreational Use and Services	97.7
3. 专业音像器材	Professional Audio and Video Equipment	100.1

注：2016年起，商品零售价格调查目录进行了微调。
Note: Since 2016, the retail price survey catalogue has been fine-tuned.

9-10 续表
Continued

项目	Item	指数 Indexes
六、文化办公用品	**Culture and office Articles**	**100.5**
七、日用品	**Articles for Daily Use**	**100.0**
1. 日用百货	General Merchandise for Daily Use	97.4
2. 厨具餐具茶具	Kitchen ware, tableware, tea set	102.6
3. 清洗用品	Cleaning Products	102.3
4. 其他日用品	Other Articles for Daily Use	99.2
八、体育娱乐用品	**Sports and Recreation Articles**	**101.3**
1. 体育户外用品	Sports and outdoors	96.3
2. 娱乐用品	Recreation Articles	103.8
九、交通、通信用品	**Transportation and Communication Appliances**	**98.2**
1. 交通运输机械	Transportation Machines	97.4
2. 通信器材	Communication Equipment	102.6
十、家具	**Furniture**	**101.6**
十一、化妆品	**Cosmetics**	**99.5**
十二、金银饰品	**Gold, Silver and Jewelry**	**109.5**
十三、中西药品及医疗保健用品	**Traditional Chinese and Western Medicals and Health Care Articles**	**106.3**
1. 医疗卫生器具	Medical apparatus	100.5
2. 中药	Herbal medicine	107.0
3. 西药	Western Medicines	108.0
4. 保健器具及用品	Health Care Articles	100.6
十四、书报杂志及电子出版物	**Books, Newspapers, Magazines and Electronic Publications**	**109.1**
1. 教材及参考书	Teaching Material and Reference Books	114.3
2. 书报杂志	Books, Newspapers and Magazines	104.5
3. 计算机办公软件	Computer office software	101.2
十五、燃料	**Fuels**	**95.9**
1. 煤炭及制品	Coal and Its Products	102.9
2. 石油及制品	Petroleum and Its Products	95.8
十六、建筑材料及五金电料	**Building Materials and Hardware**	**100.4**
1. 建筑装璜材料	Building Decoration Materials	100.3
2. 五金水暖	Hardware	100.6

主要统计指标解释

居民消费价格指数 是反映一定时期内城乡居民所购买的生活消费品价格和服务项目价格变动趋势和程度的相对数，是对城市居民消费价格指数和农村居民消费价格指数进行综合汇总计算的结果。该指数可以观察和分析消费品的零售价格和服务价格变动对城乡居民实际生活费支出的影响程度。

商品零售价格指数 是反映一定时期内城乡商品零售价格变动趋势和程度的相对数。商品零售价格的变动直接影响到城乡居民的生活支出和国家的财政收入，影响居民购买力和市场供需的平衡，影响到消费与积累的比例关系。因此，该指数可以从一个侧面对上述经济活动进行观察和分析。

工业生产者出厂价格指数 是反映一定时期内全部工业产品出厂价格总水平的变动趋势和程度的相对数，包括工业企业售给本企业以外所有单位的各种产品和直接售给居民用于生活消费的产品。该指数可以观察出厂价格变动对工业总产值及增加值的影响。

工业生产者购进价格指数 是反映工业企业作为生产投入，而从物资交易市场和能源、原材料生产企业购买原材料、燃料和动力产品时，所支付的价格水平变动趋势和程度的统计指标，是扣除工业企业物质消耗成本中的价格变动影响的重要依据。

房地产价格指数 是反映一定时期内房地产价格变动趋势和程度的相对数，包括新建住宅销售价格指数、二手住宅销售价格指数。

Explanatory Notes on Main Statistical Indicators

Consumer Price Indices reflect the trend and degree of changes in prices of consumer goods and services purchased by urban and rural households during a given period. They are obtained by combining the Urban Consumer Price Indices and the Rural Consumer Price Indices. The Indices enable the observation and analysis of the degree of impact of the changes in the prices of retailed goods and services on the actual living expenses of urban and rural residents.

Retail Price Indices reflect the trend and degree of change in retail prices of commodities during a given period. The change in retail prices of commodities directly affect the living expenditure of urban and rural residents, government revenue, purchasing power of residents and the equilibrium of market supply and demand, and the ratio of consumption to accumulation. Therefore, the retail price indices are useful to analyze the changes of the above economic activities.

Producer Price Indices for Industrial Producers reflect the trend and degree of changes in general ex-factory prices of all industrial products during a given period, including sales of industrial products by an industrial enterprise to all units outside the enterprise, as well as sales of consumer goods to residents. It can be used to analyze the impact of ex-factory prices on gross output value and value-added of the industrial sector.

Purchasing Price Indices for Industrial Producers reflect changes in the level and degree of prices paid by industrial enterprises when they purchase production input such as raw materials, fuels and power from the market or from other energy or raw materials producing enterprises. These indices provide important basis for measuring the material consumption of industrial enterprises after removing influence of price changes.

Price Indices for Real Estate reflect the trend and degree of changes in prices of real estate during a given period, including sales price indices for newly constructed residential buildings and secondhand residential buildings.

人民生活 10

PEOPLE'S LIVING CONDITIONS

简 要 说 明

一、本篇资料的主要内容

本篇资料主要反映了全市居民的家庭收支、居住、家庭消费构成、耐用消费品拥有量等方面的情况。

二、本篇资料的来源

本篇资料中相关数据来源于居民收支调查年报，由国家统计局青岛调查队住户调查处整理提供。

Brief Introduction

I. Main Content

This section mainly reflects the residents´ household income and expenditure, housing, household consumption structure, quantity of durable consumer goods possessed and other information.

II. Source of Data

The relevant data in this material comes from the annual report of the residents´ income and expenditure survey, which is provided by the NBS Survey Office in Qingdao.

10-1 城市居民收支（1978-2014 年）
INCOME AND EXPENDITURE OF URBAN RESIDENTS (1978–2014)

年份 Year	城市居民人均可支配收入（元） Annual Per Capita Disposable Income of Urban Households (yuan)	城市居民人均消费性支出（元） Per Capita Consumption Expenditure of Urban Households (yuan)	城市恩格尔系数（%） Engel coefficient (%)
1978	336	321	
1979	380	360	
1980	537	495	
1981	500	490	57.8
1982	528	484	61.6
1983	549	510	63.7
1984	665	580	62.8
1985	733	681	58.6
1986	882	806	59.2
1987	1089	996	58.1
1988	1225	1278	55.9
1989	1455	1439	57.8
1990	1624	1507	58.4
1991	1856	1767	57.4
1992	2138	1956	57.0
1993	2668	2445	51.8
1994	3880	3479	53.2
1995	5357	4606	52.5
1996	5602	5079	51.8
1997	6222	5525	48.2
1998	6554	5565	46.4
1999	7282	5981	44.5
2000	8016	6677	42.5
2001	8731	6849	41.9
2002	8721	7344	40.5
2003	10075	8056	39.3
2004	11089	9002	38.0
2005	12920	9883	37.6
2006	15328	11945	36.4
2007	17856	13376	37.0
2008	20464	14999	37.4
2009	22368	16080	38.5
2010	24998	17531	37.4
2011	28567	19297	37.5
2012	32145	20391	36.5
2013	35227	22060	36.5
2014	38294	24016	35.7

注：2002 年开始城市居民可支配收入为新计算口径。

Note: From 2002 on, disposable income of urban residents are counted by new gauges.

10-2 农村居民收支（1978-2014 年）
INCOME AND EXPENDITURE OF RURAL RESIDENTS (1978-2014)

年份 Year	农民人均纯收入（元）Annual Per Capita Net Income of Rural Households (yuan)	农村居民人均生活消费支出（元）Per Capita Consumption Expenditure of Rural Households (yuan)	农村恩格尔系数（%）Engel coefficient (%)
1978	146	109	59.3
1979	153	129	58.4
1980	209	142	54.9
1981	218	163	44.3
1982	273	199	52.9
1983	399	277	52.8
1984	452	304	50.0
1985	567	376	47.8
1986	647	474	46.4
1987	730	462	42.9
1988	820	439	38.8
1989	876	510	38.9
1990	952	494	41.5
1991	1021	546	41.3
1992	1029	572	41.7
1993	1255	743	42.7
1994	1694	1384	54.5
1995	2225	1641	55.7
1996	2625	2173	50.5
1997	2599	2150	52.9
1998	3177	2119	49.5
1999	3415	2150	47.3
2000	3637	2380	43.2
2001	3901	2618	41.2
2002	4195	2820	38.9
2003	4530	2988	38.0
2004	5080	3353	38.7
2005	5806	3737	37.5
2006	6546	4203	36.6
2007	7477	4736	37.2
2008	8509	5303	37.7
2009	9249	5832	36.4
2010	10550	6662	35.5
2011	12370	7661	36.6
2012	13990	8653	36.2
2013	15731	9786	34.9
2014	17461	10808	33.8

10-3 城乡居民住房面积（1990-2014 年）
HOUSING AREA OF URBAN AND RURAL RESIDENTS（1990-2014）

年份 Year	城市居民人均现住房建筑面积（平方米） Per Capita Home Floor Area of Urban Residents (square meter)	农村居民人均居住面积（平方米） Per Capita Housing Area of Rural Residents (square meter)
1990	14.16	19.60
1995	17.12	23.03
2000	20.76	25.88
2001	21.86	26.59
2002	22.76	27.00
2003	23.73	27.00
2004	24.22	27.99
2005	22.96	29.54
2006	23.73	30.82
2007	23.72	30.95
2008	26.83	30.73
2009	26.71	31.39
2010	27.42	30.97
2011	27.67	31.73
2012	27.86	32.32
2013	29.12	33.50
2014	29.80	34.20

10-4 全体居民家庭基本情况（2015 年）
BASIC INFORMATION ON ALL HOUSEHOLDS (2015)

指标名称	Name	单位	Unit	2015 年	2014 年	2015 年比 2014 年增长（±%）2015/2014 (±%)
人均可支配收入	**Per Capita Disposable Income**	**元**	**yuan**	**32885**	**30273**	**8.6**
（一）工资性收入	Income from Wages and Salaries	元	yuan	20068	18348	9.4
（二）经营净收入	Net Income from Household Operations	元	yuan	6480	6035	7.4
（三）财产净收入	Income from Properties	元	yuan	2522	2396	5.2
（四）转移净收入	Income from Transfers	元	yuan	3815	3494	9.2
人均消费支出	**Per Capita Consumption Expenditure**	**元**	**yuan**	**21326**	**19653**	**8.5**
（一）食品烟酒	Food, Tobacco and Liquor	元	yuan	6459	5970	8.2
（二）衣着	Clothing	元	yuan	2096	1944	7.8
（三）居住	Residence	元	yuan	4584	4316	6.2
（四）生活用品及服务	Household Facilities, Articles and Services	元	yuan	1485	1374	8.1
（五）交通通信	Transportation and Communication	元	yuan	3226	2905	11.0
（六）教育文化娱乐	Education, Cultural and Recreation Services	元	yuan	1830	1654	10.6
（七）医疗保健	Health Care and Medical Services	元	yuan	1115	1002	11.2
（八）其他用品和服务	Other Goods and Services	元	yuan	531	488	8.8
城镇居民人均现住房建筑面积	**Per Capita Building Space in Urban Areas**	**平方米**	**sq.m**	**31.5**		
农村居民人均现住房建筑面积	**Per Capita Living Space in Rural Areas**	**平方米**	**sq.m**	**32.4**		

注：自 2015 年开始，全市城乡住户调查统一使用一体化改革后的数据，与原数据相比，城乡居民收支指标的调查范围和口径均存较大变化。原“城市居民人均可支配收入”调整为“城镇居民人均可支配收入”；原“农民人均纯收入”调整为“农村居民人均可支配收入”。2014 年数据也为新口径，与 2015 年年鉴数据不一致。2014 年农村居民住房为拥有面积，2015 年为现住房建筑面积。

Note: Since 2015, the city's urban and rural household surveys have uniformly used the data after the integration reform. Compared with the original data, the survey scope and caliber of the income indicators of urban and rural residents have changed significantly. The"per capita disposable income of residents in cities was changed to" per capita disposable income of urban residents" , the "per capita net income of farmers" was changed to "per capita disposable income of rural residents. Data in 2014 were counted by new gauge and they are different from the data in last year' s yearbook. As for the statistics of rural resident homes, the owned house area was taken in 2014, but in 2015, the construction area was counted.

10-5 全体居民家庭基本情况（2016年）
BASIC INFORMATION ON ALL HOUSEHOLDS (2016)

指标名称	Name	单位	Unit	2016年	2015年	2016年比2015年增长（±%）2016/2015（±%）
人均可支配收入	**Per Capita Disposable Income**	**元**	**yuan**	**35680**	**32885**	**8.5**
（一）工资性收入	Income from Wages and Salaries	元	yuan	21700	20068	8.1
（二）经营净收入	Net Income from Household Operations	元	yuan	7011	6480	8.2
（三）财产净收入	Income from Properties	元	yuan	2781	2522	10.3
（四）转移净收入	Income from Transfers	元	yuan	4188	3815	9.8
人均消费支出	**Per Capita Consumption Expenditure**	**元**	**yuan**	**23256**	**21326**	**9.0**
（一）食品烟酒	Food, Tobacco and Liquor	元	yuan	6983	6459	8.1
（二）衣着	Clothing	元	yuan	2271	2096	8.4
（三）居住	Residence	元	yuan	5018	4584	9.5
（四）生活用品及服务	Household Facilities, Articles and Services	元	yuan	1607	1485	8.2
（五）交通通信	Transportation and Communication	元	yuan	3479	3226	7.8
（六）教育文化娱乐	Education, Cultural and Recreation Services	元	yuan	2075	1830	13.4
（七）医疗保健	Health Care and Medical Services	元	yuan	1233	1115	10.6
（八）其他用品和服务	Other Goods and Services	元	yuan	590	531	11.2
城镇居民人均现住房建筑面积	**Per Capita Building Space in Urban Areas**	**平方米**	**sq.m**	**31.7**	**31.5**	**0.6**
农村居民人均现住房建筑面积	**Per Capita Living Space in Rural Areas**	**平方米**	**sq.m**	**33.2**	**32.4**	**2.5**

10-6 全体居民家庭基本情况（2017 年）
BASIC INFORMATION ON ALL HOUSEHOLDS (2017)

指标名称	Name	单位	Unit	2017 年	2016 年	2017 年比 2016 年增长（±%）2017/2016（±%）
人均可支配收入	**Per Capita Disposable Income**	**元**	**yuan**	**38763**	**35680**	**8.6**
（一）工资性收入	Income from Wages and Salaries	元	yuan	23514	21700	8.4
（二）经营净收入	Net Income from Household Operations	元	yuan	7485	7011	6.8
（三）财产净收入	Income from Properties	元	yuan	3082	2781	10.8
（四）转移净收入	Income from Transfers	元	yuan	4682	4188	11.8
人均消费支出	**Per Capita Consumption Expenditure**	**元**	**yuan**	**25232**	**23256**	**8.5**
（一）食品烟酒	Food, Tobacco and Liquor	元	yuan	7489	6983	7.2
（二）衣着	Clothing	元	yuan	2467	2271	8.6
（三）居住	Residence	元	yuan	5454	5018	8.7
（四）生活用品及服务	Household Facilities, Articles and Services	元	yuan	1747	1607	8.7
（五）交通通信	Transportation and Communication	元	yuan	3753	3479	7.9
（六）教育文化娱乐	Education, Cultural and Recreation Services	元	yuan	2347	2075	13.1
（七）医疗保健	Health Care and Medical Services	元	yuan	1350	1233	9.5
（八）其他用品和服务	Other Goods and Services	元	yuan	625	590	6.0
城镇居民人均现住房建筑面积	**Per Capita Building Space in Urban Areas**	**平方米**	**sq.m**	**32.7**	**31.7**	**3.2**
农村居民人均现住房建筑面积	**Per Capita Living Space in Rural Areas**	**平方米**	**sq.m**	**34.8**	**33.2**	**4.8**

10-7 全体居民家庭基本情况（2018 年）
BASIC INFORMATION ON ALL HOUSEHOLDS (2018)

指标名称	Name	单位	Unit	2018 年	2017 年	2018 年比 2017 年增长（±%） 2018/2017 (±%)
人均可支配收入	**Per Capita Disposable Income**	**元**	**yuan**	**42019**	**38763**	**8.4**
（一）工资性收入	Income from Wages and Salaries	元	yuan	25303	23514	7.6
（二）经营净收入	Net Income from Household Operations	元	yuan	8027	7485	7.3
（三）财产净收入	Income from Properties	元	yuan	3475	3082	12.8
（四）转移净收入	Income from Transfers	元	yuan	5214	4682	11.3
人均消费支出	**Per Capita Consumption Expenditure**	**元**	**yuan**	**27316**	**25232**	**8.3**
（一）食品烟酒	Food, Tobacco and Liquor	元	yuan	7787	7489	4.0
（二）衣着	Clothing	元	yuan	2538	2467	2.9
（三）居住	Residence	元	yuan	6365	5454	16.7
（四）生活用品及服务	Household Facilities, Articles and Services	元	yuan	1837	1747	5.1
（五）交通通信	Transportation and Communication	元	yuan	4084	3753	8.8
（六）教育文化娱乐	Education, Cultural and Recreation Services	元	yuan	2571	2347	9.5
（七）医疗保健	Health Care and Medical Services	元	yuan	1480	1350	9.6
（八）其他用品和服务	Other Goods and Services	元	yuan	654	625	4.6
城镇居民人均现住房建筑面积	**Per Capita Building Space in Urban Areas**	**平方米**	**sq.m**	**32.9**	**32.7**	**0.8**
农村居民人均现住房建筑面积	**Per Capita Living Space in Rural Areas**	**平方米**	**sq.m**	**35.9**	**34.8**	**3.1**

10-8 全体居民家庭基本情况（2019 年）
BASIC INFORMATION ON ALL HOUSEHOLDS (2019)

指标名称	Name	单位	Unit	2019 年	2018 年	2019 年比 2018 年增长（±%） 2019/2018 (±%)
人均可支配收入	**Per Capita Disposable Income**	**元**	**yuan**	**45452**	**42019**	**8.2**
（一）工资性收入	Income from Wages and Salaries	元	yuan	27164	25303	7.4
（二）经营净收入	Net Income from Household Operations	元	yuan	8685	8027	8.2
（三）财产净收入	Income from Properties	元	yuan	3850	3475	10.8
（四）转移净收入	Income from Transfers	元	yuan	5753	5214	10.3
人均消费支出	**Per Capita Consumption Expenditure**	**元**	**yuan**	**29501**	**27316**	**8.0**
（一）食品烟酒	Food, Tobacco and Liquor	元	yuan	8325	7787	6.9
（二）衣着	Clothing	元	yuan	2657	2538	4.7
（三）居住	Residence	元	yuan	6969	6365	9.5
（四）生活用品及服务	Household Facilities, Articles and Services	元	yuan	1957	1837	6.5
（五）交通通信	Transportation and Communication	元	yuan	4369	4084	7.0
（六）教育文化娱乐	Education, Cultural and Recreation Services	元	yuan	2904	2571	12.9
（七）医疗保健	Health Care and Medical Services	元	yuan	1600	1480	8.1
（八）其他用品和服务	Other Goods and Services	元	yuan	720	654	10.2
城镇居民人均现住房建筑面积	**Per Capita Building Space in Urban Areas**	**平方米**	**sq.m**	**31.9**	**32.9**	**(3.3)**
农村居民人均现住房建筑面积	**Per Capita Living Space in Rural Areas**	**平方米**	**sq.m**	**37.0**	**35.9**	**3.1**

10-9 城镇居民家庭基本情况（2015 年）
BASIC CONDITIONS OF URBAN HOUSEHOLDS (2015)

指标名称	Name	单位	Unit	2015 年	2014 年	2015 年比 2014 年增长（±%）2015/2014（±%）
人均可支配收入	**Per Capita Disposable Income**	**元**	**yuan**	**40370**	**37346**	**8.1**
（一）工资性收入	Income from Wages and Salaries	元	yuan	25040	23034	8.7
（二）经营净收入	Net Income from Household Operations	元	yuan	6277	5818	7.9
（三）财产净收入	Income from Properties	元	yuan	3580	3436	4.2
（四）转移净收入	Income from Transfers	元	yuan	5473	5058	8.2
人均消费支出	**Per Capita Consumption Expenditure**	**元**	**yuan**	**26052**	**24122**	**8.0**
（一）食品烟酒	Food, Tobacco and Liquor	元	yuan	7856	7295	7.7
（二）衣着	Clothing	元	yuan	2685	2497	7.5
（三）居住	Residence	元	yuan	5607	5302	5.8
（四）生活用品及服务	Household Facilities, Articles and Services	元	yuan	1819	1686	7.9
（五）交通通信	Transportation and Communication	元	yuan	3810	3455	10.3
（六）教育文化娱乐	Education, Cultural and Recreation Services	元	yuan	2264	2057	10.0
（七）医疗保健	Health Care and Medical Services	元	yuan	1352	1227	10.2
（八）其他用品和服务	Other Goods and Services	元	yuan	659	603	9.3

注：本表数据为新口径，2014 年数据与 2015 年年鉴数据不一致。

Note: The data in this sheet is in line with new statistic caliber, which leads to the inconsistency between the data of 2014 and of 2015.

10-10 城镇居民家庭基本情况（2016年）
BASIC CONDITIONS OF URBAN HOUSEHOLDS (2016)

指标名称	Name	单位	Unit	2016年	2015年	2016年比2015年增长（±%）2016/2015（±%）
人均可支配收入	**Per Capita Disposable Income**	**元**	**yuan**	**43598**	**40370**	**8.0**
（一）工资性收入	Income from Wages and Salaries	元	yuan	26898	25040	7.4
（二）经营净收入	Net Income from Household Operations	元	yuan	6846	6277	9.1
（三）财产净收入	Income from Properties	元	yuan	3909	3580	9.2
（四）转移净收入	Income from Transfers	元	yuan	5945	5473	8.6
人均消费支出	**Per Capita Consumption Expenditure**	**元**	**yuan**	**28285**	**26052**	**8.6**
（一）食品烟酒	Food, Tobacco and Liquor	元	yuan	8473	7856	7.9
（二）衣着	Clothing	元	yuan	2882	2685	7.4
（三）居住	Residence	元	yuan	6105	5607	8.9
（四）生活用品及服务	Household Facilities, Articles and Services	元	yuan	1962	1819	7.8
（五）交通通信	Transportation and Communication	元	yuan	4089	3810	7.3
（六）教育文化娱乐	Education, Cultural and Recreation Services	元	yuan	2553	2264	12.8
（七）医疗保健	Health Care and Medical Services	元	yuan	1490	1352	10.2
（八）其他用品和服务	Other Goods and Services	元	yuan	731	659	10.8

10-11 城镇居民家庭基本情况（2017 年）
BASIC CONDITIONS OF URBAN HOUSEHOLDS (2017)

指标名称	Name	单位	Unit	2017 年	2016 年	2017 年比 2016 年增长（±%） 2017/2016 (±%)
人均可支配收入	**Per Capita Disposable Income**	**元**	**yuan**	**47176**	**43598**	**8.2**
（一）工资性收入	Income from Wages and Salaries	元	yuan	28992	26898	7.8
（二）经营净收入	Net Income from Household Operations	元	yuan	7299	6846	6.6
（三）财产净收入	Income from Properties	元	yuan	4297	3909	9.9
（四）转移净收入	Income from Transfers	元	yuan	6588	5945	10.8
人均消费支出	**Per Capita Consumption Expenditure**	**元**	**yuan**	**30569**	**28285**	**8.1**
（一）食品烟酒	Food, Tobacco and Liquor	元	yuan	9059	8473	6.9
（二）衣着	Clothing	元	yuan	3117	2882	8.1
（三）居住	Residence	元	yuan	6605	6105	8.2
（四）生活用品及服务	Household Facilities, Articles and Services	元	yuan	2121	1962	8.1
（五）交通通信	Transportation and Communication	元	yuan	4399	4089	7.6
（六）教育文化娱乐	Education, Cultural and Recreation Services	元	yuan	2875	2553	12.6
（七）医疗保健	Health Care and Medical Services	元	yuan	1624	1490	9.0
（八）其他用品和服务	Other Goods and Services	元	yuan	769	731	5.2

10-12 城镇居民家庭基本情况（2018年）
BASIC CONDITIONS OF URBAN HOUSEHOLDS (2018)

指标名称	Name	单位	Unit	2018年	2017年	2018年比2017年增长（±%）2018/2017（±%）
人均可支配收入	**Per Capita Disposable Income**	**元**	**yuan**	**50817**	**47176**	**7.7**
（一）工资性收入	Income from Wages and Salaries	元	yuan	30955	28992	6.8
（二）经营净收入	Net Income from Household Operations	元	yuan	7836	7299	7.4
（三）财产净收入	Income from Properties	元	yuan	4789	4297	11.4
（四）转移净收入	Income from Transfers	元	yuan	7237	6588	9.9
人均消费支出	**Per Capita Consumption Expenditure**	**元**	**yuan**	**32890**	**30569**	**7.6**
（一）食品烟酒	Food, Tobacco and Liquor	元	yuan	9318	9059	2.9
（二）衣着	Clothing	元	yuan	3168	3117	1.7
（三）居住	Residence	元	yuan	7751	6605	17.3
（四）生活用品及服务	Household Facilities, Articles and Services	元	yuan	2207	2121	4.0
（五）交通通信	Transportation and Communication	元	yuan	4765	4399	8.3
（六）教育文化娱乐	Education, Cultural and Recreation Services	元	yuan	3122	2875	8.6
（七）医疗保健	Health Care and Medical Services	元	yuan	1764	1624	8.6
（八）其他用品和服务	Other Goods and Services	元	yuan	795	769	3.4

10-13 城镇居民家庭基本情况（2019 年）
BASIC CONDITIONS OF URBAN HOUSEHOLDS (2019)

指标名称	Name	单位	Unit	2019 年	2018 年	2019 年比 2018 年增长（±%） 2019/2018 (±%)
人均可支配收入	**Per Capita Disposable Income**	**元**	**yuan**	**54484**	**50817**	**7.2**
（一）工资性收入	Income from Wages and Salaries	元	yuan	32921	30955	6.4
（二）经营净收入	Net Income from Household Operations	元	yuan	8455	7836	7.9
（三）财产净收入	Income from Properties	元	yuan	5234	4789	9.3
（四）转移净收入	Income from Transfers	元	yuan	7874	7237	8.8
人均消费支出	**Per Capita Consumption Expenditure**	**元**	**yuan**	**35266**	**32890**	**7.2**
（一）食品烟酒	Food, Tobacco and Liquor	元	yuan	9877	9318	6.0
（二）衣着	Clothing	元	yuan	3276	3168	3.4
（三）居住	Residence	元	yuan	8449	7751	9.0
（四）生活用品及服务	Household Facilities, Articles and Services	元	yuan	2333	2207	5.7
（五）交通通信	Transportation and Communication	元	yuan	5062	4765	6.3
（六）教育文化娱乐	Education, Cultural and Recreation Services	元	yuan	3503	3122	12.2
（七）医疗保健	Health Care and Medical Services	元	yuan	1893	1764	7.3
（八）其他用品和服务	Other Goods and Services	元	yuan	873	795	9.9

10-14 农村居民家庭基本情况（2015 年）
BASIC CONDITIONS OF RURAL HOUSEHOLDS (2015)

指标名称	Name	单位	Unit	2015 年	2014 年	2015 年比 2014 年增长（±%）2015/2014 (±%)
人均可支配收入	**Per Capita Disposable Income**	**元**	**yuan**	**16730**	**15434**	**8.4**
（一）工资性收入	Income from Wages and Salaries	元	yuan	9337	8517	9.6
（二）经营净收入	Net Income from Household Operations	元	yuan	6919	6489	6.6
（三）财产净收入	Income from Properties	元	yuan	236	216	9.3
（四）转移净收入	Income from Transfers	元	yuan	238	212	12.4
人均消费支出	**Per Capita Consumption Expenditure**	**元**	**yuan**	**11127**	**10277**	**8.3**
（一）食品烟酒	Food, Tobacco and Liquor	元	yuan	3442	3188	8.0
（二）衣着	Clothing	元	yuan	826	784	5.3
（三）居住	Residence	元	yuan	2377	2248	5.8
（四）生活用品及服务	Household Facilities, Articles and Services	元	yuan	765	720	6.2
（五）交通通信	Transportation and Communication	元	yuan	1965	1751	12.2
（六）教育文化娱乐	Education, Cultural and Recreation Services	元	yuan	895	809	10.6
（七）医疗保健	Health Care and Medical Services	元	yuan	604	532	13.5
（八）其他用品和服务	Other Goods and Services	元	yuan	253	245	3.3

注：本表数据为新口径，2014 年与去年年鉴数据不一致。

Note: The data in this table is a new caliber, and the data in 2014 and last year's yearbook are inconsistent.

10-15 农村居民家庭基本情况（2016 年）
BASIC CONDITIONS OF RURAL HOUSEHOLDS (2016)

指标名称	Name	单位	Unit	2016 年	2015 年	2016 年比 2015 年增长（±%）2016/2015 (±%)
人均可支配收入	**Per Capita Disposable Income**	**元**	**yuan**	**17969**	**16730**	**7.4**
（一）工资性收入	Income from Wages and Salaries	元	yuan	10074	9337	7.9
（二）经营净收入	Net Income from Household Operations	元	yuan	7381	6919	6.7
（三）财产净收入	Income from Properties	元	yuan	256	236	8.6
（四）转移净收入	Income from Transfers	元	yuan	258	238	8.2
人均消费支出	**Per Capita Consumption Expenditure**	**元**	**yuan**	**12006**	**11127**	**7.9**
（一）食品烟酒	Food, Tobacco and Liquor	元	yuan	3651	3442	6.1
（二）衣着	Clothing	元	yuan	905	826	9.5
（三）居住	Residence	元	yuan	2586	2377	8.8
（四）生活用品及服务	Household Facilities, Articles and Services	元	yuan	814	765	6.4
（五）交通通信	Transportation and Communication	元	yuan	2113	1965	7.5
（六）教育文化娱乐	Education, Cultural and Recreation Services	元	yuan	1004	895	12.2
（七）医疗保健	Health Care and Medical Services	元	yuan	658	604	9.0
（八）其他用品和服务	Other Goods and Services	元	yuan	275	253	8.8

10-16 农村居民家庭基本情况（2017年）
BASIC CONDITIONS OF RURAL HOUSEHOLDS (2017)

指标名称	Name	单位	Unit	2017年	2016年	2017年比2016年增长（±%）2017/2016（±%）
人均可支配收入	**Per Capita Disposable Income**	**元**	**yuan**	**19364**	**17969**	**7.8**
（一）工资性收入	Income from Wages and Salaries	元	yuan	10882	10074	8.0
（二）经营净收入	Net Income from Household Operations	元	yuan	7913	7381	7.2
（三）财产净收入	Income from Properties	元	yuan	280	256	9.0
（四）转移净收入	Income from Transfers	元	yuan	289	258	12.2
人均消费支出	**Per Capita Consumption Expenditure**	**元**	**yuan**	**12928**	**12006**	**7.7**
（一）食品烟酒	Food, Tobacco and Liquor	元	yuan	3869	3651	6.0
（二）衣着	Clothing	元	yuan	971	905	7.3
（三）居住	Residence	元	yuan	2801	2586	8.3
（四）生活用品及服务	Household Facilities, Articles and Services	元	yuan	885	814	8.8
（五）交通通信	Transportation and Communication	元	yuan	2262	2113	7.0
（六）教育文化娱乐	Education, Cultural and Recreation Services	元	yuan	1129	1004	12.4
（七）医疗保健	Health Care and Medical Services	元	yuan	717	658	9.0
（八）其他用品和服务	Other Goods and Services	元	yuan	294	275	6.8

10-17 农村居民家庭基本情况（2018年）
BASIC CONDITIONS OF RURAL HOUSEHOLDS (2018)

指标名称	Name	单位	Unit	2018年	2017年	2018年比2017年增长（±%）2018/2017 (±%)
人均可支配收入	**Per Capita Disposable Income**	**元**	**yuan**	**20820**	**19364**	**7.5**
（一）工资性收入	Income from Wages and Salaries	元	yuan	11684	10882	7.4
（二）经营净收入	Net Income from Household Operations	元	yuan	8487	7913	7.3
（三）财产净收入	Income from Properties	元	yuan	310	280	10.8
（四）转移净收入	Income from Transfers	元	yuan	339	289	17.1
人均消费支出	**Per Capita Consumption Expenditure**	**元**	**yuan**	**13885**	**12928**	**7.4**
（一）食品烟酒	Food, Tobacco and Iquor	元	yuan	4098	3869	5.9
（二）衣着	Clothing	元	yuan	1020	971	5.1
（三）居住	Residence	元	yuan	3024	2801	8.0
（四）生活用品及服务	Household Facilities, Articles and Services	元	yuan	945	885	6.7
（五）交通通信	Transportation and Communication	元	yuan	2445	2262	8.1
（六）教育文化娱乐	Education, Cultural and Recreation Services	元	yuan	1245	1129	10.3
（七）医疗保健	Health Care and Medical Services	元	yuan	794	717	10.6
（八）其他用品和服务	Other Goods and Services	元	yuan	314	294	6.9

10-18 农村居民家庭基本情况（2019 年）
BASIC CONDITIONS OF RURAL HOUSEHOLDS (2019)

指标名称	Name	单位	Unit	2019 年	2018 年	2019 年比 2018 年增长（±%） 2019/2018 (±%)
人均可支配收入	**Per Capita Disposable Income**	**元**	**yuan**	**22573**	**20820**	**8.4**
（一）工资性收入	Income from Wages and Salaries	元	yuan	12580	11684	7.7
（二）经营净收入	Net Income from Household Operations	元	yuan	9270	8487	9.2
（三）财产净收入	Income from Properties	元	yuan	344	310	11.1
（四）转移净收入	Income from Transfers	元	yuan	379	339	12.0
人均消费支出	**Per Capita Consumption Expenditure**	**元**	**yuan**	**14899**	**13885**	**7.3**
（一）食品烟酒	Food, Tobacco and Liquor	元	yuan	4393	4098	7.2
（二）衣着	Clothing	元	yuan	1091	1020	6.9
（三）居住	Residence	元	yuan	3222	3024	6.5
（四）生活用品及服务	Household Facilities, Articles and Services	元	yuan	1004	945	6.3
（五）交通通信	Transportation and Communication	元	yuan	2611	2445	6.8
（六）教育文化娱乐	Education, Cultural and Recreation Services	元	yuan	1389	1245	11.5
（七）医疗保健	Health Care and Medical Services	元	yuan	856	794	7.9
（八）其他用品和服务	Other Goods and Services	元	yuan	333	314	6.0

10-19 全体居民家庭消费构成
HOUSEHOLDS CONSUMPTION STRUCTURE

项目	Item	2014年		2015年		2016年	
		年人均支出金额（元）Per Capita Annual Expenditure (yuan)	占消费支出的比重（%）Percentage to Consumption Expenditure (%)	年人均支出金额（元）Per Capita Annual Expenditure (yuan)	占消费支出的比重（%）Percentage to Consumption Expenditure (%)	年人均支出金额（元）Per Capita Annual Expenditure (yuan)	占消费支出的比重（%）Percentage to Consumption Expenditure (%)
消费支出	**Consumption Expenditure**	**19653**	**100**	**21326**	**100**	**23256**	**100**
（一）食品烟酒	Food, Tobacco and Liquor	5970	30.4	6459	30.3	6983	30.0
（二）衣着	Clothing	1944	9.9	2096	9.8	2271	9.8
（三）居住	Residence	4316	21.9	4584	21.5	5018	21.6
（四）生活用品及服务	Household Facilities, Articles and Services	1374	7.0	1485	7.0	1607	6.9
（五）交通通信	Transportation and Communication	2905	14.8	3226	15.1	3479	15.0
（六）教育文化娱乐	Education, Cultural and Recreation Services	1654	8.4	1830	8.6	2075	8.9
（七）医疗保健	Health Care and Medical Services	1002	5.1	1115	5.2	1233	5.3
（八）其他用品和服务	Other Goods and Services	488	2.5	531	2.5	590	2.5

10-19 续表
Continued

项目	Item	2017年		2018年		2019年	
		年人均支出金额（元）Per Capita Annual Expenditure (yuan)	占消费支出的比重（%）Percentage to Consumption Expenditure (%)	年人均支出金额（元）Per Capita Annual Expenditure (yuan)	占消费支出的比重（%）Percentage to Consumption Expenditure (%)	年人均支出金额（元）Per Capita Annual Expenditure (yuan)	占消费支出的比重（%）Percentage to Consumption Expenditure (%)
消费支出	**Consumption Expenditure**	**25232**	**100**	**27316**	**100**	**29501**	**100**
（一）食品烟酒	Food, Tobacco and Liquor	7489	29.7	7787	28.5	8325	28.2
（二）衣着	Clothing	2467	9.8	2538	9.3	2657	9.0
（三）居住	Residence	5454	21.6	6365	23.3	6969	23.6
（四）生活用品及服务	Household Facilities, Articles and Services	1747	6.9	1837	6.7	1957	6.6
（五）交通通信	Transportation and Communication	3753	14.9	4084	15.0	4369	14.8
（六）教育文化娱乐	Education, Cultural and Recreation Services	2347	9.3	2571	9.4	2904	9.9
（七）医疗保健	Health Care and Medical Services	1350	5.4	1480	5.4	1600	5.4
（八）其他用品和服务	Other Goods and Services	625	2.4	654	2.4	720	2.5

10-20 城镇居民家庭消费构成
COMPOSITION OF URBAN HOUSEHOLDS CONSUMPTION

项目	Item	2014年		2015年		2016年	
		年人均支出金额（元）Per Capita Annual Expenditure (yuan)	占消费支出的比重（%）Percentage to Consumption Expenditure (%)	年人均支出金额（元）Per Capita Annual Expenditure (yuan)	占消费支出的比重（%）Percentage to Consumption Expenditure (%)	年人均支出金额（元）Per Capita Annual Expenditure (yuan)	占消费支出的比重（%）Percentage to Consumption Expenditure (%)
消费支出	**Consumption Expenditure**	**24122**	**100**	**26052**	**100**	**28285**	**100**
（一）食品烟酒	Food, Tobacco and Liquor	7295	30.2	7856	30.2	8473	30.0
（二）衣着	Clothing	2497	10.4	2685	10.3	2882	10.2
（三）居住	Residence	5302	22.0	5607	21.5	6105	21.6
（四）生活用品及服务	Household Facilities, Articles and Services	1686	7.0	1819	7.0	1962	6.9
（五）交通通信	Transportation and Communication	3455	14.3	3810	14.6	4089	14.4
（六）教育文化娱乐	Education, Cultural and Recreation Services	2057	8.5	2264	8.7	2553	9.0
（七）医疗保健	Health Care and Medical Services	1227	5.1	1352	5.2	1490	5.3
（八）其他用品和服务	Other Goods and Services	603	2.5	659	2.5	731	2.6

10-20 续表
Continued

项目	Item	2017年		2018年		2019年	
		年人均支出金额（元）Per Capita Annual Expenditure (yuan)	占消费支出的比重（%）Percentage to Consumption Expenditure (%)	年人均支出金额（元）Per Capita Annual Expenditure (yuan)	占消费支出的比重（%）Percentage to Consumption Expenditure (%)	年人均支出金额（元）Per Capita Annual Expenditure (yuan)	占消费支出的比重（%）Percentage to Consumption Expenditure (%)
消费支出	**Consumption Expenditure**	**30569**	**100**	**32890**	**100**	**35266**	**100**
（一）食品烟酒	Food, Tobacco and Liquor	9059	29.6	9318	28.3	9877	28.0
（二）衣着	Clothing	3117	10.2	3168	9.6	3276	9.3
（三）居住	Residence	6605	21.6	7751	23.6	8449	24.0
（四）生活用品及服务	Household Facilities, Articles and Services	2121	6.9	2207	6.7	2333	6.6
（五）交通通信	Transportation and Communication	4399	14.4	4765	14.5	5062	14.3
（六）教育文化娱乐	Education, Cultural and Recreation Services	2875	9.4	3122	9.5	3503	9.9
（七）医疗保健	Health Care and Medical Services	1624	5.3	1764	5.4	1893	5.4
（八）其他用品和服务	Other Goods and Services	769	2.6	795	2.4	873	2.5

10-21 农村居民家庭消费构成
COMPOSITION OF RURAL HOUSEHOLDS CONSUMPTION

项目	Item	2014年		2015年		2016年	
		年人均支出金额（元）Per Capita Annual Expenditure (yuan)	占消费支出的比重（%）Percentage to Consumption Expenditure (%)	年人均支出金额（元）Per Capita Annual Expenditure (yuan)	占消费支出的比重（%）Percentage to Consumption Expenditure (%)	年人均支出金额（元）Per Capita Annual Expenditure (yuan)	占消费支出的比重（%）Percentage to Consumption Expenditure (%)
消费支出	**Consumption Expenditure**	**10277**	**100**	**11127**	**100**	**12006**	**100**
（一）食品烟酒	Food, Tobacco and Liquor	3188	31.0	3442	30.9	3651	30.4
（二）衣着	Clothing	784	7.6	826	7.4	905	7.5
（三）居住	Residence	2248	21.9	2377	21.4	2586	21.5
（四）生活用品及服务	Household Facilities, Articles and Services	720	7.0	765	6.9	814	6.8
（五）交通通信	Transportation and Communication	1751	17.0	1965	17.7	2113	17.6
（六）教育文化娱乐	Education, Cultural and Recreation Services	809	7.9	895	8.0	1004	8.4
（七）医疗保健	Health Care and Medical Services	532	5.2	604	5.4	658	5.5
（八）其他用品和服务	Other Goods and Services	245	2.4	253	2.3	275	2.3

10-21 续表
Continued

项目	Item	2017年		2018年		2019年	
		年人均支出金额（元）Per Capita Annual Expenditure (yuan)	占消费支出的比重（%）Percentage to Consumption Expenditure (%)	年人均支出金额（元）Per Capita Annual Expenditure (yuan)	占消费支出的比重（%）Percentage to Consumption Expenditure (%)	年人均支出金额（元）Per Capita Annual Expenditure (yuan)	占消费支出的比重（%）Percentage to Consumption Expenditure (%)
消费支出	**Consumption Expenditure**	**12928**	**100**	**13885**	**100**	**14899**	**100**
（一）食品烟酒	Food, Tobacco and Liquor	3869	29.9	4098	29.5	4393	29.5
（二）衣着	Clothing	971	7.5	1020	7.3	1091	7.3
（三）居住	Residence	2801	21.7	3024	21.8	3222	21.6
（四）生活用品及服务	Household Facilities, Articles and Services	885	6.8	945	6.8	1004	6.8
（五）交通通信	Transportation and Communication	2262	17.5	2445	17.6	2611	17.5
（六）教育文化娱乐	Education, Cultural and Recreation Services	1129	8.7	1245	9.0	1389	9.3
（七）医疗保健	Health Care and Medical Services	717	5.5	794	5.7	856	5.8
（八）其他用品和服务	Other Goods and Services	294	2.4	314	2.3	333	2.2

10-22 城镇住户每百户家庭主要耐用品拥有量（1980-2019 年）
OWNERSHIP OF MAJOR DURABLE CONSUMER GOODS PER 100 URBAN HOUSEHOLDS (1980-2019)

年份 Year	家用电脑（台） Computer (set)	钢琴（架） Piano (set)	空调器（台） Air Conditioner (set)	淋浴热水器（台） Shower Water Heater (unit)	洗衣机（台） Washing Machine (set)	电冰箱（台） Household Refrigerator (set)	家用汽车（辆） Automobile (unit)	彩色电视机（台） Color TV (set)	移动电话（部） Call Phone (unit)	照相机（架） Camera (set)
1980										2
1981					12			1		2
1982					22			2		4
1983					27	1		6		6
1984					30	2		8		8
1985					36	4		18		14
1986					40	5		25		15
1987					52	18		34		18
1988					61	33		47		21
1989					67	50		59		22
1990					66	62		68		26
1991					70	76		82		33
1992		1	0	13	73	83		81		39
1993		2	1	18	83	86		88		50
1994		4	1	17	81	89		92		51
1995		4	3	34	82	89		100		61
1996		5	7	40	83	92		105		63
1997	1	5	9	47	83	93		111	3	63
1998	8	5	17	53	83	92		111	7	69
1999	11	4	22	61	83	94		117	15	69
2000	19	2	25	66	83	94		120	30	70
2001	20	2	24	66	84	93		128	36	69
2002	32	2	38	75	89	93	1	123	80	73
2003	41	3	48	76	91	93	0	125	106	70
2004	46	3	55	79	93	93	2	124	128	68
2005	55	4	69	84	92	95	4	118	153	72
2006	71	8	89	88	97	99	6	125	187	82
2007	75	7	98	93	100	107	8	122	194	83
2008	75	5	94	90	95	103	13	116	191	67
2009	82	7	98	91	96	105	18	118	199	71
2010	86	8	99	91	97	107	20	119	208	71
2011	95	8	103	92	98	108	22	117	219	77
2012	101	9	104	93	98	108	29	115	231	79
2013	105	10	104	93	98	107	32	118	232	79
2014	105	10	104	98	99	105	34	109	235	79
2015	80	9	91	91	91	94	50	101	215	57
2016	86		98	93	90	96	58	100	212	63
2017	80		101	94	91	95	60	100	205	
2018	81		120	101	100	108	62	107	228	
2019	89		126	99	100	111	64	110	233	

10-23 农村住户每百户家庭主要耐用品拥有量（1985-2019年）
OWNERSHIP OF MAJOR DURABLE CONSUMER GOODS PER 100 RURAL HOUSEHOLDS (1985-2019)

年份 Year	家用电脑（台） Computer (set)	空调器（台） Air Conditioner (set)	热水器（台） Water Heater (unit)	自行车（辆） Bicycle (unit)	洗衣机（台） Washing Machine (set)	电冰箱（台） Household Refrigerator (set)	彩色电视机（台） Color TV (set)	移动电话（部） Call Phone (unit)	照相机（架） Camera (set)	家用汽车（辆） Automobile (unit)
1985				147	0.3		3		1	
1986				165	1.1	0.3	4.5		1	
1987				148	2.4	0.5	7		2	
1988				154	2.4	1	9		2	
1989				170	3	1	12		2	
1990				164	4	2	13		2	
1991				173	5	4	16		2	
1992				178	5	7	20		2	
1993				203	7	14	26		2	
1994				204	9	21	35		7	
1995				203	16	28	43		6	
1996				198	13	33	46		8	
1997				191	15	36	56		13	
1998				184	17	39	63		15	
1999				185	20	42	74		10	
2000				165	28	47	86		13	
2001				153	28	53	92		13	
2002				152	36	58	98		16	
2003	6	5	33	137	39	60	100	45	16	2
2004	8	8	39	142	48	68	105	68	21	2
2005	14	14	53	138	57	77	109	91	21	5
2006	17	15	54	116	63	87	112	114	14	7
2007	19	19	63	118	70	94	113	132	17	8
2008	25	23	68	124	76	97	114	148	19	9
2009	28	25	71	127	79	99	115	160	21	11
2010	34	30	75	128	82	102	117	170	21	12
2011	44	32	76	114	85	100	112	202	18	15
2012	55	37	85	119	91	102	114	216	21	16
2013	61	45	88	111	93	105	116	221	26	23
2014	61	49	85		93	102	106	225	24	26
2015	46	54	86		92	105	110	219	21	41
2016	56	70	89		96	107	113	226	21	45
2017	52	78	90		98	106	110	223		48
2018	45	93	88		97	109	105	232		43
2019	42	98	96		98	108	104	227		40

主要统计指标解释

常住人员 指住户成员中，经常在家居住、或者调查期内居住时间超过一半的人员，以及本住户供养的学生。

可支配收入 指调查户在调查期内获得的、可用于最终消费支出和储蓄的总和，即调查户可以用来自由支配的收入。可支配收入既包括现金，也包括实物收入。按照收入的来源，可支配收入包含四项，分别为：工资性收入、经营净收入、财产净收入和转移净收入。计算公式为：

可支配收入 = 工资性收入 + 经营净收入 + 财产净收入 + 转移净收入

居民人均可支配收入是按居民家庭常住人口计算的平均每人可支配收入

消费支出 指住户用于满足家庭日常生活消费需要的全部支出。根据用途不同，消费支出可划分为食品烟酒、衣着、居住、生活用品及服务、交通通信、教育文化娱乐、医疗保健、其他用品及服务八大类。根据来源不同，消费支出可划分为现金消费支出、实物消费支出（含自产自用、来自单位、来自政府和其他社会组织）。

Explanatory Notes on Main Statistical Indicators

Permanent resident refers to residents that live usually in home or more than half of the survey period and students that are supported by them.

Disposable income refers to sum of all income earned within the survey period that can be used for deposit and expense on final consumption, which means the income that can be disposed freely by residents. The disposable income includes not only cash, but also income in kinds, which shall be categorized into four kinds according to source of incomes: salary income, net operating income, net property income, net transfer income. Computing formula is as follows:

Disposable income = salary income + net operating income + net property income + net transfer income

Disposable income per capita of residents is the average disposable income per person calculated based on the number of permanent residents of the family.

Consumer spending refers to all spending of residents to cover daily life consumption demands. According to different usages, the consumer spending shall be classified into eight categories: food, cigarettes and alcohol, clothing, housing, daily use articles and services, transportation & communication, education, culture & entertainment, medical and health care, other articles and services. According to sources, the consumer spending shall be classified as cash consumer spending, consumer spending in kinds (including self-produced, from the unit, from government and other social organization) .

农　业 11

AGRICULTURE

简要说明

一、本篇资料的主要内容

本篇资料主要反映了全市农业生产和农村经济的基本情况，主要包括农林牧渔业总产值、中间消耗、增加值、农村劳动力、耕地、主要农产品产量、农业机械年末拥有量、农业机械化和电气化以及农田水利建设等方面的资料。

二、本篇资料的来源

1. 本篇资料中耕地面积资料来源于市自然资源和规划局。

2. 水产品产量等相关资料来源于市海洋发展局。

3. 农业机械化等相关资料来源于市农业农村局。

4. 农田水利灌溉等相关资料来源于市水务管理局。

5. 植树造林等相关资料来源于市园林和林业局。

三、说明

本篇按照国家统计局规定，根据 2016 年第三次全国农业普查结果对 2007 年至 2017 年历史数据进行了核定和修正。

本篇资料由市统计局农村统计处、国家统计局青岛调查队农村调查处整理提供。

Brief Introduction

I. Main Content

Data in this chapter show the basic conditions of agricultural production and rural economy, mainly including agricultural output, intermediate consumption, value added, rural labor force, cultivated land, output of main agricultural produces, agricultural machinery and electrification in rural areas and basic construction on irrigation and drainage.

II. Source of Data

1. Data on area of cultivated land are provided by Qingdao Natural Resources and Planning Bureau.

2. Data on output of aquatic products are provided by Qingdao Marine Development Bureau.

3. Data on Agricultural machinery are provided by Qingdao Rural Agriculture Bureau.

4. Data on farmland water conservancy are provided by Qingdao Water Administration Bureau.

5. Data on forest planting are provided by Qingdao Landscape and Forestry Bureau.

III. Explain

This chapter is in accordance with the provisions of the State Statistical Bureau. According to the results of the third national agricultural census in 2016, the historical data from 2007 to 2017 were verified and revised.

Data in this chapter are compiled by the Division of Countryside Statistics of Qingdao Municipal Bureau of Statistics and Division of Rural Household Survey of Survey Office of the National Bureau of Statistics in Qingdao.

11-1 农村基本情况（2000-2019 年）
BASIC STATISTICS ON RURAL AREA (2000-2019)

项目	Item	单位	Unit	2000	2005	2008	2009	2010	2011	2012
一、乡村户数人口、劳动力	**Rural Households Population and Labor Force**									
乡村户数	Rural Households	万户	10 000 households	148	151	152	152	155	155	156
乡村人口数	Rural Population	万人	10 000 persons	483	479	480	485	487	489	491
乡村从业人员数	Rural Employed Population	万人	10 000 persons	255	258	271	275	276	277	277
#男	Male	万人	10 000 persons	137	138	144	146	147	147	146
#女	Female	万人	10 000 persons	118	120	126	129	129	131	130
二、年末实有耕地面积	**Year-end Area of Cultivated Land**	万公顷	**10 000 hectares**	**48**	**42**	**42**	**42**			**53**
三、农用机械总动力	**Total Agricultural Machinery Power**	万千瓦	**10 000 kW**	**459**	**620**	**697**	**719**	**764**	**784**	**798**
拖拉机	Tractors	台	unit	126981	163032	176156	180171	200208	202022	206290
四、农村用电量	**Electricity Consumed in Rural Areas**	万千瓦时	**10 000 kW·h**	**189651**	**372645**	**424292**	**426306**	**426819**	**431646**	**426815**
五、农用化肥施用量（折纯）	**Consumption of Chemical Fertilizer (convert to pure amount)**	万吨	**10 000 tons**	**33**	**33**	**31**	**30**	**30**	**29**	**29**
六、有效灌溉面积	**Irrigated Area**	万公顷	**10 000 hectares**	**30**	**30**	**31**	**32**	**33**	**33**	**33**

11-1 续表
Continued

项目	Item	单位	Unit	2013	2014	2015	2016	2017	2018	2019
一、乡村户数人口、劳动力	**Rural Households Population and Labor Force**									
乡村户数	Rural Households	万户	10 000 households	155	157	155	155	140	131	127
乡村人口数	Rural Population	万人	10 000 persons	491	494	495	497	453	419	407
乡村从业人员数	Rural Employed Population	万人	10 000 persons	277	277	275	273	246	224	211
#男	Male	万人	10 000 persons	147	147	145	145	131	119	112
#女	Female	万人	10 000 persons	131	130	130	128	115	105	99
二、年末实有耕地面积	**Year-end Area of Cultivated Land**	**万公顷**	**10 000 hectares**	**53**	**52**	**52**	**52**	**52**	**52**	**52**
三、农用机械总动力	**Total Agricultural Machinery Power**	**万千瓦**	**10 000 kW**	**809**	**827**	**854**	**698**	**728**	**738**	**751**
拖拉机	Tractors	台	unit	206300	205065	207809	211689	214799	215668	216496
四、农村用电量	**Electricity Consumed in Rural Areas**	**万千瓦时**	**10 000 kW·h**	**359139**	**404380**	**401122**	**385434**	**382437**	**377858**	**388484**
五、农用化肥施用量（折纯）	**Consumption of Chemical Fertilizer (convert to pure amount)**	**万吨**	**10 000 tons**	**29**	**29**	**28**	**28**	**28**	**27**	**27**
六、有效灌溉面积	**Irrigated Area**	**万公顷**	**10 000 hectares**	**30**	**32**	**32**	**33**	**33**	**33**	**33**

注：1. 农机机械总动力 2016 年为新统计口径，扣除农用运输汽车数据。
　　2. 乡村从业人员数 2018 年为新统计口径。

Note: 1. Data of total power of agricultural machinery of 2016 is based on the new statistic caliber, deducted by the data of agricultural vehicle.
　　2. Rural labor force of 2018 is based on the new statistic caliber.

11-2 乡村从业人员数（1985-2019年）

RURAL EMPLOYED POPULATION (1985-2019)

单位：万人(10 000 persons)

年份 Year	合计 Total	农林牧渔业 Farming, Forestry, Animal Husbandry and Fishery	工业 Industry	建筑业 Construction
1985	225.09	147.89	32.92	15.62
1988	238.93	146.00	44.46	17.51
1989	242.70	151.16	44.65	16.46
1990	247.29	155.20	44.48	16.17
1991	253.01	160.31	45.49	15.87
1992	258.23	160.04	47.00	17.25
1993	259.18	159.22	44.04	20.20
1994	258.34	155.74	43.70	21.52
1995	258.66	154.08	44.06	22.33
1996	256.34	151.10	43.08	21.80
1997	258.60	153.07	41.66	22.02
1998	258.50	152.79	40.79	21.68
1999	256.82	149.11	42.18	22.32
2000	254.62	143.59	42.76	22.99
2001	253.98	132.46	47.76	24.66
2002	254.08	119.98	53.66	26.52
2003	257.67	118.27	55.65	26.65
2004	258.91	112.05	60.32	28.36
2005	257.87	103.03	65.59	29.03
2006	264.70	102.28	71.46	28.16
2007	268.31	100.63	74.70	30.97
2008	270.71	100.90	74.82	30.87
2009	274.74	102.64	75.42	31.23
2010	276.04	102.45	76.32	32.10
2011	277.24	102.73	76.87	32.57
2012	276.97	102.24	76.82	32.36
2013	277.32	104.48	76.42	31.15
2014	276.90			
2015	274.77			
2016	273.43			
2017	245.92			
2018	223.54			
2019	210.57			

注：乡村从业人员数2018年起为新统计口径。

Note: Rural labor force of 2018 is based on the new statistic caliber.

11-2 续表
Continued

单位：万人(10 000persons)

年份 Year	交通运输仓储和邮电业 Transport, Postal and Telecommunication Services	批发零售贸易、餐饮业 Wholesale and Retail Trades and Catering Services	金融保险业 Financial and Insurance	其他劳动力 Other Labour Force
1985	5.23	0.06	19.76	3.61
1988	5.89	0.09	20.40	4.58
1989	6.00	0.12	19.95	4.36
1990	6.11	0.12	20.71	4.50
1991	6.09	0.13	20.52	4.60
1992	7.02	0.16	21.74	5.02
1993	8.93	0.16	20.65	5.98
1994	6.48	10.10		20.80
1995	7.11	10.71		20.37
1996	7.33	11.78		21.25
1997	7.62	12.40		21.83
1998	8.02	13.32		21.90
1999	8.19	14.03		20.99
2000	8.39	16.10		20.79
2001	9.02	17.80		22.28
2002	10.00	20.07		23.85
2003	9.96	20.60		26.54
2004	10.20	24.08		22.96
2005	10.70	25.88		22.34
2006	11.66	25.31		24.37
2007	11.61	27.61		21.16
2008	11.06	28.76		22.09
2009	11.40	29.03		22.75
2010	11.78	28.85		22.01
2011	11.89	29.34		21.02
2012	11.96	29.56		21.11
2013	11.92	29.48		20.33
2014				
2015				
2016				
2017				
2018				
2019				

11-3　分市、区乡村户数、人口、从业人员(2019年)
RURAL HOUSEHOLDS, POPULATION AND LABOR FORCE BY REGION (2019)

市、区名称	Region	乡村户数(万户) Rural Households (10 000 households)	乡村人口数(万人) Rural Population (10 000 persons)	乡村从业人员数(万人) Rural Employed Population (10 000 persons)	#男 Male Laborer	#女 Female Laborer	#种植业 Planting
全市	**Whole Municipality**	**127.44**	**407.34**	**210.57**	**111.96**	**98.61**	**74.52**
崂山区	Laoshan District	4.45	13.33	7.26	3.91	3.35	2.01
西海岸新区	West Coast New Area	18.23	58.27	27.91	14.92	12.99	8.02
黄岛区	Huangdao District	18.23	58.27	27.91	14.92	12.99	8.02
保税港区	Qingdao Free Trade Port Area of China						
城阳区	Chengyang District	11.07	30.73	16.88	8.93	7.95	0.93
城阳区(不含高新区)	Chengyang District (Excluding High tech District)	11.07	30.73	16.88	8.93	7.95	0.93
高新区	High tech District						
即墨区	Jimo District	23.26	75.90	37.87	20.27	17.60	13.11
胶州市	Jiaozhou	15.79	52.03	27.04	14.01	13.03	8.59
平度市	Pingdu	35.38	115.93	59.83	31.76	28.08	28.16
莱西市	Laixi	19.26	61.16	33.78	18.16	15.62	13.71

11-4 主要年份农、林、牧、渔业总产值(按现价计算)

MAJOR YEAR'S GROSS OUTPUT VALUE OF FARMING, FORESTRY, ANIMAL HUSBANDRY AND FISHERY (CURRENT PRICE)

单位:万元 (10 000 yuan)

年份 Year	农、林、牧、渔业总产值 Gross Output Value of Farming, Forestry, Animal Husbandry and Fishery	农业产值 Farming	林业产值 Forestry	牧业产值 Animal Husbandry	渔业产值 Fishery
1949	16511	14755	325	1200	231
1952	24428	21353	479	1888	708
1957	26189	22717	644	2218	610
1962	15356	13257	230	1243	626
1965	25123	21488	854	2110	671
1970	44078	36889	1851	3817	1521
1975	93213	79208	2144	7923	3938
1978	121497	94397	3112	17293	6695
1980	149436	117547	2953	22215	6721
1985	299139	215729	8986	53894	20530
1987	378981	263066	5949	73271	36695
1989	463952	303679	19134	91885	49254
1990	579877	381287	13801	119208	65581
1991	664779	417111	12875	144909	89884
1992	703433	400471	15252	150942	136768
1993	989763	509601	20845	232143	227174
1994	1424074	763366	23101	356734	280873
1995	1923771	1021413	26765	503999	371594
1996	2317434	1145399	29100	692362	450573
1997	2047712	939922	24052	578443	505295
1998	2386303	1198043	16760	633735	537765
1999	2382320	1169596	17122	618020	577582
2000	2483256	1116397	19102	692782	654975
2001	2615228	1135816	20433	758313	700666
2002	2688532	1110671	23157	796007	758697
2003	2759692	1062576	36183	859915	801018
2004	2967389	1181009	32831	937494	816055
2005	3205057	1265695	25246	1070831	843285
2006	3396096	1360755	23546	1076254	855131
2007	3665342	1460800	20801	1143644	916648
2008	3995027	1723855	24356	1195857	907793
2009	4070777	1771982	22133	1133732	980995
2010	4802184	2197935	19090	1225222	1181911
2011	5345885	2188072	19049	1500469	1426786
2012	5672486	2270097	20221	1510234	1633469
2013	6105875	2547805	21875	1553621	1711549
2014	6279086	2644851	22266	1559709	1739234
2015	6123485	2469656	21789	1529587	1814625
2016	6690910	2844023	27741	1621935	1777293
2017	6978980	3003367	30891	1663278	1830324
2018	7369968	3290651	36575	1631422	1920519
2019	7781197	3600911	43066	1671765	1936932

注:2007 年 -2017 年数据为根据第三次农业普查结果核定修正后数据。
Note: The 2007-2017 data are the approved revised data based on the results of the third agricultural census.

11-5 分市、区农、林、牧、渔业总产值（2019年，现价）
GROSS OUTPUT VALUE OF FARMING, FORESTRY, ANIMAL HUSBANDYRY AND FISHERY BY REGION (2019, CURRENT PRICE)

单位：万元 (10 000 yuan)

市、区名称	Region	农、林、牧、渔业总产值 Gross Output Value of Farming, Forestry, Animal Husbandry and Fishery	农业 Farming	林业 Forestry	牧业 Animal Husbandry	渔业 Fishery	服务业 Services
全市	**Whole Municipality**	**7781197**	**3600911**	**43066**	**1671765**	**1936932**	**528523**
崂山区	Laoshan District	131460	16327	912		92774	21448
西海岸新区	West Coast New Area	1477097	508621	6270	146844	718424	96937
黄岛区	Huangdao District	1477097	508621	6270	146844	718424	96937
保税港区	Qingdao Free Trade Port Area of China						
城阳区	Chengyang District	303960	34341	1477	21579	240627	5937
城阳区（不含高新区）	Chengyang District (Excluding High tech District)	67373	34086	1194	18093	11720	2279
高新区	High tech District	236587	255	283	3486	228906	3657
即墨区	Jimo District	1437082	468899	6395	229724	602447	129618
胶州市	Jiaozhou	1065691	507472	7624	190938	263628	96029
平度市	Pingdu	2015467	1361102	9931	541256	9727	93452
莱西市	Laixi	1350440	704150	10457	541424	9305	85103

11-6 农、林、牧、渔业总产值、增加值（2019年）
VALUE-ADDED OF FARMING, FORESTRY, ANIMAL HUSBANDRY AND FISHERY (2019)

单位：万元 (10 000 yuan)

		总计 Total	农业 Farming	林业 Forestry	牧业 Animal Husbandry	渔业 Fishery	服务业 Services
总产值	**Gross Output Value**	**7781197**	**3600911**	**43066**	**1671765**	**1936932**	**528523**
中间消耗	**Intermediate Expenditure**	**3419104**	**1474966**	**15667**	**886206**	**776041**	**266223**
中间物质消耗	Intermediate Expenditure of Matter	2505989	1118112	9721	712285	494222	171649
对非农生产部门的劳动支出	Expenditure of Labour Services to Nonagricultural Production Development	913115	356855	5946	173921	281819	94574

11-7 分市、区农、林、牧、渔业增加值（2019年）
VALUE-ADDED OF FARMING, FORESTRY, ANIMAL HUSBANDRY AND FISHERY BY REGION (2019)

单位：万元 (10 000 yuan)

市、区名称	Region	增加值 Added Value	农业 Farming	林业 Forestry	牧业 Animal Husbandry	渔业 Fishery	服务业 Services
全市	**Whole Municipality**	**4362093**	**2125946**	**27398**	**785558**	**1160891**	**262299**
崂山区	Laoshan District	76729	8447	567		57266	10449
西海岸新区	West Coast New Area	832480	282242	3942	69141	430426	46729
黄岛区	Huangdao District	832480	282242	3942	69141	430426	46729
保税港区	Qingdao Free Trade Port Area of China						
城阳区	Chengyang District	175098	19133	925	9629	142572	2840
城阳区（不含高新区）	Chengyang District (Excluding High tech District)	36307	18982	746	7986	7522	1071
高新区	High tech District	138792	151	179	1642	135050	1769
即墨区	Jimo District	810945	274713	4194	109935	357506	64596
胶州市	Jiaozhou	613135	307650	5014	91736	160453	48283
平度市	Pingdu	1143263	832412	6048	250675	6354	47774
莱西市	Laixi	710442	401349	6707	254443	6314	41628

11-8 主要年份耕地面积与播种面积
MAJOR YEAR'S CULTIVATED AND SOWN AREA

单位：万公顷（10 000 hectares）

年份 Year	年末实有耕地面积 Year-end Area of Cultivated Land	农作物播种面积 Sown Area of Farm Crops	#粮食作物 Grain Crops	#经济作物 Economic Crops
1949		93.47	84.00	7.20
1952		97.53	85.07	10.80
1957		97.87	87.07	10.53
1962		81.47	72.53	5.80
1965		82.80	71.80	8.33
1970		80.73	68.27	10.07
1975		79.82	65.84	11.01
1978		77.60	63.60	10.40
1980		75.87	60.33	12.00
1985		78.27	57.33	15.73
1987		76.67	55.87	15.93
1989		74.78	54.28	16.06
1990		76.85	56.99	15.53
1991		76.98	56.89	15.69
1992		76.96	56.37	15.64
1993	56.90	77.75	56.22	15.71
1994		76.61	54.08	16.20
1995		76.54	53.71	15.65
1996	55.01	77.26	54.81	14.90
1997		75.04	52.32	14.40
1998		77.18	53.05	14.54
1999		77.56	50.61	13.24
2000		76.47	45.07	13.98
2001		73.69	41.91	14.54
2002		72.32	40.83	13.95
2003		67.82	36.05	14.50
2004		71.33	41.40	14.11
2005	42.10	75.02	49.93	11.89
2006	41.29	74.86	49.79	11.75
2007	41.31	64.13	39.16	24.98
2008	41.79	65.29	42.56	22.73
2009	41.87	63.72	42.01	21.72
2010		64.10	42.65	21.45
2011		64.53	43.84	20.70
2012	52.81	64.36	43.95	20.40
2013	52.55	66.16	45.69	20.48
2014	52.42	66.70	46.75	19.95
2015	52.22	67.10	47.93	19.17
2016	52	68.19	48.49	19.70
2017	51.86	67.32	47.79	19.54
2018	51.86	68.37	48.11	20.26
2019	51.62	66.73	47.50	19.23

注：1. 2009 年前本表数据由市统计局提供 .
2. 2010 年起，耕地面积由国土部门提供，粮食作物面积由青岛调查队提供，经济作物面积由市统计提供。
3. 2007 年 -2017 年农作物播种面积为根据第三次农业普查结果核定修正后数据。
4. 耕地面积由市自然资源和规划局错年提供，2019 年数据为 2018 年度变更调查耕地数。

Note: 1. Those of before 2009 were provided by the National Bureau of Statistics.
2. From 2010, data on area of cultivated land are provided by Ministry of Land and Resources, area of grain crops are provided by Nation Bureau of Statistics in Qingdao, area of economic crops are provided by Nation Bureau of Statistics.
3. Sown Area of Farm Crops from 2007 to 2017 is revised according to the results of the third agricultural census.
4. Arable land data provided by the land department next year, the 2019 data is the number of cultivated land surveyed in 2018.

11-9 分市、区耕地面积（2019 年）
AREA OF CULTIVATED LAND BY REGION (2019)

单位：公顷 (hectares)

市、区名称	Region	年末耕地面积 Year-end Area of Cultivated Land	#旱田 Dry Farmland
全市	**Whole Municipality**	**516213**	**272377**
崂山区	Laoshan District	896	864
西海岸新区	West Coast New Area	73685	71360
黄岛区	Huangdao District	73685	71360
保税港区	Qingdao Free Trade Port Area of China		
城阳区	Chengyang District	6450	5058
城阳区（不含高新区）	Chengyang District (Excluding High tech District)	6450	5058
高新区	High tech District		
即墨区	Jimo District	98918	85813
胶州市	Jiaozhou	62720	23477
平度市	Pingdu	184286	12874
莱西市	Laixi	89228	72901

11-10 分市、区农作物播种面积（2019 年）
SOWN AREA OF FARM CROPS BY REGION (2019)

单位：万公顷（10 000 hectares）

市、区名称	Region	总播种面积 Total Sown Area	#粮食 Grain	#棉花 Cotton	#花生 Peanut	#烟叶 Tobacco	#蔬菜 Vegetable
全市	**Whole Municipality**	**66.73**	**47.50**	**0.03**	**7.48**	**0.02**	**10.75**
崂山区	Laoshan District	0.06	0.01		0.01		0.04
西海岸新区	West Coast New Area	7.73	4.86		1.94	0.02	0.83
黄岛区	Huangdao District	7.73	4.86		1.94	0.02	0.83
保税港区	Qingdao Free Trade Port Area of China						
城阳区	Chengyang District	0.31	0.18		0.00		0.12
城阳区（不含高新区）	Chengyang District (Excluding High tech District)	0.31	0.18		0.00		0.12
高新区	High tech District						
即墨区	Jimo District	10.05	7.79		1.21		0.98
胶州市	Jiaozhou	8.91	6.14	0.00	0.68	0.00	2.05
平度市	Pingdu	27.12	19.88	0.03	2.06	0.00	4.74
莱西市	Laixi	12.55	8.63		1.59		2.00

11-11 分市、区部分农作物产量（2019年）
OUTPUT OF FARM CROPS BY REGION (2019)

单位：吨 (ton)

市、区名称	Region	粮食 Grain	棉花 Cotton	花生 Peanut	烟叶 Tobacco	蔬菜 Vegetable
全市	**Whole Municipality**	**3026054**	**434**	**342424**	**551**	**6261517**
崂山区	Laoshan District	975		229		11087
西海岸新区	West Coast New Area	253459		95630	475	589894
黄岛区	Huangdao District	253459		95630	475	589894
保税港区	Qingdao Free Trade Port Area of China					
城阳区	Chengyang District	9420		103		41462
城阳区（不含高新区）	Chengyang District (Excluding High tech District)	9420		103		41462
高新区	High tech District					
即墨区	Jimo District	428639		43332		573468
胶州市	Jiaozhou	359110	4	29001	11	1074812
平度市	Pingdu	1424802	430	98647	65	2773659
莱西市	Laixi	549651		75482		1197135

11-12 分市、区部分农作物单位面积产量（2019年）
OUTPUT OF FARM CROPS PER HECTARE BY REGION (2019)

单位：千克 / 公顷 (kg/hectares)

市、区名称	Region	粮食 Grain	棉花 Cotton	花生 Peanut	烟叶 Tobacco	蔬菜 Vegetable
全市	**Whole Municipality**	**6371**	**1569**	**4577**	**2282**	**58242**
崂山区	Laoshan District	6991		3075		31539
西海岸新区	West Coast New Area	5212		4935	2355	71220
黄岛区	Huangdao District	5212		4935	2355	71220
保税港区	Qingdao Free Trade Port Area of China					
城阳区	Chengyang District	5144		4197		35183
城阳区（不含高新区）	Chengyang District (Excluding High tech District)	5144		4197		35183
高新区	High tech District					
即墨区	Jimo District	5505	1560	3585		58598
胶州市	Jiaozhou	5847	1569	4283	3068	52304
平度市	Pingdu	7166		4781	1791	58532
莱西市	Laixi	6371		4758		59937

11-13 主要年份农作物总产量
MAJOR YEAR'S OUTPUT OF FARM CROPS

单位：吨 (ton)

年份 Year	粮食 Grain	#小麦 Wheat	#玉米 Corn	棉花 Cotton	花生 Peanut	水果 Fruit	蔬菜 Vegetable
1949	723190	158815	25810	1280	71080	9955	356015
1952	967640	200380	58130	6025	115585	13468	284050
1957	921920	210690	141540	3520	90445	18869	625220
1962	628930	104340	53010	1280	35470	8366	524455
1965	917635	180610	135595	6090	88390	16034	465850
1970	1175985	243945	244530	16490	96280	33907	541145
1975	1899540	430135	420095	15390	98495	59206	693970
1978	1900850	514570	510635	8720	114370	82819	921140
1980	2164415	520045	819930	19630	160670	80840	996565
1985	2331060	961055	739455	19335	475270	200515	1253075
1987	2626029	996165	1030926	13819	394296	249655	1489250
1989	2654334	993406	1084441	14638	391782	288757	1664238
1990	2998246	1265157	1210687	17490	413636	292366	1786041
1991	3180893	1421143	1285043	25965	446880	294349	1837265
1992	2675641	1235755	981490	8160	321145	341415	2030327
1993	3164812	1463759	1248780	15344	419109	383368	2705349
1994	3106562	1392977	1252952	8326	494827	423024	3002318
1995	3291587	1480385	1365167	8177	510662	478685	3221507
1996	3390033	1513479	1466668	4001	486574	505711	3405056
1997	2523064	1584478	743199	2000	308233	438398	3333181
1998	3469821	1627261	1484182	4159	546786	529592	4036992
1999	3331124	1501182	1499775	3668	572941	606800	5459140
2000	2780481	1353445	1169649	2077	534174	651591	6649322
2001	2539257	1143679	1178851	3409	579441	675244	6250361
2002	2383802	1085936	1094731	3755	557714	579703	6847570
2003	2221697	931787	1117704	5324	568798	677361	7305618
2004	2650952	1301791	1202063	7216	580290	748516	6720886
2005	3150203	1535471	1478616	4042	503941	737300	5792110
2006	3039266	1548928	1372166	3954	471853	827755	6051239
2007	2319354	1118044	1106106	3546	495458	1366106	6180515
2008	2602592	1234264	1279002	3163	470424	1276385	6164760
2009	2590287	1276029	1228485	3213	467937	1294706	5743437
2010	2553744	1206593	1272970	2411	439872	1267226	5895190
2011	2678626	1213908	1386365	2375	441237	1262896	5948249
2012	2707295	1242299	1396704	2334	456372	1201836	5826702
2013	2791826	1295227	1432355	2057	440426	1217969	5906625
2014	2780244	1302282	1418469	1392	394461	1188690	6134061
2015	2878062	1332125	1497121	1279	342034	1189312	5988945
2016	2940668	1345273	1551200	408	365207	1207498	5915380
2017	2968896	1264073	1670338	420	383668	1187041	6277779
2018	3100964	1376646	1690817	977	384918	1092176	6443615
2019	3026054	1426280	1544645	434	342424	1185951	6261517

注：2007 年 -2017 年数据为根据第三次农业普查结果核定修正后数据。

Note: Agricultural data from 2007 to 2017 are revised according to the results of the third agricultural census.

11-13 续表 1 分市、区部分蔬菜产量（2019 年）
Continued OUTPUT OF SOME VEGETABLES BY CITY AND DISTRICT (2019)

单位：吨 (ton)

市、区名称	Region	蔬菜 Vegetable	#大白菜 Cabbage	#芹菜 Celery	#胡萝卜 Carrot	#马铃薯 Potato
全市	**Whole Municipality**	**6261517**	**1311604**	**156243**	**540781**	**1186366**
崂山区	Laoshan District	11087	5236	45	88	2309
西海岸新区	West Coast New Area	589894	308579	22185	902	98371
黄岛区	Huangdao District	589894	308579	22185	902	98371
保税港区	Qingdao Free Trade Port Area of China					
城阳区	Chengyang District	41462	4834	1341		3534
城阳区（不含高新区）	Chengyang District (Excluding High tech District)	41462	4834	1341		3534
高新区	High tech District					
即墨区	Jimo District	573468	111187	13975	57551	99871
胶州市	Jiaozhou	1074812	255108	56348	5774	394514
平度市	Pingdu	2773659	444709	30598	261159	532766
莱西市	Laixi	1197135	181951	31750	215307	55002

11-13 续表 2 分市、区部分蔬菜产量（2019 年）
Continued OUTPUT OF SOME VEGETABLES BY CITY AND DISTRICT (2019)

单位：吨 (ton)

市、区名称	Region	#黄瓜 Cucumber	#西红柿 Tomato	#大葱 Green onion	#蒜头 Garlic	#食用菌 Edible fungi
全市	**Whole Municipality**	**384339**	**348282**	**781769**	**107536**	**54751**
崂山区	Laoshan District	428	173	121	39	
西海岸新区	West Coast New Area	11552	33559	3574	1291	36567
黄岛区	Huangdao District	11552	33559	3574	1291	36567
保税港区	Qingdao Free Trade Port Area of China					
城阳区	Chengyang District	9588	7909	479	9	696
城阳区（不含高新区）	Chengyang District (Excluding High tech District)	9588	7909	479	9	696
高新区	High tech District					
即墨区	Jimo District	52744	25104	55288	5026	14024
胶州市	Jiaozhou	21563	14772	53489	589	434
平度市	Pingdu	33491	73735	654446	90935	2015
莱西市	Laixi	254974	193031	14372	9648	1015

11-14 分市、区猪、羊及家禽存养量（2019年）
HOGS, SHEEP, GOATS AND POULTRY IN STOCK BY REGION (2019)

单位：万头、万只 (10 000 head)

市、区名称	Region	年末生猪存养量 Hoga in Stock (year-end)	#母猪 Sow	牛 Cattle and Buffaloes	#奶牛 Cows	年末羊存养量 Sheep and Goats in Stock (year-end)	年末家禽存栏 Poultry stock at the eng of the year	#蛋鸡 Laying Hen
全市	**Whole Municipality**	**155.15**	**17.76**	**16.07**	**8.43**	**19.96**	**6018.12**	**1414.76**
崂山区	Laoshan District							
西海岸新区	West Coast New Area	23.95	2.55	0.93	0.05	3.50	598.40	170.69
黄岛区	Huangdao District	23.95	2.55	0.93	0.05	3.50	598.40	170.69
保税港区	Qingdao Free Trade Port Area of China							
城阳区	Chengyang District	1.12	0.06	0.17	0.17	0.15	33.68	22.97
城阳区（不含高新区）	Chengyang District (Excluding High tech District)	0.66	0.02	0.15	0.15	0.12	14.43	13.02
高新区	High tech District	0.46	0.04	0.02	0.02	0.03	19.25	9.95
即墨区	Jimo District	21.12	2.65	1.71	1.08	1.67	971.09	402.26
胶州市	Jiaozhou	17.51	2.16	1.26	0.34	4.35	342.91	222.31
平度市	Pingdu	57.38	6.65	4.86	0.80	7.32	2055.67	276.06
莱西市	Laixi	34.07	3.70	7.14	5.99	2.97	2016.37	320.48

11-15 分市、区肉、蛋、奶产量（2019年）
OUTPUT OF MEAT, EGGS AND MILK BY REGION (2019)

单位：万吨 (10 000 tons)

市、区名称	Region	肉类产量 Output of Meat	#猪肉 Port	#禽肉 Poultry Meat	禽蛋 Poultry Eggs	牛羊奶 Milk
全市	**Whole Municipality**	**52.78**	**20.58**	**30.14**	**20.04**	**28.88**
崂山区	Laoshan District					
西海岸新区	West Coast New Area	6.46	3.24	2.39	2.39	0.88
黄岛区	Huangdao District	6.46	3.24	2.39	2.39	0.88
保税港区	Qingdao Free Trade Port Area of China					
城阳区	Chengyang District	0.20	0.13	0.06	0.32	0.56
城阳区（不含高新区）	Chengyang District (Excluding High tech District)	0.10	0.08	0.01	0.18	0.51
高新区	High tech District	0.10	0.05	0.05	0.14	0.05
即墨区	Jimo District	6.96	2.88	3.95	5.65	3.63
胶州市	Jiaozhou	3.48	2.37	0.89	3.11	1.69
平度市	Pingdu	18.31	7.34	10.45	4.05	2.99
莱西市	Laixi	17.37	4.62	12.41	4.51	19.13

11-16 分市、区渔业养殖面积
AQUACULTURE AREA BY REGION

单位：公顷 (hectare)

市、区名称	Region	2019年 养殖面积 Aquaculture Area	2019年 #海水 Seawater	2019年 #淡水 Fresh Water	2018年 养殖面积 Aquaculture Area	2018年 #海水 Seawater	2018年 #淡水 Fresh Water
全市	**Whole Municipality**	**34460**	**31516**	**2944**	**35259**	**32344**	**2915**
崂山区	Laoshan District	986	986	0	1600	1600	
西海岸新区	West Coast New Area	11864	11438	426	12076	11650	426
黄岛区	Huangdao District	11864	11438	426	12076	11650	426
保税港区	Qingdao Free Trade Port Area of China						
城阳区	Chengyang District	7005	6741	264	6728	6465	263
城阳区（不含高新区）	Chengyang District (Excluding High tech District)						
高新区	High tech District						
即墨区	Jimo District	10801	10600	201	11146	10878	268
胶州市	Jiaozhou	2442	1751	691	2276	1751	525
平度市	Pingdu	430		430	463		463
莱西市	Laixi	932		932	970		970

11-17 分市、区水产品总产量（2019年）
OUTPUT OF AQUATIC PRODUCTS BY REGION (2019)

单位：吨 (ton)

市、区名称	Region	水产品总产量 Output of Aquatic Products	#养殖产量 Aquaculture Output	#捕捞产量 Catch	#鱼类 Fish	#甲壳类 Crust	#贝类 Shellfish	#藻类 Algae
全市	**Whole Municipality**	**1007899**	**197374**	**810525**	**154311**	**57304**	**734072**	**7752**
崂山区	Laoshan District	39198	19727	19471	11537	6607	18062	1120
西海岸新区	West Coast New Area	350553	62744	287809	83840	17207	218645	3000
黄岛区	Huangdao District	350553	62744	287809	83840	17207	218645	3000
保税港区	Qingdao Free Trade Port Area of China							
城阳区	Chengyang District	231740	40120	191620	15723	6544	190333	104
城阳区（不含高新区）	Chengyang District (Excluding High tech District)							
高新区	High tech District							
即墨区	Jimo District	283896	50096	233800	14470	21901	232908	
胶州市	Jiaozhou	99290	24509	74781	25595	4972	71151	3460
平度市	Pingdu	1120		1120	1049	68	1049	68
莱西市	Laixi	2102	178	1924	2097	5	1924	

11-18 分市、区植树及造林面积（2019年）
OUTPUT OF AQUATIC PRODUCTS BY REGION (2019)

市、区名称	Region	当年造林面积（公顷）Area of Afforestation in the Year (hectare)	育苗数量（万株）Number of Seedlings (10 000trees)	森林抚育作业面积（公顷）Forest Tending Area (hectare)	零星（四旁）植树（万株）Surrounding Tree Planting (10 000trees)
全市	**Whole Municipality**	**9637**	**11169.1**	**7294**	**298.8**
崂山区	Laoshan District		29.0	200	6.9
西海岸新区	West Coast New Area	1518	4031.9	1333	
黄岛区	Huangdao District	1518	4031.9	1333	
保税港区	Qingdao Free Trade Port Area of China				
城阳区	Chengyang District	101	520.0	667	40.0
城阳区（不含高新区）	Chengyang District (Excluding High tech District)				
高新区	High tech District				
即墨区	Jimo District	1024	2900.0	1600	
胶州市	Jiaozhou	1894	614.5	667	54.9
平度市	Pingdu	2503	2960.0	2160	110.0
莱西市	Laixi	2597	113.6	667	87.0

11-19 分市、区水果产量（2019年）
AREA OF FORESTATION AND OUTPUT OF FRUITS BY REGION (2019)

单位：吨 (ton)

市、区名称	Region	水果总产量 Output of Fruits (ton)	#园林水果 Garden Fruits	#瓜果类水果 Melon Fruits
全市	**Whole Municipality**	**1185951**	**745127**	**440825**
崂山区	Laoshan District	7206	7116	89
西海岸新区	West Coast New Area	125743	97950	27794
黄岛区	Huangdao District	125743	97950	27794
保税港区	Qingdao Free Trade Port Area of China			
城阳区	Chengyang District	18374	16652	1722
城阳区（不含高新区）	Chengyang District (Excluding High tech District)	18374	16652	1722
高新区	High tech District			
即墨区	Jimo District	42507	24026	18481
胶州市	Jiaozhou	57264	39655	17610
平度市	Pingdu	492419	265451	226969
莱西市	Laixi	442438	294278	148160

11-19 续表
Continued

单位：吨 (ton)

市、区名称	Region	#苹果 Apple	#梨 Pear	#桃 Peach	#葡萄 Grape	#杏 Apricot	#山楂 Hawthorn	#西瓜 Watermelon	#甜瓜 Muskmelon
全市	**Whole Municipality**	**281910**	**96810**	**127731**	**155163**	**11192**	**2325**	**263312**	**116159**
崂山区	Laoshan District	68	65	1734	13	1451	4	–	–
西海岸新区	West Coast New Area	41643	3812	19936	3123	349	71	21038	1144
黄岛区	Huangdao District	41643	3812	19936	3123	349	71	21038	1144
保税港区	Qingdao Free Trade Port Area of China								
城阳区	Chengyang District	656	117	6073	5176	3821		8	
城阳区（不含高新区）	Chengyang District (Excluding High tech District)	656	117	6073	5176	3821		8	
高新区	High tech District								
即墨区	Jimo District	6447	1595	10839	2683	103	36	11836	2752
胶州市	Jiaozhou	15570	3679	9414	4226	5367	71	15773	270
平度市	Pingdu	79502	23139	51585	78959	102	282	189888	3722
莱西市	Laixi	138023	64404	28150	60984	1	1860	24769	108271

11-20 分市、区果园、茶园面积和茶叶产量（2019年）
AREA OF ORCHARD AND TEA GARDEN AND PRODUCTION OF TEA BY CITY AND DISTRICT (2019)

单位：公顷 (hectare)，吨 (ton)

市、区名称	Region	果园面积 Area of Orchards	#苹果园 Apple Orchard	#梨园 Pear Orchard	#葡萄园 Vineyard	#桃园 Peach Orchard	茶园面积 Area of Tea Plantations	茶叶产量 Tea Yield
全市	**Whole Municipality**	**29446**	**8315**	**3242**	**4511**	**6073**	**3940**	**4467**
崂山区	Laoshan District	636	3	3	1	66	1155	1320
西海岸新区	West Coast New Area	5729	1118	154	156	1544	2334	2545
黄岛区	Huangdao District	5729	1118	154	156	1544	2334	2545
保税港区	Qingdao Free Trade Port Area of China							
城阳区	Chengyang District	853	32	6	170	263	68	105
城阳区（不含高新区）	Chengyang District (Excluding High tech District)	853	32	6	170	263	68	105
高新区	High tech District							
即墨区	Jimo District	1357	303	160	127	534	316	487
胶州市	Jiaozhou	1365	410	100	113	403	24	5
平度市	Pingdu	9952	2603	793	2027	1609	42	6
莱西市	Laixi	9554	3847	2026	1918	1654		

11-21 主要年份主要农业机械拥有量
MAJOR YEAR'S OWNERSHIP OF AGRICULTURAL MACHINERY

年份 Year	农业机械总动力（万千瓦）Total Agricultural Machinery Power (10 000kW)	农用拖拉机 Agricultural Tractors 混合台 set	千瓦 kW	大、中型机引农具（万台）Large and Medium Towing Farm Machinery (10 000 sets)	排灌机械 Drainage and Irrigation Machinery 台 set	万千瓦 10 000kW
1949						
1952						
1957	0.22	59	2.2	0.01		
1962	2.47	254	11.47	0.06		
1965	3.49	296	13.2	0.08		
1970	10.40	602	7 963	0.07		
1975	43.94	6447	103 476	0.48		
1978	75.45	15576	309 287	1.02		
1980	110.44	24278	502 731	1.72		
1985	174.76	33097	506 217	1.71	67794	54.92
1990	253.52	55363	680 903	2.03	105574	74.63
1991	250.58	57404	691 332	2.20	134900	73.77
1992	253.94	57182	684 182	2.28	124800	82.68
1993	261.24	56335	678 161	2.34	144460	78.96
1994	278.41	58698	688 886	2.39	147259	80.81
1995	289.23	56391	657 025	2.28	138625	73.98
1996	303.57	59698	680 447	2.32	148313	81.53
1997	326.72	66841	744 424	2.42	155629	88.09
1998	364.21	87226	894 985	2	156565	86.68
1999	411.44	105743	1 075 907	3	170875	96.20
2000	459.21	126981	1 253 210	3	182646	108.26
2001	496.27	141409	1 394 114	4	178437	104.18
2002	534.92	152920	1 537 544	5	182799	107.35
2003	560.94	160676	1 666 185	5	192930	109.44
2004	599	168061	1 818 276	5	192144	110
2005	620	163032	1757177	6	188689	112
2006	651	171155	1890402	6	192010	116
2007	680	173326	1958047	7	195050	118
2008	697	176156	2034453	8	208711	134
2009	719	180171	2266697	9	207648	134
2010	764	200208	2331867	10	190770	123
2011	784	202022	2649283	10	189834	127
2012	798	206290	2759004	10	190134	127
2013	809	206309	2968332	10	190433	127
2014	827	205065	2960438	10	190584	128
2015	854	207809	3176870	10	191152	128
2016	698	211689	3372681	10	191283	128
2017	728	214799	3550005	11	191417	128
2018	738	215668	3668505	0.8	232943	
2019	752	216496	3769281	1.7	232952	

注：大、中型机引农具 2018 年为新统计口径，只统计功率 58.8 千瓦以上机引农具。

Note: Large and medium type agricultural tools are the new statistical caliber in 2018, and only the statistical power is 58.8 kilowatts or more.

11-22 主要年份农业机械化用电量、化肥施用量

MAJOR YEAR'S MECHANIZATION, ELECTRICITY AND CHEMICAL FERTILIZER CONSUMPTION

年份 Year	有效灌溉面积（公顷）Irrigated Area (hectare)	配套机电井（眼）Number of Electromechanical Well (unit)	机耕面积（公顷）Area of Motorized Cultivation (hectare)	机播面积（公顷）Area of Motorized Planting (hectare)	机收面积（公顷）Area of Motorized Harvesting (hectare)	农村用电量（万千瓦时）Electricity Consumption in Rural Area (10 000kW·h)	化肥施用量（折纯万吨）Chemical Fertilizer Consumption (convert to 10 000tons)
1949	8340						
1952	14980						
1957	59353		12800	13			0.19
1962	55213	191	65680	927	927	55	0.10
1965	80000	125	11433	573	247	128	0.55
1970	147613	3947	143700	2527	133	1208	1.76
1975	233980	12820	248867	54507	953	2522	2.77
1978	276660	21017	329213	178533	15060	13975	3.64
1980	296606	22472	444800	187980	55333	20492	12.06
1985	302647	42925	366786	148433	56447	41524	11.66
1990	274680	56821	426680	220593	143133	67616	20.47
1991	281500	58987	431293	254266	192946	81200	22.53
1992	281610	62100	438533	270453	207780	88024	22.60
1993	284080	63954	439300	260287	225807	102501	28.04
1994	286750	64877	436820	262846	238693	121307	28.73
1995	287020	64651	435213	271707	250267	134284	31.45
1996	289320	65237	438947	280480	235933	143740	31.36
1997	292130	66783	442213	308267	266147	150971	28.99
1998	294120	64109	442920	359447	285513	153113	32.0
1999	294790	64734	440967	396180	286367	169337	32.6
2000	295190	65179	439980	346480	292787	189651	32.5
2001	296980	65547	436576	382870	265730	228069	31.7
2002	294310	65588	433660	364680	267690	256453	31.1
2003	292410	65406	415790	404980	256600	299425	31.9
2004	292520	65501	415220	454800	314680	330609	32.5
2005	296450	65303	409610	493240	367740	372644	33.0
2006	303070	65981	403980	493750	398700	413762	32.6
2007	305760	66400	400480	499590	429630	425715	33.9
2008	313920	66828	404080	517540	455120	424292	31.1
2009	322710	67027	404080	538220	481176	426306	30.2
2010	328960	67242	578726	558611	499248	426819	29.9
2011	331690	62104	600451	567947	547108	431646	29.4
2012	333850	62112	610382	627701	566653	426815	29.1
2013	302790	170008	410601	627701	566653	359138	29.1
2014	321670	169491	411355	590798	545360	404380	28.9
2015	323400	155074	417991	640022	600696	401122	28.5
2016	327600	135057	362912	561022	511000	385434	28.37
2017	329620	139342	360085	566264	516763	382437	27.83
2018	331240	136785	359238	578082	531733	377858	27.05
2019	329390	136963	353624	563689	527199	388484	26.71

11-23 分市、区农业机械化和电气化（2019 年）
MECHANIZATION AND ELECTRIFICATION IN AGRICULTURE BY REGION (2019)

市、区名称	Region	农村用电量（万千瓦小时）Electricity Consumed in Rural Areas (10 000kW · h)	机耕作业面积 Area of Motorized Cultivation (hectare)	机播地面积 Area of Motorized Planting (hectare)	机收面积 Area of Motorized Harvesting (hectare)
			面积 Area（公顷）(hectare)		
全市	**Whole Municipality**	**388484**	**353623**	**563689**	**527199**
崂山区	Laoshan District	9391			
西海岸新区	West Coast New Area	58023	43857	66600	60783
黄岛区	Huangdao District	58023	43857	66600	60783
保税港区	Qingdao Free Trade Port Area of China				
城阳区	Chengyang District	48454	915	782	827
城阳区（不含高新区）	Chengyang District (Excluding High tech District)	48454	915	782	827
高新区	High tech District				
即墨区	Jimo District	62676	47550	86241	82169
胶州市	Jiaozhou	101857	52038	79998	78185
平度市	Pingdu	72384	144955	232178	209432
莱西市	Laixi	35699	68998	105191	100397

11-24 分市、区农用化肥施用量（2019 年）
CONSUMPTION OF CHEMICAL FERTILIZERS BY REGION (2019)

单位：吨（折纯）(convert to pure amount)

市、区名称	Region	农用化肥施用量 Consumption of Chemical Fertilizers	氮肥 Nitrogenous Fertilizer	磷肥 Phosphate Fertilizer	钾肥 Potash Fertilizer	复合肥 Compound Fertilizer	附：平均每公顷耕地施用化肥量（折纯千克）Annotation: Consumption of Chemical Fertilizer Per Hectare (convert to pure volume)
全市	**Whole Municipality**	**267105**	**36144**	**10799**	**14053**	**206108**	**517**
崂山区	Laoshan District	423	27	26	4	366	472
西海岸新区	West Coast New Area	31165	5708	2391	3553	19512	423
黄岛区	Huangdao District	31165	5708	2391	3553	19512	423
保税港区	Qingdao Free Trade Port Area of China						
城阳区	Chengyang District	619	113	52	56	398	96
城阳区（不含高新区）	Chengyang District (Excluding High tech District)	619	113	52	56	398	96
高新区	High tech District						
即墨区	Jimo District	32445	9836	2163	1031	19414	328
胶州市	Jiaozhou	34305	5510	822	3735	24238	547
平度市	Pingdu	114956	5713	2013	3475	103755	624
莱西市	Laixi	53192	9239	3331	2198	38425	596

11-25 分市、区农田水利情况（2019 年）
FARMLAND WATER CONSERVANCY BY REGION（2019）

市、区名称	Region	有效灌溉面积（公顷）Irrigated Area (hectare)	有效灌溉面积占耕地面积比重（%）Percentage of Irrigated Area to Area of Cultivated Land (%)	机电井数（眼）Number of Electromechanical Well (unit)
全市	**Whole Municipality**	**329390**	**63.8**	**136963**
崂山区	Laoshan District	520	58.0	1024
西海岸新区	West Coast New Area	42990	58.3	10027
黄岛区	Huangdao District	42990	58.3	10027
保税港区	Qingdao Free Trade Port Area of China			
城阳区	Chengyang District	1990	30.9	1027
城阳区（不含高新区）	Chengyang District (Excluding High tech District)	1990	30.9	1027
高新区	High tech District			
即墨区	Jimo District	59560	60.2	35190
胶州市	Jiaozhou	39710	63.3	17726
平度市	Pingdu	130590	70.9	44856
莱西市	Laixi	54030	60.6	27113

11-26 分市、区主要农业机械拥有量（2019 年）
OWNERSHIP OF MAJOR AGRICULTURAL MACHINERY BY REGION (2019)

市、区名称	Region	农业机械总动力（万千瓦）Agricultural Machinery Power (10 000kW)	平均每公顷耕地拥有量（千瓦）Power Per Hectare of Cultivated Land (kW)	大中型拖拉机 Large and Medium Tractors		小型拖拉机 Small Tractors	
				台 set	千瓦 kW	台 set	千瓦 kW
全市	**Whole Municipality**	**751.7**	**14.6**	**44982**	**2279932**	**171514**	**1489355**
崂山区	Laoshan District						
西海岸新区	West Coast New Area	82.8	11.2	2716	131539	44740	282911
黄岛区	Huangdao District	82.8	11.2	2716	131539	44740	282911
保税港区	Qingdao Free Trade Port Area of China						
城阳区	Chengyang District	30.7	47.6	400	21893	1500	10100
城阳区（不含高新区）	Chengyang District (Excluding High tech District)	30.7	47.6	400	21893	1500	10100
高新区	High tech District						
即墨区	Jimo District	112.2	11.3	4373	243516	34623	318920
胶州市	Jiaozhou	110.2	17.6	4856	328980	20649	301865
平度市	Pingdu	279.9	15.2	25140	1200612	33723	320365
莱西市	Laixi	135.8	15.2	7497	353392	36279	255194

11-26 续表
Continued

市、区名称	Region	机引犁（部）Towing Ploughs (unit)	机引耙（部）Towing Rakes (unit)	粮食加工机械（台）Grain Processing Machinery (unit)	油料加工机械（部）Oil Processing Machinery (unit)	棉花加工机械（部）Cotton Processing Machinery (unit)	饲草料加工机械（台套）Forage Processing Machinery (unit)
全市	**Whole Municipality**	**160429**	**32233**	**25683**	**9144**	**132**	**22548**
崂山区	Laoshan District						
西海岸新区	West Coast New Area	32937	109	1117	256		2999
黄岛区	Huangdao District	32937	109	1117	256		2999
保税港区	Qingdao Free Trade Port Area of China						
城阳区	Chengyang District	1200	200	1605	520	17	338
城阳区（不含高新区）	Chengyang District (Excluding High tech District)	1200	200	1605	520	17	338
高新区	High tech District						
即墨区	Jimo District	19959	1680	3529	1472		1481
胶州市	Jiaozhou	15145	5242	3050	2125		3589
平度市	Pingdu	21850	16500	4372	1421	6	7538
莱西市	Laixi	69338	8502	12280	3350	109	6603

主要统计指标解释

农业总产值 是以货币表现的农、林、牧、渔业全部产品的总量，它反映一定时期内农业生产的总规模和总成果。

农、林、牧、渔业的统计范围是：

（1）农业包括农作物种植业和其他农业。

农作物种植业包括谷物、豆类、薯类、棉、油料、糖料、麻类、烟叶、蔬菜、药材、瓜类和其他农作物的种植，以及茶园、桑园、果园的生产经营。其他农业包括采集野生植物的果实、纤维、树胶、树脂、油料以及柴草、野生药材、菌类等及农民家庭兼营的商品性工业。

（2）林业包括林木的栽培（不包括茶园、桑园和果园的栽培、管理和收获等活动）、林产品的采集和村及村以下合作经济组织和农户的竹木采伐。

（3）牧业包括除渔业养殖以外的一切动物饲养和放牧，以及野生动物的捕猎和饲养。

（4）渔业包括水生动物和海藻类植物的养殖和捕捞。

粮食产量 指稻谷、小麦、玉米、高粱等谷物及薯类和豆类的全社会产量。包括国有经济经营的、集体统一经营的和农民家庭经营的粮食产量，还包括工矿企业办的农场和其他生产单位的产量。其产量计算方法，豆类按去豆荚后的干豆计算；薯类（不包括芋头、木薯和马铃薯）按 5 公斤鲜薯折 1 公斤粮食计算；马铃薯作为蔬菜统计；其他粮食一律按脱粒后的原粮计算。

水产品产量 指人工养殖的水产品和天然生长的水产品的捕捞量．包括海水的鱼类、虾蟹类、贝类和藻类以及内陆水域的鱼类、虾蟹类和贝类，不包括淡水生植物。

猪、牛、羊肉产量 指当年出栏并已屠宰、除去头蹄下水后带骨头肉（即胴体重）的重量。其统计范围为全社会。

农用化肥施用量 指本年内实际用于农业生产的化肥数量，包括氮肥、磷肥、钾肥和复合肥。化肥施用量要求按折纯量计算数量。折纯量是指把氮肥、磷肥、钾肥分别按含氮、含五氧化二磷、含氧化钾的百分之百成分进行折算后的数量。复合肥按其所含主要成分折算。

公式：折纯量 = 实物量 × 某种化肥有效成分含量的百分比

农业机械总动力 指用于农、林、牧、渔业生产的各种动力机械的动力总和。动力机械包括耕作、排灌、种植、植物保护、收获、农产品加工、运输、畜牧、渔业、农田水利等各种机械。不包括专门用于乡办工业、基本建设、非农业运输、科学试验和教学等非农业生产方面用的动力机械与作业机械的数量。

Explanatory Notes on Main Statistical Indicators

Gross Output Value of Agriculture refers to the total volume of products of farming, forestry, animal husbandry, and fishery expressed in the monetary terms. It reflects the overall scale and achievements of agricultural production during a given period of time.

The scope of statistics on farming, forestry, animal husbandry, and fishery are as follows:

Farming includes cultivation of farm crops and other agricultural activities.

Cultivation of farm crops include cultivation of grain crops, legume crops, tuber-crops, cotton, oil-bearing crops, sugar crops, and cultivation and management of tea plantations, mulberry fields and orchards. Other agricultural activities include harvesting wild fruits, fiber, tree gum, resin, oil-bearing plants, firewood, wild medicinal herbs, fungus, and rural-household commodity industries.

Forestry refers to planting trees of various kinds (excluding tea plantations, mulberry fields and orchards), collection of forestry products and cutting and felling of bamboo and trees by villages and other cooperative organizations under village level.

Animal husbandry refers to raising and grazing of all kinds of farm animals except fishing and aquatic cultivating, and hunting and rising of wild animals.

Fishery refers to cultivation and catching of fish and other aquatic products and cultivation and collection of seaweed and other aquatic plants.

Grain Output refers to the total output of rice, wheat, corn, sorghum, millet and other miscellaneous grains as well as tubers and bean in the whole country including grains produced by states farms, collective unit, industrial enterprises and mines, output of beans refers to dry beans without pods, the output of tubers (excluding taros,cassava and potatoes) was converted into that of grain at the ratio 5:1, i. e. 5 kilograms of fresh tubers was equivalent to 1 kilogram of grain. Statistics of potatoes as vegetables. Output of all other grains refers to husked grain.

Output of Aquatic Products refers to catches of both artificially cultured and naturally grown aquatic products, including fish, shrimps, crabs and shellfish in sea and inland water as well as seaweed. Freshwater plants are not included.

Output of Pork, Beef, and Mutton refers to the meat of slaughtered hogs, cattle, sheep and goats with head, feet, and offal taken away. Data refers to the production of the whole country.

Consumption of Chemical Fertilizers in Agriculture refers to the quantity of chemical fertilizers applied in agriculture in the year, including nitrogenous fertilizer, phosphate fertilizer, potash fertilizer, and compound fertilizer. The consumption of chemical fertilizers is required in calculation to convert the gross weight into weight containing 100% effective component (e.g. 100% nitrogen content in nitrogenous fertilizer, 100% phosphorous pent oxide contents in phosphate fertilizer, 100% potassium oxide contents in potash fertilizer) . Compound fertilizer is converted with its major component. The formula is:

Volume of effective component= physical quantity x effective component of certain chemical fertilizer (%)

Total Power of Agriculture Machinery Refers to the total mechanical power of machinery used in farming forestry animal husbandry and fishery, including machines used for ploughing, irrigation and drainage, crop growing, plant protection, harvesting, farm product processing, transport, stock breeding, fishery and water conservancy, machinery employed for non agricultural purposes such as township industry, capital construction, non–agricultural transport, scientific experiments and for teaching is excluded.

12 工 业

INDUSTRY

简要说明

一、本篇资料的主要内容

本篇资料主要反映了全市工业生产和基本效益情况，主要包括工业企业单位数、历年工业总产值、规模以上工业、国有控股工业、国有工业、集体工业、外商投资和港澳台投资工业、大中型工业企业的主要经济指标、相关的财务分析指标和主要工业产品产量等方面的内容。

二、本篇资料的来源

本篇中规模以上工业资料来源于工业统计年报，由市统计局工业统计处整理提供。

Brief Introduction

I. Main Content

Data in this chapter show the basic condition of industrial production and benefit in Qingdao, mainly including the number of industrial enterprises, gross industrial output value and indices, the output of major industrial products and major economic and relevant financial indicators of industrial enterprises. Industrial enterprises include enterprises above designated size, state share-holding enterprises, state owned enterprises, collective owned enterprises, foreign funded enterprises, enterprises with funds from Hong Kong, Macao and Taiwan, large and medium sized enterprises.

II. Source of Data

Data on industry above designated size are based on the annual report of industrial statistics, and prepared by the Division of Industry Statistics of Qingdao Municipal Bureau of Statistics.

12-1 规模以上工业企业单位数
NUMBER OF INDUSTRIAL ENTERPRISES ABOVE DESIGNATED SIZE

单位：个 (unit)

项 目	Item	1985 年	1990 年	1995 年	2000 年	2005 年	2006 年
总 计	**Total**	**2411**	**2997**	**4987**	**1504**	**3697**	**4567**
一、按经济类型分	**Grouped by Economic Types**						
国有企业	State-owned	502	568	1084	179	76	74
集体企业	Collective-owned	1907	2386	2731	226	87	72
其他经济类型企业	Other Economic Types	2	43	1172	1099	3534	4421
# 外商及港澳台商投资企业	Foreign Funded Enterprises and Enterprises with Funds from Hong Kong, Macao and Taiwan		35	1027	593	1658	1952
二、按轻重工业分	**Grouped by Light and Heavy Industries**						
轻工业	Light Industry	1398	1730	2858	891	1942	2313
重工业	Heavy Industry	1013	1267	2129	613	1755	2254
三、按企业规模分	**Grouped by Size of Enterprises**						
大型企业	Large	26	42	89	202	51	51
中型企业	Medium	80	168	216	229	441	469
小型企业	Small	2305	2787	4480	1073	3205	4047
四、按行业分	**Grouped by sectors**						
黑色金属矿采选业	Mining of Non-ferrous Metal Ores		4	6	1	2	5
有色金属矿采选业	Mining of Non-ferrous Metal Ores	2	7	9	7	5	5
非金属矿采选业	Mining and Processing of Nometal Ores	43	70	87	29	34	31
食品制造业	Manufacture of Foods	244	324	437	170	121	137
# 粮食及饲料加工	Processing of Grain and Feed	62	57	60	27		
饮料制造业	Manufacture of Beverage	31	44	74	23	29	28
# 饮料酒	Beverage Liquor	20	28	27	19	20	25

注：1. 规模以上工业企业为年主营业务收入 2000 万元及以上的工业法人企业。
2. 2010 年以前为国有及年主营业务收入 500 万元以上的非国有工业企业。
3. 本表 1998 年以前为乡及乡以上工业企业单位数 。
4. 2012 年行业分类按 2011 年发布的《国民经济行业分类》（GB/T4754-2011）重新划分。

Note: 1. Industrial enterprises above designated size refers to industrial enterprises with revenue from principal business over 20 million yuan.
2. Before 2010, industrial enterprises above designated size referred to all the state-owned enterprises and non-state enterprises with revennue from principal business over 5 million yuan.
3. Before 1998, the number of industrial enterprises refer to those at and above county level.
4. The seetors are grouped by "Classification Code of the Sectors of the National Economy" (GB/T4754-2011) in 2012.

12-1 续表 1
Continued

单位：个 (unit)

项 目	Item	2007 年	2008 年	2009 年	2010 年	2011 年
总 计	**Total**	**5032**	**5628**	**5895**	**5674**	**4727**
一、按经济类型分	**Grouped by Economic Types**					
国有企业	State-owned	63	65	163	61	147
集体企业	Gollective-owned	72	61	59	53	31
其他经济类型企业	Other Economic Types	4897	5502	5673	5560	4549
#外商及港澳台商投资企业	Foreign Funded Enterprises and Enterprises with Funds from Hong Kong, Macao and Taiwan	2091	2217	2244	2037	1618
二、按轻重工业分	**Grouped by Light and Heavy Industries**					
轻工业	Light Industry	2489	2704	2805	2635	2131
重工业	Heavy Industry	2543	2924	3090	3039	2596
三、按企业规模分	**Grouped by Size of Enterprises**					
大型企业	Large	53	48	50	52	50
中型企业	Medium	489	519	502	525	516
小型企业	Small	4490	5061	5343	5097	4161
四、按行业分	**Grouped by sectors**					
黑色金属矿采选业	Mining of Non-ferrous Metal Ores	7	23	22	12	12
有色金属矿采选业	Mining of Non-ferrous Metal Ores	5	6	6	4	
非金属矿采选业	Mining and Processing of Nometal Ores	33	30	26	26	23
食品制造业	Manufacture of Foods	156	158	174	167	127
#粮食及饲料加工	Processing of Gren and Feed					
饮料制造业	Manufacture of Beverage	33	40	42	42	36
#饮料酒	Beverage Liquor					

12-1 续表 2
Continued

单位：个 (unit)

项 目	Item	1985 年	1990 年	1995 年	2000 年	2005 年	2006 年
烟草制品业	Manufacture of Tobacco	2	2	5	3	2	2
纺织业	Manufacture of Textile	169	225	330	132	300	327
纺织服装、鞋、帽制造业	Manufacture of Textile Wearing Apparel. Footware and Caps	171	194	322	95	272	339
皮革、毛皮、羽毛(绒)及其制品业	Manufacture of Leather, Fur, Feather and Related Products	56	64	161	64	167	194
木材加工制品业	Processing of Wood and Wood Products	71	89	116	19	40	53
家具制造业	Manufacture of Furniture	61	72	88	10	72	103
造纸及纸制品业	Manufacture of Paper and Paper Products	66	74	110	56	102	128
印刷业和记录媒介的复制	Printing, Reproduction of Recording Media	61	81	215	23	44	59
文教体育用品制造业	Manufacture of Articles For Culture, Education and Sport Activities	31	27	93	48	89	91
石油、煤炭及其他燃料加工业	Oil, coal and other fuel processing industries	2	3	13	5	10	6
化学原料及制品	Manufacture of Raw Chemical Materials and Chemical Products	106	156	278	81	178	233
医药制造业	Manufacture of Medicines	16	14	39	20	30	46
化学纤维制造业	Manufacure of Chemical Fibers	2	4	26	15	14	13
橡胶制品业	Manufacture of Rubber	53	57	143	48	116	170
塑料制品业	Manufacture of Plastics	103	131	237	64	153	179
非金属矿物制品业	Manufacture of Non-mettallic Mineral Products	230	245	275	62	161	218
黑色金属压延加工业	Smelting and Pressing of Ferrous Metals	11	13	31	15	41	45
有色金属压延加工业	Smelting and Pressing of Non-ferrous Metals	6	8	19	9	28	40
金属制品业	Manufacture of Metal Products	161	186	372	88	186	250
通用设备制造业	Manufacture of General Purpose Machinery	320	398	320	94	299	397
交通运输制造业	Manufacture of Electrical Machinery and Equipment	104	114	358	52	151	194
电气机械及器材制造业	Manufacture of Electrication Machinery and Equipment	86	96	211	79	214	249
通信设备、计算机及其他电子设备制造业	Manufacture of Communication Equipment, Computers and Other Electronic Equipment	32	31	79	34	123	140
仪器仪表及文化、办公用机械制造业	Manufacture of Measuring Instruments and Machinery for Cultural Activity and Office Work	28	33	70	20	40	44
水的生产和供应业	Production and Supply of Water	8	12	12	8	10	10
电力、热力的生产和供应业	Production and Supply of Electric Power and Heat Power	10	16	20	17	27	32
燃气生产和供应业	Production and Supply of Gas	1	4	3	2	5	6
其他工业	Other Industrial Sectors	46	48	209	63	166	534

12-1 续表 3
Continued

单位：个 (unit)

项 目	Item	2007 年	2008 年	2009 年	2010 年	2011 年
烟草制品业	Manufacture of Tobacco	2	2	2	1	1
纺织业	Manufacture of Textile	340	330	322	287	229
纺织服装、鞋、帽制造业	Manfacture of Textile Wearing Apparel. Footware and Caps	362	418	434	392	295
皮革、毛皮、羽毛（绒）及其制品业	Manufacture of Leather, Fur, Feather and Related Products	197	209	210	211	160
木材加工制品业	Processing of Wood and Wood Products	64	66	68	68	49
家具制造业	Manufacture of Furniture	119	130	133	117	97
造纸及纸制品业	Manufacture of Paper and Paper Products	126	133	133	138	101
印刷业和记录媒介的复制	Printing, Reproduction of Recording Media	63	74	79	92	58
文教体育用品制造业	Manufacture of Articles For Culture, Education and Sport Activities	97	96	99	90	75
石油、煤炭及其他燃料加工业	Oil, coal and other fuel processing industries	7	7	9	8	7
化学原料及制品	Manufacture of Raw Chemical Materials and Chemical Products	261	276	275	262	231
医药制造业	Manufacture of Medicines	48	49	56	52	44
化学纤维制造业	Manufacure of Chemical Fibers	12	13	14	12	10
橡胶制品业	Manufacture of Rubber	183	211	214	196	187
塑料制品业	Manufacture of Plastics	199	227	234	233	169
非金属矿物制品业	Manufacture of Non-mettallic Mineral Products	259	311	320	327	303
黑色金属压延加工业	Smelting and Pressing of Ferrous Metals	39	24	27	31	29
有色金属压延加工业	Smelting and Pressing of Non-ferrous Metals	40	41	40	35	34
金属制品业	Manufacture of Metal Products	271	347	376	361	294
通用设备制造业	Manufacture of General Purpose Machinery	473	535	592	597	521
交通运输制造业	Manufacture of Electrical Machinery and Equipment	217	264	290	296	263
电气机械及器材制造业	Manufacture of Electrication Machinery and Equipment	274	303	300	281	230
通信设备、计算机及其他电子设备制造业	Manufacture of Communication Equipment, Computers and Other Electronic Equipment	152	163	168	167	124
仪器仪表及文化、办公用机械制造业	Manufacture of Measuring Instruments and Machinery for Cultural Activity and Office Work	47	47	55	54	39
水的生产和供应业	Production and Supply of Water	10	13	14	14	11
电力、热力的生产和供应业	Production and Supply of Electric Power and Heat Power	34	36	39	38	36
燃气生产和供应业	Production and Supply of Gas	7	13	13	14	11
其他工业	Other Industrial Sectors	895	1033	1109	1049	921

12-1 续表 4
Continued

单位：个 (unit)

项 目	Item	2012 年	2013 年	2014 年	2015 年
总计	**Total**	**4817**	**4917**	**4790**	**4876**
一、按经济类型分	**Grouped by Economic Types**				
国有企业	State-owned	144	140	132	141
集体企业	Gollective-owned	28	24	19	15
其他经济类型企业	Other Economic Types	4645	4753	4639	4720
# 外商及港澳台商投资企业	Foreign Funded Enterprises and Enterprises with Funds from Hong Kong, Macao and Taiwan	1599	1551	1445	1361
二、按轻重工业分	**Grouped by Light and Heavy Industries**				
轻工业	Light Industry	2153	2190	2080	2095
重工业	Heavy Industry	2664	2727	2710	2781
三、按企业规模分	**Grouped by Size of Enterprises**				
大型企业	Large	98	97	91	89
中型企业	Medium	596	599	568	566
小微型企业	Small& Micro-Enterprises	4123	4221	4131	4221
四、按行业分	**Grouped by sectors**				
黑色金属矿采选业	Mining of Ferrous Metal Ores	10	11	8	7
有色金属矿采选业	Mining of Non-ferrous Metal Ores				
非金属矿采选业	Mining and processing of Nometal Ores	14	13	7	6
农副食品加工业	Processing of Food from Agricultural Products	454	468	444	458
食品制造业	Manufacture of Foods	129	123	109	116
酒、饮料和精制茶制造业	Manufacture of Liquor, Beverage and Refind Tea	34	35	34	38
烟草制品业	Manufacture of Tobacco	1	1	1	1
纺织业	Manufacture of Textile	181	175	146	133
纺织服装、服饰业	Manufacture of Texitile Wearing Apparel	312	283	249	244

注：国家统计局根据《国民经济行业分类》(GB/T 4754-2017)，对《三次产业划分规定 (2012)》中行业类别进行了对应调整，其中"石油加工、炼焦和核燃料加工业"更名为"石油、煤炭及其他燃料加工业"，并将 2011 版《国民经济行业分类》4500 中部分内容和 4120 全部内容调到此类。

Note: According to the national economic industry classification (GB/ T 4754-2017), the National Bureau of Statistics carries out a corresponding adjustment to the three industries according to the classification of the national economy (GB/ T 4754-2017), in which the petroleum processing, coking and nuclear fuel processing industry is changed to petroleum, coal and other fuel processing industries, and the content of part of the content and 4,120 of the 2011 edition of the national economy industry category 4,500 are transferred to this category.

12-1 续表 5
Continued

单位：个 (unit)

项　目	Item	2016 年	2017 年	2018 年	2019 年
总计	**Total**	**4431**	**3569**	**3508**	**3536**
一、按经济类型分	**Grouped by Economic Types**				
国有企业	State-owned	128	131	145	175
集体企业	Gollective-owned	11	5	4	5
其他经济类型企业	Other Economic Types	4292	3433	3359	3356
#外商及港澳台商投资企业	Foreign Funded Enterprises and Enterprises with Funds from Hong Kong, Macao and Taiwan	1205	1037	938	868
二、按轻重工业分	**Grouped by Light and Heavy Industries**				
轻工业	Light Industry	1875	1522	1448	1400
重工业	Heavy Industry	2556	2047	2060	2136
三、按企业规模分	**Grouped by Size of Enterprises**				
大型企业	Large	85	78	76	86
中型企业	Medium	516	459	383	386
小微型企业	Small& Micro-Enterprises	3830	3032	3049	3064
四、按行业分	**Grouped by sectors**				
黑色金属采选业	Mining of ferrous metal Ores	1			0
有色金属采选业	Mining of non-ferrous Metal Ores			1	1
非金属矿采选业	Mining and processing of Nometal Ores	5	2	1	2
农副食品加工业	Processing of Food from Agricultural Products	419	338	331	304
食品制造业	Manufacture of Foods	115	111	115	123
酒、饮料和精制茶制造业	Manufacture of Liquor, Beverage and Refind Tea	33	18	17	13
烟草制品业	Manufacture of Tobacco	0	0	0	0
纺织业	Manufacture of Textile	111	91	93	103
纺织服装、服饰业	Manufacture of Textile Wearing Apparel	206	152	144	132

12-1 续表 6
Continued

单位：个 (unit)

项 目	Item	2012 年	2013 年	2014 年	2015 年
皮革、毛皮、羽毛及其制品和制鞋业	Manufacture of Leather, Fur, Feather & Its Products Footwear	177	148	124	116
木材加工和木、竹、藤、棕、草制品业	Processing of Timbers, Manufacture of Wood, Bamboo, Rattan, Palm and Straw Products	34	40	32	34
家具制造业	Manufacture of Furniture	103	107	96	98
造纸和纸制品业	Manufacture of Paper and Paper Producls	100	71	54	52
印刷和记录媒介复制业	Printing, Reproduction of Recording Media	80	121	150	156
文教、工美、体育和娱乐用品制造业	Manufacture of Articles for Culture, Arts & Crafts, Sports and Entertaiment	263	335	348	345
石油、煤炭及其他燃料加工业	Oil, coal and other fuel processing industries	8	8	9	9
化学原料和化学制品制造业	Manufacture of Chemical Raw Material and Chemical Products	224	240	246	249
医药制造业	Manufacture of Medicines	45	49	50	54
化学纤维制造业	Manufacure of Chemical Fibers	9	8	8	8
橡胶和塑料制品业	Manufacture of Rubber and Plastic	350	345	331	310
非金属矿物制品业	Manufacture of Non-mettallic Mineral Products	325	333	330	338
黑色金属冶炼和压延加工业	Smelting and Pressing of Ferrous Metals	105	93	87	83
有色金属冶炼和压延加工业	Smelting and Pressing of Non-ferrous Metals	37	36	38	39
金属制品业	Manufacture of Metal Products	399	389	380	388
通用设备制造业	Manufacture of General Purpose Machinery	362	382	395	402
专用设备制造业	Manufacture of Special Purpose Machinery	312	322	314	336
汽车制造业	Manufacture of Vehicle	136	141	145	158
铁路、船舶、航空航天和其他运输设备制造业	Manufacture of Transport Equipment for Railway, Shipping, Aerospace and other uses	145	146	152	168
电气机械和器材制造业	Manufacture of Electrical Machinery & Equipment	202	212	217	226
计算机、通信和其他电子设备制造业	Manufactuter of Computer, Communication Equipment and Other Electronic Equipment	137	136	141	147
仪器仪表制造业	Manufacture of Measuring Instrument	41	49	52	58
其他制造业	Manufacture of Other Products	18	17	13	15
废弃资源综合利用业	Recycling and Disposal of Waste Resources	4	6	6	5
金属制品、机械和设备修理业	Maintenance of Metal Products, Machinery and Equipment	7	7	7	6
电力、热力生产和供应业	Production and Supply of Electric Power and Heat Power	36	39	40	43
燃气生产和供应业	Production and Supply of Gas	12	13	12	14
水的生产和供应业	Production and Supply of water	11	15	15	16

12-1 续表 7
Continued

单位：个 (unit)

项 目	Item	2016 年	2017 年	2018 年	2019 年
皮革、毛皮、羽毛及其制品和制鞋业	Manufacture of Leather, Fur, Feather & Its Products Footwear	89	58	47	39
木材加工和木、竹、藤、棕、草制品业	Processing of Timbers, Manufacture of Wood, Bamboo, Rattan, Palm and Straw Producls	31	27	22	28
家具制造业	Manufacture of Furniture	88	65	64	59
造纸和纸制品业	Manufacture of Paper and Paper Producls	50	40	40	43
印刷和记录媒介复制业	Printing, Reproduction of Recording Media	137	110	101	88
文教、工美、体育和娱乐用品制造业	Manufacture of Ariticles for Culture, Arts & CraftsSports and Entertaiment	310	222	179	131
石油、煤炭及其他燃料加工业	Oil, coal and other fuel processing industries	9	9	8	10
化学原料和化学制品制造业	Manufacture of Chemical Raw Material and Chemical Products	223	176	171	165
医药制造业	Manufacture of Medicines	47	35	34	40
化学纤维制造业	Manufacure of Chemical Fibers	6	7	8	7
橡胶和塑料制品业	Manufacture of Rubber and Plastic	281	250	252	268
非金属矿物制品业	Manufacture of Non-mettallic Mineral Products	315	228	218	234
黑色金属冶炼和压延加工业	Smelting and Pressing of Ferrous Metals	73	27	30	25
有色金属冶炼和压延加工业	Smelting and Pressing of Non-ferrous Metals	30	23	24	29
金属制品业	Manufacture of Metal Products	348	289	278	295
通用设备制造业	Manufacture of General Purpose Machinery	383	301	316	318
专用设备制造业	Manufacture of Special Purpose Machinery	311	233	245	243
汽车制造业	Manufacture of Vehicle	154	156	168	200
铁路、船舶、航空航天和其他运输设备制造业	Manufacture of Transport Equipment for Railway, Shipping, Aerospace and other uses	156	150	155	164
电气机械和器材制造业	Manufacture of Electrical Machinery & Equipment	211	184	186	184
计算机、通信和其他电子设备制造业	Manufactuter of Computer, Communication Equipment and Other Electronic Equipment	140	128	114	117
仪器仪表制造业	Manufacture of Measuring Insturment	50	46	49	59
其他制造业	Manufacture of Other Products	16	10	11	11
废弃资源综合利用业	Recycling and Disposal of Waste Resources	6	3	3	3
金属制品、机械和设备修理业	Maintenance of Metal Products, Machinery and Equipment	5	6	6	3
电力、热力生产和供应业	Production and Supply of Electric Power and Heat Power	42	43	44	58
燃气生产和供应业	Production and Supply of Gas	14	14	15	14
水的生产和供应业	Production and Supply of water	16	17	18	23

12-2 分市、区规模以上工业企业数（2019 年）
NUMBER OF ALL INDUSTRIAL ENTERPRISES BY REGION (2019)

单位：个 (unit)

市、区名称	Region	规模以上 Above Designated	按轻重工业分 Grouped by Light and Heavy Ind		按企业规模分 Grouped by Size of Enterprises		
			轻工业 Light Industry	重工业 Heavy Industry	大型企业 Large	中型企业 Medium	小微型企业 Small& Micro-Enterprises
全　市	**Whole Municipality**	**3536**	**1400**	**2136**	**86**	**386**	**3064**
市南区	Shinan District	10	4	6	1	3	6
市北区	Shibei District	56	15	41	3	9	44
李沧区	Licang District	94	20	74		7	87
崂山区	Laoshan District	87	38	49	6	12	69
西海岸新区	West Coast New Area	818	228	590	34	106	678
黄岛区	Huangdao District	770	211	559	29	100	641
保税港区	Qingdao Free Trade Port Area of China	48	17	31	5	6	37
城阳区	Chengyang District	662	266	396	13	66	583
城阳区（不含高新区）	Chengyang District (Excluding High tech District)	556	247	309	12	53	491
高新区	High tech District	106	19	87	1	13	92
即墨区	Jimo District	521	248	273	10	63	448
胶州市	Jiaozhou	610	256	354	7	60	543
平度市	Pingdu	407	183	224	6	35	366
莱西市	Laixi	270	141	129	5	25	240

12-2 续表
Contiued

单位：个 (unit)

市、区名称	Region	按经济类型分 Grouped by Economic Types			
		国有企业 State-owned	集体企业 Collective-wned	其他经济 Others	#外资及港澳台商企业 Foreign Funded Enterprises and Enterprises with Funds from Hong Kong, Macao and Taiwan
全　市	**Whole Municipality**	**175**	**5**	**3356**	**868**
市南区	Shinan District	4		6	2
市北区	Shibei District	14	1	41	11
李沧区	Licang District	11		83	13
崂山区	Laoshan District	8		79	24
西海岸新区	West Coast New Area	62		756	212
黄岛区	Huangdao District	62		708	188
保税港区	Qingdao Free Trade Port Area of China			48	24
城阳区	Chengyang District	28	1	633	211
城阳区（不含高新区）	Chengyang District (Excluding High tech District)	12	1	543	166
高新区	High tech District	16		90	45
即墨区	Jimo District	12		509	123
胶州市	Jiaozhou	9	1	600	117
平度市	Pingdu	19	2	386	88
莱西市	Laixi	7		263	67

12-3 历年全部工业总产值
GROSS INDUSTRIAL OUTPUT VALUE OVER THE YEARS

单位：万元 (10 000 yuan)

年 份 Year	工业总产值 Gross Industrial Output Value	轻工业产值 Light Industry	重工业产值 Heavy Industry
1949	21605	18494	3111
1950	34010	28720	5290
1951	53538	44600	8938
1952	84295	69258	15037
1953	115222	74716	40506
1954	126064	80604	45460
1955	118935	86956	31979
1956	144833	93809	51024
1957	142920	101202	41718
1958	217648	92407	125241
1959	282610	84376	198234
1960	291451	77043	214408
1962	120738	64233	56505
1963	139542	83630	55912
1964	177273	108884	68389
1965	215536	141765	73771
1966	252896	152304	100592
1967	287739	163627	124112
1968	299814	175791	123489
1969	296814	188860	107954
1970	345212	202903	142309

注：本表按当年价格计算，1995 年开始工业总产值按新规定计算。
Note: The data in this form are calculated at current price. Since 1995, new regulations have been adopted in calculating gross industrial output value.

12-3 续表 1
Continued

单位：万元 (10 000 yuan)

年 份 Year	工业总产值 Gross Industrial Output Value	轻工业产值 Light Industry	重工业产值 Heavy Industry
1971	365770	216172	149598
1972	378266	230309	147957
1973	377943	245371	132572
1974	237219	154054	83165
1975	402541	261418	141123
1976	439793	278514	161279
1977	490669	296728	193941
1978	565503	336817	228686
1979	625227	379276	245951
1980	677690	442078	235612
1981	707434	479954	227480
1982	732705	474767	257938
1983	816793	513759	303034
1984	918364	569080	349284
1985	1113891	699524	414367
1986	1316230	833864	482366
1987	1703830	1065873	637957
1988	2481594	1451215	1030379
1989	3191643	1857019	1334624
1990	3571845	2057968	1513878

12-3 续表 2
Continued

单位：万元 (10 000 yuan)

年 份	Year	工业总产值 Gross Industrial Output Value	轻工业产值 Light Industry	重工业产值 Heavy Industry
1991	1991	3986427	2318257	1668170
1992	1992	4826834	2835728	1991106
1993	1993	5929236	3422107	2507129
1994	1994	8456974	4931262	3525712
1995	1995	9412635	5579637	3832998
1996	1996	11173672	6793007	4380665
1997	1997	13704735	8620710	5084025
1998	1998	15794106	10153634	5640472
1999	1999	16822436	10918827	5903609
2000	2000	19408338	12433214	6975124
2001	2001	22398464	14368582	8029882
2002	2002	25794324	14811106	10983218
2003	2003	31195595	17306539	13889056
2004	2004	39590783	21473202	18117581
2005	2005	50017829	24697792	25320037
2006	2006	59188120	28686826	30501294
2007	2007	74306364	33463071	40843293
2008	2008	89467300	37871227	51596073
2009	2009	102556155	42715781	59840374
2010	2010	116148345	44954630	71193715
2011	2011	132779629	50854938	81924691

12-3 续表 3
Continued

单位：万元 (10 000 yuan)

年　份	Year	工业总产值 Gross Industrial Output Value	轻工业产值 Light Industry	重工业产值 Heavy Industry
2012	2012	153102565	60516341	92546833
2013	2013	168971805	66799317	102172488
2014	2014	174442125	67683545	106758580
2015	2015	180194299	71176748	109017551
2016	2016	174157133	68552071	105605062
2017	2017	130197343	48954201	81243142
2018	2018	113897787	39054621	74843166
"一五"时期合计	"First Five-Year Plan" Period	647974	437287	210687
"二五"时期合计	"Second Five-Year Plan" Period	1077075	388406	688669
1963-1965 年合计	1963-1965	532351	334279	198072
"三五"时期合计	"Third Five-Year Plan" Period	1481941	883485	598456
"四五"时期合计	"Fourth Five-Year Plan" Period	1761739	1107324	654415
"五五"时期合计	"Fifth Five-Year Plan" Period	2798882	1733413	1065469
"六五"时期合计	"Sixth Five-Year Plan" Period	4289187	2737084	1552103
"七五"时期合计	"Seventh Five-Year Plan" Period	12265142	7265939	4999204
"八五"时期合计	"Eighth Five-Year Plan" Period	32612106	19087323	13524783
"九五"时期合计	"Ninth Five-Year Plan" Period	76903287	48919392	27983895
"十五"时期合计	"Tenth Five-Year Plan" Period	168996995	92657221	76339774
"十一五"时期合计	"Eleventh Five-Year Plan" Period	175336465	73641456	101695009
"十二五"时期合计	"Twelveth Five-Year Plan" Period	809490422	317030889	492420143

12-4 规模以上工业企业主要指标（2019年）
MAIN INDICATORS OF INDUSTRIAL ENTERPRISES ABOVE DESIGNATED SIZE (2019)

项目	Indicator	企业单位数（个）Number of Enterprises (unit)
总 计	**Total**	**3536**
按注册登记类型分	**Grouped by Status of Registration**	
国有及国有控股企业	State-owned and State-holding Enterprises	200
集体企业	Collective-owned Enterprises	5
股份有限公司	Share-holding Corporations Ltd	123
外商投资企业	Foreign Funded Enterprises	678
港澳台商投资企业	Invested by HongKong, Macao and Taiwan	190
按轻重工业分	**Grouped by Light and Heavy Industries**	
轻工业	Light Industry	1400
重工业	Heavy Industry	2136
按企业规模分	**Grouped by Size of Enterprises**	
大型企业	Large	86
中型企业	Medium	386
小微型企业	Small & Micro-Enterprises	3064
按所在地分	**Grouped by Location**	
市南区	Shinan District	10
市北区	Shibei District	56
李沧区	Licang District	94
崂山区	Laoshan District	87
西海岸新区	West Coast New Area	818
黄岛区	Huangdao District	770
保税港区	Qingdao Free Trade Port Area of China	48
城阳区	Chengyang District	662
城阳区（不含高新区）	Chengyang District (Excluding High tech District)	556
高新区	High tech District	106
即墨区	Jimo District	521
胶州市	Jiaozhou	610
平度市	Pingdu	407
莱西市	Laixi	270
按行业分	**Grouped by sector**	
煤炭开采和洗选业	Mining and Washing of Coal	
石油和天然气开采业	Extraction of Petroleum and Natural Gas	
黑色金属矿采选业	Mining of Ferrous Metal Ores	
有色金属矿采选业	Mining of Non-ferrous Metal Ores	1
非金属矿采选业	Mining and Processing of Nometal Ores	2
开采辅助活动	Auxiliary Activities of Mining	
其他采矿业	Mining of Other Ores	

单位：万元 (10 000 yuan)

资产合计 Total Assets	流动资产年合计 Total Current Assets	固定资产净值 Net Value of Fixed Assets
107570064	**67794361**	**18829543**
43071368	26965979	8451211
66279	51566	7198
28687533	16533234	1934619
23938131	17993421	3937978
5620834	3857498	1128656
29617062	17081592	3920801
77953002	50712769	14908743
48772190	31490656	6046461
25517074	15496416	5904778
33280800	20807288	6878304
1029354	360735	524587
3557833	1860718	958886
2636308	1477822	556009
4452026	2974120	529488
44386280	27547068	7411176
43474591	26976748	7172694
911688	570320	238481
19496401	13497171	2702289
15720018	11095593	1995365
3776383	2401578	706924
10896007	7120455	1794103
9209079	6107769	1537707
6839193	3424654	1617075
5067584	3423848	1198225
70937	3813	50964
14943	9595	3177

12-4 续表 1
Continued

项目	Indicator	营业收入 Revenue from Principal Business
总　计	**Total**	**92444172**
按注册登记类型分	**Grouped by Status of Registration**	
国有及国有控股企业	State-owned and State-holdinig Enterprises	33912865
集体企业	Collective-owned Enterprises	82398
股份有限公司	Share-holding Corporations Ltd	16481638
外商投资企业	Foreign Funded Enterprises	21957347
港澳台商投资企业	Invested by HongKong, Macao and Taiwan	5384131
按轻重工业分	**Grouped by Light and Heavy Industries**	
轻工业	Light Industry	28516721
重工业	Heavy Industry	63927451
按企业规模分	**Grouped by Size of Enterprises**	
大型企业	Large	35965710
中型企业	Medium	25167210
小微型企业	Small & Micro-Enterprises	31311252
按所在地分	**Grouped by Location**	
市南区	Shinan District	330282
市北区	Shibei District	3914587
李沧区	Licang District	3438217
崂山区	Laoshan District	3069589
西海岸新区	West Coast New Area	34589938
黄岛区	Huangdao District	33389640
保税港区	Qingdao Free Trade Port Area of China	1200298
城阳区	Chengyang District	16311460
城阳区（不含高新区）	Chengyang District (Excluding High tech District)	13839406
高新区	High tech District	2472054
即墨区	Jimo District	11082380
胶州市	Jiaozhou	8159892
平度市	Pingdu	7037011
莱西市	Laixi	4510817
按行业分	**Grouped by sector**	
煤炭开采和洗选业	Mining and Washing of Coal	
石油和天然气开采业	Extraction of Petroleum and Natural Gas	
黑色金属矿采选业	Mining of Ferrous Metal Ores	
有色金属矿采选业	Mining of Non-ferrous Metal Ores	16073
非金属矿采选业	Mining and Processing of Nometal Ores	8634
开采辅助活动	Auxiliary Activities of Mining	
其他采矿业	Mining of Other Ores	

单位：万元 (10 000 yuan)

营业成本 Cost of Principal Business	营业税金及附加 Taxes and Extra Charges on Principal Business	利润总额 Total Profits	全部从业人员年平均人数（人） Annual Average Employed Persons (person)
77699187	**1580541**	**4765786**	**659639**
28185959	1285239	1911143	113343
73788	596	3429	912
13586823	137067	1028694	82390
18119036	156256	1457460	182885
4522596	28358	301385	42094
23786521	189381	1433926	267572
53912666	1391160	3331859	392067
30088872	275028	2317575	179945
20596932	1144744	1279636	205158
27013383	160769	1168575	274536
314142	10827	833	3248
3511441	21661	104093	14144
2689632	413897	75024	14417
2258071	22202	320904	23369
28810055	853728	2071479	185939
27814690	849316	1985918	170662
995365	4411	85560	15277
13339156	93774	1059410	127646
11399546	78515	918550	107811
1939609	15259	140861	19835
9734767	46773	512745	95111
7045812	41497	260457	86432
6068339	54395	168785	63972
3927771	21787	192056	45361
8986	790	1531	213
6840	304	-637	246

12-4 续表 2
Continued

项目	Indicator	企业单位数(个) Number of Enterprises (unit)
农副食品加工业	Processing of Food from Agricultural Products	304
食品制造业	Manufacture of Foods	123
酒、饮料和精制茶制造业	Manufacture of Liquor, Beverage and Refind Tea	13
烟草制品业	Manufacture of Tobacco	
纺织业	Manufacture of Textile	103
纺织服装、服饰业	Manufacture of Textile Wearing Apparel	132
皮革、毛皮、羽毛及其制品和制鞋业	Processing of Leather, Fur, Feather & Its Products Footwear	39
木材加工和木、竹、藤、棕、草制品业	Processing of Timbers, Manufacture of Wood, Bamboo, Rattan, Palm and Straw Products	28
家具制造业	Manufacture of Furniture	59
造纸和纸制品业	Manufacture of Paper and Paper Products	43
印刷和记录媒介复制业	Printing, Reproduction of Recording Media	88
文教、工美、体育和娱乐用品制造业	Manufacture of Articles for Culture, Arts & Crafts, Sports and Entertainment	131
石油、煤炭及其他燃料加工业	Oil, coal and other fuel processing industries	10
化学原料和化学制品制造业	Manufacture of Chemical Raw Material and Chemical Products	165
医药制造业	Manufacture of Medicines	40
化学纤维制造业	Manufacture of Chemical Fibers	7
橡胶和塑料制品业	Manufacture of Rubber and Plastic	268
非金属矿物制品业	Manufacture of Non-mettallic Mineral Products	234
黑色金属冶炼和压延加工业	Smelting and Pressing of Ferrous Metals	25
有色金属冶炼和压延加工业	Smelting and Pressing of Nonferrous Metals	29
金属制品业	Manufacture of Metal Products	295
通用设备制造业	Manufacture of General Purpose Machinery	318
专用设备制造业	Manufacture of Special Purpose Machinery	243
汽车制造业	Manufacture of Vehicle	200
铁路、船舶、航空航天和其他运输设备制造业	Manufacture of Transport Equipment for Railway, Shipping, Aerospace and other uses	164
电气机械和器材制造业	Manufacture of Electrical Machinery & Equipment	184
计算机、通信和其他电子设备制造业	Manufacture of Compute, Communication Equipment and Other Electronic Equipment	117
仪器仪表制造业	Manufacture of Measuring Instrument	59
其他制造业	Manufacture of Other Products	11
废弃资源综合利用业	Recycling and Disposal of Waste Resources	3
金属制品、机械和设备修理业	Manufacture of Metal Products, Machinery and Equipment	3
电力、热力生产和供应业	Production and Supply of Electric Power and Heat Power	58
燃气生产和供应业	Production and Supply of Gas	14
水的生产和供应业	Production and Supply of Water	23

单位：万元 (10 000 yuan)

资产合计 Total Assets	流动资产合计 Total Current Assets	固定资产净值 Net Value of Fixed Assets
4296121	3129011	587092
2923997	1881854	637215
3055169	1448007	333203
838841	640173	149537
1610700	929507	179521
323002	218611	72033
100922	82943	11972
467315	365377	59167
379758	258834	97455
830057	491248	178943
751038	491556	167315
2462481	1591281	680806
6082617	3006750	1466915
1415631	861178	279391
102096	34651	16612
4591404	2336074	1435118
3649068	2660704	628695
2313168	1057547	818582
645609	226523	252836
3922995	2355622	695160
6879235	4518570	1078731
5290980	3745898	712792
13463269	11645277	1297383
12167036	8545465	1372115
14383998	7669587	1014070
5385307	3936745	642561
1630111	1329532	123112
165799	117272	26319
15757	8152	3406
6999	6769	83
4541704	1470315	2265193
1334856	247912	878974
1457144	472009	613093

12-4 续表 3
Continued

项目	Indicator	营业收入 Revenue from Principal Business
农副食品加工业	Processing of Food from Agricultural Products	7728763
食品制造业	Manufacture of Foods	2231931
酒、饮料和精制茶制造业	Manufacture of Liquor, Beverage and Refind Tea	2499116
烟草制品业	Manufacture of Tobacco	
纺织业	Manufacture of Textile	1128525
纺织服装、服饰业	Manufacture of Textile Wearing Apparel	1796314
皮革、毛皮、羽毛及其制品和制鞋业	Processing of Leather, Fur, Feather & Its Products Footwear	585121
木材加工和木、竹、藤、棕、草制品业	Processing of Timbers, Manufacture of Wood, Bamboo, Rattan, Palm and Straw Products	166732
家具制造业	Manufacture of Furniture	504615
造纸和纸制品业	Manufacture of Paper and Paper Products	474099
印刷和记录媒介复制业	Printing, Reproduction of Recording Media	832371
文教、工美、体育和娱乐用品制造业	Manufacture of Articles for Culture, Arts & Crafts, Sports and Entertainment	901927
石油、煤炭及其他燃料加工业	Oil, coal and other fuel processing industries	5693377
化学原料和化学制品制造业	Manufacture of Chemical Raw Material and Chemical Products	5069784
医药制造业	Manufacture of Medicines	989045
化学纤维制造业	Manufacture of Chemical Fibers	49282
橡胶和塑料制品业	Manufacture of Rubber and Plastic	3676104
非金属矿物制品业	Manufacture of Non-mettallic Mineral Products	3267618
黑色金属冶炼和压延加工业	Smelting and Pressing of Ferrous Metals	3039482
有色金属冶炼和压延加工业	Smelting and Pressing of Nonferrous Metals	685343
金属制品业	Manufacture of Metal Products	3761346
通用设备制造业	Manufacture of General Purpose Machinery	5493198
专用设备制造业	Manufacture of Special Purpose Machinery	3674028
汽车制造业	Manufacture of Vehicle	10475908
铁路、船舶、航空航天和其他运输设备制造业	Manufacture of Transport Equipment for Railway, Shipping, Aerospace and other uses	8485977
电气机械和器材制造业	Manufacture of Electrical Machinery & Equipment	9197409
计算机、通信和其他电子设备制造业	Manufacture of Computer, Communication Equipment and Other Electronic Equipment	6191759
仪器仪表制造业	Manufacture of Measuring Instrument	1043129
其他制造业	Manufacture of Other Products	167522
废弃资源综合利用业	Recycling and Disposal of Waste Resources	16328
金属制品、机械和设备修理业	Manufacture of Metal Products, Machinery and Equipment	15462
电力、热力生产和供应业	Production and Supply of Electric Power and Heat Power	1433945
燃气生产和供应业	Production and Supply of Gas	818328
水的生产和供应业	Production and Supply of Water	325577

单位：万元 (10 000 yuan)

营业成本 Cost of Principal Business	营业税金及附加 Taxes and Extra Charges on Principal Business	利润总额 Total Profits	全部从业人员年平均人数（人） Annual Average Employed Persons (person)
7225286	15011	104507	46405
1809987	13478	140290	16973
1965331	64639	123071	12264
1020789	5577	7326	13959
1592113	12003	62943	38748
514068	3378	12135	19443
158129	749	-3689	1907
431363	2710	12397	9958
427126	2553	10451	4735
698886	4550	31820	10472
774497	6041	26979	18082
4404516	1032937	161725	2269
4315323	24071	267774	24601
392592	11479	227300	9827
43563	280	1113	602
3102465	20038	74744	40675
2821029	19951	148045	22339
2742743	16123	94120	6650
612792	4073	16525	3441
3324624	20166	91833	40177
4536716	29463	256116	52212
2897875	22413	211811	35336
9126629	78214	635739	46808
6858540	55575	768128	49721
7218225	47661	702347	54602
5476296	27969	321066	42823
700830	7058	115651	10844
142448	1285	11547	3550
15100	134	344	62
11808	91	987	250
1412137	12509	-51550	12615
573890	3931	178117	2358
335647	13338	3182	4472

12-5 按行业分国有及国有控股工业企业主要指标（2019 年）
MAIN INDICATORS OF STATE-OWNED AND STATE-HOLDING INDUSTRIAL ENTERPRISES BY INDUSTRIAL SECTOR (2019)

项目	Indicator	企业单位数（个）Number of Enterprises (unit)
总计	**Total**	**175**
煤炭开采和洗选业	Mining and Washing of Coal	
石油和天然气开采业	Extraction of Petroleum and Natural Gas	
黑色金属矿采选业	Mining of Ferrous Metal Ores	
有色金属矿采选业	Mining of Non-ferrous Metal Ores	1
非金属矿采选业	Mining and Processing of Nometal Ores	1
开采辅助活动	Auxiliary Activities of Mining	
其他采矿业	Mining of Other Ores	
农副食品加工业	Processing of Food from Agricultural Products	
食品制造业	Manufacture of Foods	3
酒、饮料和精制茶制造业	Manufacture of Liquor, Beverage and Refind Tea	2
烟草制品业	Manufacture of Tobacco	
纺织业	Manufacture of Textile	
纺织服装、服饰业	Manufacture of Textile Wearing Apparel	
皮革、毛皮、羽毛及其制品和制鞋业	Manufacture of Leather, Fur, Feather & Its Products Footwear	
木材加工和木、竹、藤、棕、草制品业	Processing of Timbers, Manufacture of Wood, Bamboo, Rattan, Palm and Straw Products	1
家具制造业	Manufacture of Furniture	
造纸和纸制品业	Manufacture of Paper and Paper Products	1
印刷和记录媒介复制业	Printing, Reproduction of Recording Media	1
文教、工美、体育和娱乐用品制造业	Manufacture of Articles for Culture, Arts & Crafts, Sports and Entertainment	
石油、煤炭及其他燃料加工业	Oil, coal and other fuel processing industries	2
化学原料和化学制品制造业	Manufacture of Chemical Raw Material and Chemical Products	10
医药制造业	Manufacture of Medicines	4
化学纤维制造业	Manufacture of Chemical Fibers	
橡胶和塑料制品业	Manufacture of Rubber and Plastic	4
非金属矿物制品业	Manufacture of Non-mettallic Mineral Products	9
黑色金属冶炼和压延加工业	Smelting and Pressing of Ferrous Metals	5
有色金属冶炼和压延加工业	Smelting and Pressing of Non-ferrous Metals	7
金属制品业	Manufacture of Metal Products	7
通用设备制造业	Manufacture of General Purpose Machinery	12
专用设备制造业	Manufacture of Special Purpose Machinery	11
汽车制造业	Manufacture of Vehicle	6
铁路、船舶、航空航天和其他运输设备制造业	Manufacture of Transport Equipment for Railway, Shipping, Aerospace and other uses	15
电气机械和器材制造业	Manufacture of Electrical Machinery & Equipment	9
计算机、通信和其他电子设备制造业	Manufacture of Computer, Communication Equipment and Other Electronic Equipment	6
仪器仪表制造业	Manufacture of Measuring Instrument	2
其他制造业	Manufacture of Other Products	1
废弃资源综合利用业	Recycling and Disposal of Waste Resources	
金属制品、机械和设备修理业	Manufacture of Metal Products, Machinery and Equipment	1
电力、热力生产和供应业	Production and Supply of Electric Power and Heat Power	33
燃气生产和供应业	Production and Supply of Gas	6
水的生产和供应业	Production and Supply of Water	15

单位：万元 (10 000 yuan)

资产合计 Total Assets	流动资产合计 Total Current Assets	固定资产净值 Net Value of Fixed Assets
42483555	**26692705**	**8245528**
70937	3813	50964
9662	6467	1242
88672	61865	2795
2464065	1015545	218717
26517	24531	1477
59427	28637	23430
11509	5696	5201
2320376	1504437	641265
2007922	539991	668644
541219	298220	131523
845459	443658	353389
331982	274494	44012
1919494	749870	758370
417097	92365	192865
327620	166910	118660
446982	288827	100072
770625	485407	221926
9072098	8489880	396925
9793572	6810063	1035205
2598487	1656709	160012
2541568	1972679	85417
16854	14294	496
39517	33250	2845
3422	3369	46
3516288	1166656	1834534
899999	138726	619550
1342188	416346	575947

12-5　续表
Continued

项目	Indicator	营业收入 Revenue from Principal Business
总计	**Total**	**33208165**
煤炭开采和洗选业	Mining and Washing of Coal	
石油和天然气开采业	Extraction of Petroleum and Natural Gas	
黑色金属矿采选业	Mining of Ferrous Metal Ores	
有色金属矿采选业	Mining of Non-ferrous Metal Ores	16073
非金属矿采选业	Mining and Processing of Nonmetal Ores	5092
开采辅助活动	Auxiliary Activities of Mining	
其他采矿业	Mining of Other Ores	
农副食品加工业	Processing of Food from Agricultural Products	
食品制造业	Manufacture of Foods	69524
酒、饮料和精制茶制造业	Manufacture of Liquor, Beverage and Refined Tea	2040068
烟草制品业	Manufacture of Tobacco	
纺织业	Manufacture of Textile	
纺织服装、服饰业	Manufacture of Textile Wearing Apparel	
皮革、毛皮、羽毛及其制品和制鞋业	Manufacture of Leather, Fur, Feather & Its Products Footwear	
木材加工和木、竹、藤、棕、草制品业	Processing of Timbers, Manufacture of Wood, Bamboo, Rattan, Palm and Straw Products	13429
家具制造业	Manufacture of Furniture	
造纸和纸制品业	Manufacture of Paper and Paper Products	50516
印刷和记录媒介复制业	Printing, Reproduction of Recording Media	4622
文教、工美、体育和娱乐用品制造业	Manufacture of Articles for Culture, Arts & Crafts, Sports and Entertainment	
石油、煤炭及其他燃料加工业	Oil, coal and other fuel processing industries	5451136
化学原料和化学制品制造业	Manufacture of Chemical Raw Material and Chemical Products	1047400
医药制造业	Manufacture of Medicines	347586
化学纤维制造业	Manufacture of Chemical Fibers	
橡胶和塑料制品业	Manufacture of Rubber and Plastic	392528
非金属矿物制品业	Manufacture of Non-metallic Mineral Products	263970
黑色金属冶炼和压延加工业	Smelting and Pressing of Ferrous Metals	2309201
有色金属冶炼和压延加工业	Smelting and Pressing of Non-ferrous Metals	171602
金属制品业	Manufacture of Metal Products	246734
通用设备制造业	Manufacture of General Purpose Machinery	791436
专用设备制造业	Manufacture of Special Purpose Machinery	437471
汽车制造业	Manufacture of Vehicle	6664547
铁路、船舶、航空航天和其他运输设备制造业	Manufacture of Transport Equipment for Railway, Shipping, Aerospace and other uses	6656848
电气机械和器材制造业	Manufacture of Electrical Machinery & Equipment	1683251
计算机、通信和其他电子设备制造业	Manufacture of Computer, Communication Equipment and Other Electronic Equipment	2566113
仪器仪表制造业	Manufacture of Measuring Instrument	13326
其他制造业	Manufacture of Other Products	48103
废弃资源综合利用业	Recycling and Disposal of Waste Resources	
金属制品、机械和设备修理业	Manufacture of Metal Products, Machinery and Equipment	5216
电力、热力生产和供应业	Production and Supply of Electric Power and Heat Power	1219545
燃气生产和供应业	Production and Supply of Gas	403999
水的生产和供应业	Production and Supply of Water	288832

单位：万元 (10 000 yuan)

营业成本 Cost of Principal Business	营业税金及附加 Taxes and Extra Charges on Principal Business	利润总额 Total Profits	全部从业人员年平均人数（人） Annual Average Employed Persons (person)
27552440	**1280699**	**1939357**	**108745**
8986	790	1531	213
3553	132	248	131
51355	610	10680	771
1616873	56329	97049	8097
17491	38	-4695	250
45732	560	73	902
3447	113	11	140
4196627	1030220	146239	1764
878906	4306	69572	3795
135483	3919	73876	2970
364630	1817	-36077	3869
231704	1391	14489	1139
2041308	14851	90723	4999
127715	2910	14070	1686
240322	1355	-20095	2707
695335	4135	-4947	5018
347989	3175	25497	3243
5812882	58874	486741	9473
5425405	42274	589640	24190
1120122	14335	221916	9674
2354602	11870	90884	7870
10423	93	895	164
45287	185	1508	106
4459	32	138	42
1235842	10104	-73732	10346
225805	3438	146700	1052
310158	12845	-3575	4134

12-6 按行业分规模以上外商投资和港澳台商投资工业企业主要指标(2019年)

MAIN INDICATORS OF FOREIGN FUNDED ENTERPRISES AND ENTERPRISES WITH FUNDS FROM HONG KONG, MACAO AND TAIWAN ABOVE DESIGNATED SIZE BY INDUSTRIAL SECTOR (2019)

项目	Indicator	企业单位数(个) Number of Enterprises (unit)
总计	**Total**	**868**
煤炭开采和洗选业	Mining and Washing of Coal	
石油和天然气开采业	Extraction of Petroleum and Natural Gas	
黑色金属矿采选业	Mining of Ferrous Metal Ores	
有色金属矿采选业	Mining of Non-ferrous Metal Ores	
非金属矿采选业	Mining and Processing of Nometal Ores	
开采辅助活动	Auxiliary Activities of Mining	
其他采矿业	Mining of Other Ores	
农副食品加工业	Processing of Food from Agricultural Products	81
食品制造业	Manufacture of Foods	41
酒、饮料和精制茶制造业	Manufacture of Liquor, Beverage and Refind Tea	6
烟草制品业	Manufacture of Tobacco	
纺织业	Manufacture of Textile	38
纺织服装、服饰业	Manufacture of Textile Wearing Apparel	49
皮革、毛皮、羽毛及其制品和制鞋业	Manufacture of Leather, Fur, Feather & Its Products Footwear	20
木材加工和木、竹、藤、棕、草制品业	Processing of Timbers, Manufacture of Wood, Bamboo, Rattan, Palm and Straw Products	5
家具制造业	Manufacture of Furniture	12
造纸和纸制品业	Manufacture of Paper and Paper Products	10
印刷和记录媒介复制业	Printing, Reproduction of Recording Media	22
文教、工美、体育和娱乐用品制造业	Manufacture of Articles for Culture, Arts & Crafts, Sports and Entertainment	43
石油、煤炭及其他燃料加工业	Oil, coal and other fuel processing industries	1
化学原料和化学制品制造业	Manufacture of Chemical Raw Material and Chemical Products	51
医药制造业	Manufacture of Medicines	9
化学纤维制造业	Manufacture of Chemical Fibers	2
橡胶和塑料制品业	Manufacture of Rubber and Plastic	54
非金属矿物制品业	Manufacture of Non-mettallic Mineral Products	37
黑色金属冶炼和压延加工业	Smelting and Pressing of Ferrous Metals	6
有色金属冶炼和压延加工业	Smelting and Pressing of Non-ferrous Metals	3
金属制品业	Manufacture of Metal Products	53
通用设备制造业	Manufacture of General Purpose Machinery	67
专用设备制造业	Manufacture of Special Purpose Machinery	41
汽车制造业	Manufacture of Vehicle	62
铁路、船舶、航空航天和其他运输设备制造业	Manufacture of Transport Equipment for Railway, Shipping, Aerospace and other uses	30
电气机械和器材制造业	Manufacture of Electrical Machinery & Equipment	40
计算机、通信和其他电子设备制造业	Manufacture of Computer, Communication Equipment and Other Electronic Equipment	50
仪器仪表制造业	Manufacture of Measuring Instrument	14
其他制造业	Manufacture of Other Products	5
废弃资源综合利用业	Recycling and Disposal of Waste Resources	
金属制品、机械和设备修理业	Manufacture of Metal Products, Machinery and Equipment	1
电力、热力生产和供应业	Production and Supply of Electric Power and Heat Power	4
燃气生产和供应业	Production and Supply of Gas	8
水的生产和供应业	Production and Supply of Water	3

单位：万元 (10 000 yuan)

资产合计 Total Assets	流动资产合计 Total Current Assets	固定资产净值 Net Value of Fixed Assets
29558965	**21850918**	**5066634**
1817244	1376085	238687
1960437	1283353	439439
219685	150287	52385
437530	343125	74241
526442	402923	65263
205021	137889	55514
48884	38737	8242
94432	68205	18928
157393	118904	33076
329425	224999	74929
380088	269343	79330
33808	20214	8774
1744492	993869	589829
273944	198690	16329
42689	26489	12706
994115	509045	424878
649173	405747	195785
187943	140274	36952
47671	34983	13657
1048212	697135	248533
1529631	1006302	355260
1287935	916860	214141
8060626	7356562	531155
2219941	1733387	230939
2513584	1668202	336985
1559565	1108118	358310
373911	327140	20142
101592	62699	20465
2514	2468	37
132788	39623	54361
456664	149491	186367
121588	39773	70997

12-6　续表
Continued

项目	Indicator	营业收入 Revenue from Principal Business
总计	**Total**	**27341478**
煤炭开采和洗选业	Mining and Washing of Coal	
石油和天然气开采业	Extraction of Petroleum and Natural Gas	
黑色金属矿采选业	Mining of Ferrous Metal Ores	
有色金属矿采选业	Mining of Non-ferrous Metal Ores	
非金属矿采选业	Mining and Processing of Nometal Ores	
开采辅助活动	Auxiliary Activities of Mining	
其他采矿业	Mining of Other Ores	
农副食品加工业	Processing of Food from Agricultural Products	3208296
食品制造业	Manufacture of Foods	1325936
酒、饮料和精制茶制造业	Manufacture of Liquor, Beverage and Refind Tea	239340
烟草制品业	Manufacture of Tobacco	
纺织业	Manufacture of Textile	660316
纺织服装、服饰业	Manufacture of Textile Wearing Apparel	794283
皮革、毛皮、羽毛及其制品和制鞋业	Manufacture of Leather, Fur, Feather & Its Products Footwear	424724
木材加工和木、竹、藤、棕、草制品业	Processing of Timbers, Manufacture of Wood, Bamboo, Rattan, Palm and Straw Products	31231
家具制造业	Manufacture of Furniture	94017
造纸和纸制品业	Manufacture of Paper and Paper Products	154971
印刷和记录媒介复制业	Printing, Reproduction of Recording Media	349073
文教、工美、体育和娱乐用品制造业	Manufacture of Articles for Culture, Arts & Crafts, Sports and Entertainment	413188
石油、煤炭及其他燃料加工业	Oil, coal and other fuel processing industries	92041
化学原料和化学制品制造业	Manufacture of Chemical Raw Material and Chemical Products	2195980
医药制造业	Manufacture of Medicines	220886
化学纤维制造业	Manufacture of Chemical Fibers	27060
橡胶和塑料制品业	Manufacture of Rubber and Plastic	888365
非金属矿物制品业	Manufacture of Non-mettallic Mineral Products	508798
黑色金属冶炼和压延加工业	Smelting and Pressing of Ferrous Metals	379320
有色金属冶炼和压延加工业	Smelting and Pressing of Non-ferrous Metals	48152
金属制品业	Manufacture of Metal Products	1270329
通用设备制造业	Manufacture of General Purpose Machinery	1670619
专用设备制造业	Manufacture of Special Purpose Machinery	884943
汽车制造业	Manufacture of Vehicle	3914301
铁路、船舶、航空航天和其他运输设备制造业	Manufacture of Transport Equipment for Railway, Shipping, Aerospace and other uses	1469792
电气机械和器材制造业	Manufacture of Electrical Machinery & Equipment	2984992
计算机、通信和其他电子设备制造业	Manufacture of Computer, Communication Equipment and Other Electronic Equipment	2187022
仪器仪表制造业	Manufacture of Measuring Instrument	322174
其他制造业	Manufacture of Other Products	92751
废弃资源综合利用业	Recycling and Disposal of Waste Resources	
金属制品、机械和设备修理业	Manufacture of Metal Products, Machinery and Equipment	6394
电力、热力生产和供应业	Production and Supply of Electric Power and Heat Power	21646
燃气生产和供应业	Production and Supply of Gas	424785
水的生产和供应业	Production and Supply of Water	35756

单位：万元 (10 000 yuan)

营业成本 Cost of Principal Business	营业税金及附加 Taxes and Extra Charges on Principal Business	利润总额 Total Profits	全部从业人员年平均人数（人） Annual Average Employed Persons (person)
22641632	**184614**	**1758844**	**224979**
3008662	5107	47446	17988
1059096	8737	84709	7637
166071	2319	15354	2503
587692	3659	10873	6924
715273	4878	12728	16703
384306	2245	4744	13567
32989	205	-4397	472
80885	868	1035	2645
136823	946	6528	1433
283837	2188	19176	4482
344409	2906	23873	9037
83838	259	3249	71
1904267	11322	54447	9241
106746	2973	66896	1494
23705	105	300	294
722051	6061	44326	10903
429329	3728	18409	4420
362847	820	2623	970
44744	238	-1012	224
1131289	8531	37964	12240
1354539	7732	100928	16061
698401	5084	24566	7938
3147824	58682	443408	18765
1094371	9314	196907	10993
2154434	20740	307217	18180
1887402	10338	132502	21948
197181	2276	62900	2907
79943	878	3494	3057
3817	48	840	133
13541	364	4913	255
378153	568	26021	1203
23169	498	5880	291

12-7 按行业分大中型工业企业主要指标（2019年）
MAIN INDICATORS OF LARGE AND MEDIUM-SIZED INDUSTRIAL ENTERPRISES BY INDUSTRIAL SECTOR (2019)

项目	Indicator	企业单位数（个）Number of Enterprises (unit)
总计	**Total**	**472**
煤炭开采和洗选业	Mining and Washing of Coal	
石油和天然气开采业	Extraction of Petroleum and Natural Gas	
黑色金属矿采选业	Mining of Ferrous Metal Ores	
有色金属矿采选业	Mining of Non-ferrous Metal Ores	
非金属矿采选业	Mining and Processing of Nometal Ores	
开采辅助活动	Auxiliary Activities of Mining	
其他采矿业	Mining of Other Ores	
农副食品加工业	Processing of Food from Agricultural Products	31
食品制造业	Manufacture of Foods	19
酒、饮料和精制茶制造业	Manufacture of Liquor, Beverage and Refind Tea	5
烟草制品业	Manufacture of Tobacco	
纺织业	Manufacture of Textile	8
纺织服装、服饰业	Manufacture of Textile Wearing Apparel	35
皮革、毛皮、羽毛及其制品和制鞋业	Manufacture of Leather, Fur, Feather & Its Products Footwear	12
木材加工和木、竹、藤、棕、草制品业	Processing of Timbers, Manufacture of Wood, Bamboo, Rattan, Palm and Straw Products	1
家具制造业	Manufacture of Furniture	9
造纸和纸制品业	Manufacture of Paper and Paper Products	2
印刷和记录媒介复制业	Printing, Reproduction of Recording Media	8
文教、工美、体育和娱乐用品制造业	Manufacture of Articles for Culture, Arts & Crafts, Sports and Entertainment	15
石油、煤炭及其他燃料加工业	Oil, coal and other fuel processing industries	2
化学原料和化学制品制造业	Manufacture of Chemical Raw Material and Chemical Products	19
医药制造业	Manufacture of Medicines	9
化学纤维制造业	Manufacture of Chemical Fibers	
橡胶和塑料制品业	Manufacture of Rubber and Plastic	20
非金属矿物制品业	Manufacture of Non-mettallic Mineral Products	14
黑色金属冶炼和压延加工业	Smelting and Pressing of Ferrous Metals	4
有色金属冶炼和压延加工业	Smelting and Pressing of Non-ferrous Metals	3
金属制品业	Manufacture of Metal Products	24
通用设备制造业	Manufacture of General Purpose Machinery	38
专用设备制造业	Manufacture of Special Purpose Machinery	29
汽车制造业	Manufacture of Vehicle	35
铁路、船舶、航空航天和其他运输设备制造业	Manufacture of Transport Equipment for Railway, Shipping, Aerospace and other uses	31
电气机械和器材制造业	Manufacture of Electrical Machinery & Equipment	41
计算机、通信和其他电子设备制造业	Manufacture of Computer, Communication Equipment and Other Electronic Equipment	32
仪器仪表制造业	Manufacture of Measuring Instrument	7
其他制造业	Manufacture of Other Products	1
废弃资源综合利用业	Recycling and Disposal of Waste Resources	
金属制品、机械和设备修理业	Manufacture of Metal Products, Machinery and Equipment	
电力、热力生产和供应业	Production and Supply of Electric Power and Heat Power	13
燃气生产和供应业	Production and Supply of Gas	2
水的生产和供应业	Production and Supply of Water	3

资产负债率 (%) Assets–Liability Ratio (%)	流动资产周转次数(次/年) Number of Times of Annual of Turnover Current Assets (time/year)	工业成本费用利润率 (%) Ratio of Profits to Industrial Costs (%)
58.46	**1.36**	**5.47**
51.49	4.22	11.14
62.74	0.9	-7.23
70.59	2.47	1.37
65.31	1.19	6.65
46.75	1.73	5.09
64.59	1.76	0.66
55.15	1.93	3.6
55.12	2.68	2.14
81.65	2.01	-2.19
63.88	1.38	2.52
62.42	1.83	2.26
61.31	1.69	3.99
58.08	1.83	3.1
53.2	3.58	3.59
51.84	1.69	5.51
37.14	1.15	29.88
74.82	1.42	2.33
57.66	1.57	2.09
62.4	1.23	4.77
71.75	2.87	3.23
53.78	3.03	2.48
51.34	1.6	2.5
54.52	1.22	4.86
53.08	0.98	6.14
64.06	0.9	6.5
58.9	0.99	9.8
58.23	1.2	8.17
47.18	1.57	5.32
60.78	0.78	12.49
68.28	1.43	7.36
47.11	2	2.17
71.19	2.28	6.85
76.68	0.98	-3.32
43.57	3.3	27.1
57.78	0.69	0.82

12-9 按行业分国有控股工业企业主要经济效益指标(2019年)

MAIN INDICATORS ON ECONOMIC BENEFIT OF STATE-OWNED AND STATE-HOLDING INDUSTRIAL ENTERPRISES BY INDUSTRIAL SECTOR (2019)

行业	Indicator	总资产贡献率(%) Ratio of Total Assets to Industrial Output Value (%)
总计	**Total**	**9.12**
煤炭开采和洗选业	Mining and Washing of Coal	
石油和天然气开采业	Extraction of Petroleum and Natural Gas	
黑色金属矿采选业	Mining of Ferrous Metal Ores	
有色金属矿采选业	Mining of Non-ferrous Metal Ores	4.92
非金属矿采选业	Mining and Processing of Nometal Ores	7.03
开采辅助活动	Auxiliary Activities of Mining	
其他采矿业	Mining of Other Ores	
农副食品加工业	Processing of Food from Agricultural Products	
食品制造业	Manufacture of Foods	13.76
酒、饮料和精制茶制造业	Manufacture of Liquor, Beverage and Refind Tea	7.67
烟草制品业	Manufacture of Tobacco	
纺织业	Manufacture of Textile	
纺织服装、服饰业	Manufacture of Textile Wearing Apparel	
皮革、毛皮、羽毛及其制品和制鞋业	Manufacture of Leather, Fur, Feather & Its Products Footwear	
木材加工和木、竹、藤、棕、草制品业	Processing of Timbers, Manufacture of Wood, Bamboo, Rattan, Palm and Straw Products	-17.27
家具制造业	Manufacture of Furniture	
造纸和纸制品业	Manufacture of Paper and Paper Products	2.33
印刷和记录媒介复制业	Printing, Reproduction of Recording Media	3.63
文教、工美、体育和娱乐用品制造业	Manufacture of Articles for Culture, Arts & Crafts, Sports and Entertainment	
石油、煤炭及其他燃料加工业	Oil, coal and other fuel processing industries	52.77
化学原料和化学制品制造业	Manufacture of Chemical Raw Material and Chemical Products	4.61
医药制造业	Manufacture of Medicines	18.53
化学纤维制造业	Manufacture of Chemical Fibers	
橡胶和塑料制品业	Manufacture of Rubber and Plastic	-3.57
非金属矿物制品业	Manufacture of Non-mettallic Mineral Products	7.25
黑色金属冶炼和压延加工业	Smelting and Pressing of Ferrous Metals	7.26
有色金属冶炼和压延加工业	Smelting and Pressing of Non-ferrous Metals	6.28
金属制品业	Manufacture of Metal Products	-4.82
通用设备制造业	Manufacture of General Purpose Machinery	2.58
专用设备制造业	Manufacture of Special Purpose Machinery	5.00
汽车制造业	Manufacture of Vehicle	6.97
铁路、船舶、航空航天和其他运输设备制造业	Manufacture of Transport Equipment for Railway, Shipping, Aerospace and other uses	8.24
电气机械和器材制造业	Manufacture of Electrical Machinery & Equipment	11.90
计算机、通信和其他电子设备制造业	Manufacture of Computer, Communication Equipment and Other Electronic Equipment	4.77
仪器仪表制造业	Manufacture of Measuring Instrument	7.09
其他制造业	Manufacture of Other Products	9.11
废弃资源综合利用业	Recycling and Disposal of Waste Resources	
金属制品、机械和设备修理业	Manufacture of Metal Products, Machinery and Equipment	12.01
电力、热力生产和供应业	Production and Supply of Electric Power and Heat Power	-0.47
燃气生产和供应业	Production and Supply of Gas	19.59
水的生产和供应业	Production and Supply of Water	1.82

资产负债率（%） Assets–Liability Ratio (%)	流动资产周转次数(次/年) Number of Times of Annual of Turnover Current Assets (time/year)	工业成本费用利润率(%) Ratio of Profits to Industrial Costs (%)
59.70	**1.24**	**6.36**
51.49	4.22	11.14
77.73	0.79	5.27
30.13	1.12	18.20
39.38	2.01	4.90
106.73	0.55	–25.92
60.22	1.76	0.15
13.21	0.81	0.24
53.45	3.62	3.42
57.36	1.94	7.04
25.39	1.17	27.60
76.29	0.88	–8.54
72.13	0.96	5.85
73.73	3.08	4.14
49.15	1.86	9.06
65.85	1.48	–7.71
60.74	2.74	–0.62
68.68	0.90	6.28
63.91	0.78	7.98
59.58	0.98	9.53
59.19	1.02	15.24
42.36	1.30	3.50
53.73	0.93	7.28
69.85	1.45	3.19
81.67	1.55	2.72
80.79	1.05	–5.47
33.41	2.91	56.34
58.02	0.69	–0.99

12-10 按行业分规模以上外商及港澳台商投资工业企业主要经济效益指标（2019 年）

MAIN INDICATORS ON ECONOMIC BENEFIT OF FOREIGN FUNDED ENTERPRISES AND ENTERPRISES WITH FUNDS FROM HONG KONG, MACAO AND TAIWAN ABOVE DESIGNATED SIZE BY INDUSTRIAL SECTOR (2019)

行业	Indicator	总资产贡献率（%） Ratio of Total Assets to Industrial Output Value (%)
总计	**Total**	**8.27**
煤炭开采和洗选业	Mining and Washing of Coal	
石油和天然气开采业	Extraction of Petroleum and Natural Gas	
黑色金属矿采选业	Mining of Ferrous Metal Ores	
有色金属矿采选业	Mining of Non-ferrous Metal Ores	
非金属矿采选业	Mining and Processing of Nometal Ores	
开采辅助活动	Auxiliary Activities of Mining	
其他采矿业	Mining of Other Ores	
农副食品加工业	Processing of Food from Agricultural Products	4.61
食品制造业	Manufacture of Foods	7.21
酒、饮料和精制茶制造业	Manufacture of Liquor, Beverage and Refind Tea	11.78
烟草制品业	Manufacture of Tobacco	
纺织业	Manufacture of Textile	5.70
纺织服装、服饰业	Manufacture of Textile Wearing Apparel	4.69
皮革、毛皮、羽毛及其制品和制鞋业	Manufacture of Leather, Fur, Feather & Its Products Footwear	4.86
木材加工和木、竹、藤、棕、草制品业	Processing of Timbers, Manufacture of Wood, Bamboo, Rattan, Palm and Straw Products	-8.33
家具制造业	Manufacture of Furniture	3.51
造纸和纸制品业	Manufacture of Paper and Paper Products	6.64
印刷和记录媒介复制业	Printing, Reproduction of Recording Media	9.85
文教、工美、体育和娱乐用品制造业	Manufacture of Articles for Culture, Arts & Crafts, Sports and Entertainment	8.33
石油、煤炭及其他燃料加工业	Oil, coal and other fuel processing industries	11.28
化学原料和化学制品制造业	Manufacture of Chemical Raw Material and Chemical Products	5.70
医药制造业	Manufacture of Medicines	30.82
化学纤维制造业	Manufacture of Chemical Fibers	0.16
橡胶和塑料制品业	Manufacture of Rubber and Plastic	6.99
非金属矿物制品业	Manufacture of Non-mettallic Mineral Products	5.12
黑色金属冶炼和压延加工业	Smelting and Pressing of Ferrous Metals	3.57
有色金属冶炼和压延加工业	Smelting and Pressing of Non-ferrous Metals	-0.76
金属制品业	Manufacture of Metal Products	6.61
通用设备制造业	Manufacture of General Purpose Machinery	8.05
专用设备制造业	Manufacture of Special Purpose Machinery	4.26
汽车制造业	Manufacture of Vehicle	7.42
铁路、船舶、航空航天和其他运输设备制造业	Manufacture of Transport Equipment for Railway, Shipping, Aerospace and other uses	10.20
电气机械和器材制造业	Manufacture of Electrical Machinery & Equipment	15.85
计算机、通信和其他电子设备制造业	Manufacture of Computer, Communication Equipment and Other Electronic Equipment	9.80
仪器仪表制造业	Manufacture of Measuring Instrument	20.85
其他制造业	Manufacture of Other Products	6.22
废弃资源综合利用业	Recycling and Disposal of Waste Resources	
金属制品、机械和设备修理业	Manufacture of Metal Products, Machinery and Equipment	49.06
电力、热力生产和供应业	Production and Supply of Electric Power and Heat Power	5.08
燃气生产和供应业	Production and Supply of Gas	8.32
水的生产和供应业	Production and Supply of Water	8.12

资产负债率（%） Assets-Liability Ratio (%)	流动资产周转次数(次/年) Number of Times of Annual of Turnover Current Assets (time/year)	工业成本费用利润率(%) Ratio of Profits to Industrial Costs (%)
55.42	**1.25**	**6.89**
66.56	2.33	1.50
70.62	1.03	6.74
59.65	1.59	6.65
50.80	1.92	1.69
50.59	1.97	1.64
51.24	3.08	1.14
78.31	0.81	-12.40
76.21	1.38	1.13
51.28	1.30	4.38
55.07	1.55	5.86
50.91	1.53	6.15
60.14	4.55	3.66
50.85	2.21	2.55
44.16	1.11	43.41
73.25	1.02	1.13
40.42	1.75	5.28
39.96	1.25	3.80
37.16	2.70	0.70
47.45	1.38	-2.14
58.99	1.82	3.10
44.56	1.66	6.42
56.79	0.97	2.92
56.11	0.53	12.97
58.22	0.85	15.46
59.61	1.79	11.45
43.65	1.97	6.43
51.83	0.98	24.44
75.61	1.48	3.89
51.80	2.59	15.28
46.70	0.55	27.55
55.67	2.84	6.26
58.24	0.90	19.54

12-11 按行业分大中型工业企业主要经济效益指标（2019年）
MAIN INDICATORS ON ECONOMIC BENEFIT OF LARGE AND MEDIUM-SIZED INDUSTRIAL ENTERPRISES BY INDUSTRIAL SECTOR (2019)

行业	Indicator	总资产贡献率(%) Ratio of Total Assets to Industrial Output Value (%)
总计	**Total**	**8.26**
煤炭开采和洗选业	Mining and Washing of Coal	
石油和天然气开采业	Extraction of Petroleum and Natural Gas	
黑色金属矿采选业	Mining of Ferrous Metal Ores	
有色金属矿采选业	Mining of Non-ferrous Metal Ores	
非金属矿采选业	Mining and Processing of Nometal Ores	
开采辅助活动	Auxiliary Activities of Mining	
其他采矿业	Mining of Other Ores	
农副食品加工业	Processing of Food from Agricultural Products	6.78
食品制造业	Manufacture of Foods	7.49
酒、饮料和精制茶制造业	Manufacture of Liquor, Beverage and Refind Tea	7.45
烟草制品业	Manufacture of Tobacco	
纺织业	Manufacture of Textile	5.90
纺织服装、服饰业	Manufacture of Textile Wearing Apparel	8.79
皮革、毛皮、羽毛及其制品和制鞋业	Manufacture of Leather, Fur, Feather & Its Products Footwear	6.49
木材加工和木、竹、藤、棕、草制品业	Processing of Timbers, Manufacture of Wood, Bamboo, Rattan, Palm and Straw Products	40.22
家具制造业	Manufacture of Furniture	7.91
造纸和纸制品业	Manufacture of Paper and Paper Products	1.98
印刷和记录媒介复制业	Printing, Reproduction of Recording Media	14.39
文教、工美、体育和娱乐用品制造业	Manufacture of Articles for Culture, Arts & Crafts, Sports and Entertainment	8.42
石油、煤炭及其他燃料加工业	Oil, coal and other fuel processing industries	52.77
化学原料和化学制品制造业	Manufacture of Chemical Raw Material and Chemical Products	6.06
医药制造业	Manufacture of Medicines	24.39
化学纤维制造业	Manufacture of Chemical Fibers	
橡胶和塑料制品业	Manufacture of Rubber and Plastic	2.64
非金属矿物制品业	Manufacture of Non-mettallic Mineral Products	6.15
黑色金属冶炼和压延加工业	Smelting and Pressing of Ferrous Metals	6.85
有色金属冶炼和压延加工业	Smelting and Pressing of Non-ferrous Metals	7.46
金属制品业	Manufacture of Metal Products	5.85
通用设备制造业	Manufacture of General Purpose Machinery	5.52
专用设备制造业	Manufacture of Special Purpose Machinery	8.85
汽车制造业	Manufacture of Vehicle	6.25
铁路、船舶、航空航天和其他运输设备制造业	Manufacture of Transport Equipment for Railway, Shipping, Aerospace and other uses	8.63
电气机械和器材制造业	Manufacture of Electrical Machinery & Equipment	7.08
计算机、通信和其他电子设备制造业	Manufacture of Computer, Communication Equipment and Other Electronic Equipment	7.29
仪器仪表制造业	Manufacture of Measuring Instrument	8.03
其他制造业	Manufacture of Other Products	5.14
废弃资源综合利用业	Recycling and Disposal of Waste Resources	
金属制品、机械和设备修理业	Manufacture of Metal Products, Machinery and Equipment	
电力、热力生产和供应业	Production and Supply of Electric Power and Heat Power	-0.56
燃气生产和供应业	Production and Supply of Gas	3.84
水的生产和供应业	Production and Supply of Water	0.44

资产负债率（%） Assets–Liability Ratio (%)	流动资产周转次数(次/年) Number of Times of Annual of Turnover Current Assets (time/year)	工业成本费用利润率(%) Ratio of Profits to Industrial Costs (%)
57.79	**1.30**	**6.31**
68.73	2.91	1.99
68.02	0.98	7.80
46.43	1.81	4.65
62.59	1.98	1.70
53.59	1.90	5.69
56.55	2.97	2.12
28.26	3.15	12.97
59.63	1.36	3.45
66.02	1.74	−0.15
47.37	1.74	8.55
38.26	1.78	7.18
53.45	3.62	3.42
53.20	1.74	5.78
29.37	1.19	32.66
56.40	1.32	1.84
60.52	1.08	5.32
71.31	2.80	4.41
28.46	1.62	16.22
50.74	1.80	2.89
53.50	1.26	5.15
56.36	1.06	8.15
64.03	0.81	7.16
58.51	0.98	9.79
57.17	1.23	9.64
43.09	1.57	5.36
72.08	0.62	13.81
80.72	1.39	2.72
78.25	0.99	−5.88
62.05	2.59	3.39
48.14	0.52	−4.79

12-12 主要年份规模以上工业主要产品产量

OUTPUT OF MAIN PRODUCTS OF INDUSTRIES ABOVE DESIGNATED SIZE IN MAJOR YEARS

年份 Year	原盐（万吨） Salt (10 000 tons)	发电量（亿千瓦小时） Electricity (100 million kW·h)	饮料酒（万吨） Beverage Liquour (10 000 tons)	#啤酒 Beer	卷烟（万箱） Cigarettes (10 000 cases)	罐头（吨） Canned Food (ton)	化学纤维（吨） Chemical Fiber (ton)	纱（吨） Yarn (ton)
1949	15.16	1.21	0.18	0.12	2.36			27447
1952	35.08	2.11	0.37	0.18	12.27			59674
1957	44.34	2.92	0.96	0.58	23.41			50699
1962	38.60	3.86	1.58	0.79	16.59		28	17939
1965	41.34	6.80	2.04	1.34	31.34		205	68082
1970	29.96	10.57	3.39	2.55	42.16		621	85591
1975	34.52	10.98	5.30	2.98	36.00		357	79516
1978	60.68	13.63	6.25	3.75	44.00	4743	1413	85233
1980	41.19	12.50	8.49	4.84	48.79	3521	2116	83389
1985	47.34	26.97	13.76	10.05	51.81	6400	1747	91839
1988	53.28	29.35	26.61	15.58	57.01	27200	3393	107720
1990	35.70	40.22	29.18	19.61	61.94		2900	100381
1991	31.39	54.60	36.75	27.38	56.19	130510	5200	96271
1992	46.24	58.63	44.59	37.01	59.37	3200	6000	99043
1993	48.88	59.39	54.74	45.92	63.46	1900	27100	91351
1994	53.02	59.62	60.00	50.92	69.20	2300	21400	86744
1995	50.84	64.69	60.85	54.16	70.96	4609	20973	79492
1996	41.39	83.02	61.79	54.40	73.04	1719	22945	66832
1997	34.11	95.12	66.64	56.06	88.32	554	26300	70402
1998	19.08	79.65	47.33	42.79	77.10		23858	66504
1999	30.30	82.00	126.21	120.10	149.00	379	29967	56431
2000	41.83	90.84	211.47	206.50	148.10	225	65362	69561
2001	31.40	85.73	279.37	274.28	142.95	99	89989	72933
2002	42.50	89.70	323.20	320.60	138.10	11690	91394	70888
2003	36.85	87.69	353.90	351.80	148.00		101752	65919
2004	34.36	89.01	393.30	390.60	147.10	10889	115187	71931
2005	10.00	98.63	439.70	435.20	150.70	10097	95887	72140
2006	15.30	124.54	101.60（本地）	95.60（本地）	95.16（本地）	1668	72381	56128
2007	19.23	155.30	118.10（本地）	112.50（本地）	100.08（本地）	1850	68746	47850
2008	15.90	164.58	132.07（本地）	124.75（本地）	100.02（本地）	1510	51751	43102
2009	5.90	172.66	137.21（本地）	127.12（本地）	100.08（本地）	4706	59852	38566
2010	11.25	181.93	144.66（本地）	141.65（本地）	102.55（本地）	1092	68654	35278
2011		173.69	164.04（本地）	156.50（本地）	104.51（本地）	41204	38640	18556
2012		174.72	174.03（本地）	163.95（本地）	106.03（本地）	35026	32371	19404
2013	1.28	180.11	194.22（本地）	185.17（本地）	108.36（本地）	30203	23647	33687
2014		178.29	169.85（本地）	164.59（本地）	112.06（本地）	23970	22053	32336
2015		173.53	162.66（本地）	157.83（本地）	111.48（本地）	36179	17419	27721
2016		175.40	168.82（本地）	164.27（本地）		53139	14839	33416
2017		181.80	163.41（本地）	159.97（本地）		85942	11565	26493
2018		192.40	165.81（本地）	162.44（本地）		43893	5545	28948
2019			177.82（本地）	174.80（本地）		5940	39091	40562

注：1998 年以前为乡及乡以上工业。

Note: Before 1998, the data refer to those at and above county level.

12-12 续表 1
Continued

年份 Year	布 (万米) Cloth (10 000 m)	印染布 (万米) Printed Fabric (10 000 m)	机制纸及纸板(万吨) Machine-made Paper and Paperboards (10 000 tons)	硫酸 (万吨) Sulfuric Acid (10 000 tons)	烧碱 (万吨) Caustic Soda (10 000 tons)	纯碱 (万吨) Soda Ash (10 000 tons)
1949	10608	2947	0.98		0.01	
1952	30069	13658	0.44		0.17	
1957	27806	16053	1.54		0.74	
1962	7444	7375	1.45	0.06	0.89	
1965	29538	13670	2.22		1.66	5.32
1970	33660	21994	3.14	0.04	2.14	12.01
1975	31242	22828	3.10	0.53	2.36	9.15
1978	36877	25797	4.55	1.32	3.61	14.04
1980	34937	22900	5.25	4.11	4.33	18.18
1985	34998	17679	6.20	3.34	5.52	26.03
1988	35890	21213	7.42	4.88	6.62	31.12
1990	34066	21446	6.02	4.86	6.73	30.48
1991	34076	19999	5.99	5.62	5.99	29.50
1992	33682	21534	5.95	6.70	5.62	34.60
1993	35912	16606	8.84	6.96	6.07	40.43
1994	43241	16387	12.36	8.33	6.48	43.36
1995	41170	17864	11.06	9.69	7.90	43.20
1996	39023	16881	11.31	10.12	7.30	46.91
1997	43615	15722	7.78	10.16	8.45	50.55
1998	40440	9864	6.91	10.33	9.25	52.80
1999	39576	4340	7.77	12.56	8.96	53.70
2000	41783	3526	10.96	12.96	10.24	56.20
2001	40640	3402	23.05	13.03	11.44	58.47
2002	47609	5592	29.92	5.00	13.80	60.70
2003	35922	10131	31.76	4.50	13.53	62.50
2004	50111	7718	36.38	14.70	14.86	60.80
2005	51307	16027	31.95	14.80	16.10	62.50
2006	55093	20867	15.50	7.00	15.90	63.95
2007	44251	18708	24.04	9.22	14.91	71.02
2008	48399	58907	22.41	13.02	12.78	72.03
2009	31048	27998	34.59	1.40	12.24	68.21
2010	17457	29631	35.43	4.07	13.87	69.35
2011	49617	28449	32.28	5.06	13.20	70.07
2012	48987	32478	22.27	7.22	13.71	63.35
2013	51646	34381	17.95	4.32	11.06	61.66
2014	44593	33653	18.26			67.85
2015	28040	25458	18.29			68.95
2016	24973	28661	18.17		11.33	
2017	23550	21530	17.39		33.89	
2018	46737	22647	14.58		35.36	
2019	11354	27528	11.52		35.11	

12-12　续表 2
Continued

年份 Year	合成氨 (万吨) Synthetic Ammonia (10 000 tons)	化学肥料 (万吨) Chemical Fertilizer (10 000 tons)	化学农药 (吨) Chemical Pesticide (ton)	油漆 (吨) Paint (ton)	染料 (吨) Dye (ton)
1949				30	599
1952				480	2855
1957			1226	1247	4307
1962		0.45	213	910	3560
1965		1.42	2	4727	8667
1970	0.98	5.89	2313	6380	9347
1975	3.46	12.46	4439	7016	5967
1978	7.17	23.66	9714	8786	5877
1980	7.24	7.82	8333	14556	2159
1985	6.31	5.16	2000	26055	4448
1988	8.72	9.41	2400	28943	5527
1990	7.56	7.55	2500	29075	5119
1991	8.52	8.04	2800	33548	5263
1992	10.45	7.85	3400	35058	4821
1993	10.70	8.02	3600	33054	4550
1994	13.04	12.39	3600	29437	5097
1995	14.98	12.62	4934	37772	7185
1996	18.67	12.62	4976	26762	7668
1997	16.94	12.52	4600	19743	11189
1998	22.36	15.30	6755	17594	8274
1999	26.09	20.19	4480	3730	7866
2000	24.64	20.04	3758	693	9306
2001	35.53	28.07	3915	1349	9757
2002	20.30	9.80	4020	1701	9826
2003	21.55	9.70	2039	2106	10734
2004	30.30	19.60	5061	1955	3961
2005	33.80	22.10	6524	1687	13979
2006	33.30	21.30	12544		26544
2007	28.22	25.70	16433	2957	28269
2008	17.93	21.51	12848	12105	18263
2009	17.71	21.23	49684		24893
2010	16.84	14.10	16450		41383
2011	10.78	9.26	23286		
2012	7.71	6.98	28801		
2013	6.48	5.10	27715		
2014			27160		
2015			36853		
2016		14.33	34993		
2017		7.38	18911		
2018		8.08	8507		
2019		8.50	17524		

12-12　续表 3
Continued

年份 Year	化学原料药（吨） Chemical Medicines (ton)	水泥（万吨） Cement (10 000 tons)	平板玻璃（万重量箱） Plate Glass (10 000 weight cases)	耐火材料（万吨） Refractory Material (10 000 tons)	粗钢（万吨） Crude Steel (10 000 tons)	钢材（万吨） Rolled-steel (10 000 tons)
1949						0.06
1952				0.78	0.36	0.41
1957				3.39	1.77	4.30
1962		2.09		2.41	4.59	2.94
1965		6.59		2.91	11.72	8.43
1970		7.35	16.31	3.23	19.38	14.56
1975	55	20.93	19.44	4.88	21.25	20.01
1978	185	35.40	8.86	5.93	31.06	27.61
1980	123	44.66	70.13	5.38	37.14	32.82
1984	7228	70.27	91.25	7.98	37.81	32.43
1985	4222	82.70	77.00	4.35	37.51	32.68
1988	7655	141.00	108.81	4.56	50.17	38.26
1990	6913	139.48	83.13	3.91	54.55	38.04
1991	4754	165.66	96.90	3.71	56.96	39.02
1992	5743	191.50	120.00	3.86	63.75	50.09
1993	6566	221.30	148.71	3.55	61.75	44.88
1994	4238	246.50	145.12	3.06	60.82	46.95
1995	1993	213.82	426.40	3.88	67.27	49.60
1996	5505	181.45	423.60	3.54	72.02	50.60
1997	1693	208.04	570.85	2.45	75.71	51.06
1998	910	131.51	509.38	0.99	84.02	64.93
1999	1691	149.41	576.50	0.59	108.10	86.58
2000	2131	137.52	556.58	0.62	101.17	93.35
2001	2534	148.67	421.51	0.51	124.45	119.77
2002	2712	140.30	405.40	0.45	145.90	142.20
2003	3288	154.90	361.40	0.47	204.80	204.30
2004	4394	181.19	163.30	0.69	225.70	230.97
2005	4430	210.80	297.50	1.04	309.70	330.30
2006	32232	232.72	418.74	1.21	325.82	375.52
2007	14139	425.53	397.79	2.38	327.00	365.55
2008	17910	363.57	599.87	3.65	300.19	350.14
2009	19086	397.66	681.02	18.46	307.89	349.63
2010	26170	442.66	662.04	8.17	300.04	333.46
2011	29337	588.08	510.05	20.02	318.27	325.89
2012	49290	556.57	494.54	33.44	252.78	274.67
2013	49081	575.66	610.21	42.34	235.53	230.39
2014	50713	597.35	612.40	39.37	214.43	212.79
2015	45923	532.36	534.99	41.13	154.56	140.63
2016	2248	600.56	576.16	108.76	188.04	191.37
2017	2775	525.42	557.44	109.84	280.97	291.85
2018	1809	284.47	561.51	27.97	309.70	319.90
2019	2616	442.47	393.64	12.18	319.25	336.19

12-12 续表 4
Continued

年份 Year	金属切削机床(台) Metal-cutting Machine Tools (unit)	锻压机械(台) Metal Forming Machinery (unit)	交流电动机(万千瓦) AC Motors (10 000 kW)
1949			0.02
1952	105		0.50
1957	76		3.61
1962	167	77	3.85
1965	526	111	6.48
1970	2353	531	14.53
1975	3213	788	15.56
1978	2558	379	21.72
1980	595	444	20.11
1985	900	607	26.08
1988	1336	737	39.60
1990	1049	440	34.28
1991	869	764	44.17
1992	1018	982	61.08
1993	1532	919	64.13
1994	1505	860	37.71
1995	972	2563	39.18
1996	1084	584	22.65
1997	449	416	20.74
1998	280		6.43
1999	251		11.10
2000	384		38.70
2001	472	2477	42.72
2002	588		68.25
2003	990		95.63
2004	1287		96.13
2005	1347		63.50
2006	3636		702.02
2007	3392	1869	119.23
2008	8381	1230	96.89
2009	668		728.03
2010	1120		101.10
2011	1194		74.08
2012	1014		104.48
2013	2689		126.82
2014	2563		114.46
2015	618		104.30
2016	588		98.70
2017	610		202.79
2018	204		230.86
2019	584		110.03

12-12　续表 5
Continued

年份 Year	钢芯铝绞线（吨） Steel-cored Aluminum Stranded Wire (ton)	家用电冰箱（万台） Home Refrigerators (10 000 sets)	家用洗衣机（万台） Home Washing Machines (10 000 sets)	彩色电视机（万台） Color TV Sets (10 000 sets)
1949				
1952				
1957				
1962				
1965	250			
1970	34			
1975	188			
1978	684			
1980	1232			
1985	2327	1.66	0.48	6.60
1988	1571	15.22	42.38	17.00
1990	1880	27.41	45.86	18.50
1991	2463	31.51	45.70	22.27
1992	2248	54.84	46.31	28.07
1993	1144	50.48	56.59	36.08
1994	287	62.50	71.34	60.15
1995	1659	107.91	64.34	60.53
1996	2265	193.80	100.94	56.68
1997	2616	257.10	171.95	124.86
1998	1725	219.23	183.67	96.83
1999	2805	259.60	256.30	285.20
2000	4202	311.10	318.50	379.40
2001	4498	396.30	367.89	455.40
2002	5825	518.20	408.6	593.20
2003	4940	598.30	471.5	671.70
2004	6608	815.03	575.06	957.90
2005	116592	908.80	614.9	1324.30
2006	46974	1290.00	649.4	1205.60
2007	22564	1421.40	769.4	1243.10
2008	29507	723.19	407.54	836.66
2009		827.21	488.72	1064.70
2010		801.22	580.87	1111.19
2011		718.54	604.55	1154.20
2012		575.01	583.6	1439.98
2013		524.35	606.65	1512.05
2014		610.07	590.95	1714.93
2015		872.09	595.11	1736.20
2016		882.22	606.74	2111.71
2017		818.65	603.4	1703.01
2018		886.58	601.72	1695.18
2019		731.81	513.71	1580.42

12-13 规模以上工业主要产品产量
OUTPUT OF MAJOR INDUSTRIAL PRODUCTS OF INDUSTRY ABOVE DESIGNATED SIZE

产品名称	Name	计算单位	Unit	2019 年	增长 (± %) Increase (± %)
冶金工业产品	**Products of Metallurgical Industry**				
粗钢	Crude Steel	万吨	10 000 tons	319.25	3.08
钢材	Rolled-steel	万吨	10 000 tons	336.19	1.53
耐火材料制品	Refractory Material	万吨	10 000 tons	12.18	-1.33
电力工业产品	**Products of Electricity Industry**				
发电量	Electricity	亿千瓦小时	100 million kW · h	180.58	-6.47
化学工业产品	**Products of Chemical Industry**				
原油加工量	Processing Amount of Crude Oill	万吨	10 000 tons	1219.14	-20.87
汽油	Petrol	万吨	10 000 tons	374.55	-20.97
柴油	Diesel Oill	万吨	10 000 tons	305.49	-20.21
燃料油	Fuel Oil	万吨	10 000 tons	17.12	-21.47
化学农药	Chemical Pesticides	万吨	10 000 tons	1.75	18.02
塑料制品	Plastic	万吨	10 000 tons	64.47	4.18
化学药品(原料)	Chemical Medicines (Paw Materials)	万吨	10 000 tons	0.26	-3.21

12-13 续表 1
Continued

产品名称	Name	计算单位	Unit	2019 年	增长 (±%) Increase (±%)
橡胶轮胎外胎	Rubber Tire Casing	万条	10 000 tires	4388.05	6.35
机械工业产品	**Products of Machinery Industry**				
工业锅炉	Industrial Boiler	蒸发量吨	ton (evaporation amount)	11822.30	-20.80
交流电动机	AC Motors	万千瓦	10 000 kW	110.03	-4.19
金属切削机床	Metal-cutting Machine	台	set	2838	7.66
改装汽车	Refitted Motor Vehicles	辆	set	19113	4.28
民用钢质船舶	Civil Steel Ships	载重吨	syn-ton	180	-77.61
电子产品	**Electronic Products**				
彩色电视机	Color TV sets	万台	10 000 sets	1580.42	20.81
电子元件	Electronice	万只	10 000 Units	2373733.60	-11.61
建材工业产品	**Products of Construction Industry**				
水泥	Cement	万吨	10 000 tons	442.47	39.10
平板玻璃	Plate Glass	万重量箱	10 000 weight cases	393.64	-30.14

12-13 续表 2
Continued

产品名称	Name	计算单位	Unit	2019 年	增长 (± %) Increase (± %)
纺织工业产品	**Products of Textile Industry**				
纱	Yarn	吨	ton	40561.81	-9.04
布	Cloth	万米	10 000 m	11353.66	-11.94
印染布	Printed Fabric	万米	10 000 m	27527.90	0.04
化学纤维	Chemical Fibers	吨	ton	39090.88	67.40
轻工产品	**Products of Light Industry**				
机制纸及纸板	Machine-made Paper and Paperboards	万吨	10 000 tons	11.52	-35.53
家用洗衣机	Home Washing Machines	万台	10 000 sets	513.71	-7.87
糖果	Sugar	吨	ton	226	55.86
食用植物油	Vegetable Oil	万吨	10 000 tons	85.48	6.27
饮料酒	Beverage Liquor	万千升	10 000 KL	175.71	7.24
# 白酒	White Spirit	万千升	10 000 KL	2.12	1.80
# 啤酒	Beer	万千升	10 000 KL	172.73	7.61
塑料制品	Plastic Products	万吨	10 000 tons	64.47	4.18
家具	Furniture	万件	10 000 articles	503.44	-19.14
家用电冰箱	Home Refrigerators	万台	10 000 sets	731.81	0.60
皮革鞋靴	Leather Shoes	万双	10 000 pairs	1866.74	-4.22
服装	Clothing	万件	10 000 articles	42237.42	-6.90

12-14 规模以上工业主要产品生产能力
PRODUCTION CAPACITY OF MAJOR PRODUCTS OF INDUSTRY ABOVE DESIGNATED SIZE

产品名称	Name	计算单位	Unit	2019年生产能力 Production Capacity of 2019	2018年生产能力 Production Capacity of 2018
发电设备容量总计 / 发电量	Total Capacity of Generation Equipment	万千瓦 / 万千瓦小时	10 000 kW/ 10 000 kW · h	420	415
化学纤维	Chemical Fiber	吨	ton	45500	44970
棉纺锭 / 纺纱量	Knitting Spindle	锭 / 吨	spindle/ton	166988	167017
棉布织机 / 布	Cotton Cloth Loom	台 / 万米	set/10 000 m	2244	2225
焦炭	Coke	吨	ton	1600000	1600000
农用氮、磷、钾化学肥料总计（折纯）	Chemical Fertilizer	吨	ton	110000	110000
水泥	Cement	吨	ton	6700000	6623200
平板玻璃	Plate Glass	重量箱	weight cases	5600000	6200000
生铁	Pig Iron	吨	ton	3220000	3220000
粗钢	Crude Steel	吨	ton	3125000	3125000
钢材	Rolled-steel	吨	ton	5171600	5171600
金属切削机床	Metal-cutting Machine	台	set	2693	2693
家用电冰箱	Home Refrigerators	台	set	10122530	10002530
房间空气调节器	Air Conditioner	台	set	14814158	14276649
移动通信手持机（手机）	Cell Phone	台	set	8400000	14400000
彩色电视机	Color TV Sets	台	set	17877000	15164000

主要统计指标解释

工业总产值　是以货币表现的工业企业在一定时期内生产的已出售或可供出售工业产品总量，它是反映一定时间内工业生产的总规模和总水平。

资产总计　指企业拥有或控制的能以货币计量的经济资源，包括各种财产、债权和其他权利。资产按其流动性（即资产的变现能力和支付能力）划分为：流动资产、长期投资、固定资产、无形资产、递延资产和其他资产。

负债合计　指企业所承担的能以货币计量，将以资产或劳务偿付的债务，偿还形式包括货币、资产或提供劳务。负债一般按偿还期长短分为流动负债和长期负债。

利润总额　指企业生产经营活动的最终成果，是企业在一定时期内实现的盈亏相抵后的利润总额（亏损以"–"号表示），它等于营业利润加上补贴收入加上投资收益加上营业外净收入再加上以前年度损益调整。

Explanatory Notes on Main Statistical Indicators

Gross Industrial Output Value　is the total volume of final industrial products produced and industrial services provided during a given period. It reflects the total achievements and overall scale of industrial production during a given period.

Total Assets　refers to the economic resources that can be measured in currency owned or controlled by an enterprise, including various properties, claims and other rights. Assets are divided into: current assets, long–term investments, fixed assets, intangible assets, deferred assets and other assets according to their liquidity (that is, the ability to realize assets and payment capabilities).

Total Liabilities　refers to the debts that an enterprise bears that can be measured in currency and will be repaid in assets or services. The form of repayment includes currency, assets or the provision of services. Liabilities are generally divided into current liabilities and long–term liabilities according to the length of the repayment period.

Total Profits　refer to the final achievements of production and operation of the enterprises, represented by the total profits after deducting losses (loss is expressed by the negative figure). It is the sum of profits from operation, income from subsidies, investment earnings, net income from activities other than operation, and adjustment of profits and losses of previous years.

规模以上服务业 13

SERVICE ENTERPRISES ABOVE DESIGNATED SIZE

简要说明

一、本篇资料的主要内容

本篇资料主要反映了全市规模以上服务业企业主要财务状况，规模以上服务业企业分行业财务状况，规模以上服务业企业分登记注册类型财务状况，分区市规模以上服务业企业财务状况等方面的内容。

二、本篇资料的来源

本篇中规模以上服务业企业资料来源于规模以上服务业统计年报，由市统计局服务业统计处整理提供。

Brief Introduction

I. Main Content

This document mainly reflects the major financial indicators of service enterprises above designated size in the city, the financial indicators of service enterprises above designated size by industry, the financial indicators of service enterprises above designated size by registration type, and the financial indicators of service enterprises above designated size in regional cities content.

This document mainly reflects the major financial indicators of service enterprises above designated size in the city, the financial indicators of service enterprises above designated size by industry, the financial indicators of service enterprises above designated size by registration type, and the financial indicators of service enterprises above designated size in regional cities content.

II. Source of Data

The data of service enterprises above designated size in this chapter are derived from the annual statistical report of service industries above designated size, which are compiled and provided by the Service Statistics Department of the Municipal Statistics Bureau.

13-1 规模以上服务业企业主要财务状况
MAIN FINANCIAL INDICATORS OF SERVICE ENTERPRISES ABOVE THE DESIGNATED

单位：亿元 (100 million yuan)

项目	Item	2019 年	2018 年	2019 年比 2018 年增长 (%) Growth Rate in 2019 Over 2018 (%)
营业收入	Business Revenue	2254.49	2014.91	11.89
营业成本	Business Costs	1838.86	1608.46	14.32
税金及附加	Tax and Extra Charges on Business	12.41	11.98	3.59
销售费用	Sales Expenses	71.82	71.52	0.42
管理费用	Management Expenses	176.52	187.16	-5.68
财务费用	Financial Expenses	36.08	33.64	7.25
营业利润	Business Profits	215.49	198.39	8.62
利润总额	Total Profits	233.03	218.66	6.57
所得税费用	Income Taxes Payable	40.57	37.02	9.59
应付职工薪酬	Employee Compensation Payable	342.78	320.14	7.07
应交增值税	Value-added Tax Payable	39.04	38.30	1.93

注：增速按可比口径计算。

Note : The growth rates are calculated on comparable coverage.

13-2 规模以上其他营利性服务业企业主要财务状况

MAIN FINANCIAL INDICATORS OF OTHER FOR-PROFIT SERVICE ENTERPRISES ABOVE THE DESIGNATED

单位：亿元 (100 million yuan)

项目	Item	2019 年	2018 年	2019 年比 2018 年增长 (%) Growth Rate in 2019 Over 2018 (%)
营业收入	Business Revenue	705.80	588.50	19.93
营业成本	Business Costs	559.97	448.25	24.92
税金及附加	Tax and Extra Charges on Business	4.64	4.32	7.41
销售费用	Sales Expenses	35.61	35.16	1.28
管理费用	Management Expenses	68.42	70.90	-3.50
财务费用	Financial Expenses	13.27	12.95	2.47
营业利润	Business Profits	22.30	24.81	-10.12
利润总额	Total Profits	34.90	30.75	13.50
所得税费用	Income Taxes Payable	7.97	6.46	23.37
应付职工薪酬	Employee Compensation Payable	100.98	97.47	3.60
应交增值税	Value-added Tax Payable	16.10	16.60	-3.01

注：增速按可比口径计算。

Note : The growth rates are calculated on comparable coverage.

13-3 规模以上服务业企业分登记注册类型财务状况

FINANCIAL INDICATORS OF SERVICE ENTERPRISES ABOVE DESIGNATED SIZE BY REGISTRATION TYPE

单位：亿元 (100 million yuan)

类别	Category	企业单位数（个）Number of Enterprises (unit)	营业收入 Business Revenue	营业成本 Business Costs	税金及附加 Tax and Extra Charges on Business
总计	**Total**	**1912**	**2254.49**	**1838.86**	**12.41**
按登记注册类型分	**by Status of Registration**				
内资企业	**Domestic Funded Enterprises**	**1799**	**1985.47**	**1647.43**	**11.20**
国有企业	State-owned Enterprises	43	105.35	71.91	0.62
集体企业	Collective-owned Enterprises	7	2.34	1.71	0.06
股份合作企业	Cooperative Enterprises	1	0.22		0.03
有限责任公司	Limited Liability Corporations	583	914.76	781.18	5.95
股份有限公司	Share-holding Corporations Limited	70	199.11	153.22	1.54
私营企业	Private Enterprises	1079	758.61	636.07	2.95
其他企业	Other Enterprises	16	5.07	3.36	0.05
港、澳、台商投资企业	**Enterprises with Funds from Hong Kong, Macao and Taiwan**	**43**	**63.49**	**49.81**	**0.41**
合资经营企业（港或澳、台资）	Joint-ventures Enterprises	24	27.14	17.88	0.13
合作经营企业（港或澳、台资）	Cooperative Enterprises	1	1.39	1.42	
港澳台商独资经营企业	Enterprises with Sole Investment	14	30.85	27.54	0.27
港澳台商投资股份有限公司	Share-holding Corporations Ltd. With Funds from Hong Kong, Macao and Taiwan	3	4.00	2.97	
其他企业	Other Enterprises	1	0.11		0.01
外商投资企业	Foreign Funded Enterprises	**70**	**205.53**	**141.62**	**0.80**
中外合资经营企业	Joint-venture Enterprises	39	164.10	108.46	0.61
中外合作经营企业	Cooperation Enterprises	3	0.70	0.26	0.05
外资企业	Foreign Investment	26	39.55	31.98	0.15
其他企业	Other Enterprises	2	1.18	0.92	-0.01

13-3 续表 1
Continued

单位：亿元 (100 million yuan)

类别	Category	销售费用 Selling Expenses	管理费用 Management Expenses	财务费用 Financial Expenses	营业利润 Business Profits
总计	**Total**	**71.81**	**176.52**	**36.06**	**215.50**
按登记注册类型分	**by Status of Registration**				
内资企业	**Domestic Funded Enterprises**	**68.14**	**155.12**	**31.16**	**167.00**
国有企业	State-owned Enterprises	4.51	8.10	0.85	18.73
集体企业	Collective-owned Enterprises	0.06	0.46	0.03	0.02
股份合作企业	Cooperative Enterprises		0.18	0.00	0.01
有限责任公司	Limited Liability Corporations	30.75	71.48	26.50	75.08
股份有限公司	Share-holding Corporations Limited	9.47	13.21	-0.18	39.35
私营企业	Private Enterprises	23.21	60.45	3.98	33.50
其他企业	Other Enterprises	0.13	1.23	-0.01	0.31
港、澳、台商投资企业	**Enterprises with Funds from Hong Kong, Macao and Taiwan**	**1.52**	**4.12**	**2.00**	**7.00**
合资经营企业(港或澳、台资)	Joint-ventures Enterprises	1.35	1.59	1.53	5.82
合作经营企业(港或澳、台资)	Cooperative Enterprises		0.05	0.05	-0.14
港澳台商独资经营企业	Enterprises with Sole Investment	0.16	2.12	0.42	0.45
港澳台商投资股份有限公司	Share-holding Corporations Ltd. With Funds from Hong Kong, Macao and Taiwan	0.01	0.26		0.87
其他企业	Other Enterprises		0.10		
外商投资企业	Foreign Funded Enterprises	**2.16**	**17.28**	**2.90**	**41.50**
中外合资经营企业	Joint-venture Enterprises	0.58	13.41	2.77	39.23
中外合作经营企业	Cooperation Enterprises	0.20	0.20	0.01	0.01
外资企业	Foreign Investment	1.34	3.59	0.13	2.13
其他企业	Other Enterprises	0.04	0.08	-0.01	0.13

13-3 续表 2
Continued

单位：亿元 (100 million yuan)

类别	Category	利润总额 Total Profits	所得税费用 Income Taxes Payable	应付职工薪酬 Employee Compensation Payable	应交增值税 Value-added Tax Payable
总计	**Total**	**233.03**	**40.57**	**342.77**	**39.05**
按登记注册类型分	**by Status of Registration**				
内资企业	**Domestic Funded Enterprises**	**183.99**	**29.93**	**309.08**	**35.60**
国有企业	State-owned Enterprises	19.58	0.41	19.48	1.98
集体企业	Collective-owned Enterprises	0.02	0.02	0.48	0.04
股份合作企业	Cooperative Enterprises	0.02			0.01
有限责任公司	Limited Liability Corporations	87.08	16.65	157.25	14.92
股份有限公司	Share-holding Corporations Limited	40.66	5.87	38.32	4.52
私营企业	Private Enterprises	36.32	6.93	92.22	14.07
其他企业	Other Enterprises	0.32	0.05	1.33	0.06
港、澳、台商投资企业	**Enterprises with Funds from Hong Kong, Macao and Taiwan**	**7.27**	**1.11**	**5.42**	**0.58**
合资经营企业(港或澳、台资)	Joint-ventures Enterprises	5.97	0.59	3.37	0.39
合作经营企业(港或澳、台资)	Cooperative Enterprises	-0.17		0.02	0.02
港澳台商独资经营企业	Enterprises with Sole Investment	0.57	0.31	1.76	0.14
港澳台商投资股份有限公司	Share-holding Corporations Ltd. With Funds from Hong Kong, Macao and Taiwan	0.89	0.21	0.17	0.03
其他企业	Other Enterprises	0.01		0.10	
外商投资企业	Foreign Funded Enterprises	**41.76**	**9.53**	**28.27**	**2.87**
中外合资经营企业	Joint-venture Enterprises	39.39	8.96	23.25	2.46
中外合作经营企业	Cooperation Enterprises		0.05	0.16	0.02
外资企业	Foreign Investment	2.23	0.49	4.72	0.38
其他企业	Other Enterprises	0.14	0.03	0.14	0.01

13-4 规模以上服务业企业分行业财务状况(2019 年)
FINANCIAL INDICATORS OF SERVICE ENTERPRISES ABOVE DESIGNATED SIZE BY SECTOR (2019)

行业	Category	企业单位数(个) Number of Enterprises (unit)	营业收入 Business Revenue	营业成本 Business Costs	税金及附加 Tax and Extra Charges on Business
总计	Total	**1912**	**2254.49**	**1838.86**	**12.41**
按行业分	**Grouped by Sector**				
交通运输、仓储和邮政业	Transport, Storage and Postal Services	675	1108.27	987.87	4.47
信息传输、软件和信息技术服务业	Information Transmission, Software and Information Technology Services	179	379.30	262.84	1.67
房地产业	Real Estate	137	63.90	47.75	1.31
租赁和商务服务业	Leasing and Business Services	468	383.88	331.11	2.45
科学研究和技术服务业	Scientific Research and Technical Services	232	196.17	125.98	1.19
水利、环境和公共设施管理业	Management of Water Conservancy, Environment and Public Facilities	37	24.53	18.62	0.23
居民服务、修理和其他服务业	Households' service, Repair and Other Services	40	24.83	16.36	0.14
教育	Education	16	7.26	4.02	0.04
卫生和社会工作	Health and Social Work	43	21.43	15.61	0.02
文化、体育和娱乐业	Culture, Sports and Entertainment	85	44.92	28.70	0.89

单位：亿元 (100 million yuan)

销售费用 Selling Expenses	管理费用 Management Expenses	财务费用 Financial Expenses	营业利润 Business Profits	利润总额 Total Profits	所得税费用 Income Taxes Payable	应付职工薪酬 Employee Compensation Payable	应交增值税 Value-added Tax Payable
35.61	**68.41**	**13.26**	**22.29**	**34.90**	**7.97**	**100.97**	**16.10**
3.09	2.03	0.05	1.07	1.23	0.54	2.71	0.57
14.54	16.88	0.95	21.63	22.89	2.59	31.15	5.69
0.23	1.71	5.84	-5.99	-5.96	0.03	0.77	0.23
8.90	37.37	7.07	-0.36	9.78	3.29	48.88	7.50
0.62	0.81	0.08	0.82	0.84	0.21	1.40	0.07
2.60	1.15	-0.20	1.73	1.81	0.44	3.34	0.64
0.08	0.47	0.00	0.08	0.09	0.02	1.63	0.11
1.39	2.33	-1.22	3.23	3.56	0.00	3.01	0.57
1.22	1.93	0.01	-0.21	-0.04	0.06	1.44	0.23
1.00	1.97	0.03	3.12	3.25	0.79	2.97	0.30
0.67	0.78	0.51	-1.28	-1.29		2.03	0.13
1.27	0.98	0.14	-1.55	-1.26		1.64	0.06

13-7 规模以上其他营利性服务业企业分市、区财务状况(2019年)

FINANCIAL INDICATORS OF OTHER FOR-PROFIT SERVICE ENTERPRISES ABOVE DESIGNATED SIZE BY REGION (2019)

区(市)	Region	企业单位数(个) Number of Enterprises (unit)	营业收入 Business Revenue	营业成本 Business Costs	税金及附加 Tax and Extra Charges on Business
全市	**Total**	**760**	**705.79**	**559.98**	**4.65**
市南区	Shinan District	166	165.56	121.72	1.21
市北区	Shibei District	108	102.73	79.19	0.66
李沧区	Licang District	98	45.89	40.60	0.29
崂山区	Laoshan District	75	153.63	116.66	0.84
西海岸新区	West Coast New Area	140	108.05	92.70	0.61
黄岛区	Huangdao District	134	106.91	92.17	0.60
保税港区	Qingdao Free Trade Port Area of China	6	1.14	0.53	0.01
城阳区	Chengyang District	96	81.31	70.31	0.65
城阳区(不含高新区)	Chengyang District (Excluding High tech District)	66	33.65	25.49	0.19
高新区	High tech District	30	47.66	44.82	0.46
即墨区	Jimo District	19	10.09	6.90	0.12
胶州市	Jiaozhou	30	22.01	18.73	0.15
平度市	Pingdu	13	8.43	6.83	0.07
莱西市	Laixi	15	8.09	6.34	0.05

单位：亿元 (100 million yuan)

销售费用 Selling Expenses	管理费用 Management Expenses	财务费用 Financial Expenses	营业利润 Business Profits	利润总额 Total Profits	所得税费用 Income Taxes Payable	应付职工薪酬 Employee Compensation Payable	应交增值税 Value-added Tax Payable
35.61	**68.40**	**13.28**	**22.29**	**34.89**	**7.97**	**101.01**	**16.10**
9.40	21.08	2.82	6.01	13.94	1.73	23.57	4.44
4.65	7.28	0.08	10.15	10.30	1.96	17.18	3.21
0.56	4.00	0.59	0.18	0.79	0.30	2.58	0.49
11.90	11.94	0.10	13.05	15.40	2.18	19.47	3.83
4.59	11.58	5.82	-6.91	-5.87	0.90	17.52	1.57
4.55	11.38	5.82	-7.25	-6.23	0.85	17.35	1.50
0.04	0.20	0.00	0.34	0.36	0.05	0.17	0.07
2.64	7.22	2.20	-0.09	0.29	0.53	11.15	1.30
1.02	4.53	0.36	1.93	1.98	0.46	7.69	0.87
1.62	2.69	1.84	-2.02	-1.69	0.07	3.46	0.43
0.89	2.35	1.10	-1.50	-1.59	0.11	2.04	0.09
0.55	0.74	0.57	0.91	1.03	0.16	5.11	0.66
0.37	0.49	-0.01	0.58	0.58	0.09	0.43	0.14
0.06	1.72	0.01	-0.09	0.02	0.01	1.96	0.37

主要统计指标解释

营业收入　指企业经营主要业务和其他业务所确认的收入总额。营业收入合计包括“主营业务收入”和“其他业务收入”。根据会计“利润表”中“营业收入”项目的本年累计数填报。

营业成本　指企业经营主要业务和其他业务所发生的成本总额。包括企业（单位）在报告期内从事销售商品、提供劳务等日常活动发生的各种耗费。包括“主营业务成本”和“其他业务成本”。根据会计“利润表”中“营业成本”项目的本年累计数填报。

税金及附加　指企业因从事生产经营活动按税法规定应缴纳的消费税、城市维护建设税、资源税、教育费附加及房产税、土地使用税、车船使用税、印花税等相关税费。根据会计“利润表”中“税金及附加”项目的本年累计数填报。

销售费用　指企业在销售商品和材料、提供劳务的过程中发生的各种费用，包括保险费、包装费、展览费和广告费、商品维修费、预计产品质量保证损失、运输费、装卸费等以及为销售本企业商品而专设的销售机构（含销售网点、售后服务网点等）的职工薪酬、业务费、折旧费等经营费用。

管理费用　指企业为组织和管理企业生产经营所发生的费用，包括企业在筹建期间内发生的开办费、董事会和行政管理部门在企业经营管理中发生的，或者应当由企业统一负担的公司经费等。根据会计“利润表”中“管理费用”项目的本年累计数填报。

财务费用　指企业为筹集生产经营所需资金等而发生的筹资费用，包括企业生产经营期间发生的利息支出（减利息收入）、汇兑损失（减汇兑收益）以及相关的手续费等。根据会计“利润表”中“财务费用”项目的本年累计数填报。

利润总额　指企业在一定会计期间的经营成果，是生产经营过程中各种收入扣除各种耗费后的盈余，反映企业在报告期内实现的盈亏总额。根据会计“利润表”中“利润总额”项目的本年累计数填报。执行《企业会计准则》或《小企业会计准则》的企业，利润总额为营业利润加上营业外收入，减去营业外支出后的金额；执行其他企业会计制度的企业，利润总额为营业利润加上投资收益、营业外收入，再减去营业外支出后的金额。

应交增值税　指按照税法规定，以销售货物、服务、无形资产、不动产或提供加工、修理修配劳务的增值额和货物进口金额为计税依据而课征的一种流转税。

Explanatory Notes on Main Statistical Indicators

Business Revenue　refers to the total income of the business recognized by business and other business. Total operating revenue includes the main business income and other operating income.Fill in according to the cumulative number of the current year's "Business Revenue " item in the "profit statement" of accounting.

Business Costs　refers to the total amount of costs incurred by an enterprise in operating its main business and other businesses. Including the enterprise (unit) in the reporting period engaged in selling goods, providing labor services and other daily activities of all kinds of consumption. Include "main business cost" and "other business cost". The current year's cumulative counting is reported according to the operating cost item in the accounting "income statement".

Taxes and surcharges　refers to the excise duty, urban maintenance and construction tax, resource tax, education surcharge,

14-1 建筑业企业生产情况（2019 年）
PRODUCTION SITUATION OF CONSTRUCTION ENTERPRISES (2019)

项目	Item	单位	Unit	合计 Total	#中央 of which: Central Enterprises	国有企业 State-owned Enterprises	集体企业 Collective Enterprises	其他所有制企业 Other Ownership Enterprises
施工企业单位数	Number of Construction Enterprises	个	unit	760	12	18	7	735
建筑业总产值	Gross Output Value of Construction	万元	1000yuan	28099476	6133705	228980	6897	27863599
#建筑工程	of which: Construction	万元	1000yuan	23989516	5005641	196722	6748	23786046
安装工程	Installation	万元	1000yuan	3397713	919491	11500	149	3386064
建筑业增加值	Value Added of Construction	万元	1000yuan	10422400				
全年竣工产值	Output Value of Buildings Completed in the Year	万元	1000yuan	11041674	2078637	23084	3432	11015159
施工房屋面积	Floor Space of Buildings under Construction	万平方米	1000sp.m	17538	2912		25	17513
#新开工	of which: Newly Operating	万平方米	1000sp.m	7322	1297		18	7304
竣工房屋面积	Floor Space of Buildings Completed	万平方米	1000sp.m	3606	481		1	3605
#住宅	of which: Residential Buildings	万平方米	1000sp.m	2170	244			2170
计算建筑业劳动生产率平均人数	Average Number of Persons for Calculating the Labor Productivity	人	person	701150	89988	7806	228	693116

14-2 建筑业企业财务状况（2019 年）
FINANCIAL SITUATION OF CONSTRUCTION ENTERPRISES (2019)

项目	Item	单位	Unit	合计 Total
流动资产	Circulating Funds	万元	10000yuan	22381111
#存货	of which：Inventory	万元	10000yuan	3468799
年末固定资产原价	Original Value of Fixed Assets（year-end）	万元	10000yuan	2292865
本年固定资产折旧	Depreciation of Fixed Assets in the Year	万元	10000yuan	132728
年末资产合计	Total Assets（year-end）	万元	10000yuan	27815589
年末负债合计	Total Liabilities（year-end）	万元	10000yuan	21301866
所有者权益合计	Total Owners' Equity	万元	10000yuan	6513723
#实收资本	Paid-in Capitals	万元	10000yuan	3554782
主营业务收入	Revenue from Principal Business	万元	10000yuan	26848393
主营业务成本	Cost of Principal Business	万元	10000yuan	24389641
主营业务税金及附加	Taxes and Extra Charges on Principal Business	万元	10000yuan	108626
管理费用	Management Expenses	万元	10000yuan	674363
利润总额	Total Profits	万元	10000yuan	787430
利税总额	Total Pre-tax Profits	万元	10000yuan	1229372
年末应收工程款	Account Receivable（year-end）	万元	10000yuan	7591257

#中央 of which: Central Enterprises	国有企业 State-owned Enterprises	集体企业 Collective Enterprises	其他所有制企业 Other Ownership Enterprises
5755874	356265	6250	22018596
709062	27722	1472	3439605
608565	72043	4398	2216424
37224	2726	235	129768
7048350	426946	13369	27375274
6053955	316582	8063	20977220
994395	110364	5306	6398054
484011	65190	5224	3484368
6335789	277614	23114	26547665
5888440	251003	21215	24117423
9324	568	84	107974
120005	11337	1320	661706
205271	9727	223	777481
236281	13914	934	1214524
1355225	184892	3858	7402508

14-3 建筑业企业主要经济效益指标（2019 年）
MAIN INDICATOR ON ECONOMIC BENEFIT OF CONSTRUCTION ENTERPRISES (2019)

项目	Item	单位	Unit	合计 Total	#中央 of which: Central Enterprises	国有企业 State-owned Enterprises	集体企业 Collective Enterprises	其他所有制企业 Other Ownership Enterprises
建筑业劳动生产率	**Labor Productivity of Construction**							
按总产值计算	In Terms of Gross Output Value	元／人	yuan/person	400763	681614	293338	302491	402004
竣工率	**Rate of Buildings completed**							
按产值计算	In Terms of Gross output Value	%	%	39.3	33.9	17.1	49.8	38.9
产值工资率	Ratio of Wages to Gross Output Value	%	%	9.4	8.6	10.2	31.3	9.3
资金利润率	Ratio of Profit to Funds	%	%	3.3	2.1	1.8	1.5	3.4
产值利润率	Ratio of Profit to Gross Output Value	%	%	2.8	3.3	4.2	3.2	2.8
流动比率	Current Ratio	%	%	111.6	100.7	124.7	80.4	115.9
资产负债率	Assets-Liability Ratio	%	%	76.5	85.8	74.1	60.3	76.6

14-4 建筑业增加值（2019 年）
VALUE ADDED OF CONSTRUCTION (2019)

单位：亿元 (100 million yuan)

市、区名称	Region	增加值 Value Added
全市总计	**Total**	**1042.24**
市南区	Shinan District	77.13
市北区	Shibei District	106.49
李沧区	Licang District	50.08
崂山区	Laoshan District	113.20
西海岸新区	West Coast New Area	307.62
黄岛区	Huangdao District	303.76
保税港区	Qingdao Free Trade Port Area of China	3.86
城阳区	Chengyang District	70.87
城阳区（不含高新区）	Chengyang District (Excluding High tech District)	
高新区	High tech District	
即墨区	Jimo District	115.18
胶州市	Jiaozhou	108.55
平度市	Pingdu	26.00
莱西市	Laixi	66.61

注：按照城阳区（不含高新区）、高新区口径无法提供核算数据。
Note：According to the statistics of Chengyang District (excluding high-tech zones) and high-tech zones, accounting data cannot be provided.

14-5 重点建筑企业一览表（2019 年）
LIST OF KEY CONSTRUCTION ENTERPRISES (2019)

序号 Precedence	企业单位名称	Name	所在地区 Location	资质等级 Qualification Criteria
1	青建集团股份公司	Qingjian Group Co., Ltd.	市北区 Shibei District	A001
2	中建八局第四建设有限公司	Fourth Construction of China Construction Eight Bureau Co., Ltd.	市南区 Shinan District	A001
3	中青建安建设集团有限公司	Zhongqing Jianan Construction Group Co., Ltd.	市南区 Shinan District	A001
4	荣华建设集团有限公司	Ronghua Construction Group Co., Ltd.	莱西市 Laixi	A001
5	德才装饰股份有限公司	Decai Decoration Limited by Share Ltd.	崂山区 Laoshan District	B103
6	中铁建工集团山东有限公司	China Railway Construction Engineering Group Shandong Co., Ltd.	崂山区 Laoshan District	A201
7	中启胶建集团有限公司	Zhongqi Rubber Construction Group Co., Ltd.	胶州市 Jiaozhou	A001
8	中铁二十局集团第四工程有限公司	Fourth Engineering of China Railway twenty Bureau Group Co., Ltd.	崂山区 Laoshan District	A103
9	中铁十七局集团第一工程有限公司	China Railway No.17 Bureau Group First Engineering Co.,Ltd	黄岛区 Huangdao District	A003
10	东亚装饰股份有限公司	East Asia Decoration Limited by Share Ltd.	市南区 Shinan District	B103
11	青岛博海建设集团有限公司	Qingdao Bohai Construction Group Co., Ltd.	市南区 Shinan District	A001
12	青岛中嘉建设集团有限公司	Qingdao Zhongjia Construction Group Co., Ltd.	市北区 Shibei District	A101
13	中建筑港集团有限公司	Zhongjian Zhu Gang Group Co., Ltd.	市北区 Shibei District	A104
14	青岛一建集团有限公司	Qingdao Yi Jian Group Co., Ltd.	市北区 Shibei District	A001
15	青岛海川建设集团有限公司	Qingdao Hai Chuan Construction Group Co., Ltd.	市北区 Shibei District	A001
16	山东兴华建设集团有限公司	Shandong Xinghua Construction Group Co., Ltd.	黄岛区 Huangdao District	A001
17	青建国际集团有限公司	Qingjian International Group Limited	市北区 Shibei District	A101
18	青岛亿联集团股份有限公司	Qingdao Yilian Group Limited by Share Ltd.	黄岛区 Huangdao District	A001
19	山东莱钢建设有限公司	Shandong Laiwu Iron and Steel Construction Co., Ltd.	市南区 Shinan District	A101
20	青岛海尔家居集成股份有限公司	Qingdao Haier Integrated Limited by Share Ltd.	胶州市 Jiaozhou	B103
21	中铁二十五局集团第五工程有限公司	Fifth Engineering Co., Ltd. of China Railway Twenty-five Bureau Group	崂山区 Laoshan District	A110
22	青岛新华友建工集团股份有限公司	Qingdao Xinhuayou Construction Engineering Group Limited by Share Ltd.	崂山区 Laoshan District	A101
23	中交一航局第二工程有限公司	Second Engineering Company Co., Ltd. of China Communications Central Airlines	市南区 Shinan District	A104
24	青岛恒生源集团建设有限公司	Qingdao Hengshengyuan Group Construction Co., Ltd.	即墨区 Jimo District	A101
25	山东荣泰建筑工程集团有限公司	Shandong Rongtai Construction Engineering Group Co., Ltd.	黄岛区 Huangdao District	A001

14-5 续表 1
Continued

序号 Precedence	企业单位名称	Name	所在地区 Location	资质等级 Qualification Criteria
26	山东电力建设第三工程有限公司	Third Engineering Co., Ltd. of Shandong Electric Power Construction	崂山区 Laoshan District	A006
27	中铁十局集团青岛工程有限公司	China Railway Ten Bureau Group Qingdao Engineering Co., Ltd.	市北区 Shibei District	A110
28	中石化第十建设有限公司	Sinopec tenth Construction Company Limited	黄岛区 Huangdao District	A109
29	青岛即建建设集团有限公司	Qingdao JiJian Construction Group Co., Ltd.	即墨区 Jimo District	A101
30	青岛瑞源工程集团有限公司	Qingdao Ruiyuan Engineering Group Co., Ltd.	黄岛区 Huangdao District	A105
31	青岛中建联合建设工程有限公司	Qingdao China Construction United Construction Engineering Co., Ltd.	崂山区 Laoshan District	A101
32	青岛海德工程集团股份有限公司	Qingdao Hyde Road and Bridge Engineering Limited by Share Ltd.	市南区 Shinan District	B111
33	青岛建祥建设集团有限公司	Qingdao Jian Xiang Construction Group Co., Ltd.	胶州市 Jiaozhou	A101
34	青岛建设集团有限公司	Qingdao Construction Group Co., Ltd.	市南区 Shinan District	B103
35	青岛第一市政工程有限公司	Qingdao First Municipal Engineering Co., Ltd.	市北区 Shibei District	A110
36	青岛德泰建设工程有限公司	Qingdao De Tai Construction Engineering Co., Ltd.	黄岛区 Huangdao District	A101
37	青岛颐金建筑装饰工程有限公司	Qingdao Yijin Building Decoration Engineering Co., Ltd.	市南区 Shinan District	B103
38	青岛平建建筑安装股份有限公司	Qingdao Pingjian Construction and Installation Co., Ltd.	平度市 Pingdu	A101
39	青岛城建集团有限公司	Qingdao Urban Construction Group Co., Ltd.	市北区 Shibei District	A110
40	青岛营上建设集团有限公司	Qingdao Yingshang Construction Group Co., Ltd.	即墨区 Jimo District	A101
41	青岛温泉建设集团有限公司	Qingdao Hot Spring Construction Group Co., Ltd.	即墨区 Jimo District	A101
42	中国石油天然气第七建设有限公司	China Petroleum and Natural Gas Seventh Construction Co., Ltd.	崂山区 Laoshan District	A109
43	青岛市房屋建设集团股份有限公司	Qingdao Housing Construction Group Limited by Share Ltd.	市北区 Shibei District	A101
44	青岛福瀛建设集团有限公司	Qingdao Fu ying Construction Group Co., Ltd.	黄岛区 Huangdao District	A101
45	青岛胶城建设集团有限公司	Qingdao Rubber City Construction Group Co., Ltd.	胶州市 Jiaozhou	A101
46	中建中新建设工程有限公司	China State Construction Zhongxin Construction Engineering Co.,Ltd	高新区 High tech District	A101
47	青岛滨海建设集团有限公司	Qingdao Binhai Construction Group Co., Ltd.	黄岛区 Huangdao District	A101
48	青岛艺高城市建设工程有限公司	Qingdao Yi Gao City Construction Engineering Co., Ltd.	市北区 Shibei District	A201
49	青岛土木建工集团有限公司	Qingdao Civil Engineering Group Co., Ltd.	黄岛区 Huangdao District	A101

14-5 续表 2
Continued

序号 Precedence	企业单位名称	Name	所在地区 Location	资质等级 Qualification Criteria
50	青岛港务局港务工程公司	Qingdao Port Bureau Port Engineering Company	黄岛区 Huangdao District	A204
51	青城建工集团有限公司	Qingcheng Construction Group Co., Ltd.	高新区 High tech District	A101
52	青岛安装建设股份有限公司	Qingdao Installation and Construction Limited by Share Ltd.	市北区 Shibei District	A112
53	青岛青房建安集团有限公司	Qingdao Qingfang Jianan Group Co., Ltd.	市南区 Shinan District	A101
54	青岛鑫兴泰建筑工程有限公司	Qingdao Xinxingtai Construction Engineering Co., Ltd.	城阳区 Chengyang District	A201
55	青岛方圆达建设集团有限公司	Qindao Fang Yuan Da Construction Group Co.,Ltd.	李沧区 Licang District	A101
56	山东国建工程集团有限公司	Shandong State Construction Engineering Group Co., Ltd.	崂山区 Laoshan District	A101
57	中诚祥建设工程有限公司	Zhongchengxiang Construction Engineering Co., Ltd.	李沧区 Licang District	A101
58	青岛新城发展建筑工程有限公司	Qingdao New Town Development Engineering Co., Ltd.	市北区 Shibei District	A101
59	青岛营海建设(集团)有限公司	Qingdao Ying hai Construction Group Co., Ltd.	胶州市 Jiaozhou	A101
60	青岛胶州湾建设集团有限公司	Qingdao Jiaozhou Bay Construction Group Co., Ltd.	胶州市 Jiaozhou	A101
61	青岛西海岸市政工程有限公司	Qingdao West Coast municipal Group Municipal Engineering Company	黄岛区 Huangdao District	A110
62	青岛环城建工集团有限公司	Qingdao Ring City Construction Engineering Group Co., Ltd.	黄岛区 Huangdao District	A101
63	青岛东建建设有限公司	Qingdao Dongjian Construction Co., Ltd.	李沧区 Licang District	A101
64	山东天诚市政公路工程有限公司	Shandong Tiancheng Municipal Highway Engineering Co., Ltd.	崂山区 Laoshan District	A110
65	青岛登科市政工程有限公司	Qingdao Dengke Municipal Engineering Co., Ltd.	城阳区 Chengyang District	A110
66	青岛公路建设集团有限公司	Qingdao Highway Construction Group Co., Ltd.	崂山区 Laoshan District	A102
67	青岛市政空间开发集团有限责任公司	Qingdao Municipal Space Development Group Ltd	市南区 Shinan District	A110
68	青岛地矿岩土工程有限公司	Qingdao Geotechnical Engineering Co., Ltd.	市南区 Shinan District	B101
69	青岛建设集团建兴工程有限公司	Qingdao construction group LITE-ON Engineering Co., Ltd.	高新区 High tech District	A101
70	青岛建设装饰集团有限公司	Qingdao Construction Decoration Group Co.,Ltd.	市南区 Shinan District	B103
71	青岛市崂山区古建建筑工程有限公司	Qingdao Laoshan ancient building engineering Co., Ltd.	崂山区 Laoshan District	A101
72	青岛昶德建设集团有限公司	Qingdao Changde Construction Group Co., Ltd.	胶州市 Jiaozhou	A101
73	青岛市益水工程股份有限公司	Qingdao Yishui Engineering Co.,Ltd.	市南区 Shinan District	A210
74	青岛康太源建设集团有限公司	Qingdao Kangtine Construction Group.Lnc.	李沧区 Licang District	A101

14-5 续表 3
Continued

序号 Precedence	企业单位名称	Name	所在地区 Location	资质等级 Qualification Criteria
75	青岛市华鲁公路工程有限公司	Qingdao Hualu Highway Engineering Co., Ltd	黄岛区 Huangdao District	A102
76	青岛三星工程有限公司	Qingdao Sanxing Engineering Co., Ltd.	城阳区 Chengyang District	A110
77	山东奥华建筑安装工程有限公司	Shandong Ao Hua Construction and Installation Engineering Co., Ltd.	市南区 Shinan District	A101
78	青岛嘉恒建设集团有限公司	Qingdao Jiaheng Construction Group Co., Ltd.	市南区 Shinan District	A101
79	青岛昆泉建设工程有限公司	Qingdao Kunquan Construction Engineering Co., Ltd.	黄岛区 Huangdao District	A101
80	青岛高新建筑安装工程有限公司	Qingdao High-tech Construction and Installation Engineering Co., Ltd.	崂山区 Laoshan District	A101
81	青岛永鑫建筑工程有限公司	Qingdao Yongxin Construction Engineering Co., Ltd.	平度市 Pingdu	A201
82	青岛望城三宝建设有限公司	Qingdao Wangcheng Sanbao Construction Co., Ltd.	莱西市 Laixi	A101
83	胶南市建筑工程公司	Jiaonan City Construction Engineering Company	黄岛区 Huangdao District	A101
84	青岛九龙建设集团有限公司	Qingdao Jiulong Construction Group Co., Ltd.	胶州市 Jiaozhou	A101
85	青岛华联装饰工程有限公司	Qingdao Hualian Decoration Engineering Co., Ltd.	市北区 Shibei District	B103
86	青岛建工集团有限公司	Qingdao Construction Engineering Group Co., Ltd.	崂山区 Laoshan District	A102
87	青岛福海洋建设集团有限公司	Qingdao Fu Ocean Construction Group Co., Ltd.	胶州市 Jiaozhou	A101
88	青岛环海工程贸易发展有限公司	Qingdao Huanhai Engineering & Trade Development Co., Ltd.	市北区 Shibei District	A201
89	青岛亿佰建工集团有限公司	Qingdao Yibai Construction Engineering Group Co., Ltd.	黄岛区 Huangdao District	A201
90	青岛宝利建设有限公司	Qingdao Baoli Construction Co., Ltd.	黄岛区 Huangdao District	A201
91	青岛东捷建设工程有限公司	Qingdao Dong jie Construction Engineering Co., Ltd.	市北区 Shibei District	A101
92	鲁建集团股份有限公司	Lu Jian Group Limited by Share Ltd.	崂山区 Laoshan District	A202
93	青岛隆昌达建设集团有限公司	Qingdao Longchangda Construction Group Co., Ltd.	胶州市 Jiaozhou	A101
94	青岛金星科技工程有限公司	Qingdao Jinxing Technology Engineering Co., Ltd.	市南区 Shinan District	B111
95	青岛金原建设集团有限公司	Qingdao Jinyuan Construction Group Co., Ltd.	黄岛区 Huangdao District	A201
96	山东世纪阳光建筑科技有限公司	Shandong Century Sunshine Construction Technology Co., Ltd.	市南区 Shinan District	B112
97	青岛建工建安集团有限公司	Qingdao Construction Engineering Jian'an Group Co., Ltd.	崂山区 Laoshan District	A101
98	青岛福堉建筑劳务有限公司	Qingdao Fuyu Construction Labor Services Co., Ltd.	李沧区 Licang District	B914
99	青岛永安建筑工程劳务有限公司	Qingdao Yongan Construction Engineering Service Co., Ltd.	李沧区 Licang District	B914
100	即墨市七级建筑工程有限公司	Jimo Seventh Grade Construction Engineering Co., Ltd.	即墨区 Jimo District	A201

主要统计指标解释

建筑业统计单位 指从事房屋、构筑物建造和设备安装活动的法人企业。建筑业法人企业应具有建筑业资质并能够独立核算，同时其应具备以下条件：①依法成立，有自己的名称、组织机构和场所，能够承担民事责任；②独立拥有和使用资产，承担负债，有权与其他单位签订合同；③独立核算盈亏，能够编制资产负债表。

建筑业总产值 是以货币形式表现的建筑业企业在一定时期内生产的建筑业产品和提供的服务的总和。建筑业总产值包括：

（1）建筑工程产值：指列入建筑工程预算内的各种工程价值。

（2）安装工程产值：指设备安装工程价值，不包括被安装设备本身的价值。

（3）其他产值：建筑业总产值中除建筑工程、安装工程以外的产值。包括房屋构筑物修理产值、非标准设备制造产值、总包企业向分包企业收取的管理费以及不能明确划分的施工活动所完成的产值。

建筑业增加值 指建筑业企业在报告期内以货币形式表现的建筑业生产经营活动的最终成果。

建筑业现价增加值 按生产法和分配法（收入法）两种方法计算，以收入法的计算结果为准，即从收入的角度出发，根据生产要素在生产过程中应得的收入份额计算。具体计算方法：经济普查年度建筑业增加值按照《经济普查年度 GDP 核算方案》计算，非经济普查年度建筑业增加值按照《非经济普查年度 GDP 核算方案》计算。

Explanatory Notes on Main Statistical Indicators

Statistical Unit in Construction refers to corporate enterprise engaged in the construction of buildings and structures and in the installation of equipment. A corporate construction enterprise should have qualification certificates with independent accounting system, and should meet the following 3 requirements: 1. being set up in line with relevant legal basis, having its full name, organization and location, and capable of taking civil liabilities; 2. independently possessing and using its assets and assuming its liabilities, and entitled to sign contracts with other institutions; and 3. making independent accounts of its profits and losses, and capable of compiling its own balance sheet.

Gross Output Value of Construction refers to total of construction products and services, expressed in money terms, produced or rendered by construction and installation enterprises during a given period of time. It includes:

1. Output value of construction projects, that is the value of projects covered by the project budgets;

2. Output value of installation projects, that is the value of the installation of equipment, (excluding the value of the equipment to be installed) ;

3. Output value of others, that is the output value of construction industry excluding that of construction projects and installation projects. It includes: output value of repair of buildings and structures; output value of non-standard equipment manufacturing; overhead expenses received by contracted enterprises to the sub-contracted enterprises and the completed output value of construction activities that have no clear definition.

Added Value Of Construction Industry refers to the final results of construction industry production and operation activities expressed in currency by construction enterprises during the reporting period.

Value Added At Current Price Of Construction Industry Calculate according to the two methods of production method and distribution method (income method). The calculation result of income method shall prevail, that is, from the perspective of income, it is calculated according to the income share of production factors in the production process. Specific calculation method: The annual added value of the construction industry in the economic census is calculated in accordance with the "Annual GDP Accounting Plan for the Economic Census", and the annual added value of the construction industry in the non–economic census is calculated in accordance with the "Non–economic Census Annual GDP Accounting Plan".

15 运输、邮电

TRANSPORT, POSTAL AND TELECOMMUNICATION SERVICES

简要说明

一、本篇资料的主要内容

本篇资料主要反映了全市交通运输业和邮电业通讯业发展的基本情况，主要包括客货运输及港口吞吐量、民用汽车拥有量、独立核算运输邮电单位主要财务指标、邮电通讯基本情况、邮政行业发展情况、快递企业发展情况、电信行业基本情况、城市轨道交通发展情况等方面的内容。

二、本篇资料的来源

1. 本篇资料中交通运输邮电资料来源于全市交通运输邮电业统计年报。

2. 交通运输资料来源于青岛市交通运输委员会、青岛市港航局、青岛市运管局、青岛港(集团)有限公司、青岛国际机场集团有限公司、青岛地铁集团有限公司。

3. 邮政业资料来源于青岛市邮政管理局、中国邮政集团公司青岛市分公司。

4. 电信业资料来源于青岛市通信管理局、中国电信集团公司山东省青岛市电信分公司、中国电信股份有限公司青岛分公司、中国联合网络通信有限公司青岛市分公司、中国移动通信集团山东有限公司青岛分公司。

5. 民用汽车拥有量资料来源于青岛市公安局交警支队车辆管理所。

本篇资料由市统计局服务业统计处整理提供。

Brief Introduction

I. Main Content

Data in this chapter show the basic conditions of the development of transport, post and telecommunications in Shandong Province, mainly including the freight traffic and passenger traffic, cargo handled at port, possession of civil motor vehicles, major financial indices and basic conditions of transport, postal and telecommunication services, development of the postal services, express company development, development of urban rail transit.

II. Source of Data

1. Data on transport are based on the annual report of transport.

2. Data on transportation are provided by Qingdao Municipal Transportation Committee, Qingdao Port and Shipping Bureau , Qingdao Transportation Management Bureau, Qingdao Port International Co.,Ltd, Qingdao International Airport Group Co.,Ltd, Qingdao Metro Group Co.,Ltd.

3. Data on postal and telecommunication are based on Qingdao Municipal Postal Administration, Qingdao Post Bureau.

4. Data on business of telecommunication services Qingdao Communication Administration, China Telecom Group Corporation Qingdao Branch of Shandong Province, China Telecom Co., Ltd. Qingdao Branch, China United Network Communications Co., Ltd. Qingdao Branch, China Mobile Communications Group Shandong Co., Ltd. Qingdao Branch.

5. Date on possession of civil motor vehicles are provided by Qingdao Municipal Public Security Bureau Traffic Police Detachment Vehicle Management Office.

Data in this chapter are prepared and provide by the Division of Industry Statistics of Qingdao Municipal Bureau of Statistics.

15-1 主要年份客货运输及港口吞吐量

MAJOR YEAR'S PASSENGER & FREIGHT TRAFFIC AND HANDLING CAPACITY OF THE PORTS

年份 Year	客运量（万人） Passenger Traffic (10000 persons)			货运量（万吨） Freight Traffic (10000 tons)			港口货物吞吐量（万吨） Volume of Freight Handled in Ports (10 000 tons)	集装箱吞吐量（万标箱） Containers (10 000 TEU)	航空旅客吞吐量（万人） Air Passenger Throughput (10 000 persons)	航空货邮吞吐量（万吨） Air Cargo and Mail Throughput (10 000 tons)
	铁路 Railways	公路 Highways	海运 Waterways	铁路 Railways	公路 Highways	海运 Waterways				
1949	327	14	9	386	162	22	73			
1952	571	49	13	447	399	44	181			
1957	1054	149	13	747	548	118	269			
1962	3100	141	39	909	524	97	391			
1965	1424	230	19	1257	690	158	524			
1970	1329	373	20	1856	736	232	695			
1975	1803	159	30	2325	817	282	1542			
1978	1986	274	49	2917	1561	528	2081			
1980	1896	713	73	2596	1642	941	1779			
1985	2063	1 894	86	3009	2303	919	2610		2.17	0.06
1988	2083	3 300	234	3418	6486	1160	3153		17.48	0.32
1990	1488	3 639	316	3741	6433	1556	3068		28.12	0.54
1991	1453	4144	366	3774	6896	1789	3194		38.36	0.70
1992	1488	4965	437	3899	6822	1981	3240		54.17	0.57
1993	1499	6436	499	4044	7685	1910	3650		70.77	0.70
1994	1564	6787		4112	8336	1804	4331		92.64	0.88
1995	1480	9785		4205	11788	2185	5165		132.71	1.26
1996	1230	10738		4415	10749	474	6056	81.1	157.61	1.73
1997	1308	11855		4466	11232	544	6944	103.3	178.68	1.96
1998	1549	11754		4028	14311	1792	7044	121.3	184.66	2.15
1999	1674	12103		3919	14550	1926	7282	154.3	203.11	2.89
2000	1780	12145		4256	17234	2998	8661	212.0	243.15	3.44
2001	1678	13686		4778	20906	3432	10423	264.0	281.01	3.62
2002	1530	14516	777	5079	24480	2530	12252	341.0	321.99	4.63
2003	1366	13132	786	4929	27241	2773	14135	424.0	349.10	5.46
2004	1496	16420	862	5119	29937	3503	16303	514.0	480.84	7.55
2005	552	17212	972	2299	31009	4471	18727	630.7	587.96	8.91
2006	810	17752	999	2790	32047	4768	22438	770.0	679.12	10.13
2007	1101	18800	1080	2781	33336	4019	26507	946.6	786.80	11.57
2008	1278	19909	1055	3225	34172	5080	30029	1037.7	820.04	13.05
2009	1425	19612	1145	3772	16297	4332	31668	1027.6	966.01	13.54
2010	1537	20460	1302	5031	17525	4407	35012	1201.0	1110.12	16.37
2011	1693	21560	791	5697	19208	4220	37971	1302.0	1171.64	16.65
2012	1881	22724	414	6126	21312	1791	41465	1450.0	1260.12	17.19
2013	2056	23588	333	6266	23270	1313	45782	1552.0	1451.67	18.62
2014	2301	5588	324	5564	19043	1434	47701	1658.0	1641.18	20.44
2015	2421	5370	288	5486	20073	1456	49749	1743.0	1820.21	20.81
2016	2701	4532	225	5569	20701	1685	51463	1805.0	2050.50	23.69
2017	3179	4534	215	6021	24716	1800	51314	1830.9	2321.06	23.21
2018	3455	4602	161	6280	27453	2502	54250	1931.5	2453.57	22.45
2019	3979	4593	186	6115	29170	2493	57736	2101.2	2555.63	25.63

注：1. 从 2014 年公路客、货运量统计口径进行调整，与以前年度不可比。
　　2. 根据市交通运输局提供数据，对航空部分吞吐量历史数据进行了修正。

Note: 1. In 2014, the Ministry of Transportation made an adjustment to the statistical gauge for highway passenger and freight transportation and the data are not comparable directly.
　　2. According to the data provided by the Municipal Transportation Bureau, some historical data of aviation throughput have been revised.

15-2 民用车辆拥有量（2019 年底）
POSSESSION OF CIVIL MOTOR VEHICLES (END OF 2019)

单位：辆 (unit)

项目	Item	合计 Total 辆数 Number	#个人 of which：Private Vehicles 辆数 Number
一、汽车	**Automobile**	**2928198**	**2534523**
1. 载客汽车	Passenger Vehicles	2637630	2375743
其中：轿车	of which：Sedan	1709742	1562033
2. 载货汽车	Trucks	273308	148820
3. 其他汽车	Other Automobile	17260	9960
二、电车	**Tram**	**125**	
三、摩托车	**Motorcycle**	**99830**	**98138**
四、农用运输车	**Agricultural Transport Vehicle**		
五、挂车	**Trailer Trucks**	**31633**	**259**
六、其他类型车	**Other Vehicles**	**141**	**2**
七、校车	**School Bus**	**2518**	**1**

补充资料：机动车驾驶员（3691405 人）Motor drivers（person）
其中：汽车驾驶员（3648794 人）of which：Automobile drivers (person)

15-3 客货运输及港口吞吐量（2019 年）
PASSENGER & FREIGHT TRAFFIC AND HANDLING CAPACITY OF THE PORTS (2019)

项目 Item	货运量（万吨）Freight Traffic (10 000 tons)	货物周转量（亿吨公里）Cargo Turnover (100million tons · km)	客运量（万人）Passenger Traffic (10 000 persons)	旅客周转量（亿人公里）Passenger Turnover (100million persons · km)	项目 Item	旅客吞吐量（万人）Passenger Throughput (10 000 persons)	货物吞吐量（万吨）Cargo Throughput (10 000 tons)	集装箱（万标箱）Containers (10 000 TEU)
总计 Total	**37779**	**1749.83**	**8758**	**196.73**	**总计 Total**	**2583**	**57762**	**2101**
铁路 Railways	6115	185.91	3979	121.36	机场 Civil Aviation	2556	26	
公路 Highways	29170	589.87	4593	75.18	港口 Ports	27	57736	2101
水运 Waterways	2493	974.05	186	0.19				

15-4 规模以上运输邮电单位主要财务指标（2019 年）
MAJOR FINANCIAL INDICATORS OF TRANSPORTATION, POST AND TELECOMMUNICATION UNITS ABOVE DESIGNATED SCALE (2019)

单位：亿元 (100 million yuan)

项目	Item	营业收入 Revenue from principal Business	营业成本 Cost of principal Business	营业利润 Operating Profits	营业税金及附加 Business taxes and surtax	利润总额 Total Profits
总计	**Total**	**1234.66**	**1066.57**	**4.99**	**168.02**	**172.47**
道路运输业	Road Transport	235.43	247.20	1.38	15.18	17.16
水上运输业	Water Transport	127.27	77.87	1.40	74.88	75.34
航空运输业	Air Transport	43.50	38.89	0.22	-0.35	0.63
管道运输业	Pipeline Transport	10.36	5.08	0.02	4.25	4.29
多式联运和运输代理业	Multimodal Transport and Transport Agent	518.72	481.81	0.49	24.47	24.96
装卸搬运和仓储业	Loading And Unloading And Storage	131.97	101.03	0.86	18.69	18.99
邮政业	Post	40.28	35.66	0.11	1.20	1.10
电信、广播电视和卫星传输服务	Telecommunications, Broadcast Television and Satellite Transmission Services	127.13	79.03	0.51	29.70	30.00

注：该表数据来源于规模以上服务业统计年报。
Note：The data in this table comes from the statistical annual report of the service industry above designated size.

15-5 邮电通讯基本情况（2019年）
BASIC CONDITIONS OF POSTAL AND TELECOMMUNICATION SERVICES (2019)

市、区名称	Region	邮政局（处）Post Office (unit)	#提供邮政全功能服务的 of which: Providing Omni-directional Postal Services	邮路总长度（公里）Length of Postal Routes (km)	邮运汽车（辆）Vehicles for Postal Services (unit)	信筒、信箱（个）Post Boxes (unit)
全市	**Total**	**265**	**214**	**5974**	**383**	**663**
市南区	Shinan District	19	8	1505	52	79
市北区	Shibei District	22	13	1743	48	92
李沧区	Licang District	9	4	71	19	31
崂山区	Laoshan District	7	4	56	14	25
西海岸新区	West Coast New Area	48	38	670	67	86
城阳区	Chengyang District	12	9	178	28	29
即墨区	Jimo District	36	34	522	47	75
胶州市	Jiaozhou	31	29	295	40	63
平度市	Pingdu	54	50	636	38	127
莱西市	Laixi	27	25	298	30	56

注：西海岸新区含保税港区数据，城阳区含高新区数据。
Note: West Coast New Area includes data from bonded port areas, and Chengyang District includes data from high-tech areas.

15-6 邮政行业发展情况
DEVELOPMENT OF THE POSTAL SERVICES

指标名称	Name	计量单位	Unit	2019 年	2018 年
一、邮政行业业务收入	**Postal Services Business Income**	亿元	**100 million yuan**	**81.68**	**62.81**
1、邮政寄递服务	Postal Delivery Service	亿元	100 million yuan	2.86	3.05
2、快递业务	Express Service	亿元	100 million yuan	65.53	50.22
二、邮政行业业务总量	**Total Business Volume Of Postal Industry**	亿元	100 million yuan	**103.55**	**82.87**
1、邮政寄递服务	Postal Delivery Service	万件	10 000 articles	18153	17449
其中：函件	Number Of Letters	万件	10 000 articles	1438	1612
包裹	Package	万件	10 000 articles	31	29
订销报纸累计数	Cumulative number of newspapers ordered and sold	万份	10 000 copies	14309	14566
订销杂志累计数	Cumulative number of magazines ordered and sold	万份	10 000 copies	646	629
汇兑	Exchange	万笔	10 000 sums	9	11
2、快递业务	Express Service	万件	10 000 articles	45325	38323
其中：同城	Same City	万件	10 000 articles	10921	10738
异地	Different Places	万件	10 000 articles	33775	27016
国际 / 港澳台	International/Hong Kong, Macao And Taiwan	万件	10 000 articles	629	569

注：该表数据由邮政管理局提供。
Note： The data in this table is provided by the postal administration.

15-7 快递企业发展情况
EXPRESS COMPANY DEVELOPMENT

指标名称	Name	计量单位	Unit	2019 年	2018 年
快递业务量	**Express Business Volume**	**万件**	**10 000 articles**	**45325**	**38323**
同城	Same City	万件	10 000 articles	10921	10738
异地	Different Places	万件	10 000 articles	33775	27016
国际及港澳台	International/ Hong Kong, Macao And Taiwan	万件	10 000 articles	629	569
快递业务收入	**Express Revenue**	**亿元**	**100 million yuan**	**65.53**	**50.22**
同城	Same City	亿元	100 million yuan	8.31	8.99
异地	Different Places	亿元	100 million yuan	37.70	27.02
国际及港澳台	International/ Hong Kong, Macao And Taiwan	亿元	100 million yuan	10.10	7.88
其他	Others	亿元	100 million yuan	9.42	6.33

注：该表数据由邮政管理局提供。
Note: The data in this table is provided by the postal administration.

15-8 电信行业基本情况
BASIC SITUATION OF TELECOM INDUSTRY

指标名称	Name	计量单位	Unit	2019 年	2018 年
一、电信业务总量（2015 年不变价）	**TOTAL TELECOMMUNICATIONS BUSINESS**	**亿元**	**100 million yuan**	**812.08**	**568.01**
其中：固定话音业务总量	Total Fixed Voice Service	亿元	100 million yuan	1.33	1.75
固定数据及互联网业务总量	Fixed Data And Total Internet Business	亿元	100 million yuan	18.39	16.20
移动话音业务总量	Total Mobile Voice Service	亿元	100 million yuan	23.84	24.96
移动数据及互联网业务总量	Total Mobile Data And Internet Services	亿元	100 million yuan	659.96	436.49
电信业务收入	Telecommunications Revenue	亿元	100 million yuan	107.35	110.28
二、电信营业网点	**Telecom Business Network**	**个**	**unit**	**438**	**469**
三、固定电话交换机总容量（含农话）	**Total Capacity Of Fixed Telephone Exchanges(Including Rural Fixed Telephone)**	**万门**	**10 000 line**	**334**	**334**
固定电话年末用户	Fixed Telephone Year-End User	万户	10 000 households	156	139
其中：新装电话	Newly Installed Telephone	万户	10 000 households	9	11
城市电话用户	Urban Telephone User	万户	10 000 households	130	112
乡村电话用户	Village Phone User	万户	10 000 households	25	33
住宅电话年末用户	Home Phone Year-End User	万户	10 000 households	42	60
城市电话用户	Urban Telephone User	万户	10 000 households	30	41
乡村电话用户	Village Phone User	万户	10 000 households	12	20
四、固定电话本地通话量	**Fixed Telephone Local Call Volume**	**万分钟**	**10 000 minutes**	**166264**	**186827**
长话电路	Long Distance Circuit	路	line	13465	13073
长途电话通话量	Long Distance Call Volume	万次	10 000 times	13852	14143
长途电话通话时长	Long-Distance Phone Call Duration	万分钟	10 000 minutes	271353	38464
五、互联网用户数	**Number Of Internet Users**	**万户**	**10 000 households**	**1502**	**1462**
固定宽带互联网用户数	Number Of Fixed Broadband Internet Users	万户	10 000 households	418	398
移动互联网用户数	Number Of Mobile Internet Users	万户	10 000 households	1084	1064

注：该表数据由青岛市通信管理局、中国电信集团公司山东省青岛市电信分公司、中国电信股份有限公司青岛分公司、中国联合网络通信有限公司青岛市分公司、中国移动通信集团山东有限公司青岛分公司等单位提供。

Note: The data in this table is provided by Qingdao Municipal Communications Administration, China Telecom Group Corporation Qingdao Branch, Shandong Province, China Telecom Co., Ltd. Qingdao Branch, China United Network Communications Co., Ltd. Qingdao Branch, China Mobile Communications Group Shandong Co., Ltd. Provided by Qingdao Branch of the company and other units.

15-8 续表
Continued

指标名称	Name	计量单位	Unit	2019 年	2018 年
六、互联网通信量	**Internet Traffic**				
固定互联网宽带使用时长	Fixed Internet Broadband Usage Time	万分钟	10 000 minutes	74618437	48342353
固定互联网宽带接入流量	Fixed Internet Broadband Access Traffic	万 G	10 000 G	328808	246534
移动互联网接入流量	Mobile Internet Access Traffic	万 G	10 000 G	95740	58600
七、光缆线路长度	**Cable Line Length**				
长途光缆线路长度	Long-Distance Cable Line Length	公里	km	4595	4405
本地网中继光缆线路长度	Line Length of Relay Optical Cable in Local Network	公里	km	11740	9950
接入网光缆线路长度	Optical Cable Line Length In Access Network	公里	km	297043	262861
八、移动通信用户	**Mobile Communication Users**				
移动电话交换机容量	Mobile Phone Switch Capacity	万户	10 000 households	3051	2946
期末移动电话用户数	Number of mobile phone users at the end of the period	万户	10 000 households	1246	1259
其中：3G 移动电话用户	3G Mobile Phone Users	万户	10 000 households	79	132
其中：4G 移动电话用户	4G Mobile Phone Users	万户	10 000 households	1003	932
九、移动电话通话量	**Mobile Phone Call Volume**				
移动电话通话时长	Mobile Phone Call Duration	万分钟	10 000 minutes	4378432	4098512
十、通信能力	**Communication Ability**				
移动电话交换机容量	Mobile Phone Switch Capacity	万户	10 000 households	3051	2930
移动电话基站数	Number Of Mobile Phone Base Stations	个	unit	63795	53337
其中：3G 移动电话基站数	Number Of 3G Mobile Phone Base Stations	个	unit	9072	8428
其中：4G 移动电话基站数	Number Of 4G Mobile Phone Base Stations	个	unit	37982	33560
十一、互联网通信能力	**Internet Communication Capability**				
互联网宽带接入端口	Internet Broadband Access Port	个	unit	8547426	7263867

注：该表数据由青岛市通信管理局、中国电信集团公司山东省青岛市电信分公司、中国电信股份有限公司青岛分公司、中国联合网络通信有限公司青岛市分公司、中国移动通信集团山东有限公司青岛分公司、中国铁通集团有限公司青岛分公司等单位提供。

Note: The data in this table is provided by Qingdao Municipal Communications Administration, China Telecom Group Corporation Qingdao Branch, Shandong Province, China Telecom Co., Ltd. Qingdao Branch, China United Network Communications Co., Ltd. Qingdao Branch, China Mobile Communications Group Shandong Co., Ltd. Provided by Qingdao Branch of the company, Qingdao Branch of China Tietong Group Co., Ltd.

15-9 城市轨道交通发展情况
DEVELOPMENT OF URBAN RAIL TRANSIT

指标名称	Name	计量单位	Unit	2019 年	2018 年
客运量	**Passenger Traffic**	万人次	**10 000 person-times**	**18753**	**15294**
日均客运量	**Average Daily Passenger**	万人次	10 000 person-times	**51**	**42**
旅客周转量	**Passenger Turnover**	万人公里	**10 000 passenger-km**	**166857**	**124411**
运营车数	**Number Of Vehicles Operated**	辆	**unit**	**596**	**522**
其中：地铁	Subway	辆	unit	596	522
轻轨	Subway	辆	unit		
运营线路总数	**Total Number Of Operating Lines**	条	**line**	**4**	**4**
其中：新增运营线路	New Operating Line	条	line		2
其中：地铁	Subway	条	line		
轻轨	Light Rail	条	line		
市域快线	City Express	条	line		2
运营线路总长度	**Total Length Of Operating Line**	公里	**km**	**176**	**172**
其中：新增运营线路长度	New Operating Line Length	公里	km	4	126
其中：地铁	Subway	公里	km	4	126
轻轨	Light Rail	公里	km		
市域快线	City Express	公里	km		
地铁站点总数	**Total Number Of Subway Stations**	个	**unit**	**83**	**80**
其中：换乘站点个数	Number Of Transfer Stations	个	unit	3	3
其中：新增站点个数	Number Of New Sites	个	unit	3	42
其中：新增换乘站点个数	Increase The Number Of Transfer Stations	个	unit		1
总开行次数	**Total Number Of Trips**	列次	**train number**	**472052**	**329849**
总运营里程	**Total Operating Mileage**	公里	**km**	**15160200**	**9149612**
列车准点率	**Train On Time Rate**	%	%	**99.99**	**99.97**

注：该表数据由青岛地铁集团有限公司提供。
Note: The data in this table is provided by Qingdao Metro Group Co., Ltd.

15-10 按行业分企业信息化及电子商务情况(2019年)
INFORMATIZATION AND E-COMMERCE OF ENTERPRISES BY INDUSTRIAL SECTOR (2019)

行业	Industry	企业数(个) Number of Enterprises (unit)	期末使用计算机数(台) Computers Used at the End of Period (unit)	每百人使用计算机数(台) Computers Used Per 100 Persons (unit)
总计	**Total**	**10201**	**547180**	**39**
采矿业	Mining	3	107	23
制造业	Manufacturing	3387	208603	33
电力、热力、燃气及水生产和供应业	Production and Supply of Electricity, Heat, Gas and Water	94	8576	44
建筑业	Construction	798	57755	24
批发和零售业	Wholesale and Retail Trades	2417	68953	54
交通运输、仓储和邮政业	Transport, Storage and Post	671	40352	39
住宿和餐饮业	Hotels and Catering Services	432	10624	25
信息传输、软件和信息技术服务业	Information Transmission, Software and Information Technology Services	178	45112	132
房地产业	Real Estate	1309	35160	55
租赁和商务服务业	Leasing and Business Services	463	20124	36
科学研究和技术服务业	Scientific Research and Technical Services	231	35810	93
水利、环境和公共设施管理业	Management of Water Conservancy, Environment and Public Facilities	36	1523	14
居民服务、修理和其他服务业	Service to Households, Repair and Other Services	40	2243	28
教育	Education	16	3031	100
卫生和社会工作	Health and Social Service	43	3637	57
文化、体育和娱乐业	Culture, Sports and Entertainment	83	5570	62

注：有电子商务交易活动的企业是指通过计算机网络开展电子商务销售或电子商务采购的企业。
Note：Enterprises with E-Commerce Transactions refers to those enterprises which performed sales or purchases through internet.

单位：亿元 (100 million yuan)

企业拥有网站数（个）Websites of Enterprises(unit)	每百家企业拥有网站数（个）Websites Per 100 Enterprises (unit)	有电子商务交易活动 With E-Commerce Transactions		电子商务销售额（万元）Sales of E-Commerce (10 000 yuan)	电子商务采购额（万元）Purchases of E-Commerce (10 000 yuan)
		企业数（个）Enterprises(unit)	比重 (%) Proportion(%)		
5636	**55**	**2651**	**26.0**	**38032793**	**25761106**
2	67				
2445	72	862	25.5	17956366	8696909
39	41	18	19.1	30206	142385
378	47	151	18.9	1278293	1213456
964	40	686	28.4	16556304	14681555
321	48	148	22.1	1051375	564673
153	35	235	54.4	325173	2915
198	111	78	43.8	583557	355278
588	45	156	11.9	30647	19180
236	51	137	29.6	73205	41646
184	80	86	37.2	55004	39872
17	47	15	41.7	34	114
17	43	11	27.5	1117	366
14	88	8	50.0	16169	668
32	74	18	41.9	825	1303
48	58	42	50.6	74519	786

15-11 区（市）企业信息化及电子商务情况（2019年）

INFORMATIZATION AND E-COMMERCE OF ENTERPRISES BY REGION (2019)

区（市）	Region	企业数（个）Number of Enterprises (unit)	期末使用计算机数（台）Computers Used at the End of Period (unit)	每百人使用计算机数（台）Computers Used Per 100 Persons (unit)
全市	**Total**	**10201**	**547180**	**39**
市南区	Shinan District	1104	92676	64
市北区	Shibei District	813	56299	51
李沧区	Licang District	709	18750	39
崂山区	Laoshan District	616	69633	54
西海岸新区	West Coast New Area	2265	121192	35
黄岛区	Huangdao District	2083	109501	35
保税港区	Qingdao Free Trade Port Area of China	182	11691	44
城阳区	Chengyang District	1416	86872	42
城阳区（不含高新区）	Chengyang District (Excluding High tech District)	1110	59711	36
高新区	High tech District	306	27161	69
即墨区	Jimo District	911	32705	27
胶州市	Jiaozhou	1154	34617	26
平度市	Pingdu	749	21717	28
莱西市	Laixi	464	12719	13

注：有电子商务交易活动的企业是指通过计算机网络开展电子商务销售或电子商务采购的企业。
Note: Enterprises with E-Commerce Transactions refers to those enterprises which performed sales or purchases through internet.

单位：亿元（100 million yuan）

企业拥有网站数（个）Websites of Enterprises(unit)	每百家企业拥有网站数（个）Websites Per 100 Enterprises (unit)	有电子商务交易活动 With E-Commerce Transactions		电子商务销售额（万元）Sales of E-Commerce (10 000 yuan)	电子商务采购额（万元）Purchases of E-Commerce (10 000 yuan)
		企业数（个）Enterprises(unit)	比重(%) Proportion(%)		
5636	**55**	**2651**	**26.0**	**38032793**	**25761106**
692	63	289	26.2	11172633	5211705
420	52	178	21.9	1304408	1517521
282	40	262	37.0	1992912	2114556
360	58	313	50.8	8767558	8307469
1278	56	309	13.6	8602728	6432657
1181	57	274	13.2	8031659	6055141
97	53	35	19.2	571069	377516
782	55	420	29.7	1057028	1197301
561	51	345	31.1	646137	800643
221	72	75	24.5	410891	396658
533	59	232	25.5	2606184	330923
694	60	468	40.6	2223376	365310
362	48	126	16.8	140554	197719
233	50	54	11.6	165412	85945

主要统计指标解释

货（客）运量　指在一定时期内，各运输部门实际运送的货物（旅客）数量。是反映运输业为国民经济和人民生活服务的数量指标，也是制定和检查运输生产计划，研究运输发展规模和速度的重要指标。货运按吨计算，客运按人计算。货物不论运输距离长短，货物类别，均按实际重量统计；旅客不论行程远近或票价多少，均按一人一次作为客运量统计。半价票、小孩票也按一人统计。

货物（旅客）周转量　指在一定时期内，由各种运输工具运送的货物（旅客）数量与其相应运输距离的乘积之总和，是反映运输业生产总成果的重要指标，也是编制和检查运输生产计划，计算运输效益、劳动生产率以及核算运输单位成本的主要基础资料。通常以吨公里和人公里为计算单位。计算货物周转量通常按发出站与到达站之间的最短距离，也就是计费距离计算。

港口货物吞吐量　指经水运进出沿海主要港区范围，并经过装卸的货物数量，包括邮件及办理托运手续的行李、包裹以及补给运输船舶的燃、物料和淡水。货物吞吐量按货物流向分为进口、出口吞吐量，按货物交流性质分为外贸货物吞吐量和国内贸易货物吞吐量。货物吞吐量的货类构成及其流向，是衡量港口生产能力大小的重要指标。

航空旅客吞吐量　指在一定时期内，通过机场进出航空港的旅客数量。

航空货邮吞吐量　指在一定时期内，通过机场进出航空港的货物和邮件数量。

邮政行业业务总量　指以货币形式表现的邮政企业为社会提供各类邮政通信服务或其他服务的总数量。计算方法为各类邮政通信服务业务的实物量分别乘以相应的不变单价，求出各类业务的货币量后加总求得。该指标反映了一定时期邮政通信业务发展的总成果，是观察邮政通信业务发展变化总趋势的综合性指标。

快递业务量　指企业收寄的各类快递业务总数量，由受理用户委托的企业负责统计。包括国内同城快递业务量、国内异地快递业务量、港澳台快递业务量、国际快递业务量。

电信业务总量　指以货币形式表示的电信企业为社会提供的各类电信服务的总数量。包括固定话音业务总量、固定数据及互联网业务总量、固定增值及其他业务总量、移动话音业务总量、移动数据及互联网业务总量、移动增值及其他业务总量。

长途光缆线路长度　指长途光缆线路的实际长度。架空的光缆按实际杆路长度统计，埋设地下、水底的光缆按沟长统计。

本地网中继光缆线路长度　指本地网内各业务节点之间，从起点至终点所经由的光缆线路实际长度。架空光缆按实际杆路长度统计，埋设地下、水底的光缆按埋设光缆的沟长统计。

移动电话基站数　指为小区服务的无线收发信设备，处理基站与移动台之间的无线通信，在移动交换机与移动台之间起中继作用，监视无线传输质量的全套设备数。

3G 移动电话基站数　指报告期末本电信企业 3G 移动通信网络上实际使用的 NoFe-B 数量。包括 TF-SCFMA 基站、WCFMA 基站和 CFMA2000 基站。

4G 移动电话基站数　指报告期末本电信企业 4G 移动通信网络上实际使用的 Node-B 数量。包括 TD-LTE 基站和 FDD-LTE 基站。

互联网宽带接入端口　指用于接入互联网用户的各类实际安装运行的宽带接入端口的数量。

网站数 指报告期末企业拥有和维护的，在互联网上可浏览的网站数，不包括企业内网。网站是指在公共互联网上，面向公众使用的，基于TCP/IP协议的计算机系统，以域名本身或者“WWW.＋域名”为网址的web站点，由地址、软件、硬件和内容组成。

电子商务销售金额 指报告期内企业（单位）借助网络订单而销售的商品和服务总额。借助网络订单指通过网络接受订单，付款和配送可以不借助于网络。

电子商务采购金额 指报告期内企业（单位）借助网络订单而采购的商品和服务总额。借助网络订单指通过网络发送订单，付款和配送可以不借助于网络。

电子商务交易平台 指在电子商务活动中为交易双方或多方提供交易撮合及相关服务的信息网络系统的总和。

Explanatory Notes on Main Statistical Indicators

Freight (Passenger)Traffic refers to the volume of freight (passenger)transported with various means. Freight transport is calculated in tons and passenger traffic is calculated in the number of persons. Despite the type of freight and traveling distance, the freight transport is calculated in the actual weight of the goods; and despite the traveling distance and ticket price, the passenger traffic is calculated by the principle that one person can be counted only once in one travel. The passengers who travel with a half price ticket or a child ticket is also calculated as one person. The freight (passenger) traffic provides a quantitative measure to show how the transport industry serves the national economy and people, and is also an important indicator for planning the transport industry and for studying the development scale and speed of the transport industry.

Freight Ton-kilometers (Passenger-kilometers) refer to the sum of the products of the volume of transported cargo (passengers) multiplying by the transport distance. It is an important indicator to reflect the achievement of transportation industry. Normally, the shortest distance between the departure station and the destination station (i.e., the payable distance) is the basis to calculate the freight ton-kilometers. This is an important indicator to show the total results of the transport industry, to prepare and examine the transport plan and to measure the efficiency, the labour productivity and the unit cost of transport.

Volume of Freight Handled in Ports refers to the volume of cargo passing in and out the harbor area of the major coastal ports and having been loaded and unloaded. The volume includes that of the postal matters, registered luggage and fuels, materials and fresh water as supplies of the ships. The volume of freight handled may be classified by direction of flow as freight for import and freight for export, or by nature of cargo as freight for domestic trade and freight for foreign trade. As an important indicator, the volume of freight handled by type of cargo and by main flow direction reflects the production capacity of ports.

Air Passenger Throughput refers to the number of passengers entering and leaving the airport through the airport in a certain period of time.

Air Cargo And Mail Throughput refers to the amount of cargo and mail entering and leaving the airport through the airport within a certain period of time.

Business Volume of Post Services refers to the total amount of post services or other services provided by the post departments for society. The calculation method is that the physical quantity of each type of postal communication service business is multiplied by the corresponding constant unit price, and the monetary quantity of each type of service is obtained and summed up. This indicator reflects the total results of the development of postal communication services in a certain period of time, and is a comprehensive indicator for observing the general trend of development and change of postal communication services.

Business Volume of Express Services refers to the total number of various types of express delivery services received and received by the enterprise, and the enterprises entrusted by the user are responsible for statistics. Including domestic city express business volume, domestic off-site express business volume, Hong Kong, Macao and Taiwan express business volume, international express business volume.

Business Volume of Telecommunication Services refers to the total number of telecommunication services provided by telecommunication enterprises in the form of money for the society. Including the total volume of fixed voice services, fixed data and total Internet services, fixed value-added and other services, total mobile voice services, total mobile data and Internet services, mobile value-added and other business.

Long-Distance Cable Line Length refers to the actual length of the long-distance cable line. The overhead optical cable is counted according to the actual length of the pole. The underground and underwater cables are counted according to the length of the trench.

Local Network Trunk Cable Length Refers to the actual length of the cable line between the service nodes in the local network and from the starting point to the destination. The overhead optical cable is counted according to the actual length of the pole. The underground and underwater optical cables are counted according to the length of the buried optical cable.

Number of Mobile Phone Base Stations refers to the wireless transceiver device serving the cell, handles the wireless communication between the base station and the mobile station, and acts as a relay between the mobile switch and the mobile station to monitor the total number of devices for wireless transmission quality.

Number of 3G Mobile Phone Base Stations refers to the number of NoFe-B actually used on the 3G mobile communication network of the telecommunications enterprise at the end of the reporting period. It includes TF-SCFMA base station, WCFMA base station, and CFMA2000 base station.

Number of 4G Mobile Phone Base Stations refers to the number of Node-B actually used on the 4G mobile communication network of the telecommunications enterprise at the end of the reporting period. It includes TD-LTE base station and FDD-LTE base station.

Internet Broadband Access Port refers to the number of broadband access ports that are actually installed and operated for accessing Internet users.

Websites refers to the number of websites owned and maintained by enterprises at the end of the reporting period, excluding the intranet. A website is a web site on the public Internet, accessible to the public, based on the TCP/IP protocol, with the domain name itself or the "WWW.+ domain name" as its URL, consisting of address, software, hardware and content.

E-commerce sales amount refers to the total amount of goods and services sold by an enterprise (unit) through online orders during the reporting period. With the help of a network order refers to the acceptance of orders over the network, payment and distribution can be made without the help of the network.

E-commerce purchase amount refers to the total amount of goods and services purchased by an enterprise (unit) through the help of a network order during the reporting period. With the help of a network order, an order is sent over the network, and payment and distribution can be made without the help of the network.

E-commerce trading platform refers to the sum of information network systems that provide transaction matching and related services for both parties or parties in e-commerce activities.

批发和零售业 16

WHOLESALE AND RETAIL TRADES

简要说明

一、本篇资料的主要内容

本篇资料主要反映了全市批发和零售业经营情况和效益情况，主要包括批发和零售业商品流转及财务情况、亿元以上商品交易市场、社会消费品零售总额等内容。

二、本篇资料的来源

本篇资料来源于批发和零售业统计年报和定期报表统计资料。由市统计局外经贸易统计处整理提供。

Brief Introduction

I. Main Content

Data in this chapter show the development of wholesale and retail trade of the whole city, mainly including the circulation and financial indices of commodities in the wholesale and retail trade, commodity exchange markets over 100 million yuan, total retail sales of consumer goods, etc.

II. Source of Data

Data in this chapter are based on annual report and regular reports of wholesale and retail trade. Data in this chapter are prepared and compiled by the Division of Trade and External Economic Relations Statistics of Qingdao Municipal Bureau of Statistics.

16-1 社会消费品零售总额（1985-2019年）
TOTAL RETAIL SALES OF CONSUMER GOODS (1985-2019)

单位：万元 (10 000 yuan)

年份 Year	消费品零售总额 Total Retail Sales of Consumer Goods	批发零售业 Wholesale and Retail Trades	住宿餐饮业 Hotels and Catering Services	其他行业 Others
1985	307222	231477	16996	18753
1986	364091	269418	21384	27118
1987	432569	310658	23319	32617
1988	590538	434572	32304	45449
1989	619941	450812	34083	56303
1990	658264	484770	35568	67863
1991	760562	566767	43320	56812
1992	888411	666911	53045	67392
1993	1381791	1029750	79918	96567
1994	1873212	1346723	126809	202134
1995	2362682	1627640	184925	304133
1996	2687133	1858214	218582	318787
1997	2979302	2084958	239542	357685
1998	3328902	2294750	274412	406348
1999	3710897	2678209	310962	385994
2000	4215480	3067944	381840	397499
2001	4824874	3498744	498046	426179
2002	5464940	4080963	625827	394750
2003	6315866	5169609	830717	315540
2004	7299288	6119422	993279	186587
2005	8479672	7118804	1146604	214264
2006	9885247	8226694	1403617	254936
2007	11805893	9702897	1783908	319089
2008	14456246	12590079	1505564	360603
2009	16728814	13761257	2464719	502838
2010	18923835	16550240	2373595	
2011	22172581	19408076	2764505	
2012	25331596	22147219	3184377	
2013	28650167	25076367	3573800	
2014	32182505	28179596	4002909	
2015	35481601	31012690	4468911	
2016	39141939	34175128	4966811	
2017	43214295	37751718	5462577	
2018	47427204	41340208	6086996	
2019	51265971	44158221	7107750	

注：1. 自2003年开始消费品零售总额不再包括制造业零售额和农民对非农居民的销售额分组。
2. 自2005年起，住宿业从其它行业调整到住宿餐饮业中。
3. 根据第二次经济普查结果，对1993年以来的历史数据进行了调整。

Note: 1. Since 2003, retail sales of manufacturing and retail sales of rural residents to urban residents are excluded in total retail sales of consumer goods.
2. Since 2005, hotels is adjusted to hotels and catering services from the others.
3. Historical data since1993 have been adjusted according to results of the Second China Economic Census.

16-2 分市、区社会消费品零售总额（2019 年）
TOTAL RETAIL SALES OF CONSUMER GOODS BY REGION (2019)

单位：万元 (10 000 yuan)

市、区名称	Region	消费品零售总额 Total Retail Sales of Consumer Goods	按行业分	
			批发零售业 Wholesale and Retail Trades	住宿餐饮业 Hotels and Catering Services
全　市	**Whole Municipality**	**51265971**	**45538680**	**5727291**
市南区	Shinan District	6516686	5484664	1032021
市北区	Shibei District	6391114	5706544	684569
李沧区	Licang District	3938380	3603009	335371
崂山区	Laoshan District	3659222	3454350	204872
西海岸新区	West Coast New Area	11171575	9732111	1439464
黄岛区	Huangdao District	11036596	9601081	1435514
保税港区	Qingdao Free Trade Port Area of China	134979	131029	3950
城阳区	Chengyang District	3798917	3390160	408757
城阳区（不含高新区）	Chengyang District (Excluding High tech District)	3649759	3259196	390562
高新区	High tech District	149158	130964	18194
即墨区	Jimo District	4589859	4224750	365109
胶州市	Jiaozhou	5377134	4775611	601523
平度市	Pingdu	3113123	2789636	323487
莱西市	Laixi	2709961	2377844	332117

16-3 限额以上批发和零售业商品购销存总额（2019年）

TOTAL PURCHASES, SALES AND STOCK OF ENTERPRISES ABOVE DESIGNATED SIZE OF WHOLESALE AND RETAIL TRADES (2019)

单位：万元 (10 000 yuan)

项目	Item	商品销售总额 Total Sales Value	#批发总额 Wholesale Value	零售总额 Retail Value	库存总额 Stock
总　计	**Total**	**86689261.1**	**71181223.1**	**15309042.2**	**4346668.6**
国有企业	State-owned Enterprises	69859.5	49040.1	20819.4	12745.0
集体企业	Collective-owned Enterprises	91284.8	89626.8	1658.0	58.2
其它企业	Other Enterprises	86528116.8	71042556.2	15286564.8	4333865.4
农、林、牧产品批发	Products Wholesale of Agriculture, Forestry and Animal Husbandry Products Wholesale	1884729.8	1875914.8	8815.0	137071.8
食品、饮料及烟草制品批发	Wholesale of Food, Beverages and Tobaccos	6154947.8	5938326.2	185902.7	381588.6
纺织、服装及家庭用品批发	Retail of Textiles, Garments and Daily Consumer Articles	11257636.7	10906416.3	350899.1	365424.4
文化、体育用品及器材批发	Wholesale of Culture, Sports Appliances and Equipment	1107919.7	1094469.8	13449.9	69608.6
医药及医疗器材批发	Wholesale of Medicines and Medical Appliances	2783954.3	2778046.1	5908.2	210840.7
矿产品、建材及化工产品批发	Wholesale of Machinery, Hardware and Electronic Equipment	39268966.4	38964319.4	146685.2	1240750.6
机械设备、五金产品及电子产品批发	Wholesale of Machinery, Hardware and Electronic Equipment	6655998.4	6549818.9	96934.6	353129.8
贸易经纪与代理	Trade Broker and Agency	375567.2	375567.2		23392.2
其它批发业	Other Wholesale not Classified Elsewhere	1416978.0	1413105.5	3872.5	20250.0
综合零售	Integrated Retail Trade	2793126.0	12820.7	2780305.3	188183.7
食品、饮料及烟草制品专门零售	Retail of Food, Beverages and Tobaccos	294815.0	57348.7	237466.3	35790.5
纺织、服装及日用品专门零售	Retail of Textiles, Garments and Daily Consumer Articles	1388174.4	222922.2	1164503.3	356822.3
文化、体育用品及器材专门零售	Retail of Culture, Sports Appliances and Equipment	290003.3	64268.6	225734.7	82747.5
医药及医疗器材专门零售	Retail of Medicines and Medical Appliances	764020.8	92839.4	671181.4	84271.4
汽车、摩托车、燃料及零配件专门零售	Retail of Motor Vehicles, Motorcycles, Fuel and Parts	5961981.2	500426.1	5461555.1	470201.4
家用电器及电子产品专门零售	Retail of Household Electric Appliances and Electronic Products	711060.2	67164.7	643895.5	47845.6
五金、家具及室内装饰材料专门零售	Retail of Hardware, Furniture and Decoration Materials	59576.7	627.2	58949.5	12238.7
货摊、无店铺及其他零售业	Non-shop and Other Retails	3519805.2	266821.3	3252983.9	266510.8

16-4 限额以上批发和零售业商品分类销售额（2019 年）
CLASSIFIED SALES OF WHOLESALE AND RETAIL AND RETAIL COMMODITIES ABOVE DESIGNATED SIZE (2019)

单位：万元 (10 000 yuan)

项目	Item	销售总额 Total Sales Value	#批发总额 Wholesale Value	零售总额 Retail Value
销售总额	**Total Sales Value**	**79272038.8**	**64218999.9**	**15053038.9**
1. 粮油、食品类	Grain & Oil and Food	4403081.6	2971225.5	1431856.1
其中：粮油类	Which of: Grain and Oil	646503.2	463720.3	182782.9
肉禽蛋类	Meat, Poultry and Eggs	1162580.9	947429.9	215151.0
水产品类	Aquatic Products	389380.4	349685.3	39695.1
蔬菜类	Vegetable and Fruit	171376.6	94784.9	76591.7
干鲜果品类	Dried and Fresh Fruit	711200.2	504437.2	206763.0
2. 饮料类	Beverages	388624.4	149630.7	238993.7
3. 烟酒类	Tobacco and Liquor	2070078.0	1760021.9	310056.1
4. 服装、鞋帽、针纺织品类	Clothing, Shoes, Hats and Textiles	3819898.3	2238790.1	1581108.2
（1）服装类	Clothing	1929504.0	949630.1	979873.9
（2）鞋帽类	Shoes and Hats	797533.3	262757.3	534776.0
（3）针纺织品类	Knitwear and Textiles	1092861.0	1026402.7	66458.3
5. 化妆品类	Cosmetics	321164.7	113060.0	208104.7
6. 金银珠宝类	Gold, Silver and Jewellery	410027.4	84086.4	325941.0
7. 日用品类	Articles for Daily Use	1000179.3	412477.0	587702.3
其中：可穿戴智能设备	Which of: Wearable smart devices	2964.6	3.8	2960.8
8. 五金、电料类	Hardware and Electrical Materials	353013.2	331213.9	21799.3
9. 体育、娱乐用品类	Sports and Recreation Articles	109527.3	16608.0	92919.3
其中：照相器材类	Which of: Photographic Apparatus	6386.9	148.8	6238.1
10. 书报杂志类	Newspapers and Magazines	182268.2	63707.4	118560.8
11. 电子出版物及音像制品类	E-journals and Video Products	7401.0	1648.8	5752.2
12. 家用电器和音像器材类	Household Appliances and Video Appliances	11070332.3	8188783.8	2881548.5
其中：能效等级为 1 级和 2 级的商品	Which of: Products with energy efficiency grades 1 and 2	2738337.5	2076981.8	661355.7
其中：智能家用电器和音像器材	Which of: Smart household appliances and audio-visual equipment	2134303.9	2035240.2	99063.7
13. 中西药品类	Traditional Chinese and Western Medicines	2492617.0	1790503.9	702113.1
其中：西药类	Which of: Western Medicines	1983176.8	1498375.4	484801.4
中草药及中成药类	Traditional Chinese Medicines	132680.5	65534.0	67146.5
14. 文化办公用品类	Cultural and Offices Appliances	1315425.5	888749.5	426676.0
其中：计算机及其配套产品	Which of: Computer and Related Products	693160.2	621208.2	71952.0
15. 家具类	Furniture	239051.8	131168.0	107883.8
16. 通讯器材类	Communication Appliances	665370.3	344810.2	320560.1
其中：智能手机	Which of: Smart phones	581672.6	298957.6	282715.0
17. 煤炭及制品类	Coal and Related Products	3417950.8	3404424.5	13526.3
18. 木材及制品类	Wood and Wooden Products	1003498.3	1003498.3	
19. 石油及制品类	Petroleum and Related Products	14064006.7	12338976.9	1725029.8
20. 化工材料及制品类	Chemical Materials and Related Products	6117951.4	6117951.4	
其中：化肥类	Which of: Fertilizers	341142.1	341142.1	
21. 金属材料类	Metal Materials	12963633.5	12963633.5	
22. 建筑及装潢材料类	Building and Decoration Materials	732208.0	690961.4	41246.6
23. 机电产品及设备类	Mechanical and Electrical Products	2292159.4	2246145.0	46014.4
其中：农机类	Which of: Agricultural Machineries	7001.9	7001.9	0.0
24. 汽车类	Automobiles	5446442.5	1768636.2	3677806.3
其中：新能源汽车	Which of: New energy vehicles	802313.0	701190.2	101122.8
25. 种子饲料类	Seeds and Feedstuff	909178.2	909178.2	
26. 棉麻类	Cotton, Flax	384143.2	383075.8	1067.4
27. 其他类	Others	3092806.5	2906033.6	186772.9

注：此表为定期报表数据。
Note: The data are from regular reports.

16-5 限额以上批发业财务状况（2019年）

FINANCIAL POSITION OF ENTERPRISES ABOVE DESIGNATED SIZE OF WHOLESALE TRADE (2019)

单位：万元 (10 000 yuan)

指标	Indicator	合计 Total	国有经济 State-owned Enterprises	集体经济 Collective-owned Enterprises	外商及港澳台经济 Foreign Funded Enterprises and Enterprises with Funds from Hong Kong, Macao and Taiwan	其它 Other Enterprises
单位数	**Number of Enterprises**	**1752**	**5**	**1**	**64**	**1682**
年末资产负债	**Year-end Assets-Liability**					
资产总计	Total Assets	29705295	45944	50803	1272584	28335964
流动资产合计	Sub-total of Current Assets	26195565	41376	48886	1030254	25075049
负债合计	Total Liabilities	24152795	39295	46863	827496	23239140
所有者权益合计	Total Owners' Equity	5552500	6649	3940	445088	5096823
损益及分配	**Loss, Profits and Distribution**					
营业收入	Revenue from Principal Business	64459403	48157	87496	2098015	62225734
营业成本	Cost of Principal Business	61462077	47723	79134	1936287	59398933
营业税金及附加	Taxes and Extra Charges on Principal Business	209252	2	142	3158	205950
营业利润	Profits from Principal Business	605736	-2052	-1218	65830	543175
其他业务利润	Profits from other Business	119882	200	0	-2085	121767
销售费用	Operating Costs	1331743	320	533	54266	1276624
管理费用	Management Expenses	669516	1716	8953	33355	625491
财务费用	Financial Expenses	205870	799	-24	9308	195788
利润总额	Total Profits	649278	161	-1225	65544	584798
经济效益	**Economic Benefit**					
商品经营费用率 %	Ratio of Operating Costs to Revenue from Principal Business	2.07	0.66	0.61	2.59	2.05
商品销售利润率 %	Ratio of Profit to Sales Revenue	1.01	0.33		3.12	0.94

16-6 限额以上零售业财务状况（2019 年）

FINANCIAL POSITION OF ENTERPRISES ABOVE DESIGNATED SIZE OF RETAIL TRADE (2019)

单位：万元 (10 000 yuan)

指标	Indicator	合计 Total	国有经济 State-owned Enterprises	集体经济 Collective-owned Enterprises	外商及港澳台经济 Foreign Funded Enterprises and Enterprises with Funds from Hong Kong, Macao and Taiwan	其它 Other Enterprises
单位数	**Number of Enterprises**	**706**	**5**	**1**	**36**	**664**
年末资产负债	**Year-end Assets-Liability**					
资产总计	Total Assets	8594262	28017	1695	938948	7625602
流动资产合计	Sub-total of Current Assets	6175585	22678	1686	767931	5383289
负债合计	Total Liabilities	7120450	23427	855	686580	6409588
所有者权益合计	Total Owners' Equity	1473813	4591	841	252368	1216013
损益及分配	**Loss, Profits and Distribution**					
营业收入	Revenue from Principal Business	14389319	18555	1441	1993727	12375597
营业成本	Cost of Principal Business	12665062	13791	1284	1607153	11042834
营业税金及附加	Taxes and Extra Charges on Principal Business	54963	58	3	10403	44499
营业利润	Profits from Principal Business	269266	2434	92	80626	186114
其他业务利润	Profits from other Business	168928			40161	128767
销售费用	Operating Costs	1007281	82		194853	812346
管理费用	Management Expenses	422277	2203	61	97917	322095
财务费用	Financial Expenses	70510	-41		1437	69113
利润总额	Total Profits	293042	2868	92	83194	206887
经济效益	**Economic Benefit**					
商品经营费用率 %	Ratio of Operating Costs to Revenue from Principal Business	7.00	0.44		9.77	6.56
商品销售利润率 %	Ratio of Profit to Sales Revenue	2.04	15.46	6.40	4.17	1.67

16-7 分市、区城乡亿元商品交易市场分布情况（2019年）
BASIC STATISTICS ON COMMODITY EXCHANGE MARKETS OF TRANSACTION VALUE OVER 100 MILLION YUAN BY REGION (2019)

市、区名称	Region	亿元商品交易市场数量（个）Number of Commodity Exchange Markets of Transaction Value over 100 Million Yuan (unit)			亿元商品交易市场成交额（亿元）Turnover of Commodity Exchange Markets of Transaction Value over 100 Million yuan (100 million yuan)		
		合计 Total	#综合市场 Integrated Markets	#专业市场 Special Markets	合计 Total	#综合市场 Integrated Markets	#专业市场 Special Markets
全　市	**Whole Municipality**	**52**	**11**	**41**	**1270**	**497**	**773**
市南区	Shinan District						
市北区	Shibei District	7	1	6	76	45	31
李沧区	Licang District	5	1	4	36	11	25
崂山区	Laoshan District	2		2	4		4
西海岸新区	West Coast New Area	7	2	5	61	18	43
黄岛区	Huangdao District						
保税港区	Qingdao Free Trade Port Area of China	1		1	20		20
城阳区	Chengyang District	2	1	1	263	262	1
城阳区（不含高新区）	Chengyang District (Excluding High tech District)						
高新区	High tech District						
即墨区	Jimo District	9	1	8	603	135	468
胶州市	Jiaozhou	10	3	7	119	9	110
平度市	Pingdu	9	2	7	89	17	71
莱西市	Laixi						

主要统计指标解释

社会消费品零售总额 指各种经济类型的批发和零售业、住宿和餐饮业以及其他行业对城乡居民和社会集团的消费品零售额总和。该指标从2003年开始不再包括制造业零售额和农民对非农居民的零售额。

商品购进总额 指从本企业(单位)以外的单位和个人购进(包括从国外直接进口)作为转卖或加工后转卖的商品。这个指标反映批发零售贸易业从国内、国外市场上购进商品的总量。商品购进总额包括:(1)从工农业生产者购进的商品;(2)从出版社、报社的出版发行部门购进的图书、杂志和报纸;(3)从各种类型的批发零售贸易企业(单位)购进的商品;(4)从其他单位购进的商品,如从机关、团体、企业、单位购进的剩余物资,从餐饮业、服务业购进的商品,从海关、市场管理部门购进的缉私和没收的商品,向居民收购的废旧商品等;(5)从国(境)外直接进口的商品,但不包括企业(单位)为自身经营用和未通过买卖行为而收入的商品以及销售退回、商品损益等。。

商品销售总额 指对本企业(单位)以外的单位和个人出售(包括对国(境)外直接出口)的商品。这个指标反映批发零售贸易业在国内市场上销售商品以及出口商品的总量。商品销售总额包括:(1)售给城乡居民和社会集团消费用的商品;(2)售给工业、农业、建筑业、运输邮电业、批发零售贸易业、餐饮业、服务业等作为生产、经营使用的商品;(3)售给批发零售贸易业作为转卖或加工后转卖的商品;(4)对国(境)外直接出口的商品。不包括:出售本企业(单位)自用的废旧包装用品,未通过买卖行为付出的商品,经本单位介绍,由买卖双方直接结算,本单位只收取手续费的业务,购货退出的商品以及商品损耗和损失等。

Explanatory Notes on Main Statistical Indicators

Total Retail Sales of Consumer Goods refers to the sum of retail sales of consumer goods sold by all sectors of the national economy to urban and rural residents and social groups. Sectors of the national economy include wholesale and retail trade, accommodation and catering trade and others.Since 2003, retail sales of manufacture and retail sales of rural residents to urban residents are excluded in total retail sales.

Total Purchases of Commodities refer to the total value of purchases of commodities by the enterprises (establishments) from other establishments or individuals (including direct import from abroad) for the purpose of re-selling, either with or without further processing of the commodities purchased. This indicator is used to show the total value of purchases of commodities by wholesale and retail establishments from domestic and overseas markets. The total purchases include: 1. agricultural and industrial products purchased from producers; 2. books, magazines and newspapers purchased from distribution departments of the publishers; 3. commodities purchased from wholesale and retail establishments of different status of registration; 4. commodities purchased from other units, such as surplus materials purchased from government agencies, enterprises or institutions, commodities purchased from catering and service establishments, confiscated goods purchased from customs authorities or market management agencies, second-hand goods and wastes purchased from residents; and 5.commodities directly imported from abroad. Excluded are commodities purchased by enterprises (establishments) for use in their own business operation, commodities obtained without buying or selling procedures, rejected commodities, etc.

Total Sales of Commodities refer to value of commodities sold by the establishments to other establishments and individuals (including direct export). This indicator is used to show the total value of sales of commodities at domestic markets and export. The total sales include: 1. commodities sold to urban and rural residents and social groups for their consumption; 2. commodities sold to establishments in industry, agriculture, construction, transportation, post and telecommunications, wholesale and retail trades, hotels and catering services, and public utility for their production and operation; 3. commodities sold to wholesale and retail establishments for re-selling, with or without further processing; and 4. commodities for direct export to other countries. Excluded are selling of waste packaging materials used by the establishments (units) themselves, commodities transferred without buying or selling procedures, commission income from brokerage in transactions for which settlement is directly handled by buyers and sellers, rejected commodities in the purchase, loss in commodities, etc.

住宿、餐饮业和旅游 17

HOTELS, CATERING SERVICES AND TOURISM

简要说明

一、本篇资料的主要内容

本篇资料主要反映了全市住宿和餐饮业的经营情况和效益情况以及旅游的基本情况，主要包括住宿和餐饮业经营情况和财务情况、涉外以及国内旅游基本情况等方面的内容。

二、本篇资料的来源

本篇资料中住宿和餐饮业经营情况和财务情况资料来源于住宿和餐饮业统计年报和定期报表统计资料；旅游资料来源于市旅游局。由市统计局外经贸易统计处整理提供。

Brief Introduction

I. Main Content

The information in this chapter mainly reflects the operating conditions and benefits of the accommodation and catering industry in the city, as well as the basic conditions of tourism, mainly including the operating conditions and financial conditions of the accommodation and catering industry, foreign-related and domestic tourism, and other aspects.

II. Source of Data

The information on the operating and financial status of the accommodation and catering industry in this article comes from the annual statistics of the accommodation and catering industry and the statistical data of the regular statements, and the tourism information comes from the Qingdao Tourism Bureau. Provided by Qingdao Municipal Bureau of Statistics of Foreign Trade and Economic Cooperation.

17-1 限额以上住宿和餐饮业法人企业经营情况（2019年）
BUSINESS CONDITIONS OF ENTERPRISES OF HOTELS AND CATERING SERVICES ABOVE DESIGNATED SIZE (2019)

单位：万元 (10 000 yuan)

项目	Item	营业额 Turnover	#客房收入 Income from Guest Rooms	餐费收入 Catering Income	商品销售收入 Income from Commodity Sales	其他收入 Other Income
总　计	**Total**	**1183612.1**	**274911.6**	**831266.0**	**19318.1**	**58116.4**
一、住宿业	**Hotels**	**492595.7**	**255931.0**	**183797.9**	**7791.0**	**45075.8**
国有企业	State-owned Enterprises	72631.0	31147.2	31165.2	1273.8	9044.8
集体企业	Collective-owned Enterprises	453.3	261.5	191.8		
其他企业	Other Enterprises	419511.4	224522.3	152440.9	6517.2	36031.0
独立门店	Freestanding Stores	432171.8	212472.3	169145.4	7541.6	43012.5
连锁总店	General Chain Stores	4354.1	3669.0	14.4		670.7
连锁直营店	Chain Store	18391.9	15274.4	2691.2	88.6	337.7
连锁加盟店	Franchise Store	37677.9	24515.3	11946.9	160.8	1054.9
其他	Others					
		88557.6	38721.5	39567.1	1756.7	8512.3
五星	Five Star Class	94492.9	40990.5	47115.9	888.2	5498.3
四星	Four Star class	45271.3	23843.6	16885.9	1107.9	3433.9
三星	Three Star class	1356.4	531.3	796.4	28.7	
二星	Two Star class	1799.6	1308.8	102.2	0.2	388.4
其他	Others	261117.9	150535.3	79330.4	4009.3	27242.9
二、餐饮业	**Catering Services**	**691016.4**	**18980.6**	**647468.1**	**11527.1**	**13040.6**
国有企业	State-owned Enterprises	4336.9	1940.0	2353.1	9.0	34.8
集体企业	Collective-owned Enterprises	1810.5	249.2	734.1	686.8	140.4
其他企业	Other Enterprises	684869.0	16791.4	644380.9	10831.3	12865.4
独立门店	Freestanding Stores	271889.5	15155.6	237672.8	6636.9	12424.2
连锁总店	General Chain Stores	298510.5		295028.9	3324.1	157.5
连锁直营店	Chain Store	18860.3	1885.0	16631.2		344.1
连锁加盟店	Franchise Store	50045.7		50045.7		
其他	Others	51710.4	1940.0	48089.5	1566.1	114.8

17-2 限额以上住宿业财务状况（2019 年）
FINANCIAL SITUATION OF HOTELS ABOVE DESIGNATED SIZE (2019)

单位：万元 (10 000 yuan)

指标	Indicator	合计 Total	国有经济 State-owned Enterprises	集体经济 Collective-owned Enterprises	外商及港澳台经济 Foreign Funded Enterprises and Enterprises with Funds from Hong Kong, Macao and Taiwan	其它 Other Enterprises
单位数	**Number of Enterprises**	**232**	**16**	**1**	**8**	**207**
年末资产负债	**Year-end Assets-Liability**					
资产总计	Total Assets	1186348	102145	1237	191417	891550
流动资产合计	Sub-total of Current Assets	648982	47115	330	70344	531194
负债合计	Total Liabilities	945323	56547	396	115106	773274
所有者权益合计	Total Owners' Equity	241026	45598	841	76311	118275
损益及分配	**Loss,Profits and Distribution**					
营业收入	Revenue from Principal Business	471850	68905	432	59526	342987
营业成本	Cost of Principal Business	150553	18175	163	18919	113296
营业税金及附加	Taxes and Extra Charges on Principal Business	6404	904	2	1685	3814
营业利润	Profits from Principal Business	-19591	1646	-2	1478	-22713
其他业务利润	Profits from other Business	7086	1535	268	1587	3696
销售费用	Operating Costs	160136	31380	254	9305	119197
管理费用	Management Expenses	156121	17802	15	22278	116026
财务费用	Financial Expenses	20550	118		6343	14089
利润总额	Total Profits	-16619	2251	-1	1428	-20297
其他	**Others**					
应付职工薪酬	Employee Compensation Payable	139655	28218	181	16395	94862
营业利润率	Operating Profit Margin	-3.52	3.27	-0.23	2.40	-5.92

17-3 限额以上餐饮业财务状况（2019 年）
FINANCIAL SITUATION OF CATERING SERVICES ABOVE DESIGNATED SIZE (2019)

单位：万元 (10 000 yuan)

指标	Indicator	合计 Total	国有经济 State-owned Enterprises	集体经济 Collective-owned Enterprises	外商及港澳台经济 Foreign Funded Enterprises and Enterprises with Funds from Hong Kong, Macao and Taiwan	其它 Other Enterprises
单位数	**Number of Enterprises**	**219**	**2**	**1**	**15**	**201**
年末资产负债	**Year-end Assets-Liability**					
资产总计	Total Assets	473648	8387	361	133019	331882
流动资产合计	Sub-total of Current Assets	236717	8161	329	29908	198319
负债合计	Total Liabilities	407633	1925	367	110025	295317
所有者权益合计	Total Owners' Equity	66015	6462	-6	22994	36565
损益及分配	**Loss, Profits and Distribution**					
营业收入	Revenue from Principal Business	653420	4091	1677	275183	372469
营业成本	Cost of Principal Business	354883	2747	1647	137314	213176
营业税金及附加	Taxes and Extra Charges on Principal Business	1364	46	4	265	1049
营业利润	Profits from Principal Business	29047	-37	22	26993	2069
其他业务利润	Profits from other Business	3229			590	2639
销售费用	Operating Costs	178410		1	80582	97827
管理费用	Management Expenses	83373	1346	3	29444	52580
财务费用	Financial Expenses	6149		0	2185	3964
利润总额	Total Profits	30950	-37	22	27273	3692
其他	**Others**					
应付职工薪酬	Employee Compensation Payable	125628	1021	317	45277	79013
营业利润率	Operating Profit Margin	4.74	-0.89	1.29	9.91	0.99

17-4 入境旅游人数（2000-2019 年）
NUMBER OF OVERSEA VISITOR ARRIVALS (2000-2019)

项目	Item	2000 年	2005 年	2008 年	2009 年	2010 年
总计	**Total**	**260592**	**684407**	**800455**	**1000670**	**1080511**
一、外国人	**Foreigner**	**177098**	**596177**	**697391**	**801424**	**826628**
# 韩国	Korea	69878	295111	340648	363181	382225
日本	Japan	67215	177121	210090	261553	242082
美国	USA	10384	23284	28998	28745	35539
俄罗斯	Russia	4820	12062	3774	9525	15793
德国	Germany	3820	10646	11261	14735	21626
新加坡	Singapore	6321	6060	10683	17453	13444
英国	UK	2798	5744	10657	9103	17639
加拿大	Canada	1865	4397	5467	7741	9279
法国	France	2491	5166	6067	7030	11766
意大利	Italy	1555	3963	3871	3747	3867
澳大利亚	Australia	1817	4257	7940	6641	8223
菲律宾	Philippines	7947	3459	2075	7800	14140
泰国	Thailand	780	3261	2236	3685	2572
印尼	Indonesia	1241	2349	1589	4221	7863
新西兰	New Zealand	442	710	1161	2029	1597
二、港澳和台湾同胞	**Chinese Compatriots from Hong Kong, Macao and Taiwan**	**60367**	**88230**	**103064**	**199246**	**253883**

17-5 入境旅游收入（2000-2019 年）
EARNINGS FROM INTERNATIONAL TOURISM (2000-2019)

项目	Item	2000 年	2005 年	2008 年	2009 年	2010 年
总计	**Total**	**118164**	**340899**	**347645**	**377000**	**399688**
旅游购物	Shopping	20742	67047	66053	70763	74104
住宿费	Accommodation	17443	37277	37198	41093	43933
餐饮费	Dining	11223	33557	33374	36569	38747
交通费	Transportation	35252	128112	9039	9877	145551
邮电费	Postal and Telecommunication	5502	18394	17382	18812	19081
文化娱乐费	Culture and Entertainment	6894	20240	20163	22394	24032
游览	Sightseeing			18773	21037	22978
其他	Other Services		36272	145663	29745	31262

单位：人次 (person-time)

2011 年	2012 年	2013 年	2014 年	2015 年	2016 年	2017 年	2018 年	2019 年
1156391	**1270113**	**1282814**	**1280526**	**1338098**	**1410494**	**1443715**	**1535733**	**1702568**
809043	**877593**	**905415**	**951732**	**996191**	**1042213**	**1056800**	**1118860**	**1258240**
298096	338383	338191	366584	389832	68010	432430	451046	507854
216755	185613	146080	135179	140762	151832	164095	174147	192257
45842	48431	54178	57907	62771	68010	73905	79392	87014
15750	26432	26519	25356	28529	30534	32540	37053	44720
26178	26311	19014	21723	23425	25456	26636	28646	33256
16626	16316	16305	19975	21310	23713	25257	26060	29001
23955	28385	19496	22817	23812	26133	28006	28942	31577
12007	11678	9727	9483	10659	11592	12544	15473	16849
12019	15595	21422	17828	19388	21836	23507	25035	27218
7028	5622	5679	7705	8747	9234	10627	11559	12904
15465	16644	11149	15339	16798	18839	20304	21491	23344
14259	7546	18630	6668	7300	7891	8489	9837	11300
3271	2369	3692	4803	5331	5784	6628	7367	8331
8128	4571	10011	6568	5692	6220	7388	9816	11161
6265	6448	1452	2549	2872	3352	4230	7367	7965
347348	**392520**	**377399**	**328794**	**342511**	**368281**	**386915**	**416873**	**444328**

单位：万元 (10 000 yuan)

2011 年	2012 年	2013 年	2014 年	2015 年	2016 年	2017 年	2018 年	2019 年
441171	**519495**	**511158**	**503900**	**566742**	**656966**	**694103**	**798374**	**1084000**
80823	93872	94055	109246	122473	141970	129381	102192	264604
59823	59378	58577	62232	69879	81004	77184	150893	134308
40191	51378	51065	44041	49589	57483	68091	122950	95717
134425	170238	180945	160492	180791	209573	249113	273842	351975
16720	23014	22950	19400	21593	25031	33248	16766	42059
36132	32832	32103	33409	36271	42045	42201	62273	70243
51705	32832	32152	44192	49930	57879	40674	33532	90839
21353	55951	39311	30888	36216	41982	54211	35927	34254

17-6 国内旅游人数及收入（2019 年）
NUMBER OF DOMESTIC TOURISTS AND INCOME (2019)

指标	Indicator	单位	Unit	2019 年
国内旅游人数	Number of Domestic Tourists	万人次	10000 person-times	11132.58
1. 过夜旅游者人数	Number of Overnight Tourists	万人次	10000 person-times	5081.28
2. 不过夜旅游者（一日游人数）	Number of Non-overnight (One-day Sightseeing) Tourists	万人次	10000 person-times	6051.3
国内旅游人均花费	Per Capita Expenditure of Domestic Tourist	元	yuan	1704.19
国内旅游收入	Earnings from Domestic Tourism	亿元	100 million yuan	1897.2
1. 接待过夜旅游者收入	Earnings from Overnight Tourists	万 元	10000 yuan	1572.68
2. 接待不过夜旅游者（一日游）收入	Earnings form Non-overnight (One-day Sightseeing) Tourists	万 元	10000 yuan	324.52

主要统计指标解释

住宿餐饮业营业额 指住宿和餐饮业法人企业、产业活动单位在经营活动中因提供服务或销售商品等取得的收入，包括客房收入、餐费收入、商品销售收入和其他收入。客房收入指住宿和餐饮业法人企业、产业活动单位在经营活动中因提供住宿服务取得的客房收入。餐费收入指住宿和餐饮业法人企业、产业活动单位因为顾客提供就餐服务取得的收入，包括经烹饪、调制加工后出售的各种食品，如主食、炒菜、凉拌菜等的收入。商品销售收入指住宿和餐饮业法人企业、产业活动单位伴随服务而出售商品所取得的收入。其他收入指营业收入中除客房收入、餐费收入、商品销售收入以外的其他收入，包括娱乐、健身和商务服务等。

国内旅游者 是指不以谋求职业、获取报酬为目的，离开惯常居住环境，到国内其它地方从事参观、游览、度假等旅游活动（包括外出探亲、疗养、考察、参加会议和从事商务、科技、文化、教育、宗教活动过程中的旅游活动），出行距离超过10公里，出游时间超过6小时，但不超过12个月的我国大陆居民。

入境旅游者 指来我国参观、访问、旅行、探亲、访友、休养、考察、参加会议和从事经济、科技、文化、教育、体育、宗教等活动的外国人、华侨、港澳和台湾同胞的人数。不包括外国在我国的常驻机构，如领事馆、通讯社、企业办事处的工作人员；来我国常住的外国专家、留学生以及在岸逗留不过夜人员。

Explanatory Notes on Main Statistical Indicators

Business Revenue of Hotels and Catering Services refer to revenue received from providing services or selling commodities by corporate enterprises and establishments engaged in hotel and catering services, including income from hotel rooms, from catering services, from selling of commodities and from other services. Income from hotel rooms refers to income of corporate enterprises and establishments by providing lodging services. Income from catering services refers to income of corporate enterprises and establishments by providing catering services, including selling of cooked or prepared foods such as stable food, cooked dishes or cold dishes. Income from selling of commodities refers to income of corporate enterprises and establishments by selling commodities that accompany the services they provide. Income from other activities refers to income received other than income from hotel rooms, catering services or selling of commodities, such as income from providing recreation, fitness or business services.

Domestic Tourists refers to residents in mainland China who are not for the purpose of seeking employment, remuneration, and leaving the usual living environment, elsewhere to engage in domestic visitors, sightseeing, vacation travel (including to go out to visit relatives, infirmary, observing, participate in the meeting and engage in business, science and technology, culture, education, religious activities in the course of tourism activities), trip distance of more than 10 km, trips longer than six hours, but not more than 12 months.

Entrance Tourists refers to foreigners, overseas Chinese, Chinese compatriots from Hong Kong, Macao and Taiwan coming to China for sight-seeing, visits, tours, family reunions, vacations, study tours, conferences and other activities of a business, scientific and technological, cultural, educational and religious nature. It does not include representatives and employees of resident institutions of foreign countries in China such as embassies, consulates, news agencies and offices of foreign companies and organizations, nor does it include long-term foreign experts or students residing in China, or persons in transition without spending a night in China.

教育、科技和文化 18

EDUCATION SCIENCE & TECHNOLOGY AND CULTURE

简 要 说 明

一、本篇资料的主要内容

本篇资料主要反映了全市教育、科技和文化事业基本情况。教育部分主要包括高等教育、中等教育、初等教育、成人教育、职业教育、幼儿园等方面的基本情况。科技部分主要包括科研机构、科学技术奖励、大中型工业企业技术开发情况。文化部分主要包括文化、文物、广播、电视、报纸杂志出版、图书出版等方面的发展状况。

二、本篇资料的来源

1. 教育部分，技工学校的资料来源于市人力资源和社会保障局，其他资料来源于市教育局。

2. 科技部分，科研机构及科技奖励资料来源于市科技局，大中型工业企业科技活动资料来源于市统计局统计调查年报。

3. 文化部分，图书、杂志、报纸出版有关资料来源于青岛出版集团、海大出版社其他资料来源于市文化广电新闻出版局。

本篇资料由市统计局人口和社会科技统计处整理提供。

Brief Introduction

I. Main Content

Data in this chapter show the basic conditions of education, science & technology and culture. Data on education show the development of higher education, secondary education, primary education, adult education, vocational education and kindergartens. Data on science & technology show the basic conditions of science research institutions, scientific and technological achievements and prizes, scientific & technological activities of large and medium-size industrial enterprises. Data on culture show the basic conditions of arts, cultural relics, broadcasting, television and publication of newspapers, magazines and books.

II. Source of Data

1.In education component, data on the basic conditions of technical schools are provided by Qingdao Municipal Bureau of Human Resources and Social Security, and the other data on education are provided by Qingdao Municipal Bureau of Education.

2. In science & technology component, data on science research institutions and scientific & technological achievements and prizes are provided by Qingdao Municipal Bureau of Science and Technology. Data on scientific and technological activities are from the annual report of scientific and technological activities, which is provided by Qingdao Municipal Bureau of Statistics.

3. In culture component, data on publication of books, magazines and newspapers are provided by Qingdao Publishing Group and Ocean University Press. The other data are provided by Qingdao Municipal Bureau of Culture, Broadcasting, Television, Press and Publication.

Data in this chapter are provided and compiled by the Division of Population and Science & Technology of Qingdao Municipal Bureau of Statistics.

18-1 各级各类学校基本情况（2019 年）

BASIC STATISTICS ON SCHOOLS BY LEVEL AND TYPE OF SCHOOL (2019)

项目	Item	学校数（所）Schools（unit）	毕业生数（人）Graduates（person）	招生数（人）New Students Enrollment(person）	在校学生数（人）Students Enrollment(person）	教职工数（人）Teachers and Staff（person）	#专任教师 of which：Full-time Teachers
研究生	Postgraduates	8	11045	17311	50043		
普通高等学校	Regular Institutions of Higher Education	24	103684	126423	415824	34259	22849
中等专业学校	Specialized Secondary Schools	6	10842	10434	30555	851	678
技工学校	Technical Schools	20	6108	9127	32733	2355	1718
职业学校	Vocational Schools	42	17790	16953	49517	7304	6189
普通中学	Regular Secondary Schools	327	120931	144983	408953	43103	39822
初中	Junior Secondary Schools	254	81400	95633	282438	26790	25250
高中	Senior Secondary Schools	73	39531	49350	126515	16313	14572
小学	Primary Schools	720	95378	107475	583784	36616	35332
特殊教育学校	Special Education Schools	13	252	425	2375	673	584
幼儿园	Kindergartens	2352	87895	107562	294768	37139	23424
成人高等学校	Adult Institutions of Higher Education	1	37436	69854	131387		
成人中等学校	Adult Institutions of Secondary Education	2	672	5	155	28	21
成人初等学校	Adult Primary Education Schools						

18-2　主要年份各级各类学校在校学生数

MAJOR YEAR´S STUDENTS ENROLLMENT OF SCHOOLS BY LEVEL AND TYPE OF SCHOOL

单位：人 (person)

年份 Year	普通高等学校 Regular Institutions of Higher Education	中等学校 Secondary Schools	中等专业学校 Specialized Secondary Schools	普通中学 Regular Secondary Schools	职业中学 Vocational Schools	技工学校 Technical Schools	小学 Primary Schools
1949	1 007	13 804	1 600	12 204			213 470
1952	2 761	27 951	3 770	24 181			413 286
1957	3 133	56 689	4 985	51 604	100		482 397
1962	4 381	62 646	2 791	58 639	243	973	522 921
1965	2 987	99 605	9 405	88 187	1 490	523	788 485
1970	320	222 521	105	220 262	2 154		728 433
1975	1 151	350 309	3 144	346 403		762	928 153
1978	3 465	464 584	4 269	457 460	2 000	865	634 905
1980	6 783	325 935	5 195	318 193	1 344	1 203	816 970
1985	10 631	327 446	11 475	279 915	33 945	2 111	691 341
1988	14 408	352 576	11 819	306 943	28 933	4 881	629 212
1990	15 433	351 365	15 118	296 163	34 568	5 516	632 314
1991	15 491	353 410	14 618	298 568	34 421	5 803	612 772
1992	16 470	367 480	14 763	307 903	38 242	6 572	585 381
1993	23 858	383 043	16 877	318 179	40 743	7 244	583 585
1994	25 018	420 077	20 582	347 667	43 734	8 094	593 419
1995	24 908	450 212	23 744	372 335	46 044	8 089	595 891
1996	26 076	468 561	26 951	382 760	50 131	8 719	607 284
1997	27 434	463 619	28 543	362 305	61 640	11 131	626 749
1998	29 507	442 525	28 757	336 918	65 989	10 861	625 308
1999	33 681	459 520	26 955	352 238	70 236	10 091	583 594
2000	46 131	497 391	25 192	398 458	63 894	9 847	534 922
2001	60 728	542 400	25 358	443 693	62 003	11 346	499 147
2002	82 539	575 599	27 421	467 628	67 085	13 465	478 634
2003	168 439	586 704	28 948	461 435	75 221	21 100	467 560
2004	201 739	598 804	30 881	436 117	101 553	30 253	476 897
2005	239 761	569 230	33 522	391 148	106 400	38 160	479 781
2006	260 339	554 308	32 051	365 192	116 487	40 578	483 892
2007	264 917	558 527	28 011	360 410	130 156	39 950	484 775
2008	269 314	582 932	25 330	373 884	143 126	40 592	477 230
2009	275157	564476	22739	377427	127792	36518	465031
2010	284788	535079	24014	380025	98560	32480	462722
2011	291453	505051	25905	373226	74892	31028	479513
2012	296645	489103	27005	369580	65419	27099	484985
2013	300246	484025	28389	365110	61594	28932	496343
2014	313486	479260	28751	362599	58170	29740	516529
2015	322260	467231	33038	355401	48590	30202	536492
2016	340875	470333	32710	356107	50927	30589	547231
2017	346328	490796	32882	372196	52539	33179	550540
2018	397982	500872	31879	385443	51440	32110	569923
2019	415824	521758	30555	408953	49517	32733	583784

18-3 主要年份普通高等学校基本情况
MAJOR YEAR´S BASIC STATISTICS ON REGULAR INSTITUTIONS OF HIGHER EDUCATION

单位：人 (person)

年份 Year	学校数（所）Schools (unit)	毕业生数 Graduates	招生数 New Students Enrollment	在校学生数 Students Enrollment	教职工数 Teachers and Staff	#专任教师 of which : Full-time Teachers
1949	1		250	1 007	779	226
1952	2	262	565	2 761	12 530	308
1957	2	356	755	3 133	1 308	622
1962	5	647	653	4 381	1 866	749
1965	3	741	529	2 987	1 539	623
1970	2	684		320	1 178	486
1975	2	460	473	1 151	1 353	582
1978	4	739	1 782	3 465	2 829	1 176
1980	6	431	1 717	6 783	4 182	1 606
1985	7	1 828	3 823	10 631	5 561	2 181
1988	7	3 496	4 687	14 408	6 875	2 499
1990	7	4 495	4 745	15 433	7 305	2 624
1991	7	4 880	4 954	15 491	7 282	2 489
1992	7	4 458	5 428	16 470	7 344	2 523
1993	7	3 140	9 449	23 858	7 366	2 520
1994	4	7 059	8 042	25 018	7 466	2 650
1995	4	7 828	7 978	24 908	7 545	2 682
1996	4	6 691	7 956	26 076	7 606	2 745
1997	4	7 091	8 503	27 434	7 790	2 813
1998	4	6 912	8 849	29 507	7 662	2 907
1999	4	7 202	11 584	33 681	7 662	2 928
2000	6	7 128	18 427	46 131	8 030	3 278
2001	6	8 991	22 787	60 728	8 706	4 058
2002	7	13 053	29 731	82 539	9 517	4 723
2003	25	25 747	61 975	168 439	18 911	10 293
2004	25	34 860	70 022	201 739	21 437	12 347
2005	25	46 114	79 725	239 761	23 078	13 894
2006	25	55 931	79 094	260 339	24 881	15 195
2007	25	68 354	78 728	264 917	25 956	16 005
2008	25	75 198	86 878	269 314	26 654	16 805
2009	25	69475	81025	275157	26983	16870
2010	25	70450	82220	284788	28145	16996
2011	22	79466	84434	291453	28151	17120
2012	22	79791	87981	296645	29445	18183
2013	22	78974	85707	300246	28958	18396
2014	22	77503	90127	313486	28944	18587
2015	24	79784	92251	322260	29620	19213
2016	26	86270	100525	340875	30390	20151
2017	25	95006	98983	346238	32013	21231
2018	25	105580	118247	397982	32628	21576
2019	24	103684	126423	415824	34259	22849

18-4 各类成人教育基本情况（2019 年）
BASIC STATISTICS ON ADULT EDUCATION (2019)

单位：人 (person)

各类学校	Schools by Type of School	学校数（所）Schools (unit)	毕业生数 Graduates	招生数 New Students Enrollment	在校学生数 Students Enrollment	教职工数 Teachers and Staff	# 专任教师 of which : Full-time Teachers
总　计	**Total**	**3**	**38108**	**69859**	**131542**	**28**	**21**
成人高等教育	Adult Higher Education	1	37436	69854	131387		
广播电视大学	Broadcasting and TV Universities						
职工、农民大学	Universities of Vocational and Agricultural Education						
函授、夜大学	Correspondence and Evening College Education						
管理干部学校	Cadre Management Schools						
成人中等教育	Adult Secondary Education	2	672	5	155	28	21
成人中等专业学校	Adult Specialized Secondary Schools	2	672	5	155	28	21

18-5 分市、区普通中学情况（2019 年）
BASIC STATISTICS ON REGULAR SECONDARY SCHOOLS BY REGION (2019)

单位：人 (person)

市、区名称	Region	普通高中 Regular Senior Secondary Schools				普通初中 Regular Junior Secondary Schools			
		学校数 Schools (unit)	毕业生数 Graduates	招生数 New Students Enrollment	在校生数 Students Enrollment	学校数 Schools (unit)	毕业生数 Graduates	招生数 New Students Enrollment	在校生数 Students Enrollment
合　计	**Whole Municipality**	**73**	**39531**	**49350**	**126515**	**254**	**81400**	**95633**	**282438**
市直属	Municipal Level	22	9939	11706	31299	3	2560	2961	8155
市南区	Shinan District					11	2480	3462	9058
市北区	Shibei District	1		214	540	24	6375	8336	22789
李沧区	Licang District	2	9	7	44	13	3414	4716	12864
崂山区	Laoshan District	2				11	2281	2962	7789
西海岸新区	West Coast New Area	12	6560	8565	20395	41	14418	16601	47939
城阳区	Chengyang District	6	2737	3427	8864	16	6248	8608	23009
即墨区	Jimo District	9	6069	6912	19000	32	12322	15532	45020
胶州市	Jiaozhou	7	4289	6833	15660	23	11060	11453	33922
平度市	Pingdu	7	6625	7171	19488	46	12519	12355	38956
莱西市	Laixi	4	3303	4431	11074	30	7068	7663	30178
高新区	High tech District	1		84	151	4	655	984	2759

18-6 分市、区职业中学、小学情况（2019年）

BASIC STATISTICS ON VOCATIONAL SECONDARY SCHOOLS AND PRIMARY SCHOOLS BY REGION (2019)

单位：人（person）

市、区名称	Region	职业中学 Vocational Secondary Schools				小学 Primary School			
		学校数 Schools (unit)	毕业生数 Graduates	招生数 New Students Enrollment	在校生数 Students Enrollment	学校数 Schools (unit)	毕业生数 Graduates	招生数 New Students Enrollment	在校生数 Students Enrollment
全　市	**Whole Municipality**	**42**	**17790**	**16953**	**49517**	**720**	**95378**	**107475**	**583784**
市直属	Municipal Level	22	3183	2227	7615		42	77	355
市南区	Shinan District					28	5115	6143	33774
市北区	Shibei District					68	8947	11211	61068
李沧区	Licang District					38	5243	8146	39995
崂山区	Laoshan District					28	3518	4350	25077
西海岸新区	West Coast New Area	10	5477	4998	15526	98	16438	19979	105824
城阳区	Chengyang District	3	930	827	3158	46	8809	12748	65554
即墨区	Jimo District	2	2232	1482	5016	166	15189	14666	84127
胶州市	Jiaozhou	1	2515	1976	6230	74	11239	11187	62724
平度市	Pingdu	1	1978	2190	4862	101	12450	11284	67972
莱西市	Laixi	3	1475	3253	7110	68	7558	6350	31067
高新区	High tech District					5	830	1334	6247

注：市直属中有一所十二年一贯制学习，校数在高中中统计。

Note: There is a 12-year consistent study in the city directly under the government, the number of schools in the high school statistics.

18-7　分市、区中小学教职工情况（2019 年）
BASIC STATSTICS ON TEACHERS AND STAFF IN SECONDARY AND PRIMARY SCHOOLS BY REGION (2019)

单位：人 (person)

市、区名称	Region	普通中学 Regular Secondary Schools		职业中学 Vocational Secondary Schools		小学 Primary School	
		教职工数 Teachers and Staff	# 专任教师 of which：Full-time Teachers	教职工数 Teachers and Staff	# 专任教师 of which：Full-time Teachers	教职工数 Teachers and Staff	# 专任教师 of which：Full-time Teachers
全　市	**Whole Municipality**	**43103**	**39822**	**7304**	**6189**	**36616**	**35332**
市直属	Municipal Level	4142	3420	2473	1964		
市南区	Shinan District	1213	1082			2149	2048
市北区	Shibei District	2603	2412			3644	3470
李沧区	Licang District	1530	1380			2128	2054
崂山区	Laoshan District	1034	977			1688	1631
西海岸新区	West Coast New Area	7101	6564	1524	1368	6330	6173
城阳区	Chengyang District	3232	2996	660	577	3192	3049
即墨区	Jimo District	6744	6360	712	623	5534	5333
胶州市	Jiaozhou	4319	4021	631	512	4263	4173
平度市	Pingdu	6222	5923	641	618	4815	4640
莱西市	Laixi	4281	4038	663	527	2519	2414
高新区	High tech District	682	649			354	347

18-8 分市、区幼儿园基本情况（2019年）
BASIC STATISTICS ON KINDERGARTENS BY REGION (2019)

单位：人 (person)

市、区名称	Region	幼儿园（所） Kindergartens (unit)	幼儿数 Children	教职工数 Teachers and Staff	#专任教师 of which : Full-time Teachers
全　市	**Whole Municipality**	2352	**294768**	**37139**	**23424**
市直属	Municipal Level				
市南区	Shinan District	67	14279	2506	1207
市北区	Shibei District	128	30645	3245	2082
李沧区	Licang District	65	24465	3124	1575
崂山区	Laoshan District	115	15132	2417	1399
西海岸新区	West Coast New Area	470	58022	7819	4890
城阳区	Chengyang District	155	28248	3973	2544
即墨区	Jimo District	436	37263	4911	3004
胶州市	Jiaozhou	351	35324	4109	2692
平度市	Pingdu	391	31778	2866	2289
莱西市	Laixi	145	15736	1675	1337
高新区	High tech District	29	3876	494	405

18-9 科研机构基本情况（1978-2019 年）
BASIC STATISTICS ON SCIENTIFIC RESEARCH INSTITUTIONS (1978-2019)

年份 Year	独立自然科研结构（个） Independent Institutions of Natural Scientific Research (unit)	独立自然科研结构中科技人员（个） Personnel of Independent Institutions of Natural Scientific Research (person)	完成科研项目（项） Number of Scientific Research Projects Completed (item)	取得科技成果（项） Number of Achievements in S&T (item)
1978	31	2701	306	306
1980			481	297
1982	41	2345	451	451
1983	48	3182	530	530
1984	53	3312	507	507
1985	52	3673	552	552
1986	63	3998	577	577
1988	101	5199	544	510
1990	141	6046	414	931
1991	72	5665	753	753
1992	71	5726	659	659
1993	69	5545	546	546
1994	69	5540	467	467
1995	59	5286	441	441
1996	58	4738	613	613
1997	54	4577	418	418
1998	52	4142	517	517
1999	58	3771	606	606
2000	54	3637	621	621
2001	50	3191	457	457
2002	52	3248	406	406
2003	53	3246	589	589
2004	50	3226	506	506
2005	50	3234	438	438
2006	50	3291	548	548
2007	50	3432	506	506
2008	42	3709	416	416
2009	43	3727	572	572
2010	44	4088	472	472
2011	47	4548	345	345
2012	48	4967	304	304
2013	48	6057	433	433
2014	50	5438	415	415
2015	54	6037	639	639
2016	57	5722	606	606
2017	57	6017	588	588
2018	58	6017	406	406
2019	58	6417	400	400

注：1991 年以后不包括民办科研机构。
Note: Since 1991, private institutions of scientific research are not included.

18-10 独立科学研究机构情况（2019 年）
BASIC STATISTICS ON INDEPENDENT INSTITUTIONS OF SCIENTIFIC RESEARCH (2019)

项目	Item	计量单位	Unit	总计 Total	中央属 Central	地方属 Local
机构数	Number of Institutions	个	unit	58	22	36
职工人数	Staff and Workers	人	person	8829	6690	2139
科技人员	Personnel Engaged in S&T	人	person	6417	4692	1725
经费收入	Funding for S&T	万元	10 000 yuan	660142.5	334704.7	325437.8
经费支出	Expenditures for S&T	万元	10 000 yuan	375760.3	289648.4	86111.9

18-11 科学技术奖励情况（2019 年）
AWARD STATISTICS ON SCIENCE AND TECHNOLOGY (2019)

项目	Item	单位	Unit	自然科学奖 Natural Science Prizes Awarded	技术发明奖 Invention Prizes Awarded	科技进步奖 Scientific and Technological Progress Prizes Awarded	科学技术功勋奖 Scientific and Technological Credit Prizes Awarded	国际科技合作奖 International S&T Cooperation Prizes Award	最高奖 Highest Prizes Award
国家级	National Level	项	Item		3	8			
特等	Special Grade								
#一等	First Prize	项	Item			1			
二等	Second Prize	项	Item		3	7			
省级	Provincial Level	项	Item	9	9	80		2	
#一等	First Prize	项	Item	1	2	9			
二等	Second Prize	项	Item	6	4	22			
三等	Third Prize	项	Item	2	3	49			
市级	Municipal Level	项	Item	10	6	132		5	2
#一等	First Prize	项	Item	2	1	12			
二等	Second Prize	项	Item	5	2	78			
三等	Third Prize	项	Item	3	3	42			

注：国际科技合作奖、最高奖不分等级。
Note: There is no grade in international scientific and technological cooperation prizes award and highest prizes award.

18-12 文化、文物事业机构、人员数（2019年）

NUMBER OF CULTURAL AND CULTURAL RELIC INSTITUTIONS AND PERSONNEL (2019)

项目	Item	文化机构数（个） Number of Cultural Institutions (unit)		文化人员数（人） Number of Cultural Personnel (Person)	
		2019年	2018年	2019年	2018年
一、艺术事业	**Art**				
1.艺术表演团体	Art Performance Troupes	9	9	852	830
2.艺术表演场所	Art Centers	9	10	194	201
3.艺术展览创作机构	Art Creation Institutions	4	5	26	28
4.艺术研究机构	Art Research Institutions				
5.艺术展览机构	Art Exhibition Institutions				
6.其他	Others				
二、图书馆事业	**Libraries**				
公共图书馆	Public Libraries	12	12	278	279
#县（区）级图书馆	County Libraries	11	11	180	170
三、群众文化事业	**Mass Culture**				
1.群众艺术馆	Mass Art Centers				
2.文化馆	Cultural Palaces	12	12	221	214
3.文化站	Cultural Centers	134	136	553	527
4.其他	Others				

18-13　文化部门艺术剧团情况（2019年）
STATISTICS ON ART TROUPES OF CULTURAL DEPARTMENT (2019)

项目	Item	剧团数（个）Number of Troupes (unit)	职工人数（人）Staff and Workers (person)	演出场次（场）Number of Performances (show)	观众人数（万人次）Number of Spectators (10000 person-times)	演出收入（万元）Income from Ticket Sales (10000 yuan)	#财政补贴（万元）Appropriation Funds (10000 yuan)
总　计	**Total**	**9**	**852**	**1991**	**136.3**	**11186.3**	**7746.3**
一、按单位性质分	**Divided by unit nature**						
事业	Career	6	413	1189	103.1	9344.7	7746.3
企业	Enterprise	3	439	802	33.2	1841.6	
二、按剧种分	**Grouped by Type of Drama**						
1. 话剧团	Drama Troupes	1	103	357	10.7	639.2	
2. 歌舞团	Song and Dance Troupes	1	253	313	12.5	1029.8	
3. 戏曲剧团	Local Opera Troupes	6	374	1259	108.1	5314.8	4095.8
#京剧	of which：Beijing Opera	1	83	132	10.0	172.6	
4. 曲艺团	Recitation and Ballad Troupes						
5. 文工团（艺术团）	Cultural and Performance Troupes	1	122	62	5.0	4202.5	3650.5

18-14　图书馆、文化馆情况
STATISTICS ON LIBRARIES AND CULTURAL CENTERS

项目	Item	单位	Unit	2019年		2018年	
				全市合计 Total	#市区 Urban Area	全市合计 Total	#市区 Urban Area
公共图书馆	**Pubilc Libraries**	个	unit	**12**	**9**	**12**	**9**
工作人员	Staff and Workers	人	person	278	229	275	225
藏书册数	Collection Books	千册	1000 copies	8121	7127	6996	6108
阅览席位	Seating Capacity of Reading Rooms	张	piece	6400	5143	6412	5351
读者人数	Readers	万人次	10000 person/times	520	454.5	482.1	419.3
文化馆	**Cultural Centers**	个	unit	**12**	**9**	**12**	**9**

主要统计指标解释

普通高等学校　指按照国家规定的设置标准和审批程序批准举办，通过国家统一招生考试，招收高中毕业生为主要培养对象，实施高等教育的全日制大学、独立设置的学院和高等专科学校、短期职业大学。

成人高等学校　指按照国家有关规定审批，招收通过全国成人高教统一招生考试的具有高中毕业或同等学历的在职从业人员，利用脱产、半脱产、业余或函授等多种形式对其实施高等学历教育，培养高等教育专科或本科毕业水平的专门人才，修业年限、课程设置和总学时数均按高等学历教育要求付诸实施的学校。包括广播电视大学、职工高等学校、农民高等学校、管理干部学院；教育学院、独立设置的函授学院等。

科技活动人员　指直接从事科技活动、以及专门从事科技活动管理和为科技活动提供直接服务，累计的实际工作时间占全年制度工作时间 10% 及以上的人员。

文化事业机构　指从事专业文化工作和为专业文化工作服务的独立建制的单独核算的单位。不包括这些单位另外举办独立核算的其他机构和各部门的业余文化组织。

Explanatory Notes on Main Statistical Indicators

Regular Institutions of Higher Education　refer to educational establishments set up according to the government evaluation and approval procedures, enrolling graduates from senior secondary schools and providing higher education courses and training for senior professionals. They include full-time universities, colleges, high professional schools, high professional vocational schools and others.

Adult Institutions of Higher Education　refer to educational establishments, set up in line with relevant rules approved by the government, enrolling staff and workers with senior secondary school or equivalent education, and providing higher education courses in many forms of correspondence, spare time, or full time for adults. Professionals thus trained receive a qualification equivalent to graduates studying regular courses at regular universities, colleges and professional colleges. Institutions of higher learning for adults include schools of high education for staff and workers, schools of high education for peasants, colleges for management cadres, pedagogical colleges, independent correspondence colleges, radio and TV universities and other educational establishments.

Personnel Engaged in S&T Activities　refer to personnel directly engaged in S&T activities, in the management of S&T activities, and in providing direct service to S&T activities, who spend over 10% of the total working hours in a year in S&T activities.

Cultural Institutions　refer to units, which have their own organizational system and independent accounting system and specialize in or serve cultural development. They exclude other establishments run by these cultural institutions and amateur cultural groups established by various departments.

19 体育、卫生和民政、司法

SPORTS, PUBLIC HEALTH AND CIVIL AFFAIRS, JUDICIAL AFFAIRS

简要说明

一、本篇资料的主要内容

本篇资料反映了全市体育、卫生、民政、司法等社会事业的基本情况。体育部分主要包括主要年份运动员、教练员、裁判员发展人数、体育运动破纪录、获奖情况。卫生部分主要包括各类卫生机构及其人员、床位数。民政部分主要包括婚姻登记、社会救济、社会福利事业基本情况、殡葬服务情况。司法部分主要包括律师、公证、调解、社会治安基本情况。

二、本篇资料的来源

1. 体育部分来源于市体育局。

2. 卫生部分来源于市卫计委。

3. 民政部分来源于市民政局。

4. 司法部分，社会治安资料来源于市公安局，其他资料来源于市司法局。

本篇资料由市统计局人口和社会科技统计处整理提供。

Brief Introduction

I. Main Content

Data in this chapter show the basic conditions of sports, public health, civil affairs and judicial affairs. Data on sports are mainly including the number of athletes, coaches and referees, conditions of record and awards. Data on public health are mainly including the number of health institutions, personnel and beds. Data on civil affairs are mainly including the conditions of marriage registration, social relief, social welfare and funeral services. Data on judicial affairs are mainly including the conditions of lawyers, notarization, mediation and social order.

II. Source of Data

1. Data on sports are provided by Qingdao Municipal Bureau of Physical.

2. Data on public health are provided by Qingdao Municipal Bureau of Health.

3. Data on civil affairs are provided by Qingdao Municipal Bureau of Civil Affairs.

4. In judicial affairs component, data on social order are provided by Qingdao Municipal Bureau of Public Security and the other data are provided by Qingdao Municipal Bureau of Justice.

Data in this chapter are provided and compiled by the Division of Population and Science & Technology of Qingdao Municipal Bureau of Statistics.

19-1 体育事业情况(2000-2019年)

STATISTICS ON SPORTS (2000-2019)

单位：人 (person)

项 目	Item	2000	2005	2007	2008	2009	2010	2011	2012	2013	2014	2015	2016	2017	2018	2019
体育部门职工人数	**Staff and Workers in Sports Commissions**	**849**	**834**	**772**	**1210**	**910**	**1015**				**847**	**795**	**857**	**654**	**682**	**784**
# 运动员	Athletes	90	87	55	452	512	287				287	259		284	1123	2259
教练员	Coaches	174	235	211	173	106	170	136					120	133	134	131
重点体校	Key Sports School	126	117	249	109	97	115	129						1061	1370	881
业余体校	Spare Time Sports Schools	142	223	145		160								1537	1846	1702
体育专业队	Professional Sports Teams	135	132	121		144	192	87	84	42	38	17	17	5	5	
优秀运动员	Excellent Athletes	90	87	55	71	72	146	57								
优秀运动队专职教练员	Full-time Coaches of Excellent Sports Teams	18	23	47	106	92	97	54				89	120			
等级裁判员发展人数	**Certified Referees**	**1114**	**275**	**781**	**205**	**292**	**212**	**510**	**558**	**512**	**514**	**490**	**167**		**511**	**347**
# 二级	Second Grades	451	275	781	181	252	169	510	484	463	514	490	116		319	122
三级	Third Grades	616														90
等级运动员发展人数	**Certified Athletes**	**343**	**260**	**108**	**310**	**512**	**229**	**436**	**362**	**362**	**283**	**259**		**176**	**327**	**829**
# 二级	Second Grades	209	260	108	281	448	229	436	256	362	283	259		176	290	730
三级	Third Grades	46														
少年级	Junior Grades	88														

19-1 续表
Continued

项 目	Item	单位	Unit	2000	2005	2007	2008	2009	2010	2011	2012	2013	2014	2015	2016	2017	2018	2019
全年获得奖牌数	**Number of Medals Won in the Year**	**枚**	**piece**	**347.5**	**669**	**481**	**494**	**602**	**754**	**829**	**746**	**659**	**576.5**	**596**	**729.5**	**3032**	**849**	**1507.5**
#国家级金牌	Golden Medals at National Level	枚	piece	45	62	61	26	30	14	105	88	90	48	51	101	104	76	142
国家级银牌	Silver Medals at National Level	枚	piece	28	48	38	21	23	7	49	100	44	21	44	56	91	81	127
省级金牌	Golden Medals at Provincial Level	枚	piece	116.5	187	116	168	207	459	225	193	174.5	202.5	149	219.5	214.5	264	428.5
省级银牌	Silver Medals at Provincial Level	枚	piece	62	174	93	122	149	116	155	110	111.5	121.5	126	135	140	161	289
体育运动破全国记录	**Records Broken the National Records**																	
项目	Number of Events	项	item		2	1		1	1	2	1						1	
人数	Number of Persons	人	person		2	1		1	1	2	1						1	
次数	Number of Times	人次	person-times		4	1		1	1	2	1						1	
体育运动破全省记录	**Records Broken the Provincial Records**																	
项目	Number of Events	项	item	7	3		2		1									
人数	Number of Persons	人	person	7	1		2		1									
次数	Number of Times	人次	person-times	7	3		2		1								15	

19-2 主要年份卫生事业基本情况
MAJOR YEAR'S BASIC STATISTICS ON PUBLIC HEALTH

年份 Year	卫生机构数（个）Health Institutions (unit)	#医院 of which: Hospitals	医疗床位数（张）Beds in Health Institutions (bed)	#医院 of which: Hospitals	卫生技术人员（个）Medical and Technical Personnel (person)	#医生 of which: Hospitals	每千人口拥有医生数（人）Number of Doctors per 1000 Population (person)	每千人口拥有床位数（张）Number of Hospital Beds per 1000 Population (bed)
1949	80	26	1079	970	2637	1292	0.32	0.27
1952	260	34	2943	1691	3748	1559	0.37	0.70
1957	624	45	5163	2656	6941	2578	0.53	1.07
1962	849	149	7167	4526	8279	2972	0.64	1.55
1965	912	162	8428	5003	9051	3586	0.73	1.72
1970	712	170	8613	6603	9591	3761	0.70	1.60
1975	959	181	10902	9078	13558	4566	0.80	1.90
1978	1192	212	13084	10709	16921	5893	1.01	2.24
1980	1253	212	14170	11345	19265	6781	1.14	2.38
1985	1517	219	18469	13214	23413	9694	1.55	2.95
1990	1563	235	23541	16586	27932	13761	2.08	3.56
1991	1579	235	23727	16796	27772	13227	1.98	3.54
1992	1562	236	24765	17269	28305	13157	1.95	3.67
1993	1540	237	24885	17469	28705	13312	1.97	3.68
1994	1335	242	24732	17882	28938	13535	1.99	3.64
1995	1347	228	25282	18126	29816	13840	2.02	3.69
1996	2216	228	24334	18344	30048	13790	2.00	3.53
1997	2193	239	25201	19046	31121	14400	2.07	3.62
1998	2190	237	24887	19083	31623	14327	2.05	3.56
1999	2185	235	25481	19798	31965	14453	2.06	3.62
2000	2911	231	24392	20057	32160	14860	2.10	3.45
2001	3199	217	24755	20313	32765	15772	2.22	3.48
2002	3050	213	21370	20662	31469	13371	1.87	2.99
2003	3111	213	23980	21605	32337	13452	1.87	3.33
2004	2923	219	25432	23465	32937	13953	1.91	3.48
2005	2609	235	30627	28564	33942	15008	2.03	4.13
2006	2834	232	28724	26653	34360	15451	2.06	3.83
2007	2006	251	30062	28107	33807	15018	1.98	3.97
2008	1985	249	32350	29874	36574	16260	2.14	4.25
2009	2017	252	32803	30527	40217	16734	2.19	4.30
2010	2147	254	36066	33383	43285	17696	2.32	4.72
2011	2549	280	39980	35600	47347	18310	2.39	5.22
2012	2607	288	47254	41186	54488	21593	2.81	6.14
2013	2936	285	44876	39725	59961	24113	3.12	5.80
2014	3126	297	47081	42961	62738	24946	3.20	6.03
2015	3146	308	48601	45066	65264	26270	3.35	6.20
2016	7564	322	50649	47309	87733	27675	3.49	6.39
2017	7927	410	55798	46282	76146	30867	3.84	6.94
2018	8027	421	53154	50842	83975	34578	4.23	6.82
2019	8317	427	60519	58492	90361	37813	4.55	7.28

注：自2016年起，卫生机构及人员包含村卫生室。

Note: Health agency and personnel includes village clinic as of 2016.

19-3 各类卫生机构、床位、人员数(2019 年底)

NUMBER OF HEALTH INSTITUTIONS, BEDS AND EMPLOYED PERSONS (END OF 2019)

项　目	Item	机构数（个）Health Institutions (unit)	床位数（张）Beds in Health Institutions (bed)	人员数（人）Personnel (person)
总　计		**8317**	**60519**	**108728**
一、医院合计	**Sub-total of Hospitals**	**427**	**58492**	**73898**
1. 医院	Hospitals	324	51311	65629
#综合医院	General Hospitals	179	32925	43643
中医医院	Hospitals Specialized in Traditional Chinese Medicine	38	6370	8154
中西医结合医院	Hospitals of Combination of Chinese and Western Medicine	5	593	835
专科医院	Specialized Hospitals	97	11060	12812
#口腔医院	Stomatological Hospitals	6	70	616
眼科医院	Ophthalmology Hospitals	9	636	829
肿瘤医院	Tumor Hospitals	2	60	107
心血管病医院	Cardiovascular Diseases Hospitals	3	1086	1138
精神病医院	Mental Hospitals	18	3794	2111
传染病医院	Infectious Disease Hospitals	2	590	542
皮肤病医院	The Skin Disease Hospital	2	100	106
骨科医院	Orthopaedics Hospitals	6	439	342
2. 卫生院	Sanitation Stations	103	7181	8269
二、社区卫生服务中心	**Neighborhood Service Centers**	**79**	**475**	**3588**
三、门诊部	**Outpatient Service Stations**	**392**	**67**	**6089**
四、诊所	**Clinics**	**2601**	**0**	**10178**
五、卫生所、医务室、护理站	**Medical Houses Nursing Station**	**323**	**20**	**999**
六、社区卫生服务站	**Neighborhood Service Stations**	**208**	**166**	**2943**
七、急救中心	**First Aid Centers**	**7**		**223**
八、采供血机构	**Institutions of Blood Collection and Supply**	**1**		**237**
九、妇幼保健院（所、站）	**Maternity and Child Care Centers**	**12**	**387**	**1550**
十、专科疾病防治院（所、站）	**Specialized Disease Prevention & Treatment Institutions**	**5**	**257**	**238**
十一、疾病预防控制中心（防疫站）	**Centers for Disease Control and Prevention (Epidemic Prevention Stations)**	**46**		**1000**
十二、卫生监督所	**Sanitation Control Stations**	**12**		**483**
十三、卫生监督检验所（站）	**Sanitation Control and Test Stations**			
十四、计划生育技术服务机构	**Family Planning Service Institutions**	**16**		**88**
十五、健康教育所（站、中心）	**Health Education Stations**			
十六、其它卫生机构	**Other Health Institutions**	**24**	**655**	**973**
十七、村卫生室	**Village clinic**	**4164**		**6241**

注：床位数指实有床位数。

Note : The number of beds refers to the number of beds actually available.

# 卫生技术人员 Medical and Technical Personnel	# 医生 Doctors	注册护士 Registered Nurses	药剂人员 Pharmacists	检验人员 Laboratory Technicians
90361	**37813**	**40864**	**4301**	**2679**
63387	**23049**	**31385**	**3395**	**2048**
56100	19968	28793	2840	1741
37857	13575	19522	1759	1111
7004	2664	3324	537	212
729	254	320	76	41
10386	3430	5578	457	374
485	241	207	6	5
583	199	333	25	20
62	31	26	2	2
950	328	468	46	28
1828	416	1237	81	43
468	159	241	25	28
88	31	39	8	6
269	105	126	10	8
7287	3081	2592	555	307
3018	**1335**	**1158**	**245**	**102**
5202	**2568**	**2145**	**204**	**133**
9982	**6042**	**3768**	**126**	**12**
969	**567**	**368**	**14**	**3**
2484	**1238**	**913**	**211**	**47**
156	**66**	**83**	**1**	**5**
171	**47**	**72**		**51**
1172	**465**	**490**	**55**	**81**
201	**85**	**69**	**14**	**15**
740	**411**	**63**	**14**	**69**
375				
24	**12**	**5**		
648	**195**	**246**	**22**	**113**
1832	**1733**	**99**		

19-4 分市、区各类卫生机构数（2019年底）

NUMBER OF HEALTH INSTITUTIONS IN VARIOUS TYPES OF CITIES AND DISTRICTS (END OF 2019)

市、区名称	Region	机构数（个）Institution (unit)	医院小计 Sub-total of Hospitals	#医院 Hospitals	#卫生院 Sanitation Stations
全 市	**Whole Municipality**	**8317**	**427**	**324**	**103**
市南区	Shinan District	412	30	30	
市北区	Shibei District	807	74	74	
李沧区	Licang District	476	24	24	
崂山区	Laoshan District	461	19	17	2
西海岸新区	West Coast New Area	1350	61	45	16
城阳区	Chengyang District	779	31	26	5
即墨区	Jimo District	1064	53	32	21
胶州市	Jiaozhou	990	38	24	14
平度市	Pingdu	1160	55	26	29
莱西市	Laixi	818	42	26	16

19-4 续表

Continued

市、区名称	Region	采供血机构 Institutions of Blood Collection and Supply	妇幼保健院（所、站）Maternity and Child Care Centers	专科疾病防治院（所、站）Specialized Disease Prevention & Treatment Institutions
全 市	**Whole Municipality**	**1**	**12**	**5**
市南区	Shinan District	1	1	1
市北区	Shibei District		2	
李沧区	Licang District		1	
崂山区	Laoshan District		1	
西海岸新区	West Coast New Area		2	2
城阳区	Chengyang District		1	
即墨区	Jimo District		1	
胶州市	Jiaozhou		1	
平度市	Pingdu		1	2
莱西市	Laixi		1	

社区卫生服务中心 Neighborhood Service Centers	社区卫生服务站 Neighborhood Service Stations	门诊部 Outpatient Service Stations	诊所、卫生所、医务室、护理站 Clinics Medical Houses	急救中心 First Aid Centers
79	**208**	**392**	**2924**	**7**
12	28	43	287	
18	57	72	578	1
14	44	37	354	
3	30	33	230	
12	20	70	463	1
12	3	68	241	1
2	20	19	268	1
4		20	219	1
		29	218	1
2	6	1	66	1

疾病预防控制中心（防疫站） Centers for Disease Control and Prevention (Epidemic Prevention Stations)	卫生监督所 Sanitation Control Stations	村卫生室 Village health room	计划生育技术服务机构 Family Planning Service Institutions	其他卫生机构 Other Health Institutions
46	**12**	**4164**	**16**	**24**
1	1			7
2	2			1
1	1			
1	1	139		4
6	1	711		1
9	1	408		4
23	1	657	16	3
1	1	702		3
1	1	851		1
1	2	696		

19-5 分市、区各类卫生床位数（2019 年底）

NUMBER OF SANITARY BEDS IN VARIOUS TYPES OF CITIES AND DISTRICTS (END OF 2019)

市、区名称	Region	床位数（张） Beds in Health Institutions (bed)	医院小计 Sub-total of Hospitals
全　市	**Whole Municipality**	**60519**	**58492**
市南区	Shinan District	7760	7037
市北区	Shibei District	15270	15221
李沧区	Licang District	3191	3158
崂山区	Laoshan District	1147	1085
西海岸新区	West Coast New Area	8057	7478
城阳区	Chengyang District	3759	3759
即墨区	Jimo District	5434	5331
胶州市	Jiaozhou	5942	5762
平度市	Pingdu	5626	5408
莱西市	Laixi	4333	4253

19-6 分市、区各类卫生人员数（2019 年底）

NUMBER OF HEALTH PERSONNEL BY CITY AND DISTRICT (END OF 2019)

市、区名称	Region	人员数（人） Personnel (person)	# 卫生技术人员 #Medical and Technical Personnel
全　市	**Whole Municipality**	**108728**	**90361**
市南区	Shinan District	15638	13158
市北区	Shibei District	26223	23135
李沧区	Licang District	8262	7248
崂山区	Laoshan District	4439	3575
西海岸新区	West Coast New Area	14535	11893
城阳区	Chengyang District	8354	6690
即墨区	Jimo District	8900	6994
胶州市	Jiaozhou	8290	6566
平度市	Pingdu	8034	6411
莱西市	Laixi	6053	4691

# 医院 Hospitals	# 卫生院 Sanitation Stations	门诊部 Outpatient Service Stations	妇幼保健院(所、站) Maternity and Child Care Centers	专科疾病防治院(所、站) Specialized Disease Centers
51311	**7181**	**67**	**387**	**257**
7037		24		10
15221		18		
3158				
1058	27			
5839	1639	4	100	129
3576	183			
4394	937	17	40	
4592	1170	4	107	
3279	2129		100	118
3157	1096		40	

# 医生 #Doctors	注册护士 Registered Nurses	药剂人员 Pharmacists	检验人员 Laboratory Technicians	其他人员 Other Personnel
37813	**40864**	**4301**	**2679**	**4830**
5049	6459	577	374	813
9547	10721	1072	669	1316
3141	3401	339	189	351
1774	1396	143	123	113
5075	5270	592	310	770
2815	2962	343	238	297
2965	2926	402	231	346
2771	2994	292	195	324
2728	2787	294	188	282
1948	1948	247	162	218

19-7 提供住宿的社会服务机构单位情况（2019年）
SITUATION OF SOCIAL SERVICE INSTITUTIONS PROVIDING ACCOMMODATION (2019)

市、区名称	Region	单位数（个） Number of Institutions (unit)	年末职工人数（人） Number of Staff and Workers at Year-end (person)	年末床位数（张） Number of Beds at Year-end (bed)
全　市	**Whole Municipality**	**245**	**5372**	**39328**
市本级	Municipal Level	3	162	1070
市南区	Shinan District	22	1070	3281
市北区	Shibei District	60	1300	8866
李沧区	Licang District	37	750	4380
崂山区	Laoshan District	13	349	2258
西海岸新区	West Coast New Area	23	484	4309
城阳区	Chengyang District	22	322	4098
即墨区	Jimo District	13	276	2837
胶州市	Jiaozhou	15	207	2992
平度市	Pingdu	24	150	2269
莱西市	Laixi	13	302	2968

19-8 社会救济情况（2019年）
BASIC STATISTICS ON SOCIAL RELIEF (2019)

市、区名称	Region	城镇居民最低生活保障人数（人） Number of Persons Receiving Minimum Living Allowance in Urban Area (Person)	城镇居民最低生活保障家庭数（户） Number of Households Receiving Minimum Living Allowance in Urban Area (household)	城镇低保资金支出（万元） Urban low-security capital expenditure (10 000 yuan)
全　市	**Whole Municipality**	**19311**	**13201**	**18546.1**
市南区	Shinan District	3069	2192	3141.5
市北区	Shibei District	11402	7620	11005.5
李沧区	Licang District	1915	1263	1755.7
崂山区	Laoshan District	101	55	89.8
西海岸新区	West Coast New Area	696	525	680.8
城阳区	Chengyang District	211	144	192.6
即墨区	Jimo District	862	622	825.7
胶州市	Jiaozhou	558	412	459
平度市	Pingdu	340	243	270.6
莱西市	Laixi	157	125	124.9

年末在院人数（人） Residences at Year-end (person)	老年人 Senior Citizens	青壮年 Young and middle-aged	少年儿童 Youth
19579	**19053**	**270**	**207**
581	91	256	201
1464	1464		
6622	6622		
2276	2276		
768	754	14	
1888	1888		
1089	1089		
1067	1067		
1112	1112		
1343	1327		
1369	1363		6

农村居民最低生活保障人数（人） Number of Persons Receiving Minimum living Allowance in Rural Area (person)	农村居民最低生活保障家庭数（户） Number of Households Receiving Minimum Living Allowance in Rural Area (household)	农村低保资金支出 （万元） Rural low-security capital expenditure (10 000 yuan)
73294	**50232**	**48311.8**
1694	917	1234.2
12217	8455	8700.4
3211	2071	2486
16925	11894	14507.2
11711	7742	6649.9
20182	13637	10990
7354	5516	3744.1

19-9 分市、区婚姻登记情况(2019 年)

BASIC STATISTICS ON MARRIAGE REGISTRATION BY REGION (2019)

市、区名称	Region	准予登记结婚 Registered Marriages		
		合计(对) Total (couple)	初婚(人) First Marriages (person)	恢复结婚(对) Resumed Marriages (couple)
全 市	**Whole Municipality**	**52311**	**70671**	**86**
市本级	Municipal Level	215	283	1
市南区	Shinan District	4592	6453	5
市北区	Shibei District	5947	7559	12
李沧区	Licang District	2979	3775	3
崂山区	Laoshan District	2562	3931	
西海岸新区	West Coast New Area	9416	12176	
城阳区	Chengyang District	4049	5783	1
即墨区	Jimo District	6379	9490	7
胶州市	Jiaozhou	5146	6843	
平度市	Pingdu	7200	9335	56
莱西市	Laixi	3826	5043	1

再婚（人）Remarriages (person)		准予登记离婚（对）Registered Divorces (couple)	涉外婚姻登记（对）Registered Marriages with Foreigner (couple)
男 Male	女 Female		
16760	**17191**	**24940**	**37**
80	67	45	37
1420	1311	2206	
2211	2124	3726	
1126	1057	1754	
623	570	846	
3255	3401	4919	
1155	1160	1731	
1587	1681	2113	
1689	1760	2406	
2371	2694	3548	
1243	1366	1646	

19-10 律师、公证、调解、社会治安基本情况(2000-2019年)

BASIC STATISTICS ON LAWYERS, NOTARIZATION, MEDIATION AND SOCIAL ORDER (2000-2019)

项目	Item	单位	Unit	2000年	2005年	2008年	2009年	2010年
一、律师工作	**Lawyers**							
律师事务所	Law Offices	个	unit	76	116	159	203	222
律师工作者	Lawyers	人	person	1439	1941	2915	3144	2487
专职	Full-time Lawyers	人	person	971	1542	1855	1934	2377
兼职(含特邀)	Part-time Lawyers	人	person	150	73	90	86	94
请常年法律顾问单位	Units with Permanent Legal Advisors	个	unit	2508	3564	4086	4457	4779
全年办理民事代理	Agent of Civil Cases	件	case	5571	11104	20547	29025	26935
刑事辩护	Defender of Criminal Cases	件	case	1755	3003	3655	3758	3964
非诉讼事件	Agent of Non-litigious Legal Affairs	件	case	5251	6501	5467	5897	4274
解答法律询问	Agent of Legal Advisory Services	件	case	58385	27880	31571	30123	21102
代写法律事务文书	Agent of Legal Documents Written on Behalf of Clients	件	case	9335	8595	9077	6015	6210
二、公证工作	**Notarization**							
公证处	Notary Offices	个	unit	15	15	13	13	13
公证人员	Notarial Personnel	人	person	152	196	214	214	214
公证员	Notaries	人	person	106	112	117	118	117
办理公证文书	Notarized Documents	件	case	120849	105787	101766	97019	94077
三、人民调解	**People's Mediation**							
人民调解委员会	People's Mediation Committees	个	unit	9750	11480	11223	9643	8014
调解人员	Mediators	人	person	34714	46735	33875	32675	27820
调解民间纠纷	Civil Disputes Mediated	件	case	18501	13658	12803	14660	20550
四、社会治安	**Social Order**							
交通事故发生次数	Traffic Accidents	次	time	15601	7051	3025	2570	2313
死亡人数	Deaths	人	person	1371	776	489	402	393
受伤人数	Injuries	人	person	8620	6639	3273	2943	2504
经济损失	Losses	万元	10000 yuan	4815.70	2208.20	991.50	854.80	811.27
火灾发生次数	Fire Accidents	次	time	3088	1948	840	773	683
死亡人数	Deaths	人	person	10	3	16	5	9
受伤人数	Injuries	人	person	43	3	13		4
经济损失	Losses	万元	10000 yuan	1531.06	550.40	979.70	865.50	5566.11

附 录

APPENDIX

2019年省内各市主要经济指标对比情况

MAJOR ECONOMIC INDICATORS ON CITIES OF THE PROVINCE (2019)

指标 Indicator	单位 Unit	全省 Whole province	青岛市 Qingdao	济南市 Jinan	淄博市 Zibo	枣庄市 Zaozhuang	东营市 Dongying
生产总值（GDP）	亿元 (100 million yuan)	71067.5	11741.3	9443.4	3642.4	1693.9	2916.2
比上年增长 YOY Growth	%	5.5	6.5	7.0	3.5	3.6	4.2
规上工业增加值比上年增长 YOY Growth of Industrial Added Value above Designated Size	%	1.2	0.6	4.2	1.3	2.1	4.4
固定资产投资比上年增长 YOY Growth of Investment Fixed Assets	%	-8.4	21.6	12.6	-44.6	-15.8	-32.6
货物进出口总额 Imports and Exports	亿元 (100 million yuan)	20420.9	5925.6	1125.1	881.0	146.4	1628.7
比上年增长 YOY Growth	%	5.8	11.2	14.7	-7.2	38.8	-0.6
#货物出口 Exports	亿元 (100 million yuan)	11130.4	3411.9	644.3	416.9	139.1	342.3
比上年增长 YOY Growth	%	5.3	7.4	1.2	0.0	41.3	-7.0
货物进口 Imports	亿元 (100 million yuan)	9290.6	2513.7	480.8	464.1	7.3	1286.4
比上年增长 YOY Growth	%	6.4	16.9	39.6	-12.8	3.4	1.3
社会消费品零售总额比上年增长 Total Retail Sales of Consumer Goods YOY Growth	%	6.4	8.1	8.1	6.2	4.9	2.2
一般公共预算收入 General Public Budget Revenue	亿元 (100 million yuan)	6526.6	1241.7	874.2	368.7	147.3	245.1
比上年增长 YOY Growth	%	0.6	0.8	7.2	-4.3	0.4	0.2
全体居民人均可支配收入 Disposable income per capita of all residents	元 yuan	31597	45452	41472	37543	26291	40602
比上年增长 YOY Growth	%	8.2	8.2	8.4	8.1	8.0	8.0
城镇居民人均可支配收入 Per Capita Disposable Income of Urban Households	元 yuan	42329	54484	51913	45237	34030	51128
比上年增长 YOY Growth	%	7.0	7.2	7.3	7.0	6.3	6.7
农村居民人均可支配收入 Per Capital Net Income of Rural Households	元 yuan	17775	22573	19454	19916	16747	19013
比上年增长 YOY Growth	%	9.1	8.4	9.1	9.0	9.1	8.7

烟台市 Yantai	潍坊市 Weifang	济宁市 Jining	泰安市 Taian	威海市 Weihai	日照市 Rizhao	临沂市 Linyi	德州市 Dezhou	聊城市 Liaocheng	滨州市 Binzhou	菏泽市 Heze
7653.5	5688.5	4370.2	2663.6	2963.7	1949.4	4600.3	3022.3	2259.8	2457.2	3410.0
5.5	3.7	3.8	6.3	3.6	7.2	3.0	6.1	3.7	4.1	6.3
5.0	−0.7	1.4	5.4	2.3	8.6	−6.2	4.8	1.8	3.2	2.2
5.0	−23.2	−3.6	−23.3	−15.0	−16.5	−23.5	−13.6	−41.2	−23.5	8.1
2904.2	1784.2	460.7	169.9	1401.4	1052.3	834.0	344.7	408.1	872.8	484.0
−4.7	10.2	8.7	7.9	0.9	17.6	23.8	17.6	−16.2	7.0	−5.3
1731.0	1128.0	284.2	132.2	920.7	406.4	678.6	203.3	206.5	311.4	175.8
−2.0	8.9	30.0	6.4	1.0	0.2	27.5	8.4	−15.1	2.5	16.0
1173.1	656.1	176.6	37.7	480.7	645.9	155.4	141.4	201.7	561.4	308.2
−8.3	12.6	−14.0	13.4	0.6	31.9	9.9	33.9	−17.3	9.7	−14.3
7.4	5.6	2.2	3.7	9.3	8.0	3.5	7.0	6.0	6.8	9.2
595.4	571.1	405.0	224.7	249.9	170.4	330.0	206.3	196.6	243.0	221.9
−6.5	0.2	1.2	2.4	−12.2	6.6	5.8	1.9	1.2	1.0	7.7
37783	32518	28055	29690	39593	27577	27619	22608	21602	28517	20673
8.3	8.2	8.3	8.4	8.1	8.7	8.1	8.9	8.8	8.1	9.6
47977	41664	37139	37695	49044	35732	37912	28536	29215	37378	28327
6.9	6.7	6.7	7.1	6.9	7.4	6.1	7.4	7.1	6.6	8.2
21218	20369	17644	18621	22171	17312	14979	16028	14816	17480	14176
9.2	8.8	9.9	9.8	8.6	9.7	9.8	10.1	9.8	8.8	10.3

2019 年十五个副省级城市主要经济指标对比表
MAJOR ECONOMIC INDICATORS ON CITIES UNDER PROVINCIAL LEVELS (2019)

指标 Indicator	单位 Unit	青岛 Qingdao	沈阳 Shenyang	大连 Dalian	长春 Changchun	哈尔滨 Haerbin
全市生产总值（GDP）	亿元 (100 million yuan)	11741.3	6470.3	7001.7	5904.1	5249.4
比上年增长 YOY Growth	%	6.5	4.2	6.5	3.0	4.4
# 第一产业 Primary Industry	亿元 (100 million yuan)	410.0	284.0	458.5	348.1	569.5
比上年增长 YOY Growth	%	1.6	3.8	3.0	2.1	2.6
第二产业 Secondary Industry	亿元 (100 million yuan)	4182.8	2178.6	2799.8	2495.4	1127.3
比上年增长 YOY Growth	%	4.7	2.4	11.9	5.3	3.1
第三产业 Tertiary Industry	亿元 (100 million yuan)	7148.6	4007.6	3743.3	3060.6	3552.6
比上年增长 YOY Growth	%	8.0	5.2	2.9	1.0	5.2
三产占比 Three-yield ratio	%	60.9	61.9	53.5	51.8	67.7
规上工业增加值比上年增长 YOY Growth of Industrial Added Value above Designated size	%	0.6	2.8	16.1	6.2	2.5
固定资产投资比上年增长 YOY Growth of Investment in Fixed Assets	%	21.6	13.2	-19.8	-19.0	7.3
社会消费品零售总额 Total Retail Sales of Consumer Goods	亿元 (100 million yuan)	5126.6	4479.6	3948.7	-	-
比上年增长 YOY Growth	%	8.1	10.6	1.8	3.9	5.6
货物进出口总额 Imports and Exports	亿元 (100 million yuan)	5925.6	1072.8	4352.8	995.8	251.5
比上年增长 YOY Growth	%	11.2	9.0	-7.5	-5.6	19.9
# 货物出口 Exports	亿元 (100 million yuan)	3411.9	315.9	1914.8	148.6	119.8
比上年增长 YOY Growth	%	7.4	-7.7	1.2	-2.6	15.7
货物进口 Imports	亿元 (100 million yuan)	2513.7	756.9	2438.0	847.1	131.7
比上年增长 YOY Growth	%	16.9	17.9	-13.3	-6.1	24.0
一般公共预算收入 General Public Budget Revenue	亿元 (100 million yuan)	1241.7	730.3	692.8	420.0	370.9
比上年增长 YOY Growth	%	0.8	1.3	-1.6	-12.1	-3.5
城镇居民人均可支配收入 Per Capita Disposable Income of Urban Households	元 (yuan)	54484	46786	46468	37844	40007
比上年增长 YOY Growth	%	7.2	6.2	6.7	7.0	5.8
农村居民人均可支配收入 Per Capita Net Income of Rural Households	元 (yuan)	22573	18124	19974	15455	18238
比上年增长 YOY Growth	%	8.4	9.6	10.3	8.6	7.7
居民消费价格指数 Consumer Price Index	上年同期 =100	103.3	102.4	102.4	102.9	102.6

注：部分城市数据未公布。
Note：Some of the urban income data has not been finalized.

南京 Nanjing	杭州 Hangzhou	宁波 Ningbo	厦门 Xiamen	济南 Jinan	武汉 Wuhan	广州 Guangzhou	深圳 Shenzhen	成都 Chengdu	西安 Xian
14030.2	15373.0	11985.1	5995.0	9443.4	16223.2	23628.6	26927.1	17012.7	9321.2
7.8	6.8	6.8	7.9	7.0	7.4	6.8	6.7	7.8	7.0
289.8	326.0	322.3	26.5	343.1	379.0	251.4	25.2	612.2	279.1
0.7	1.9	2.3	0.7	1.3	3.0	3.9	5.2	2.5	4.3
5040.9	4875.0	5782.9	2494.0	3265.2	5988.9	6454.0	10495.8	5244.6	3167.4
6.7	5.0	6.2	9.7	7.8	6.5	5.5	4.9	7.0	7.6
8699.5	10172.0	5879.9	3474.6	5835.1	9855.3	16923.2	16406.1	11155.9	5874.6
8.6	8.0	7.9	6.6	7.0	8.2	7.5	8.1	8.6	6.8
62.0	66.2	49.1	58.0	61.8	60.7	71.6	60.9	65.6	63.0
7.0	5.1	6.4	8.6	4.2	4.4	5.1	4.7	7.8	6.9
8.0	11.6	8.1	9.0	12.6	9.8	16.5	18.8	10.0	1.1
6135.7	6215.0	4473.7	1731.9	5162.2	7449.6	–	6582.9	7478.4	–
5.2	8.8	7.7	12.2	8.1	8.9	7.8	6.7	9.9	6.0
4828.2	5596.8	9170.3	6412.9	1103.3	2441.4	9995.8	29773.9	5822.7	3243.1
11.8	6.7	6.9	6.9	17.9	13.8	1.9	–0.6	16.9	–1.8
3006.9	3612.7	5969.6	3528.7	622.5	1363.5	5258.0	16709.0	3309.8	1730.2
20.2	5.7	7.6	5.7	5.2	7.2	–6.2	2.7	20.6	–11.6
1821.3	1984.1	3200.6	2884.2	480.8	1077.9	4737.8	13064.9	2512.9	1512.9
0.3	8.5	5.8	8.3	39.6	23.4	12.7	–4.7	12.3	12.4
1580.0	1966.0	1468.5	768.3	874.2	1564.1	1697.2	3773.2	1483.0	702.6
7.5	7.7	6.4	1.8	7.2	2.3	4.0	6.5	7.9	2.6
64372	66068	64886	59018	51913	51706	65052	62522	45878	41850
8.5	8.0	7.9	8.5	7.3	9.2	8.5	8.7	8.9	8.1
27636	36255	36632	24802	19454	24776	28868	–	24357	14588
9.4	9.2	8.9	10.7	9.1	9.4	10.9	–	10.0	9.8
103.1	103.1	103.0	103.0	103.3	103.2	103.0	103.4	102.8	102.7

2019 年副省级城市之外部分城市主要经济指标情况

THE MAIN ECONOMIC INDICATORS OF SOME OTHER CITIES THAN THE SUB-PROVINCIAL CITY FOR (2019)

指标 Indicator	单位 Unit	北京 Beijing	天津 Tianjin	上海 Shanghai	重庆 Chongqing	苏州 Suzhou	无锡 Wuxi
全市生产总值（GDP）	亿元 (100 million yuan)	35371.3	14104.3	38155.3	23605.8	19235.8	11852.3
同比增长 Year-on-year growth	%	6.1	4.8	6.0	6.3	5.6	6.7
#第一产业 Primary Industry	亿元 (100 million yuan)	113.7	185.2	103.9	1551.4	196.7	122.5
同比增长 Year-on-year growth	%	-2.5	0.2	-5.0	3.6	-6.5	-2.4
第二产业 Secondary Industry	亿元 (100 million yuan)	5715.1	4969.2	10299.2	9496.8	9130.2	5627.9
同比增长 Year-on-year growth	%	4.5	3.2	0.5	6.4	5.1	7.6
第三产业 Tertiary Industry	亿元 (100 million yuan)	29542.5	8949.9	27752.3	12557.5	9908.9	6101.9
同比增长 Year-on-year growth	%	6.4	5.9	8.2	6.4	6.3	6.0
第三产业增加值占 GDP 比重 Proportion taken by the added value in GDP for the Tertiary Industry	%	83.5	63.5	72.7	53.2	51.5	51.5
规模以上工业增加值同比增长 YOY Growth of Industrial Added Value above Designated Size	%	3.1	3.4	0.4	6.2	2.8	7.8
固定资产投资同比增长 YOY Growth of Investment in Fixed Assets	%	-2.4	13.9	5.1	5.7	8.3	6.1
社会消费品零售总额 Total Retail Sales of Consumer Goods	亿元 (100 million yuan)	12270.1	5516.1	13497.2	8667.3	6088.8	3983.4
同比增长 Year-on-year growth	%	4.4	-0.3	6.5	8.7	6.0	8.5
进出口总额 Imports and Exports	亿元 (100 million yuan)	28663.5	7346.0	34046.8	5792.8	21987.2	6366.6
同比增长 Year-on-year growth	%	5.4	-9.1	0.1	11.0	-5.9	3.3
#出口总额 Exports	亿元 (100 million yuan)	5167.8	3017.8	13720.9	3712.9	13232.8	3821.2
同比增长 Year-on-year growth	%	6.1	-5.9	0.4	9.4	-3.1	2.1
一般公共预算收入 General Public Budget Revenue	亿元 (100 million yuan)	5817.1	2410.3	7165.1	2134.9	2221.8	1036.3
同比增长 Year-on-year growth	%	0.5	14.4	0.8	-5.8	4.8	2.4
城镇居民人均可支配收入 Per Capita Disposable Income of Urban Households	亿元 (100 million yuan)	67756	46119	73615	37939	68629	61915
同比增长 Year-on-year growth	%	8.7	7.3	8.2	8.7	8.1	8.6
农村居民人均可支配收入 Per Capita Consumption Expenditure Of Rural Residents	亿元 (100 million yuan)	-	24804	33195	15133	35152	33574
同比增长 Year-on-year growth	%	-	7.5	9.3	9.8	8.4	9.1
居民消费价格指数 Consumer Price Index	%	102.3	102.7	102.5	102.7	103.0	102.9